Sports Illustrated™
THE BASEBALL VAULT

Sports Illustrated™

THE BASEBALL VAULT

Great Writing from the
Pages of *Sports Illustrated*

TRIUMPH
B O O K S

Library of Congress Cataloging-in-Publication Data available upon request

This book is available in quantity at special discounts for your group or organization. For further information, contact:
   Triumph Books LLC
   814 North Franklin Street
   Chicago, Illinois 60610
   (312) 337-0747
   www.triumphbooks.com

Printed in U.S.A.
ISBN: 978-1-63727-499-6
Design by Patricia Frey

THE BASEBALL VAULT
CONTENTS

DISTANT REPLAY

Lost in History. 3
BY WILLIAM NACK | AUGUST 19, 1996

The Barrio Boys. 16
BY ALEXANDER WOLFF | JUNE 27, 2011

LEGENDS

The Legacy of the Last Great Player on the Last Great Team 31
BY RICHARD HOFFER | AUGUST 21, 1995

The Left Arm of God 35
BY TOM VERDUCCI | JULY 12, 1999

From the Hill to the Hall 50
BY HERBERT WARREN WIND | MARCH 2, 1959

Cardinal Virtue 65
BY JOE POSNANSKI | AUGUST 2, 2010

THE NEGRO LEAGUES

Baseball's Forgotten Pioneers. 77
BY SHELLEY SMITH | MARCH 30, 1992

The Guiding Light 80
BY STEVE WULF | SEPTEMBER 19, 1994

No Place in the Shade 91
BY MARK KRAM | JUNE 20, 1994

THE STORYTELLERS

The Sound of Summer 101
BY STEVE RUSHIN | JULY 30, 2001

The Endless Summer of Bob Uecker 104
BY LUKE WINN | JULY 1, 2013

The Spirit of St. Louis. 113
BY RICK REILLY | MAY 7, 2001

The Voice of Baseball 116
BY TOM VERDUCCI | MAY 10, 2016

COLORFUL CHARACTERS

The Hub Hails Its Hobbling Hero. 131
BY PETER GAMMONS | NOVEMBER 10, 1986

What's in a Name? 137
BY ALEXANDER WOLFF | JULY 2, 2007

The Passing of a Counterfeit Bill 142
BY RICK REILLY | SEPTEMBER 24, 2007

Kid Glove. 145
BY L. JON WERTHEIM | JULY 2, 2018

The Hit Man Hits Back. 153
BY PETER GAMMONS | FEBRUARY 6, 1989

Randy (Macho Man) Savage's Dream Was to Make It to the Majors 165
BY JEFF PEARLMAN | MAY 23, 2011

Tamed Fury 173
BY S.L. PRICE | JULY 19, 2018

The Many Lives of Slammin' Sammy 188
BY JASON BUCKLAND AND BEN REITER | JULY 2, 2018

PERSONAL REFLECTIONS

A Time for All Us Children 201
BY FRANK DEFORD | MARCH 27, 1978

Here's to Opening Day, and a Kid's Belief That Anything Can Happen 208
BY JOE POSNANSKI | APRIL 5, 2010

Farewell, Teddy Ballgame...213
BY LEIGH MONTVILLE | JULY 15, 2002

Mets Autographs...221
BY ALEXANDER WOLFF | SEPTEMBER 15, 1986

Tinker to Evers to Chance...to Me................................233
BY TIM LAYDEN | DECEMBER 3, 2012

Penitence Race 247
BY DAVID SIMON | OCTOBER 12, 2015

THE GAME WITHIN THE GAME

The First to Be Free...259
BY LEIGH MONTVILLE | APRIL 16, 1990

Waiting Game 273
BY JACK McCALLUM | JUNE 25, 2001

Keep Your Eye on the Balls......................................279
BY EMMA BACCELLIERI | SEPTEMBER 6, 2021

Remembering the Best (and Worst) of Pitchers at the Plate............286
BY STEVE RUSHIN | MARCH 31, 2021

Take Me Out to...the Winter Meetings in Vegas, Baby, Vegas 293
BY JOE POSNANSKI | DECEMBER 22, 2008

THE MODERN AGE

The Metrics System..307
BY ALBERT CHEN | AUGUST 22, 2016

'This Should Be the Biggest Scandal in Sports'......................313
BY STEPHANIE APSTEIN AND ALEX PREWITT | JUNE 4, 2021

Kim Ng Made History. Now Comes the Hard Part 323
BY STEPHANIE APSTEIN | MARCH 23, 2021

The Ohtani Rules...331
BY TOM VERDUCCI | SEPTEMBER 14, 2021

Houston's Grand Experiment 339
BY BEN REITER | JUNE 30, 2014

*Playing for the Yankees Has Its Perks. In-Flight Internet
    Is Not One of Them* 351
BY STEPHANIE APSTEIN | MARCH 15, 2023

The Last Ordinary Inning 355
BY EMMA BACCELLIERI | MARCH 11, 2021

UNFORGETTABLE MOMENTS

End of the Glorious Ordeal 361
BY RON FIMRITE | APRIL 15, 1974

The Year, the Moment and Johnny Podres 365
BY ROBERT CREAMER | JANUARY 2, 1956

A Series to Savor 370
BY STEVE RUSHIN | NOVEMBER 4, 1991

It Happened 377
BY TOM VERDUCCI | NOVEMBER 14, 2016

A Death in the Baseball Family 386
BY S.L. PRICE | SEPTEMBER 24, 2007

No-No Regrets 400
BY PHIL TAYLOR | JUNE 15, 2015

At the End of the Curse, a Blessing 409
BY TOM VERDUCCI | December 12, 2004

DISTANT REPLAY

AUGUST 19, 1996

Lost in History

From 1929 to 1931, the Philadelphia A's were the best
team in baseball, with four future Hall of Famers
and a lineup that dominated Babe Ruth's legendary
Yankees. So why hasn't anyone heard of them?

BY WILLIAM NACK

In his box festooned with bunting along the third base line, President
Herbert Hoover had just quietly flashed the sign that the fifth game of the
1929 World Series was over. The President had buttoned up his overcoat. At
his side, his wife, Lou, had taken the cue and pulled on her brown suede
gloves. Around them Secret Service men were arranging a hasty presidential
exit from Philadelphia's Shibe Park. Yogi Berra had not yet illuminated the
world with his brilliant baseball epiphany—"It ain't over till it's over"—so
how on earth were the Hoovers to know?

It was nearing 3:15 p.m. on Monday, Oct. 14, and the Chicago Cubs
were beating the Philadelphia Athletics 2–0 behind the elegant two-hit
pitching of starter Pat Malone. For eight innings, bunching a potpourri of
off-speed pitches around a snapping fastball, Malone had benumbed one
of the most feared batting orders in the history of baseball. At its heart
were Al Simmons, who batted .334 and hit 307 home runs over his major
league career; Jimmie Foxx, who once hit a home run with such force that
it shattered a wooden seat three rows from the top of the upper deck at
Yankee Stadium; and Mickey Cochrane, who batted .331 in the '29 regular
season and is widely regarded as one of the finest hitting catchers ever to
play the game.

Now it was the last of the ninth in a game Chicago had to win to stay alive in the Series. The Cubs were down three games to one, and all they needed to return the Series to Chicago was one more painless inning from Malone. Out at shortstop, scuffing the dirt, a 22-year-old Ohio country boy named Woody English had been watching Malone cut down the A's one by one. Only Simmons and Bing Miller, Philadelphia's rightfielder, had been able to rap out hits, a measly pair of singles.

Of the 50 players who suited up that day for the two teams, only English survives, and the 89-year-old former All-Star remembers savoring the prospect of returning to Wrigley Field for Game 6. "Malone could throw real hard, and he was throwing very well," English recalls. "All we needed was three more outs and we were back in Chicago for the last two games. It looked like we had it salted away."

As things would turn out, only the peanuts were salted. For this was the '29 Series, which had already proved to be one of the wildest, most twisting, most dramatic Fall Classics of all time. By the bottom of the ninth inning of Game 5, 24 Series records had been either broken or tied. The Cubs had struck out 50 times, and their surpassing second baseman, Rogers Hornsby, had fanned eight times.

This was the Series in which A's manager and part owner Connie Mack had stunned everyone in baseball by reaching around his pitching rotation—the strongest of its era, anchored by the sensational southpaw Robert (Lefty) Grove—and handing the ball in the opener to an aging, sore-armed righthander named Howard Ehmke. This was the Series in which Philadelphia, losing 8–0 in the seventh inning of Game 4, had come back swinging in what is still the most prolific inning of scoring in more than 90 years of Series history. Finally, this was the Classic that crowned a regular season in which the A's had won 104 American League games and finished a thumping 18 ahead of the second-place New York Yankees, the vaunted pinstripes of Babe Ruth, Lou Gehrig, Tony Lazzeri and Bill Dickey.

The 1927 Yankees, who won 110 games and finished 19 ahead of second-place Philadelphia, are traditionally venerated as the finest team ever assembled. In fact, according to most old-timers who played in that era, the 1927 and '28 Yankees and the 1929 and '30 Athletics matched up so closely that they were nearly equal, with the A's given the nod in fielding and pitching and the Yankees in hitting.

"I pitched against both of them, and you could flip a coin," recalls Willis Hudlin, 90, who won 157 games for the Cleveland Indians between 1926 and 1940. "They both had power and pitching. A game would be decided on who was pitching and what kind of a day he had. You could throw a dart between 'em."

In truth, the chief difference between the two teams had less to do with how they played in any given game than with where they played their home games. Many veteran baseball observers believe that the Yankees' far more exalted status in history is due largely to the fact that they played in New York, in media heaven, where the manufacture of myth and hype is a light industry. Regardless, these observers agree that those old A's were the finest baseball team to play in Philadelphia and the greatest team that almost no one remembers.

"Those A's never got the credit they deserved," says Shirley Povich, 91, the retired sports editor of *The Washington Post*, who covered both teams. "The A's were victims of the Yankee mystique. Perhaps the 1927 Yankees were the greatest team of all time. But if there was a close second, perhaps an equal, it was those A's. They are the most overlooked team in baseball."

Indeed, from 1929 to '31 the A's were a juggernaut quite as formidable as the Yankees had been between '26 and '28. Both teams won three consecutive pennants and two of three World Series; both teams lost a seven-game Series to the St. Louis Cardinals (the Yanks in '26 and the A's in '31). Statistically the New York and Philadelphia mini-dynasties were remarkably even: The A's had a record of 313–143 (.686) between 1929 and '31; the Yanks, 302–160 (.654) between 1926 and '28. And while Philadelphia scored six fewer runs than the Yankees—2,710 to 2,716—the A's had five fewer runs scored against them: 1,992 to 1,997. That represents a difference between the two teams, in net scoring, of *only one run.*

The Yankees had the best single year at the plate, hitting .307 and scoring 975 runs in 1927. The Athletics' strongest offensive showings came in '29, when they batted .296, and '30, when they scored 951 runs. On defense the A's were clearly superior; over their three-year reign they committed only 432 errors, 167 fewer than the Yankees made during their period of hegemony.

Old-timers assert that if there was any position where those forgotten '29 A's had the edge over the '27 Yankees, it was behind the plate. The Yankees platooned two mediocre catchers, Pat Collins and Johnny Grabowski. In contrast, the A's started Cochrane, a lifetime .320 hitter who competed with the kind of fiery abandon that would one day characterize Pete Rose. On top of all that, Cochrane played his pitchers like violins.

The finest of them was the sullen, hard-assed Grove—"the greatest lefthanded pitcher I ever saw," says Chief Hogsett, 92, who won 63 games for three American League teams between 1929 and '38. Grove was the premier stopper of his era. "He could shut you out any day," Hudlin says. "The Yankees didn't have any pitcher that overpowering."

The Athletics had no compromising weakness. "They had it all," says Ray Hayworth, 92, who caught for the Detroit Tigers from 1926 to '38. "Great pitching and great hitting and exceptional defense. And they first proved themselves to be a great baseball team in the '29 Series."

In the bottom of the ninth that Oct. 14 at Shibe, Malone quickly fanned Walter French, the pinch hitter who led off for the A's, and English again sensed that Game 5 belonged to the Cubs. He was not alone. Hundreds of people in the crowd of nearly 30,000 began watching the game over their shoulders as they made for the exits. Then, just as surely as Malone had the game in hand, it all began to unravel. The pitcher had two strikes on Max Bishop, the A's second baseman, when Bishop slashed a single past Chicago third baseman Norm McMillan and down the line in left. At once the departing crowds stopped in the aisles and at the exits and turned around. Even President Hoover decided not to forsake his seat.

Next up at the plate was Philadelphia centerfielder George Haas. His sad eyes and long, tapered face had inspired his nickname, Mule, but there was nothing plodding about his baseball. Haas was a fluid, quick-jump fielder and, when the screws were tightening, a ferociously intense all-fields hitter. He had batted .313 during the regular season. In fact, he was one of six A's—along with Simmons (.365), Foxx (.354), Miller (.335), Cochrane (.331) and Jimmy Dykes (.327)—who had hit over .310 with more than 400 at bats that year. Haas was heard muttering an oath as he went into the box. The curse, according to *Chicago Tribune* columnist Westbrook Pegler, was "a noise which the baseball players bandy back and forth from bench to bench during the season and the intent is strictly contumelious."

Malone studied the signs from catcher Zack Taylor and fired his first pitch right into Haas's wheelhouse, and the Mule struck the ball flush, lifting it in a high arc past rightfielder Kiki Cuyler and toward the row houses on North 20th Street, where hundreds of people sitting on makeshift rooftop bleachers and leaning out windows saw the ball bounce on the pavement. For eight innings, according to one writer, Shibe had been as solemn as "a convention of morticians." Suddenly it erupted. "The place went up in a roar," English recalls.

Bishop skipped over second base and then slowed down, waiting for Haas to catch up to him, and shook Mule's hand before trotting on toward home. From the presidential box the mayor of Philadelphia, Harry Mackey, sitting two seats to the left of Hoover, vaulted over the railing and embraced Haas as he swam into the arms of teammates gathered at the dugout.

Up in the press box the rhapsodies began. Cy Peterman, writing for *The Evening Bulletin* of Philadelphia, penned this ode to the homer by Haas:

"They sing of joy when long lost sons come home. They prate of happiness when wars are done. But did you ever see a homer in the ninth that tied the score? There, ladies and gentlemen, is joy."

Standing at short, English could feel the game slipping away. In front of him Malone stepped off the mound toward home and stuck out his jaw at his catcher, yelling angrily, "You asked for that one!"

Taylor walked forward and tried to calm Malone. "How was I to know?" the catcher asked. "Bear down now and win it back in the 10th. You're the one to do it."

Just then, up to the plate went the menacing Cochrane, who was hitting .429 in the Series. Malone settled down at once and got the A's catcher to bounce a ground ball to Hornsby for the second out. The pitcher was now one out away from extra innings, but his woes were far from over. The Philadelphia leftfielder, Simmons, with his weak ankles and heavy thighs, went lumbering to the batter's box like Br'er Bear in the Uncle Remus tales, carrying on his shoulder his 38-inch-long club. At times like this nobody, except perhaps Foxx, could stir the crowds at Shibe the way the former Aloysius Harry Szymanski, the son of a Polish immigrant from Milwaukee, could.

Simmons was known as Bucketfoot Al for his unorthodox hitting stroke: Instead of stepping toward the pitcher when he swung, he stepped toward third base, into the bucket. As awkward as the maneuver looked, however, Simmons unfailingly leaned into pitches, driving through them with his left shoulder. Most pitchers were terrified of him because he could drive the ball to all parts of the park. "He had the best power to the opposite field of any hitter I saw," says Hayworth. "He used to hit the ball over the rightfield scoreboard like a lefthanded hitter."

Indeed, for years Simmons's line drives beat like distant drums off the right-centerfield fence at Shibe. On the eve of the '29 Series, in *The Evening Bulletin*, Ty Cobb had called Simmons "the gamest man in baseball with two strikes on him." Whenever the A's were compared to the Yankees, Simmons was Gehrig to Foxx's Ruth.

For kids who haunted the perimeters of Shibe, Simmons was the grist of legend. This was a time when players often lived in private homes near the ballparks where they played. Simmons lived at 2745 North 20th Street, across the street from Shibe's rightfield fence, in a second-floor bedroom in the home of Mr. and Mrs. A.C. Conwell. Simmons was a notoriously late sleeper, and the discreet Mrs. Conwell would ask neighborhood boys to awaken the star so he would not miss batting practice. One of the lads was Jerry Rooney, whose family lived three doors away, and at age four, he recalls, he entered Simmons's room and whispered to him, "It's time to wake up, Al. You're in a slump, and it's time to go to batting practice."

He was in no slump now. Simmons had an oft-expressed contempt for pitchers. "They're trying to take bread and butter out of my mouth," he used to say. Going to bat against Malone, Simmons treated the pitcher as if he were throwing batting practice. On the second pitch Simmons stepped in the bucket and lofted a drive to right center that looked like a home run. It fell just short, but by the time centerfielder Hack Wilson played the ricochet off the scoreboard, the crowd was on its feet, singing, and Simmons was pulling up at second.

Malone walked Foxx intentionally, setting up a force at three bases, and then Miller stepped into the box, looking for a curve that never came.

Shibe Park, which had opened in 1909, occupied a single city block of North Philly. The stadium, bounded by streets on all four sides, was at the center of a predominantly Irish neighborhood of row houses and small factories. Like a ballpark in a Norman Rockwell painting, Shibe had knotholes in the wooden fence in rightfield where dozens of smudge-nosed boys lined up daily to peer in, as if looking into a giant magic egg. To hear old-timers in Philadelphia remember it, Shibe was a stunning shag rug of deepest green, its paths and boxes and pitcher's mound immaculately manicured, in the middle of a city blackened by factory chimneys and coal-burning locomotives. "Shibe was this perfect place," says Walt Garvin, a 76-year-old Philadelphia native. "Everything was green. No advertisements on the fences. Neat and clean and perfectly kept."

The Phillies played in the dilapidated Baker Bowl, six blocks east of Shibe on Lehigh Avenue, and attending one of their games in those days was tantamount to slumming. From the first year a Philadelphia team played in the World Series—back in 1905, when the New York Giants defeated the A's four games to one—until the Whiz Kids won the pennant for the Phillies in 1950, this was an American League city, a town whose heart belonged to the A's.

That first Athletics-Giants Series, not incidentally, had powerful social overtones. It set the tall, reserved, lace-curtain Irishman from Massachusetts, Cornelius McGillicuddy, against the scrappy shanty Irishman from New York, John McGraw. But the 1905 Series represented something broader than the class divisions among the immigrant Irish on the Eastern seaboard. It symbolized the historic struggle for primacy between the two largest and most prosperous cities in the U.S.: New York and Philadelphia.

In Colonial days Boston had been the first U.S. city in size and importance. But by the end of the 18th century Philadelphia had become ascendant, and so it remained until the mid-1800s, when New York took over as the economic and cultural mecca of the New World. In the early days of the

20th century Philadelphia was the nation's second city, and its teams' most memorable clashes on baseball diamonds—first against the Giants and later against the Yankees—expressed the city's aspiration to reclaim its place as the nation's center.

"The battle between New York and Philadelphia in baseball was symbolic of that battle for urban supremacy," says Bruce Kuklick, Nichols Professor of American History at Penn and author of *To Every Thing a Season: Shibe Park and Urban Philadelphia*. And at the center of the battle, always, was Mack.

It was he who pieced together the powerful A's team that whipped Chicago in the 1910 World Series, four games to one, and then twice crushed the Giants, 4–2 in 1911 and 4–1 in 1913. And it was Mack who, after selling the stars of those teams to avoid a bidding war with the emerging Federal League, ultimately retooled the A's into an even better team through a series of remarkably sage moves in 1923, the year he bought a curveball artist named Rube Walberg; in '24, the year he took rookies Simmons and Bishop to spring training; and in '25, the year he obtained Cochrane and Grove from minor league clubs and, at the urging of one of his retired sluggers, Frank (Home Run) Baker, picked up a grinning, moonfaced farm boy from the Eastern Shore of Maryland: Foxx.

Thus the A's acquired four future Hall of Famers—Simmons, Grove, Cochrane and Foxx—in two remarkable years. By 1928, still fishing, Mack had plucked Haas out of the minors and added a strapping 6'4" graduate of Swarthmore College, George Earnshaw, who threw a blazing heater and a nasty snake. By then Mack was also recycling through Shibe some of the greatest has-beens in the annals of the game, including Cobb and fellow outfielder Tris Speaker. John Rooney, Jerry's brother, recalls the day in 1928, when he was five, that his father took him to the roof of their row house at 2739 North 20th Street. Pointing to the A's outfielders, the elder Rooney said, "See those three men? I want you to remember them. They are Ty Cobb, Tris Speaker and Al Simmons. Three of the greatest ballplayers of all time."

The Yankees won successive World Series in 1927 and '28, but the latter year it took all they had to keep the salty, emerging A's from stealing the pennant. New York finished 2½ games in front of Philadelphia, but what hurt Athletics fans was not so much losing but losing to the *Yankees*. "They were terribly disliked in Philadelphia," says Allen Lewis, who in 1928 was an 11-year-old A's fan and who later would become a baseball writer for the *Philadelphia Inquirer* and a member of the Veterans Committee of the Baseball Hall of Fame. "The papers used to write 'Noo Yawk Yankees.' It was ridiculous, but they did."

All of which made '29 the sweeter for the waiting. The A's clinched the pennant on Sept. 14. They had become the new irresistible force in baseball. And while Mack had a superb pitching rotation—Grove finished 20–6 and Earnshaw 24–8—it was he, the manager, who threw the most sweeping curve in World Series history. Two weeks before the season's end, Mack secretly decided to start the Series with Ehmke, a 35-year-old journeyman who had pitched fewer than 55 innings during the year. Mack confided his decision to Ehmke, sending him to scout the Cubs, but told no one else.

The press speculated that Earnshaw or Grove would pitch in the opening game, and not even Ehmke believed that Mack would enable him to fulfill his dream of starting in a World Series. As the players warmed up at Wrigley Field, Mack refused to name his starter. At one point Ehmke sat down on the bench next to his manager. "Is it still me, Mr. Mack?" he asked.

"It's still you," Mack said.

Fifteen minutes before game time, Ehmke took off his jacket and started to warm up. Jaws dropped in both dugouts. Grove and Earnshaw stared at each other in disbelief. Ehmke hadn't pitched in weeks. Simmons was sitting next to Mack, and he could not restrain himself. "Are you gonna pitch him?" Simmons asked.

"You have any objections to that?" Mack answered. Simmons shook his head. "If you say so, it's all right with me," he replied.

Over the next three hours, in one of the most dazzling performances in World Series history, Ehmke struck out 13 batters, then a Series record, with a bewildering array of sneaky-quick fastballs and off-speed curves. Looking loose-jointed and nonchalant, Ehmke at times seemed half asleep. "He looked like he didn't give a damn what happened," English recalls. "He threw that big, slow curveball that came in and broke away from righthanders." All but one Cubs starter, first baseman Charlie Grimm, hit from the right side, and Ehmke twice struck out Chicago's toughest batters—Hornsby, Wilson and Cuyler—throwing junk. "Ehmke was a change from the guys we were used to, who threw hard," English says. "Not many pitchers used that stuff against us."

Ehmke went all nine innings and won the game 3–1. Mack would relish that victory the rest of his days. "It was beautiful to watch," he would recall years later.

"That was the surprise of the century," says Hudlin. "Nobody would have done that but Connie Mack. Howard just wasn't that kind of pitcher. I don't know how Connie figured it. A hunch, I guess. Then Howard went out and made monkeys out of the Cubs."

Ehmke's memorable pitching aside, the Series of '29 showed why that year's Athletics, if overshadowed by the '27 Yankees, have been admired by baseball insiders as one of the best teams in history. Foxx, the first baseman who was known as both Double X and the Beast, hit 33 home runs and batted in 117 runs during the season, and twice he hit prodigious homers in the World Series to put the A's in front to stay: a 400-foot solo shot in Game 1, in which Ehmke pitched so brilliantly, and a three-run line drive that helped propel Philadelphia to a 9–3 victory in Game 2, in which Grove and Earnshaw fanned 13 Cubs between them.

Foxx retired after the 1945 season with 534 home runs, 1,921 RBIs and a lifetime batting average of .325, but numbers hardly express the high and delicious drama he brought to the plate. He used to cut off the sleeves of his uniform to show off his picnic-roast arms, and he could drive balls 500 feet on a line with a whip of his powerful wrists. Stories of his most titanic clouts have all the ingredients of myth. "I think he had more power than Ruth or Gehrig," says Mel Harder, who won 223 games for the Indians between 1928 and '47.

It was Lefty Gomez, the Hall of Fame pitcher for the Yankees, who threw the ball that Foxx drove into the upper deck in Yankee Stadium, splintering the back of that seat. Many years later Gomez was sitting at home with his wife watching U.S. astronauts on television as they walked the surface of the moon collecting rocks in a sack. At one point an astronaut picked up what appeared to be a white object.

"I wonder what that is," said Gomez's wife.

"That's the ball Foxx hit off me in New York," Gomez replied.

After winning the first two games of the '29 Series at Wrigley, the A's went home to Shibe looking for a sweep. The Cubs won the third game 3–1 behind the pitching of Guy Bush, but that merely set up the most spectacular game of the Series—one that drew upon the resources of Philadelphia's most formidable pitcher and all the power of its batting order.

By the middle of the seventh inning of Game 4, the Cubs were winning 8–0, and they were riding the A's mercilessly. In the dugout Bush had been celebrating each run by donning a blanket as if it were a headdress and doing what one writer described as "a mock Indian war dance" along the Cubs' bench.

Mack was at the point of surrendering the game when a frustrated Simmons, who earlier had swung so hard on a third strike that he had fallen down, took a cut at Charlie Root's third pitch in the bottom of the seventh and struck a thunderous home run that bounced on the roof of the pavilion in left, making the score 8–1. Four successive A's batters then hit singles: Foxx to right; Miller to center; Dykes to left, scoring Foxx; and shortstop Joe Boley to right center, scoring Miller. With the score 8–3, George Burns, hitting for pitcher Ed Rommel, popped up to English for the first out.

After Bishop singled to center, scoring Dykes, Cubs manager Joe McCarthy called on Art Nehf to relieve Root, who was booed as he walked off the field. "They ought to have cheered him," English says.

On every afternoon of the '29 Series thousands of people jammed City Hall Plaza in downtown Philly to hear the play-by-play piped through speakers and to follow the movement of steel figures on a large magnetic scoreboard. Hundreds watched from open windows at City Hall and nearby office buildings. On other city corners thousands more gathered around P.A. systems that blared the play-by-play. During Game 4 the crowd's voices rose each time the A's scored in the seventh.

Haas went to the plate to face Nehf. The Mule stroked a low liner to center. English turned and saw Wilson lose the ball in the sun. "It went over his head," English says, "and he turned and ran for it." Boley scored. Bishop chased him home. The ball rolled to the wall. Haas rounded third and raced to the plate for an inside-the-park home run. In the A's dugout Dykes pounded on the man standing next to him. "We're back in the game!" Dykes shouted. Reeling under Dykes's blows, the man fell against the bats and spilled them. It was the spindly Mack.

Never once had Dykes seen his manager leave the bench. Mack usually just sat there, dressed in a dark suit, like an undertaker, and moved his fielders around with a wave of his scorecard. But he left his seat that day. "I'm sorry," said Dykes.

The 67-year-old skipper just smiled. "That's all right, Jimmy," he said. "Wasn't it wonderful?"

At Mason's Dance Hall in Philly, in a crowd gathered around a radio set on a table, 12-year-old Carmen Cangelosi leaped to his feet, screaming, as the announcer described Haas galloping home: "They're gonna win now! They're gonna win now!" City Hall Plaza erupted in howls.

The score was 8–7. Nehf walked Cochrane and was relieved by Sheriff Blake. Simmons met Blake with a single to left. Foxx then singled through the box, scoring Cochrane and tying the game up. At Philadelphia's Franklin Field, where Allen Lewis was in a football crowd of 30,000 watching Penn play Virginia Poly, the makeshift baseball scoreboard in the west stands had shown the Cubs leading 8–0. "And then the crowd erupted," says Lewis. "In the bottom of the seventh, they put '8' up on the board. Play on the field stopped, and the players all turned around and looked up. I can still see that today."

Malone was brought into the game to face Miller. Trying to brush the batter back, Malone grazed him with the first pitch, loading the bases. All that English remembers of the waning moments of that historic seventh was the ball cracking off Dykes's bat and flying into deep left, and Riggs

Stephenson going back and reaching up but fumbling the ball. "He should have made the catch," English says. The ball bounced off the wall. Simmons and Foxx scored.

The A's led 10–8. Malone then fanned Boley and Burns to end the inning.

When Mack called on Grove to pitch the last two innings, not a boy in all of Philly doubted the game's outcome. Grove was a lanky 6'3", and in his windup he looked like an oil rig: His head and hands and torso rose and dipped rhythmically—once, twice, three times—until they rose a final time and he fired. "I can still hear Grove's fastball popping into Cochrane's glove," says former A's fan John McLaughlin, 77. No one in Grove's day threw a baseball harder, and there are those who believe he threw the hardest of all time.

The Washington Post's Povich remembers a day in the mid-1930s when Bob Feller was the phenom of the hour and was to pitch at Washington's Griffith Stadium against the Senators. The retired Walter Johnson, an old friend of Povich's, was living in Maryland, and Povich invited him out to Griffith to see the kid with the heater, once clocked at 103 mph. "Walter was the most modest man you would ever know," Povich says. "And he's looking at Feller for a couple of innings and saying, 'Oh, he's fast!' Then a little while later he says, 'Oh, my! He's fast!' And then I popped the question: 'Does he throw as fast as you did?' And Walter said, 'No. And I don't think he's as fast as Lefty Grove.'"

Grove's best fastball came in at the letters and rose out of the strike zone. "If you took it, it would be a ball," English says. "But if you had two strikes on you, you couldn't take it. It was that close, and he had great control."

Tales of Grove's exploits abound. One afternoon while leading the Yankees 1–0 in the ninth inning, Grove gave up a triple to the leadoff hitter, shortstop Mark Koenig. Throwing nothing but darts, Grove then struck out Ruth, Gehrig and Bob Meusel. On nine pitches.

Grove had a Vesuvian temper that was quite as famous as his fastball, and he left behind him a trail of wrecked watercoolers and ruined lockers. There were many days when players, particularly skittish rookies, dared not speak to him as he observed the world from the long shadows of his bony scowl. One day in 1931, against the woeful St. Louis Browns, Grove was trying to win his 17th straight game without a loss—and thereby set an American League record—when a young outfielder named Jim Moore, substituting for the ailing Simmons, misjudged an easy fly ball and, ultimately, cost Grove the game, 1–0. Grove swept into the clubhouse like the Creature from the Black Lagoon. He picked up a wooden chair and smashed it into splinters. He then tried to rip off his locker door and settled for kicking it in. His rage unappeased, he tore off his uniform, sending buttons flipping like

tiddlywinks, and shredded it like a rag. He bellowed, "Where is Simmons? He
could have caught that ball in his back pocket!" Grove refused to speak to
anyone for a week, and it was years before he forgave Simmons for staying
out sick that day.

After his team stormed back to take the lead in Game 4 of the '29 Series,
Grove took to the mound for the final two innings. He faced six batters and
blew the ball past four of them. Hornsby, swinging late, flied to Miller to end
the game.

There were celebrations in the streets of Philadelphia that night. The A's
miraculous victory was the biggest story of the day. No wonder Hoover and
his wife went north behind the locomotive *President Washington* to be on
hand for Game 5.

Prohibition was still the law, and as Hoover walked across the field to
Shibe's presidential box at 1 p.m., the crowd chanted, "Beer! Beer! We want
beer!" What the crowd ended up with was something even headier: Simmons
standing on second with the score tied in the bottom of the ninth, and Bing
Miller, known as Old Reliable, at the plate. Miller was looking for his favorite
pitch—"He was the best curveball hitter in the league," old-timer Hayworth
says—so Malone whipped two fastballs past him for strikes.

"I thought, It will be another fast one," Miller would later recall. So he
shortened his grip and moved closer to the plate. Malone threw another
fastball, and Miller swung. To this day English can see the ball flying over
Hornsby's head, dropping in right center and rolling toward the fence.
Simmons charged home to win the game 3–2. The Series was over.

Mack always said that the 1929 World Series was the greatest he ever
saw, and that a diorama of that final moment should be built and set in a
special corner at Cooperstown: Here is Wilson chasing Miller's double to the
fence. Over there is Simmons plowing toward home, his spikes chopping up
dirt on the path. In the middle is Malone, standing on the mound with his
head down. And there is Hoover on his feet, applauding, and Mayor Mackey
leaping from the box again, this time tossing his hat in the air, while all the
A's charge out of the dugout onto a perfectly manicured patch of green.

It was the last World Series game that America would watch in innocence.
Fifteen days later, on Black Tuesday—Oct. 29, 1929—the stock market would
crash, and the country would begin to slide into the Great Depression.
Nothing would ever be the same. While the A's would win the World Series
again in 1930 and a third straight pennant in '31, their fate would mirror
the desperate nature of the times. By the end of 1932, scrambling to stay
afloat financially, Mack had sold Simmons, Dykes and Haas to the Chicago
White Sox for $100,000. In December '33 Mack sent Grove, Walberg and

Bishop to the Boston Red Sox for $125,000 and two nobodies, and Cochrane to the Tigers for $100,000 and one nobody. Foxx hit 58 home runs in 1932 and another 128 in the three years after that, but following the '35 season, Mack sold him to the Red Sox for $150,000 and two players. Through the 1930s and '40s the A's never got near another pennant and often had the worst team in baseball.

Of course, New York won the battle for urban supremacy. The A's were Philadelphia's last illusion of ascendancy. The poignant aftermath to all this was that the Yankees led the lobby that drove the A's out of Philadelphia and into Kansas City for the 1955 season. Like conquered slaves, the Kansas City A's became a sort of farm team for the Yankees, and over the years they helped feed New York players such as Roger Maris and Clete Boyer. The A's moved to Oakland in 1968 and won three straight World Series, from 1972 to '74. Then, when owner Charles Finley began feeling financial pressures, much as Mack had years before, the Yankees fed on Oakland's remains. Two of the A's best players, Jim (Catfish) Hunter and Reggie Jackson, figured prominently on the Yankees' 1977 and '78 championship teams.

The A's of '29 to '31 left a generation of Philadelphians with memories of what it was like to have a team that ate the great Yankees for dinner, with Cubs on the side. Today, most fans who recall the A's of that era well are in or nearing their 80's. What they all remember most vividly is that '29 World Series—the day Ehmke whipped the Cubs, the day the A's scored 10 in the seventh and the day Simmons scored from second to win the final game.

Carmen Cangelosi still remembers sitting in Mason's Dance Hall and listening to that seventh inning of Game 4 on the radio. "That inning made me a baseball fan for life," says Cangelosi, 78, a retired graphic artist. "I was an Athletics fan for life. I still know all the players. I know where they played. I know their nicknames: Bucketfoot Al. Double X. Old Reliable. Lefty. Mule. I know that 10-run inning and who scored and how they scored. Just like it was yesterday at Mason's. I remember when they won the World Series. There was a buzz in the air. An energy. You felt good about yourself, about your city, about everybody around you."

JUNE 27, 2011

The Barrio Boys

In 1949 El Paso's Bowie Bears, a team of poor Hispanic players who were too unworldly to be intimidated by their more affluent Anglo opponents, came from nowhere to win Texas's first high school baseball championship

BY ALEXANDER WOLFF

You'd saw off a broomstick for a bat. For a ball you'd beg spools of thread from the textile plant, enough to wrap into a wad you could seal with carpenter's tape. You'd go back to that factory for cloth remnants to sew together for a glove, which you'd stuff with cotton you picked at the ranch on the fringe of the barrio.

That's what you did as a kid of Mexican blood in El Paso during the 1940s to play the game that, more than anything else, could make you an American. But to become a champion at that game—to beat all Anglo comers in a world that belonged to them—how would you do that?

Borders are shape-shifting things: sometimes barriers, sometimes membranes, sometimes overlooks from which one people take the measure of another. If you were to transport yourself to the El Paso of 1949 and take up a position as far south as possible—by the north shore of the Rio Grande, in a netherland not wholly of the U.S. but not of Mexico either—you'd be a cutoff throw from Bowie High School, the only public secondary school in the U.S. then dedicated to educating Mexican-Americans. The people of south and east El Paso dealt every day with two kinds of border. The geographical one at their backs reminded them of their Mesoamerican heritage. The aspirational border just to the north, an east-west highway through downtown, was a tantalizing gateway to their country of choice.

16

Andy Morales, a member of the 1949 Bowie High baseball team, used to walk the eight blocks from his home up to Alameda Avenue, the local stretch of U.S. Highway 80, the artery that ran from San Diego to the Georgia coast. Beyond the avenue lay the Anglos' turf, where a Mexican-American would think twice before entering. Instead they focused on the road. "My friends and I, we'd compete counting out-of-state license plates on Alameda," Morales says. "I set the record one Saturday: 39 in a two-hour period." Plate-spotting gave Morales and his buddies a chance to glimpse the energy of a country ready to burst after the end of World War II, a place where they gradually came to believe they belonged.

They would owe that awakening in large part to the game they loved. Bowie High didn't field a baseball squad until 1946, when a wiry, energetic man, not 5'6", arrived from San Antonio to start one. Three years later the Bowie team included Morales, the wisecracking second baseman who never took a book home from school because there wasn't enough light to read by; Javier (Lefty) Holguin, the pitcher with a knuckleball so loco that nobody would play catch with him; Jose (Rocky) Galarza, the smoky-eyed third baseman to whom Bowie coeds dedicated yearbook pages; and Ramon Camarillo, the catcher whose hunches came to him in dreams.

Despite poverty that made them scrounge for equipment and wonder if they'd have enough food to eat, and despite discrimination that subjected them to stinging slurs and other indignities from Anglos, these boys and the other 11 players on the 1949 Bowie Bears would win the first Texas high school baseball tournament ever staged.

Bowie High sat in El Paso's Second Ward, or Segundo Barrio, home to the city's leach field and sewage-treatment plant. A smelting operation, stockyards and a meatpacking company further fouled the air. Nowhere in the U.S. did more babies die of diarrhea. The barrio had no paved streets, much less sidewalks, streetlights or parks, and 50,000 people packed themselves into less than one square mile, about twice the population density of New York City. Those not living in adobe hovels were warehoused in presidios like the ones in which Camarillo and Bowie first baseman Tony Lara grew up, where as many as 175 families—at least 700 people—were shoehorned into a single block of two-story tenement buildings, with one communal cold-water commode serving each row of two-room apartments. Compared with Anglo El Paso, the Second Ward was, Camarillo said, "like another country."

One might have expected Bowie's '49ers to be cowed by their more affluent, better equipped Anglo opponents, but, Lara says, "we were so dumb, we didn't know how to be intimidated." This obliviousness was carefully cultivated. Bowie's baseball coach made sure his players didn't wallow in want and ethnic victimization, diverting them instead with such requirements as daily classroom attendance, executing the hit-and-run and mastering the nuances of English by speaking nothing else around him. "With Nemo there were no heroes," says Gus Sambrano, a shortstop on the 1949 team. "He was the leader. His message was, 'You have leadership; follow.' We were the followers."

William Carson (Nemo) Herrera was a *fronterizo*, a child of the borderland like his players, and he probably knew them better than their parents did. He was born in Brownsville, Texas, in 1900; his father, Rodolfo, had immigrated after losing his landholdings in the political unrest that would lead to the Mexican Revolution, and his mother, Carolina, had roots in the Canary Islands. The family moved to San Antonio when Nemo was seven, and by age 13 he had become the bat boy of the San Antonio Bronchos of the Texas League. He steeped himself in the game. His speed and tenacity served him well in basketball as well as baseball at Brackenridge High. He would excel at both sports at Southwestern University in Georgetown, Texas, and play semipro baseball during summers.

After graduating he became the head basketball coach and assistant football coach at Beaumont (Texas) High for a year before joining Gulf Oil's subsidiary in Tampico, Mexico. There he progressed from pipeline work to the payroll department while playing second base on the company team.

In July 1927, during his fourth year in Tampico, Herrera was spiked during an industrial-league game and wound up in the town's American hospital. Within a month he had married the head nurse on the floor, Mary Leona Hatch, an Anglo who had been orphaned as a girl near Opelousas, La. A year later Herrera took a job as baseball and basketball coach at Lanier High in San Antonio's West Side barrio, where he would spend 18 years, including all of the Depression. His basketball teams rarely had much size, so he introduced what later generations would recognize as a full-court press, "only we called it a man-to-man-all-over-the-court defense," Herrera would say. Five times his teams reached the state final four, winning titles in 1943 and '45. Herrera acquired enough of a reputation for Texas A&M to offer him its basketball coaching job, but he turned it down for the stability of public school work. In 1946 Bowie came calling, offering a better salary and the benefits of a desert climate for Mary Leona, who suffered from hay fever, and Bill, one of their two sons, who had asthma.

Herrera's new high school belied the squalor of the Segundo Barrio. When the city expanded the school in 1941 onto what had once been a slag heap, a complex of athletic fields girdled by cottonwoods and elms bloomed in the floodplain of the Rio Grande. Signs throughout the school warned students to speak only English, and special pronunciation classes walked them through phonemes and diphthongs. "I once asked the girl sitting in front of me for a piece of paper in Spanish," Sambrano recalls. "I got suspended, and my mom and dad said, 'This was the first time, and it'll be the last!'"

La Bowie, as it was called, was a temple of assimilation. When President Franklin D. Roosevelt federalized the all-Hispanic Company E of the Texas National Guard's 141st Infantry Regiment late in 1940, half the soldiers had been Bowie Bears. Forty former Bowie students gave their lives during World War II, most of them as members of Company E, whose ranks were steadily thinned through the Italian campaign, from Salerno to San Pietro to the slaughter at the Rapido River, where over two days in January 1944 German soldiers killed, wounded or captured virtually every GI not swept to his death by the current. At the outset of the 1948–49 school year Bowie dedicated a memorial to its fallen 40, and an ROTC color guard concluded each day with a retreat ceremony, lowering the flag that flew above that cenotaph.

Herrera worked to make baseball one of Bowie's tools of Americanization. He set up a summer league in the barrio and placed kids on American Legion and commercially sponsored teams. Then he bird-dogged the games, nudging prospects he liked to go out for the Bowie varsity the following spring. (A decade later, after *Brown v. Board of Education* forced El Paso to close all-black Douglass High School, Herrera enticed a bilingual African-American kid from the South Side to enroll at Bowie; future NCAA-champion basketball coach Nolan Richardson would star for Nemo in hoops as well as baseball.)

El Paso was a military town, and eventually Nemo took his guys to play base teams at Fort Bliss and Biggs Field, where they often outperformed their older, bigger, stronger hosts. "We went out on the field against those base teams not knowing any better," says Morales, attributing many of the Bowie boys' victories to Herrera's enforced obliviousness. Always the Bears ate at the mess. "Those were the only days we'd get three square meals," Morales says.

The Growler, the school newspaper, could have taken its name from the sound in a Bowie student's stomach. Mary Leona Herrera would pack her husband off to work each day with extra sandwiches, which he left in plain sight so they could be "stolen" by his famished boys. As their stomachs filled up, so did their heads. Molding his baseball teams in the image of his basketball squads, Herrera played small ball before it, too, had a name. "We used to work on some plays for hours and hours," says Morales. "We won games on details, not because we hit the ball out of the park."

Herrera spent Saturday mornings chasing down truants. "He'd say to me, 'I'm gonna kick their butts if they're not back in school,'" remembers Bill Herrera, 77, who would accompany his father on his rounds. But back at Bowie, Nemo would just as doggedly plead the cases of those same kids to principal Frank Pollitt.

The coach treated his baseball diamond like a drawing-room carpet, picking stray pebbles off the infield. And he encouraged teasing for its democratizing effect. One day first baseman Lorenzo Martinez showed up at practice with a new glove, bought across the river in Juàrez. "It smelled like a dead salmon," Morales recalls. "Nemo said, 'You paid for that?' The madder Martinez got, the more Nemo encouraged us to give it to him.

"Nemo had a wide nose with huge nostrils, and when he got mad he looked like a raging bull. We used to joke that we should all get toreador capes." One day, as a few Bears nursed beers in a Juàrez cantina, Herrera walked in. They figuratively reached for their capes. "I'll tell you the truth," he said. "I'd rather see you guys drink beer than soda pop. Soda pop will ruin your health."

If a Bear took only one thing away from his coach, it was a credo that became an incantation. "It's not who you are or where you're from," Nemo would say. "It's who you become." The last of those words synced with the striving of the postwar generation, with the American Dream, with all those cars whizzing east and west on Highway 80.

By the spring of 1949 the new coach's spadework had begun to pay off. A San Antonio sportswriter noted "the wonderful spirit" of the Bowie baseball team—"the way the pitchers bear down, the sharp fielding and baserunning reminiscent of the old St. Louis Gashouse Gang." *The Aztec*, the Bowie yearbook, had already gone to press by the time the Bears edged El Paso High, the Anglo school on the North Side, to win the district title, so beneath a team photo the editors had written, *Good Luck to you, Team, and when these Aztecs reach you, may you have lived up to those early-season forecasts.*

When the Bears reached Lamesa, Texas, for the best-of-three bi-district playoffs against Lamesa High, their appearance on the sidewalks caused gawkers to pour out of storefronts. "You'd have thought the circus had come to town," Sambrano recalls. Some people made cracks like, "Why don't you speak English?" and "Remember the Alamo," while others called the players "hot tamales" and "greasy Mexicans."

Herrera found a restaurant that would serve the team, but not in its largely empty dining room; tables and chairs were hastily set up in the kitchen. The Bears' coach rarely brought up the discrimination his boys faced, for fear they might be tempted to use it as an excuse. Herrera regarded prejudice as the problem of the prejudiced, Sambrano says, best met with an even temper and devotion to the task at hand.

Bowie's Ruben Porras three-hit Lamesa to win the series opener 9–1, and the next day Trini Guillen scattered five hits in the 8–0 shutout that clinched the bi-district title. "Those guys were big," Sambrano remembers, "but we had what they didn't: speed." Against the Golden Tornados, the El Paso *Herald-Post* reported, the Bears "made a race track out of the diamond." In the first inning of each game Bowie scored a run on a lone hit and either an error or a walk.

By sweeping Lamesa, Bowie earned a trip to Austin for the single-elimination quarterfinals of the state tournament. "If memory serves," Lara recalls drily, "there were eight teams, and we were rated 10th to win it all."

Racial segregation still prevailed in Texas during the 1940s, but Mexican-Americans confounded the easy dichotomies of black and white. In Lubbock, where the team made a rest stop on the way to Austin, a sign in one window read, NO DOGS OR MEXICANS. "I remember seeing two drinking fountains, one COLORED and one WHITE," Morales says. "Me being brown, I didn't know which was for me. I asked a husky Anglo guy which one I was supposed to use." Morales took the man's reply ("I don't give a s---") as permission to use the white one.

In Austin, while most of the other visiting teams stayed in hotels, the Bowie team had to sleep on Army cots set up beneath the stands of Memorial Stadium, the football field on the Texas campus, and to make the long slog across the field to the Longhorns' field house to use the bathroom. But to Herrera's naive boys, the unusual accommodations only heightened the adventure. They lined the cots up like hurdles and ran races. When Hispanic businesses and social organizations back home sent telegrams of support, the Bears delighted in the spectacle of a Western Union messenger driving his motorcycle up the stadium ramp for deliveries. One day four players ventured downtown to see a movie and were bewildered when they were told, "Mexicans sit upstairs." They waited for the usher to turn a corner, then scrambled into seats in the orchestra in the dark. "We watched *The Streets of Laredo*," shortstop Ruben Rodriguez recalls, "with William Holden."

Facing Stephenville High in the quarterfinals, Bowie made another display of first-inning resourcefulness, scoring three runs on two hits. The press had expected Herrera to start his ace, Guillen, who was 7–0 for the season. One reporter wondered why the Bowie coach instead "gambled with his Number 2 pitcher."

"Number 1, Number 2, who can tell?" Herrera replied, leaving unsaid that Guillen had just spent four days in the hospital with strep throat.

Porras—"the dark-skinned righthander," as the *Austin American-Statesman* described him—struck out six while limiting Stephenville to two hits in the 5–1 victory.

The wisdom of using his ace sparingly became clear the next day, in the semifinal against Waco High. The game lasted three hours. Guillen held up until the fourth, when Waco touched him for two runs and Herrera brought Porras on in relief.

With the score tied at two in the sixth, Rodriguez stole third, then sprinted for home on a long fly ball. "I would have scored easily tagging up and that would have won us the game," Rodriguez remembers, "but me like a dummy forgot there was only one out. The ball was caught, and I got doubled up. Nemo almost strangled me, he was so mad."

The score remained tied at two into the 10th, when Waco loaded the bases with nobody out. Suddenly Herrera yelled in Spanish, "Watch the guy on third! He's gonna steal!" Camarillo called for a pitchout and picked the runner off. It was the only time any '49er can remember Herrera addressing the players in Spanish. Camarillo then cut down another runner trying to advance to third during the rundown, and during the next at bat he caught one more trying to steal second.

In the following inning Bowie centerfielder Fernie Gomez, his back to home plate, preserved the tie by running down a long drive with a catch that his teammates would recognize in Willie Mays's famous World Series play five years later. But in the top of the 12th Waco took a 3–2 lead on a double and Morales's two-base error. That might have doomed Bowie had Morales not delivered a reversal of fortune in the bottom of the inning. With Bears on second and third, Morales hit a grounder that eluded the Waco second baseman to tie the game. Then the fates squared accounts with Rodriguez too: His quailing single dropped into short centerfield to send Gomez home with the game-winner.

Neither of El Paso's daily papers sent a reporter to the tournament, so people back home followed Bowie's progress through the collect calls Herrera placed to KTSM Radio. His boys, Herrera said in his call after the Waco game, "just don't know when to quit. They're eating well and hitting that ball, and that wins ball games." Surely it's one of the few times a coach has credited a victory to eating well.

In the final, Austin's Stephen F. Austin High, the tournament's No. 1 seed, enjoyed more than home field advantage. The Maroons hadn't lost to another high school all season, even beating the Longhorns' freshmen. They had swept Robstown in their bi-district series by a combined score of 36–1 and in the semifinals eliminated Denison 12–0. The Boston Braves would soon sign the Maroons' ace, righthander Jack Brinkley, to a $65,000 bonus. Brinkley had allowed only one hit in his quarterfinal start, a 2–0 win over Lubbock.

In the final Herrera intended to counter Brinkley by pitching Guillen, but before game time he asked his catcher, Camarillo, for his thoughts. Camarillo nominated Lefty Holguin, arguing that the knuckleballer would keep the Maroons off-balance. (Camarillo later confessed that he volunteered Holguin because he had dreamed the Bears would win the title with him on the mound.) Herrera agreed—Guillen could still barely speak, and Porras had pitched 15 innings in two days—with the proviso that Holguin would get the hook if he became wild. "When you've got just one left," Herrera would later say, "that's who you pitch."

During Austin's half of the first inning, each Maroons hitter returned to the dugout with the same verdict: Holguin was "just a good batting-practice pitcher," as one told his coach, according to the *Austin American-Statesman.* "We'll get him next inning."

The next inning came, and the next and the next, yet Austin couldn't muster a hit off Holguin. Meanwhile, Bowie seized a 1–0 lead in its usual fashion, jumping on a couple of first-inning errors. But after Holguin walked two Maroons in the fourth, Herrera was true to his word, lifting Lefty for Guillen. In the sixth inning Bears rightfielder Ernesto Guzman tripled, and two infield errors on a grounder by Lara allowed both Bears to cross, putting Bowie up 3–0.

In the last inning Austin finally kindled to life. Brinkley, the pitcher, led off with a single and advanced to second on a walk. Guillen struck out the next man, but Brinkley scored after Galarza misplayed a slow roller, leaving runners on second and third. The next Austin hitter sent a single to right to knock in a second run, and as the Maroons' third base coach waved the tying run home, the favorites looked to seize their chance.

That's when all of Bowie's preparation—the harping on details, the numbing repetition, the many games against military-base teams around El Paso—paid its biggest dividend. From right Guzman sent the ball on a line. Morales, the cutoff man, let it go through to Camarillo, who fixed a tag on the Maroons' base runner for the second out.

On the play at the plate another Maroon, also representing the tying run, made his way to second base. An infield hit edged him to third. Whereupon the next Austin hitter slapped a sharp ground ball.

At least some of the 2,700 fans there that night must have wondered what the Bowie shortstop was thinking, dropping to one knee. "I was ready to block it, just in case," Rodriguez says. "I said, 'This damn ball's not going through me.'" He caught the ball cleanly, stood up and whipped it across the diamond. Cradled safely in Lara's borrowed glove, the ball made the urchins of El Paso lords of all Texas.

"There was no celebration when it was over," Morales recalls. "We took it as part of how Nemo raised us—we just picked up our belongings and walked out of there."

The Bowie players don't recall shaking hands with their opponents. And though the Bears received a trophy—"I mean, it must be about three feet high," Herrera marveled in his collect call that night—there was no formal presentation or other official act recognizing that Bowie had won Texas's inaugural baseball championship. The Bears had scratched out nothing but unearned runs to win the final, and to a typical Texan of the time it must have seemed that an alien team had seized the title by alien means. The *Austin American-Statesman* reacted as if Pancho Villa had just led a raid over the border: *Amigo, the Bowie Bears have come and gone. And they have taken with them the state baseball championship. They took it Wednesday night through a weird assortment of hits, errors, jinxes and other sundry items which ultimately meant Bowie 3, Austin 2.*

After the Bears had packed up for the ride home, a few rocks hit their bus. "There were two cops there who didn't do anything," Rodriguez recalls. When a restaurant near Fort Stockton, 240 miles from home, wouldn't serve the Bowie party, Herrera ferried food to the bus.

Around noon the following day, as the team rumbled along Highway 80 over the El Paso County line, a sheriff's deputy on a motorcycle flashed his lights to pull the bus over. One player wondered if they'd hit somebody. When the officer stepped aboard, it was to inform the driver that Bowie students were affixing a STATE CHAMPS banner to the side of the bus and that he'd be providing a police escort to the terminal. "As the bus approached downtown there were people lining both sides of the street," Lara recalls. "A lot of Anglos were cheering for us too."

The minor league El Paso Texans threw a Bowie Night that weekend, and the Bears were feted with several banquets the following week. "We can't give them anything," one city official told the local paper, "but we can sure feed them."

Still, the Bears sensed that even in their hometown, they were given a second-class celebration. Instead of the mayor meeting them at the bus station, as had been announced, an alderman did the honors. "At the depot some guy came up to Nemo and gave him a box with a shirt in it," Morales remembers. "When [El Paso's] Austin High won the district in football, their coach got a brand new car."

None of the players stopped by the terminal's baggage room to claim luggage. "We all carried paper bags with our stuff off the bus," Morales says. "I walked a mile, hopped the streetcar, then walked the eight blocks home."

The night before the team had left for Austin, students in a Bowie home economics class stayed up late preparing hard-boiled eggs for the players to eat on the trip. The Bears had won, one of those coeds would say at a Bowie reunion years later, "*porque jugaron con huevos.*" Because they played with eggs—that is, with balls.

Sixty years would pass before another team from El Paso County claimed a state baseball title. In 2009, Socorro High, a school with a Hispanic enrollment of more than 95%, ventured to the Austin suburb of Round Rock to beat Austin Westlake and Lufkin for the Class 5A crown. Early in the semifinal a knot of Westlake supporters unfurled a Confederate flag, chanted "We speak English!" and waved their I.D.'s. "If we can have something like that in our day and age," says Jesus Chavez, Bowie's current principal and a former Socorro administrator, "I can't even imagine what they went through in 1949."

A month after their victory the Socorro players visited Bowie to present championship rings—not awarded in 1949—to the eight surviving Bears. A new Bowie High sits on an old melon field that in '49 was part of Mexico but in 1963 passed into the U.S. as part of the Chamizal Settlement between the two countries.

If the borderland remains its protean self, in one respect it's as hard as a barrier can be: While Juàrez becomes an ever more Hobbesian hell of drug violence, in which more than 8,000 people have been murdered over the past three years, El Paso remains virtually immune. Bowie nonetheless serves the second-poorest zip code in the U.S. The annual median income in the Segundo Barrio languishes below $20,000, and 68.8% of the children in Bowie's catchment area are considered at risk. Chavez says, "This school is about facing adversity, moving forward and beating the odds."

The 1949 Bears and their young counterparts from Socorro gathered near the commemorative display in Bowie's Fine Arts Building, where a visitor can punch up audio of Nemo Herrera's collect calls back to KTSM Radio. The 400 people on hand included Peter Contreras, assistant athletic director of the state's University Interscholastic League, the high school sanctioning body that hadn't seen fit to properly lodge or honor the Bears 60 years earlier. That Contreras is Hispanic is only one of uncountable examples of how times have changed. As for the old slights, the '49ers were "always very restrained how they responded," says Reyes Mata, the South

Side native who helped organize the event. "They always maintained their dignity."

What did they become, Nemo Herrera's barrio boys from El Paso and San Antonio? Judges and produce barons and big-city postmasters. Mechanics and firefighters and civil servants. Opticians and claims adjusters and veterans, many of them decorated. An outsized number chose Nemoesque professions: teaching, educational administration, coaching.

Rocky Galarza, the old third baseman, put an open-air boxing ring behind his South Side tavern. He plucked kids off the streets, and if the streets pulled them back, as they briefly did eventual WBF lightweight champ Juan (Ernie) Lazcano, Galarza would simply wait until they returned, wiser, to the sanctuary of his ring. The best ones ultimately made their way to L.A. or Dallas or Houston, where someone else cashed in on them; Galarza, in cowboy boots and jeans, his black hair flowing as he worked a guy out, simply turned to the next kid to save. One night in 1997 one of Galarza's barmaids shot and killed him in his sleep. Seven years later, on the eve of a title fight in Las Vegas, Lazcano told Bill Knight of the *El Paso Times*, "Sometimes, when I'm asleep, I still see him, still hear him. He's telling me, 'Come on, Champ, don't give up. Feint. Don't just stand there. Move your feet.' It's nice to know, isn't it, that if you do something special for people the way Rocky did, that you live on through them?"

Andy Morales, the license-plate-spotting second baseman, also "went Nemo," as the old Bears put it. After winning a football scholarship to New Mexico and serving in Korea with the Navy, he became baseball coach at El Paso's Austin High. There, in the early '70s, he taught the game to an Anglo kid named Chris Forbes, who grew up to coach Socorro to that 2009 state title. Morales followed the Bulldogs as they made a familiar way east through the draw, to Midland and greater Austin, as excited as he had been as a Bowie Bear. He was amazed that a dozen spirit buses would make the trip from El Paso for the final.

As for Herrera himself, he remained at Bowie until 1960. "The [Bowie] boys knew little of fundamentals," he said upon leaving, "and I was told I couldn't teach them. But I did." He took a post at another barrio high school, Edgewood of San Antonio. After one year Herrera—by now known as *el viejo*, the old man—returned to El Paso to coach baseball at Coronado High, a new, largely Anglo school on the outskirts of town. "I couldn't get those guys to do a damn thing," he would say. "They had a car in the parking lot and a gal on their arm."

Upon reaching the mandatory retirement age of 70, he returned one last time to San Antonio, working as director of civilian recreation at Kelly Air Force Base for 10 years before retiring again. He died in 1984. Herrera remains the only Texas high school coach to have won state titles in two sports, and his name can be found throughout the barrios of the two cities: on a scholarship fund, an elementary school and a baseball field in El Paso; and on a scholarship fund, a basketball court and the Kelly Air Force Base civilian rec center in San Antonio. "It's almost a competition between the two cities to see who can honor Nemo the most," says his son Charles, 75.

Of the eight members of the 1949 Bowie Bears still living, the five in El Paso gather for breakfast every few months at a Mexican restaurant on the East Side. Listen in, and you'll hear the sounds of baseball: chatter, needling, kibitzing, stories that reach across the years and often involve their old coach. Not that it matters particularly, but the banter is much more likely to be in English than in Spanish. And just so you know, Morales says, "For 60 years we've never lost a conversation."

LEGENDS

AUGUST 21, 1995

The Legacy of the Last Great Player on the Last Great Team

SPORTS ILLUSTRATED's obituary for legendary New York Yankees slugger Mickey Mantle, who died in August of 1995 at the age of 63 due to cancer in his liver

BY RICHARD HOFFER

Mickey Mantle, with his death Sunday at 63, passes from these pages forever and becomes the property of anthropologists, people who can more properly put the calipers to celebrity, who can more accurately track the force of personality. We can't do it anymore, couldn't really do it to begin with. He batted this, hit that. You can look it up. Hell, we do all the time. But there's nothing in our library, in all those numbers, that explains how Mantle moves so smoothly from baseball history into national legend, a country's touchstone, the lopsided grin on our society.

He wasn't the greatest player who ever lived, not even of his time perhaps. He was a centerfielder of surprising swiftness, a switch-hitter of heart-stopping power, and he was given to spectacle: huge home runs (his team, the New York Yankees, invented the tape-measure home run for him); huge seasons (.353, 52 HRs, 130 RBIs to win the Triple Crown in 1956); one World Series after another (12 in his first 14 seasons). Yet, for one reason or another, he never became Babe Ruth or Joe DiMaggio—or, arguably, even Willie Mays, his exact contemporary.

31

But for generations of men, he's the guy, has been the guy, will be the guy. And what does that mean exactly? A woman beseeches Mantle, who survived beyond his baseball career as a kind of corporate greeter, to make an appearance, to surprise her husband. Mantle materializes at some cocktail party, introductions are made, and the husband weeps in the presence of such fantasy made flesh. It means that, exactly.

It's easy to account, at least partly, for the durability and depth of his fame: He played on baseball's most famous team during the game's final dominant era. From Mantle's rookie season in 1951—the lead miner's son signed out of Commerce, Okla., for $1,100—to his injury-racked final year in 1968, baseball was still the preeminent game in the country. This was baseball B.C. (Before Cable), and a nation's attention was not scattered come World Series time. Year in, year out, men and boys in every corner of the country were given to understand during this autumnal rite that there really was only one baseball team and that there really was only one player: No. 7, talked with a twang, knocked the ball a country mile. But it was more than circumstance that fixed Mantle in the national psyche; he did hit 18 World Series home runs, a record, over the course of 65 of the most watched games of our lives.

Even knowing that, acknowledging the pin-striped pedigree, the fascination still doesn't add up. If he was a pure talent, he was not, as we found out, a pure spirit. But to look upon his youthful mug today, three decades after he played, is to realize how uncluttered our memories of him are. Yes, he was a confessed drunk; yes, he shorted his potential—he himself said so. And still, looking at the slightly uplifted square jaw, all we see is America's romance with boldness, its celebration of muscle, a continent's comfort in power during a time when might did make right. Mantle was the last great player on the last great team in the last great country, a postwar civilization that was booming and confident, not a trouble in the world.

Of course, even had he not reflected the times, Mantle would have been walking Americana. His career was storybook stuff, hewing more to our ideas of myth than any player's since Ruth. Spotted playing shortstop on the Baxter Springs Whiz Kids, he was delivered from a rural obscurity into America's distilled essence of glamour. One year Mantle is dropping 400 feet into the earth, very deep into Oklahoma, to mine lead on his father's crew, another he's spilling drinks with Whitey Ford and Billy Martin at the Copa.

A lesson reaffirmed: Anything can happen to anybody in this country, so long as they're daring in their defeats and outsized in victory. Failure is forgiven of the big swingers, in whom even foolishness is flamboyant. Do you remember Mantle in Pittsburgh in the 1960 Series, twice whiffing in

Game 1 and then, the next day, crushing two? Generations of men still do. The world will always belong to those who swing from the heels.

Still, Mantle's grace was mostly between the lines; he developed no particular bonds beyond his teammates, and he established no popularity outside of baseball. As he was dying from liver cancer, none of the pre-tributes remarked much on his charm. And, as he was dying from a disease that many have presumed was drinking-related, there was a revisionist cast to the remembrances. Maybe he wasn't so much fun after all.

But, back then, he most certainly was. Drunkenness had a kind of high-life cachet in the '50s: It was manly, inasmuch as you were a stand-up guy who could be counted on to perform the next afternoon, and it was glamorous. Down the road, as Mantle would later confess from the other side of rehabilitation, it was merely stupid. But palling around with Billy and Whitey—just boys, really, they all had little boys' names—it amounted to low-grade mischief. Whatever harm was being done to families and friends, it was a small price to pay for the excitement conferred upon a workaday nation.

In any event, we don't mind our heroes flawed, or even doomed. Actually, our interest in Mantle was probably piqued by his obvious destiny, the ruin he often foretold. As a Yankee he was never a whole person, having torn up his knee for the first time in his first World Series in '51. Thereafter, increasingly, he played in gauze and pain, his prodigal blasts heroically backlit by chronic injury. But more: At the hospital after that '51 incident, Mantle learned that his father, Mutt, admitted to the same hospital that same day, was dying of Hodgkin's disease. It was a genetic devastation that had claimed every Mantle male before the age of 40. The black knowledge of this looming end informed everything Mickey did; there was little time, and every event had to be performed on a grand scale, damn the consequences. Everything was excused.

As we all know, having participated in this gloomy death watch, it didn't end with that kind of drama. It was Billy, the third of Mantle's four sons, who came down with Hodgkin's, and who later died of a heart attack at 36. Mickey lived much longer, prospering in an era of nostalgia, directionless in golf and drinking, coasting on a fame that confounded him (Why was this man, just introduced to him, weeping?).

Then Mantle, who might forever have been embedded in a certain culture, square-jawed and unchanged, did a strange thing. Having failed to die in a way that might have satisfied the mythmakers, he awoke with a start and checked himself into the Betty Ford Center. This was only a year and a half ago, and, of course, it was way too late almost any way you figure it. Still, his remorse seemed genuine. The waste seemed to gall him, and his anger shook the rest of us.

The generation of men who watched him play baseball, flipped for his cards or examined every box score must now puzzle out the attraction he held. The day he died there was the usual rush for perspective and the expected sweep through the Yankee organization. They said the usual things. But former teammate Bobby Murcer reported that he had talked to the Mick before he had gone into the hospital the final time—neither a liver transplant nor chemotherapy could arrest the cancer or stop his pain—and Mantle, first thing, asked how a fund-raiser for children affected by the Oklahoma City bombing was going, something he and Murcer, also from Oklahoma, were involved in. It was odd, like the sudden decision to enter rehab and rescue his and his family's life, and it didn't really square with our idea of Mantle.

But let's just say you were of this generation of men, that you once had been a kid growing up in the '50s, on some baseball team in Indiana, and you remember stitching a No. 7 on the back of your KIRCHNER'S PHARMACY T-shirt, using red thread and having no way of finishing off a stitch, meaning your hero's number would unravel indefinitely and you would have to do it over and over, stupid and unreformed in your idolatry. And today here's this distant demigod, in his death, taking human shape. What would you think now?

JULY 12, 1999

The Left Arm of God

He was a consummate artist on the mound, the most dominant
player of his time, yet he shunned fame and always put team
above self. On the field or off, Sandy Koufax was pitcher perfect

BY TOM VERDUCCI

He sat in the same booth every time. It was always the one in back, farthest
from the door. The trim, darkly handsome man would come alone, without
his wife, nearly every morning at six o'clock for breakfast at Dick's Diner
in Ellsworth, Maine, about 14 miles from their home. He often wore one of
those red-and-black-checkered shirts you expect to see in Maine, though
he wasn't a hunter. He might not have shaved that morning. He would
walk past the long counter up front, the one with the swivel stools that,
good Lord, gave complete strangers license to strike up a conversation. He
preferred the clearly delineated no-trespassing zone of a booth. He would
rest those famously large hands on the Formica tabletop, one of those mini-
jukeboxes to his left and give his order to Annette, the waitress, in a voice as
soft and smooth as honey.

He came so often that the family who ran the diner quickly stopped
thinking of him as Sandy Koufax, one of the greatest pitchers who ever
lived. They thought of him the way Koufax strived all his life to be thought
of, as something better even than a famous athlete: He was a regular.

Dick Anderson and his son Richard, better known as Bub, might glance
up from their chores when Koufax walked in, but that was usually all. One
time Bub got him to autograph a napkin but never talked baseball with
him. Annette, Bub's sister, always worked the section with that back booth.

35

For three years Koufax came to the diner and not once did he volunteer information to her about his life or his career. It was always polite small talk. Neighborly. Regular.

Koufax was 35, five years since his last pitch, in 1966, when he came eagerly, even dreamily, to Maine, the back booth of America. He had seen a photo spread in *Look* magazine about the Down East country homestead of a man named Blakely Babcock, a 350-pound Burpee Seed salesman, gentleman farmer and gadfly whom everybody called Tiny. Tiny would invite neighbors and friends over for cookouts and dinner parties, during which he liked to consume great quantities of food, then rub his huge belly and bellow laughingly to his wife, "So, what's for dinner, Alberta?" Tiny's North Ellsworth farmhouse caught Koufax's fancy at just about the same time one of his wife's friends was renovating her farmhouse in Maine. Wouldn't it be perfect, Koufax thought, to live quietly, almost anonymously, in an old farmhouse just like Tiny's?

Alberta Babcock was pulling a hot tin of sweet-smelling blueberry muffins from the oven when Koufax first saw the place in person, and the old Cape-style house was filled with so many flowers that it looked like a watercolor come to life. Koufax was sold, and on Oct. 4, 1971, Sanford and Anne Koufax of Los Angeles, as they signed the deed, took out a 15-year, $15,000 mortgage from Penobscot Savings Bank and bought what was known as Winkumpaugh Farm from Blakely and Alberta Babcock for about $30,000. A cord was cut. The rest of Sandy Koufax's life had begun.

The Babcocks had lived in the farmhouse since 1962, but no one was exactly sure how old the place was. Property records were lost to a fire at Ellsworth City Hall in 1933, and records from 1944 list the farmhouse's age even then only as "old." Nestled on the side of a small mountain off a dusty dirt road called Happytown Road and around the corner from another called Winkumpaugh Road, the farmhouse was the perfect setting for a man hoping to drop out of sight, even if that man was a beloved American icon who mastered the art of pitching as well as anyone who ever threw a baseball. A man so fiercely modest and private that while at the University of Cincinnati on a basketball scholarship, he didn't tell his parents back in Brooklyn that he was also on the baseball team. The man whose mother requested one of the first copies of his 1966 autobiography, *Koufax*, so she could find out something about her son. ("You never told *me* anything," she said to him.) The man who in 1968, two years after retiring with three Cy Young Awards, four no-hitters and five ERA titles, mentioned nothing of his baseball career upon meeting a pretty young woman named Anne who was redecorating her parents' Malibu beach house. Koufax did offer to help her paint, though. It wasn't until several days later that she learned his identity—and he learned hers: She was the daughter of actor Richard Widmark. They were married six months later in her father's West Los Angeles home in front of about a dozen people.

The last two years that Anne and Sandy Koufax lived at Winkumpaugh Farm were the first in his life when he was bound by neither school nor work. After commuting from Maine during the summer of 1972 for his sixth season as a television commentator for NBC, he quit with four years left on his contract. He loathed the work. He could tell you every pitch thrown by every pitcher in a game without having written anything down, but there was a problem: He didn't like to talk about himself. At a meeting before Game 5 of the 1970 World Series, fellow announcer Joe Garagiola noted that Cincinnati's starting pitcher, Jim Merritt, had an injured arm. "I said, 'Sandy, what a perfect thing to talk about. That's what you had, too.'" Garagiola says. "But he said he didn't want to talk about himself. He wouldn't do it."

"Every time he had to leave Maine to work one of those games, it broke his heart," says MaJo Keleshian, a friend and former neighbor who attended Sarah Lawrence College with Anne. She still lives without a television on land she and her husband bought from Koufax. "He was very happy here. He came here to be left alone."

Since then only his address has changed—and many times, at that. Joe DiMaggio, baseball's other legendary protector of privacy, was practically Rodmanesque compared with Koufax. DiMaggio was regal, having acquired even the stiff-handed wave of royalty. We watched the graying of DiMaggio as he played TV pitchman and public icon. Koufax is a living James Dean, the aura of his youth frozen in time; he has grayed without our even knowing it. He is a sphinx, except that he doesn't want anyone to try to solve his riddle.

Koufax was the kind of man boys idolized, men envied, women swooned over and rabbis thanked, especially when he refused to pitch Game 1 of the 1965 World Series because it fell on Yom Kippur. And when he was suddenly, tragically, done with baseball, he slipped into a life nearly monastic in its privacy.

One question comes to mind: Why? Why did he turn his back on Fame and Fortune, the twin sirens of celebrity? Why did the most beloved athlete of his time carve out a quiet life—the very antithesis of the American dream at the close of the century? For the answer I will go searching for the soul of Sandy Koufax, which seems as mysterious as the deepest Maine woods on a moonless night.

Bob Ballard is a retiree in Vero Beach, Fla., who works part time as a security guard at Dodgertown, the sleepiest spring training site in all of baseball. Sometime around 1987 he told the secretary who worked for

Peter O'Malley, then the owner of the Dodgers, how much he would enjoy getting an autograph from Koufax for his birthday. A few days later Koufax, working for the Dodgers as a roving pitching instructor, handed Ballard an autographed ball and said, "Happy birthday."

Every year since then, on or about Ballard's birthday, Koufax has brought the old man an autographed ball. Koufax delivered on schedule this year for Ballard's 79th birthday. "He's a super, super guy," says Ballard. "Very courteous. A real gentleman. A lot nicer than these players today."

It is a lovely day for golf. I am standing in the tiny pro shop of the Bucksport (Maine) Golf Club, a rustic, nine-hole track. The parking lot is gravel. Even the rates are quaint: $15 to play nine holes, $22 for 18, and you are instructed to play the white tees as the front nine, then the blue tees as the back nine. There is no valet parking, no tiny pyramids of Titleists on the scrubby range, no MEMBERS ONLY signs, no attitude. This is Koufax's kind of place. I am standing in the imprint of his golf spikes, a quarter-century removed. He was a member of the Bucksport Golf Club, one of its more enthusiastic members.

It wasn't enough that he play golf, he wanted to be good enough to win amateur tournaments. Koufax was working on the engine of a tractor one day when a thought came to him about a certain kind of grip for a golf club. He dropped his tools, dashed into his machine shop, fiddled with a club and then raced off to the Bucksport range. He was still wearing dungaree shorts and a grease-splattered shirt when he arrived. "That's how dedicated to the game he was," says Gene Bowden, one of his old playing partners.

Koufax diligently whittled his handicap to a six and entered the 1973 Maine State Amateur. He advanced to the championship flights by draining a 30-foot putt on the 18th hole. He missed the next cut, though, losing on the last hole of a playoff.

Koufax is exacting in every pursuit. Ron Fairly, one of his Dodgers roommates, would watch with exasperation as Koufax, dressed suavely for dinner in glossy alligator shoes, crisply pressed slacks and a fruit-colored alpaca sweater, would fuss over each hair in his sideburns. "Reservation's in 15 minutes, and it's a 20-minute ride," Fairly would announce, and Koufax would go right on trimming until his sideburns were in perfect alignment.

He brought that same meticulousness to Maine. It wasn't enough to dabble in carpentry and home electronics—he built and installed a sound system throughout the house. It wasn't enough to cook—he became a gourmet cook, whipping up dishes not by following recipes but by substituting ingredients and improvising by feel. Later in life it wasn't enough to jog; he ran a marathon. He didn't just take up fishing, he moved to Idaho for some of the best salmon fishing in the world. He defines himself by the fullness of his life and the excellence he seeks in every corner of it, not the way the rest of the word defines him: through the narrow prism of his career as a pitcher. "I think he pitched for the excellence of it," Keleshian says. "He didn't set out to beat someone or make anyone look bad. He used himself as his only measure of excellence. And he was that way in everything he did. He was a fabulous cook, but he was almost never quite satisfied. He'd say, Ah, it needs a little salt or a little oregano, or something. Once in a great while he'd say, Ah-ha! That's it!"

Walt Disney, John Wayne, Kirk Douglas, Daryl Zanuck and all the other Hollywood stars who held Dodgers season tickets when Koufax was the biggest star in America never came to Winkumpaugh Farm. The fans never came, either, though a fat sack of fan mail arrived every week, even seven years after he last threw a pitch. The place was perfect, all right. He could move about without fuss, without having to talk about his least favorite subject: himself. "He did say once that he'd rather not talk baseball and his career," Bowden says. "And we never did."

"When Hideo Nomo was getting really, really big, Sandy told me, 'He'd better learn to like room service,'" O'Malley says. "That's how Sandy handled the attention." Koufax almost never left his hotel room in his final two seasons for the Dodgers. It wasn't enough that he move to a creaky, charmingly flawed farmhouse in Maine with a leaky basement, he quickly bought up almost 300 acres adjacent to it.

Not even the serenity of Maine, though, could quell Koufax's wanderlust. After three years he decided the winters were too long and too cold. The farmhouse needed constant work. His stepfather took ill in California. Koufax sold Winkumpaugh Farm on July 22, 1974, leaving for the warmer but still rural setting of Templeton, Calif., in San Luis Obispo County.

Koufax is 63, in terrific shape and, thanks to shoulder surgery a few years back, probably still able to get hitters out. (In his 50s Koufax was pitching in a fantasy camp when a camper scoffed after one of his pitches, "Is that all you've got?" Koufax's lips tightened and his eyes narrowed—just about all the emotion he would ever show on the mound—and he unleashed a heater that flew damn near 90 mph.)

The romance with Anne ended with a divorce in the early '80s. He remarried a few years later, this time to a fitness enthusiast who, like Anne, had a passion for the arts. That marriage ended in divorce last winter. Friends say Koufax is delighted to be on his own again. Says Lou Johnson, a former Dodgers teammate, "He has an inner peace that's really deep-rooted. I wish I had that."

He is the child of a broken marriage who rejected everything associated with his father, including his name. Sanford Braun was three years old when Jack and Evelyn Braun divorced, and his contact with Jack all but ended about six years later when Jack remarried and stopped sending alimony payments. Evelyn, an accountant, married Irving Koufax, an attorney, a short time later. "When I speak of my father," he wrote in his autobiography, "I speak of Irving Koufax, for he has been to me everything a father could be." Koufax rarely spoke to Jack Braun, and not at all during his playing days. When the Dodgers played at Shea Stadium, Jack would sit a few rows behind the visitors' dugout and cheer for the son who neither knew nor cared that he was there.

Now there is but one Koufax bearing that name. He has no children, no immediate family—both his mother and stepfather are deceased. The death of his only sibling, a sister, in 1997, had a profound impact on a man who has struggled to deal with the deaths of friends and other players from his era. "People react to death differently," O'Malley says. "Sandy takes a death very, very, very hard."

He has a small circle of close friends, and many other buddies who always seem to be one or two phone numbers behind him. "It sounds odd, but he's very home-oriented," Keleshian says, "yet very nomadic."

His list of home addresses since he stopped playing baseball reads like a KOA campground directory: North Ellsworth, Maine; Templeton and Santa Barbara, Calif.; Idaho; Oregon (where his second wife ran a gallery); North Carolina (where he and his second wife kept horses); and Vero Beach—not to mention extensive trips to Hawaii, New Zealand and Europe. This spring he was looking for a new place to spend the summer and once again had his eye on rural New England. "He doesn't say much about what he's up to," says Bobby McCarthy, a friend who owns a Vero Beach restaurant that Koufax prefers to frequent when it's closed. "We'll be sitting in the restaurant in the morning, and that night I'll see he's at a Mets game in New York. And he hadn't said anything that morning about going there. But that's Sandy."

At 8:30 on a lovely Sunday morning in March, I attend a chapel service in the Sandy Koufax Room at Dodgertown. Players and coaches in their fabulously white Dodgers uniforms are there, but not Koufax. The Dodgers give glory to Jesus Christ every Sunday in a conference room named for the greatest Jewish ballplayer who ever lived. Outside the room is a picture of a young Koufax, smiling, as if he is in on the joke.

Don Sutton is a native of Clio, Ala., who reached the big leagues at age 21 in 1966, which is to say he got there just in time. His first season in the majors was Koufax's last. Says Sutton, "I saw how he dressed, how he tipped, how he carried himself and knew that's how a big leaguer was supposed to act. He was a star who didn't feel he was a star. That's a gift not many people have."

Tommy Hutton, who grew up in Los Angeles, also made his big league debut for the Dodgers in '66, entering the ninth inning at first base as Koufax finished off the Pirates 5–1 on Sept. 16. Says Hutton, now a broadcaster for the Marlins, "I'll never forget this. After the game he came up to me and said, 'Congratulations.' Ever since then, I've always made it a point to congratulate a guy when he gets into his first game."

I am standing in a tunnel under the stands behind home plate at Dodger Stadium on a clear summer night in 1998. Koufax is about 75 feet in front of me, seated on a folding chair on the infield while the Dodgers honor Sutton with the retirement of his number before a game against the Braves. When the program ends, Sutton and all his guests—former Dodgers Ron Cey and Steve Garvey among them—march past me toward an elevator that will take them to a stadium suite. All except Koufax. He is gone. Vanished. I find out later that as soon as the ceremony was over, he arose from his chair, walked briskly into the Dodgers dugout and kept right on going into the team parking lot and off into the night. "That's Sandy," said one team official. "We call him the Ghost."

I am searching for an apparition. I never saw Koufax pitch, never felt the spell he held over America. I had just turned six when Koufax walked into the Sansui room of the Regent Beverly Wilshire Hotel on Nov. 18, 1966, to announce his retirement from baseball. To have missed his brilliance heightens the fascination. For me he is black-and-white newsreel footage shot from high behind home plate, and an inexhaustible supply of statistics that border on the absurd. A favorite: Every time he took the mound, Koufax was twice as likely to throw a shutout as he was to hit a batter.

Koufax was 30 years old when he quit. Women at the press conference cried. Reporters applauded him, then lined up for his autograph. The world, including his teammates, was shocked. In the last 26 days of his career, including a loss in the 1966 World Series, Koufax started seven times, threw five complete-game wins and had a 1.07 ERA. He clinched the pennant for Los Angeles for the second straight year with a complete game on two days' rest. Everyone knew he was pitching with traumatic arthritis in his left elbow, but how bad could it be when he pitched like that?

It was this bad: Koufax couldn't straighten his left arm—it was curved like a parenthesis. He had to have a tailor shorten the left sleeve on all his coats. Use of his left arm was severely limited when he wasn't pitching. On bad days he'd have to bend his neck to get his face closer to his left hand so that he could shave. And on the worst days he had to shave with his right hand. He still held his fork in his left hand, but sometimes he had to bend closer to the plate to get the food into his mouth.

His elbow was shot full of cortisone several times a season. His stomach was always queasy from the cocktail of anti-inflammatories he swallowed before and after games, which he once said made him "half-high on the mound." He soaked his elbow in an ice bath for 30 minutes after each game, his arm encased in an inner tube to protect against frostbite. And even then his arm would swell an inch. He couldn't go on like this, not when his doctors could not rule out the possibility that he was risking permanent damage to his arm.

Not everyone was shocked when Koufax quit. In August 1965 he told Phil Collier, a writer for *The San Diego Union-Tribune* to meet him in a room off the Dodgers' clubhouse. Koufax and Collier often sat next to each other on the team's charter flights, yapping about politics, the economy or literature. "Next year's going to be my last year," Koufax told Collier. "The damn thing's all swelled up. And I hate taking the pills. They slow my reactions. I'm afraid someone's going to hit a line drive that hits me in the head."

Koufax didn't tell anyone else, and he made Collier promise not to write the story. So they shared that little secret throughout the 1966 season. When the Dodgers went to Atlanta, Collier whispered to Koufax, "Last time here for you." And that is exactly how Koufax pitched that season, as if he would never pass this way again. He won a career-high 27 games, pushing his record in his final six seasons to 129–47. He was 11–3 in his career in 1–0 games. In 1965 and '66 he was 53–17 for the club that scored fewer runs than all but two National League teams.

"He's the greatest pitcher I ever saw," says Hall of Famer Ernie Banks. "I can still see that big curveball. It had a great arc on it, and he never bounced it in the dirt. Sandy's curve had a lot more spin than anybody else's—it spun like a fastball coming out of his hand—and he had the fastball of a pure strikeout pitcher. It jumped up at the end. The batter would swing half a foot under it. Most of the time we knew what was coming, because he held his hands closer to his head when he threw a curveball, but it didn't matter. Even though he was tipping off his pitches, you still couldn't hit him."

Koufax was so good, he once taped a postgame radio show with Vin Scully *before* the game. He was so good, the relief pitchers treated the night before his starts the way a sailor treats shore leave. On one rare occasion in which Koufax struggled to go his usual nine innings—he averaged 7.64 per start from '61 to '66—manager Walter Alston visited his pitcher while a hungover Bob Miller warmed in the bullpen.

"How do you feel, Sandy?" Alston asked.

"I'll be honest with you, Skip," Koufax said. "I feel a hell of a lot better than the guy you've got warming up."

On Nov. 17, 1966, Collier came home from watching the Ice Capades and was greeted with this message from his babysitter: "Mr. Koufax has been trying to call you for a couple of hours." Collier knew exactly what it was about. He called Koufax.

"I'm calling the wire services in the morning," Koufax told him. "Is there anything you need from me now?"

"Sandy," Collier said, "I wrote that story months ago. It's in my desk drawer. All I have to do is make a call and tell them to run it."

Says Collier, "It was the biggest story I'll ever write. They ran it across the top of Page One with a big headline like it was the end of World War II."

I have gotten ahold of Koufax's home telephone number in Vero Beach, but I do not dare dial it. Even from afar I can feel the strength of this force field he has put around himself. To puncture it with a surprise phone call means certain disaster. I have read that Koufax so hated the intrusions of the telephone during his playing days that he once took to stashing it in his oven. Buzzie Bavasi, the Dodgers' general manager, would have to send telegrams to his house saying, "Please call."

I don't call. I am an archeologist—dig I must, but with the delicate touch of brushes and hand tools. I enlist the help of Koufax's friends. Now I understand why people I talk to about Koufax are apprehensive. They ask, Does Sandy know you're doing this story? (Yes.) It's as if speaking about him is itself a violation of his code of honor.

There is a 58-year-old health-care worker in Portchester, N.Y., named David Saks who attended Camp Chi-Wan-Da in Kingston, N.Y., in the summer of 1954. Koufax, who is from Brooklyn, was his counselor. "He was this handsome, strapping guy, a great athlete who had professional scouts trying to sign him," Saks says. "I was 13. He was 18. We all were in awe of him. But even then there were signs that he wanted people to avoid fussing about him to the nth degree."

Saks needed a day to think before agreeing to share two photographs he has from Camp Chi-Wan-Da that include the teenage Koufax. "Knowing how he is...," Saks explains. Saks has neither seen nor spoken to Koufax in 45 years. He does, however, have recurring dreams about happy reunions with him.

In Vero Beach, where Koufax spends much of his time now, the townsfolk choose not to speak his name when they come upon him in public. They will say, "Hello, Mr. K.," when they run into him at the post office or, "Hello, my good friend," rather than tip off a tourist and risk creating one of those moments Koufax detests.

"Sandy has a quiet, productive way about him," says Garagiola, president of the Baseball Assistance Team (BAT), a charity that helps former players in medical or financial straits. Garagiola sometimes calls Koufax to ask him to speak with former players who are particularly hurting. "He can't really understand that," Garagiola says. "He's got a great streak of modesty. He'll say, 'What do they want to talk to me for?' He is a Hall of Famer in every way. He'll make an impact. You won't know it and I won't know it, but the guy he's helping will know it. Above anything else, I'll remember him for his feelings for fellow players."

There was an outfielder named Jim Barbieri who joined the Dodgers during the 1966 pennant race. He was so nervous that he would talk to himself in the shower, and the pressure so knotted his stomach that he once threw up in the locker room. One day Koufax motioned toward Barbieri in the dugout and said to Fairly, "I have a responsibility to guys like him. If I pitch well from here on out, I can double that man's income." Koufax, who was referring to World Series bonus money, went 8–2 the rest of the season. From 1963 to '66 he was 14–2 in September, with a 1.55 ERA.

Earlier in that 1966 season a television network offered Koufax $25,000 to allow their cameras to trail him on and off the field. Koufax said he would do it for $35,000, and only if that money was divided so that every Dodgers player, coach and trainer received $1,000.

Koufax attends Garagiola's BAT dinner in New York City every winter, and always draws the biggest crowd among the many Hall of Famers who sign autographs during the cocktail hour. "I grew up in Brooklyn," says Lester Marks of Ernst and Young, which secured the Koufax table this year. "I went to Ebbets Field all the time. I'm 52. I thought seeing Sandy Koufax pitch was the thrill of a lifetime, but meeting him as an adult was an even bigger thrill. My guests were shocked at what a down-to-earth gentleman he is."

After this year's dinner I walked through the crowded ballroom toward Koufax's table, only to see him hustle to a secured area on the dais. He posed for pictures with the Toms River, N.J., Little League world champions. Then he was gone, this time for a night of refreshments in Manhattan with New York Mets pitcher Al Leiter, as close to a protege as Koufax has in baseball.

I should mention that I did meet Sandy Koufax a few years ago, before I embarked on this quest to find out what makes him run. I was at Dodgertown, standing next to the row of six pitching mounds adjacent to the Dodgers' clubhouse. "Sacred ground," as former Dodgers pitcher Claude Osteen calls it, seeing as it was here that Branch Rickey hung his famous strings, forming the borders of a strike zone at which every Dodgers pitcher from Newcombe to Koufax to Sutton to Hershiser took aim. (Koufax was so wild as a rookie that pitching coach Joe Becker took him to a mound behind the clubhouse so he would not embarrass himself in front of teammates and fans.) Tan and lean, Koufax looked as if he had just come in from the boardwalk to watch the Los Angeles pitchers throw. He was dressed in sandals, a short pair of shorts and a polo shirt. I said something to him about the extinction of the high strike. Koufax said that he hadn't needed to have that pitch called a strike in order to get batters to swing at his high heater. When I followed up with a question about whether baseball should enforce the high strike in today's strike zone, Koufax's face tightened. I could almost hear the alarms sounding in his head, his warning system announcing, This is an interview! He smiled in a polite but pained way and said in almost a whisper, "I'd rather not," and walked away.

When chatty reporters aren't around, that lonely pedestal called a pitching mound still gives Koufax great pleasure. He is the James Bond of pitching coaches. His work is quick, clean, stylish in its understatement and usually done in top-secret fashion. He has tutored Cleveland's Dwight Gooden and L.A.'s Chan Ho Park on their curveballs and Houston's Mike Hampton on his confidence; convinced L.A.'s Kevin Brown that it was O.K. to lead his delivery with his butt; and taught former Dodger Orel Hershiser to push off the rubber with the ball of his foot on the dirt and the heel of his foot on the rubber. Hershiser removed some spikes from the back of his right shoe so that he could be more comfortable with Koufax's style of pushing off.

Koufax has tried since 1982 to teach his curveball technique to Mets closer John Franco. "I can't do it," Franco says. "My fingers aren't big enough to get that kind of snap." Koufax was God's template for a pitcher: a prizefighter's back muscles for strength, long arms for leverage and long fingers for extra spin on his fastball and curveball. The baseball was as low as the top of his left ankle when he reached back to throw in that last calm moment of his delivery—like a freight train cresting a hill—just before he flung the weight and force of his body toward the plate.

His overhand curveball was vicious because his long fingers allowed him to spin the ball faster than anybody else. Most pitchers use their thumb to generate spin, pushing with it from the bottom of the ball and up the back side. Koufax could place his thumb on the top of the ball, as a guide— similar to the way a basketball player shooting a jumper uses his off-hand on the side of the ball—because his long fingers did all the work, pulling down on the baseball with a wicked snap. On the days he wasn't pitching Koufax liked to hold a ball with his fastball and curveball grips because he believed it would strengthen the muscles and tendons in his left hand by just the tiniest bit.

Koufax may be the best pitching coach alive, though he wants no part of that job's high visibility or demands on his time. He cannot be pinned down any easier than a tuft of a dandelion blown free by the wind. After quitting NBC in February 1973, Koufax didn't take another job until 1979, when he explained that his return to the Dodgers as a roving minor league pitching coach was partly due to financial concerns. Koufax pitched 12 years in the majors and made only $430,500 in salary. He has steadfastly rejected endorsement offers and supplements his income with perhaps two card shows a year.

In the '80s Koufax enjoyed staying under the big league radar by doing his coaching for the Dodgers at the minor league level, in places such as San Antonio, Albuquerque and Great Falls, Mont., where he liked to stay up late talking pitching with the players and staff. He likes helping young players. In Great Falls he saw the potential of a righthander the organization was down on for being too hot-tempered. "He's got the best arm on the staff," Koufax said. "Stay with this guy." He was right about John Wetteland, the Texas Rangers' closer, now in his 11th season as one of the most reliable short relievers in baseball.

Koufax abruptly quit the Dodgers in February 1990. O'Malley had thought he was doing Koufax a favor by ordering the farm director to cut back on Koufax's assignments in 1989, but Koufax told O'Malley, "I just don't think I'm earning what you're paying me." He also was ticked off when one of the Dodgers bean counters bounced back an expense report to him over a trivial matter. Since then Koufax has worked on an ad hoc basis, ready to help his friends. Fox baseball analyst Kevin Kennedy, who carries a handwritten note from Koufax in his wallet, invited him to spring training in 1993 when Kennedy was managing the Texas Rangers. Koufax stayed one week, insisting that he wear an unmarked jersey with a plain blue cap rather than the team's official uniform. "He really enjoyed it," says Osteen, who was Kennedy's pitching coach. "Every night we'd go out to dinner and just talk baseball deep into the night. At the end of the week he said, 'You know, I've really had a good time.' I was floored. For him to acknowledge how he felt was a major, major thing. Believe me. I could tell he had missed the game. But at the same time, after a week of it he was ready to go back to his own private life. One week was enough."

Last year Koufax visited the Mets' camp in Port St. Lucie, Fla., as a favor to owner Fred Wilpon, a former teammate at Lafayette High School in Brooklyn, and Dave Wallace, the Mets' pitching coach who befriended Koufax when Wallace was working in the Dodgers' minor league system. Koufax sat in front of the row of lockers assigned to the Mets' pitchers and began talking. A crowd grew, pulling into a tight circle like Boy Scouts around a campfire.

Koufax looked at Leiter—also a lefthander—and said, "Al, you've had a nice career. Pitched in the World Series. But you can be better."

"I know," Leiter said. "Can you help me?"

Koufax liked that. He showed Leiter how he used to push off the rubber. He asked Leiter about where he aimed a certain pitch, and when Leiter said, "I'm thinking outer half—" Koufax cut him off. "Stop!" he said. "You never think outer *half*. You think a *spot* on the outside corner. Think about throwing the ball *through* the back corner of the plate, not to it."

What Koufax stressed most was that Leiter needed to pitch away more to righthanded hitters. Koufax lived on fastballs on the outside corner. Leiter, who says that many hitters today dive into the ball, prefers to pound cut fastballs on their fists. But Koufax showed Leiter how to make the ball run away from righthanders by changing the landing spot of his right foot by one inch and by letting his fingers come off slightly to the inside half of the ball. And Koufax shared the lesson that saved his career, the lesson it took him six years in the big leagues to learn: A fastball will behave better, with just as much life and better control, if you throttle back a little. "Taking the grunt out of it," is how Koufax put it.

In 1961 Koufax was a career 36–40 pitcher with awful control problems. He was scheduled to throw five innings in the Dodgers spring training B game against the Twins in Orlando, but the other pitcher missed the flight, and Koufax said he'd try to go seven. His catcher and roommate, Norm Sherry, urged him to ease up slightly on his fastball, throw his curve and hit his spots. Koufax had nothing to lose; manager Walter Alston and the front office were at the A game. Cue the chorus of angels and dramatic lighting. Koufax *got it*. He threw seven no-hit innings and, as he wrote in his book, "I came home a different pitcher from the one who had left."

A few weeks after Koufax spoke to the Mets' staff, an excited Wilpon approached Leiter in the clubhouse and said, "I don't know what you did with Sandy, but he wants you to have his home number. I've never known him to do this before with any player. If you ever want to talk with him, just give him a call."

Leiter says he rang the dial-a-legend line three or four times. "I wasn't sure what to do," he says. "I didn't want to call so much where he would think I was taking advantage of our friendship. On the other hand, I didn't want to not call, and he'd think, 'That guy is blowing me off.' It's kind of delicate, you know what I mean? But Sandy's cool. Real cool." At 32, Leiter had the best season of his career (17–6, 2.47). "I accepted the idea of throwing outside more," he says. "The times when I did it fairly often were the three or four most dominating games I had all year."

Koufax likes to slip into Dodgertown during spring training unnoticed, parking his Saab convertible or his Jeep Wagoneer in a back lot, visiting with O'Malley if he sees the shades open to Villa 162 and watching pitchers throw on the sacred ground of the practice mounds. He has noticed that there are a lot more microphones and cameras at Dodgertown since Rupert Murdoch bought the team last year. He is not happy about that.

I am chatting with Bobby McCarthy, Koufax's friend from Vero Beach, during an exhibition game at Dodgertown when Dave Stewart, a former Koufax pupil (who himself coached the pennant-winning San Diego Padres pitching staff last year), stops by. "We were talking about Sandy," McCarthy says.

"Oh, yeah?" Stewart says. "I just saw him in the clubhouse."

I bolt, but when I get to the clubhouse, the Ghost has vanished. I can practically smell the ethereal contrails.

A few days later I get the official word from a member of Koufax's inner circle: "He doesn't want to talk. He's at the point where he doesn't care what people write; he just doesn't want to say anything. Sorry."

I fire my last bullet. The home phone number. I haven't needed to muster this kind of courage to dial a telephone since I asked my date to our high school prom. The phone rings. I remember the code: The answering machine is on if he's in town, off if he's not. The phone just keeps ringing.

It is Opening Day of the 1999 season. I am standing before the house at Winkumpaugh Farm. Or what is left of it. It burned to the ground 22 days ago.

I am staring at a cement hole in the ground filled with ash and garbage and the stump of a chimney. Standing with me is Dean Harrison, a 45-year-old intensive-care nurse who grew up in West Orange, N.J., rooting for Koufax. He bought the property last year and lives in a house farther up the hill. When his power goes out during a winter storm, he calls the utility company and says, "The Koufax line is out." And they know exactly where the problem is. He knows the history of the place.

Koufax sold Winkumpaugh Farm to Herbert Haynes of Winn, Maine, who sold it three months later to John and Kay Cox of Mare Island, Calif. Cox was an absentee landlord, renting it when he could. Young people used it as a party house. Necessary repairs were left undone. By the time Henderson bought it last fall, Winkumpaugh Farm was in awful shape. "I wanted to save it," he says. "I was about 30 years too late." He finally decided to donate the farmhouse to the Ellsworth Fire Department.

When the fire company went out to the house on March 14, patches of ground were showing through what was left of winter's last snowfall.

The first thing the firemen did was grab pieces of Sandy Koufax's life for themselves. They pulled up floorboards and planks of clapboard siding. A policeman, Tommy Jordan, tossed some switch plates, two faucet handles and a small pile of bricks into the back of his squad car.

After this bit of scavenging, the firefighters practiced a few rescues with a controlled fire, then they scattered hay on Winkumpaugh Farm's old wood floors and torched it. The old place went up quick as kindling, gone before a tear could fall to the snow.

After the fire burned out, Keleshian reached into the smoldering ruin and took some ancient square-headed nails. She also took some of the farmhouse's charcoaled remains, with which she plans to sketch from memory two drawings of Winkumpaugh Farm—one for Anne and one for Sandy.

The early spring sun holds me in its warmth as it begins to sink behind the mountain beyond the valley. The quiet of North Ellsworth is profound, disturbed only by the gentle whisper of the wind through the pines and the bare branches of the oak, beech, birch and apple trees.

The farmhouse is gone, and yet I see it clearly. I see the weather vane atop the tiny cupola, the second-floor dormers, the screened-in porch and the white sign under the eaves that says WINKUMPAUGH FARM in black letters. I can hear classical music playing through homemade speakers. I can smell dinner wafting through the cozy house. Without the recipe in front of him, Sandy is making his grandmother's stuffed cabbage. He is surrounded by friends, laughter, the glow of a wood-burning stove and the warmth of walls lined with hardbound books. He is home.

Koufax always hated it when people described him as a recluse, and I have come to understand how wrong that label is. A recluse doesn't touch so many people with lifelong lessons of generosity, humility and the Zen of the curveball.

I have rebuilt his farmhouse in my mind, and it is sturdier and more beautiful this way. Why shouldn't I do the same when taking the measure of the man who once lived there? Must every blank be filled in, leaving us no room to construct parts of him as we wish? What we don't see can help us keep him forever young, unflinchingly true to himself, forever an inspiration.

Looking at the ruins of Winkumpaugh Farm at my feet, I realize that I no longer need that Vero Beach phone number. I have found Sandy Koufax.

MARCH 2, 1959

From the Hill to the Hall

On the eve of a new spring training season, Yogi Berra looms
larger than ever as one of baseball's great personalities

BY HERBERT WARREN WIND

One fine day last autumn Yogi Berra, the affluent Yankee, had a relatively
free stretch to enjoy himself. That is, there was no bottling convention to
attend on behalf of the Yoo-Hoo chocolate drink company (in which he
has a considerable investment), no business to transact with Mr. George
Weiss, no television or banquet appearances, no household chores of any
particular urgency, and he and Phil Rizzuto, his old friend and guide, had
been able to make their two visits (one to a hospital and the other to an
orphanage) quite early in the morning. A little before noon, Berra returned
to his hillside home on the wooded outskirts of Tenafly, N.J. and, finding
it bare of Mrs. Berra (who was out shopping) and the two oldest of his
three sons (who were at school), he played for a few minutes with Dale (his
youngest), who is 2 years old, helped the maid to locate the old baseball-
type golf cap he was looking for and headed for the White Beeches golf
course in Haworth. Yogi drives a gray Pontiac with the license plate YB 8,
eight being the number on his Yankee uniform. Unlike most Americans, for
whom lack of sufficient recognition is a besetting problem, Berra's problem
is to avoid too much recognition, and the identifying license plate is one of
the few luxuries in the other direction that he allows himself.

White Beeches is a relaxed and friendly club, just right for a budding
squire who has his feet firmly on the ground. After his round—an 86 which
was better than the figures indicated, since a strong November wind was

out—Yogi sat around for about an hour in the grill with his foursome. One of them, a skiing buff, wanted to know if Yogi would be interested in going up to Tremblant with him on his next trip there. Before Yogi had time to reply, a third party piped up, "Casey would love that, huh? The news you were trying out the ski slopes." Berra, who makes it a point to avoid discussing Yankee business and personalities whenever possible, let that serve as his answer. The conversation shortly after this got around to the colossal amount of time wives and children spend on the telephone nowadays. One member of the group, a soldier of progress who spoke with a tone of endorsement, informed the others that you could now get a special phone installed for the teenagers in your family who wanted to talk with their teen-age friends.

"Your boys will be needing one soon," he suggested to Berra.

"Well, they won't be getting one," Yogi said. "I want to do all I can for my kids," he added softly, "but, golly, that isn't one of them."

Yogi had dinner at home with his wife Carmen and their two oldest, Larry, who is 9, and Timmy, 7, and then was off for Clifton, another New Jersey town about 20 miles away, in which the Berra-Rizzuto Alleys, a gleaming 40-lane emporium, are located. The alleys were officially opened last spring, but each time Yogi enters the building he feels the same intense glow of pride he did on opening night. This particular evening he was set to bowl for the team representing the Glendale Display and Advertising Co., and in his office changed into his bowling shoes and the green-and-black Glendale bowling shirt. He bowls for that team on Wednesdays, and on Mondays for a team of Yankees whose star is Bill Skowron (who has about a 160 average) and whose roster includes Phil Rizzuto, Elston Howard, Johnny Kucks, Ralph Houk and Gil McDougald. Since he had about 20 minutes in hand before the evening match was scheduled to begin, Berra moseyed down to the Dugout Restaurant for a cup of coffee and then made a quick tour of the rest of the premises. In the Stadium Lounge, where the bar is built in the shape of Yankee Stadium, he chatted about business with his brother Johnny, who is in charge there, and cast an approving eye at the large blowup photograph of the décolleté songstress who was to appear there that weekend. As he returned to the promenade behind the alleys, a middle-aged man, attired in the purple-and-white bowling shirt of a local bank, came up to him and told him how wonderful the alleys looked. "The whole place," he said, "is so spotless you would think you fellows opened it yesterday." Berra lights up like a child at certain compliments, and did so then. "You know who works for the company that polishes our alleys, Tommy?" he said with exuberance. "McDougald, Gil." This was the first of a slew of chats, long and short, in which Yogi was enmeshed the rest of the evening. A very homey atmosphere obtains at the alleys. Berra seemed to know everyone who approached him, most of them by name, and each of the patrons wanted to know how business was and seemed personally pleased at Yogi's report that things were going pretty good and Phil now thought the main problem was getting enough business during the daylight hours. At 9 o'clock the match between Seabert's Delicatessen and Glendale Display got under way. Yogi had a very good evening for him, rolling an even 200 on his first string, his high for the year, and finishing with a respectable three-string total of 504.

Just before he entered the office to change out of his bowling togs, a superbouncy woman of vaguely 30 who appeared to know Yogi well—and everyone else at the alleys for that matter—handed Yogi a small package tied in a bright ribbon. "It's a gift from me to you," she instructed him. "You should make sure you open it in private." He did, so to speak, in the office, where Freddy Rizzuto, Phil's brother who is the alleys' assistant manager, was on duty. The contents turned out to be a carton of the cigarettes Yogi endorses and a selection of six comic books. Mixed emotions, including one that indicated they'll-do-it-everytime, came over Yogi's face. "Well, Freddy," he said at length in an administrative tone, "I can always give the books to my kids."

Yogi left for home shortly after 11. In the main lobby there is a large glass case in which four magnificent American League MVP plaques, the one which Rizzuto won and the three Yogi won, are on display. Yogi slowed down his stride and looked at the case for just a moment. Then he half-walked and half-trotted out into the night.

It is pleasant to contemplate the good fortune which has come the way of Lawrence Peter Berra. If it is coming to any athlete, he has it coming to him. Aside from being a person of unusual decency and natural charm, he has, from a fairly inauspicious beginning in the big leagues, achieved over the last dozen years a place among the memorable players in the long history of the game—one of that extremely small number of players who have performed in the years following World War II who is a certainty to be elected to the Hall of Fame. Over and above this, Berra is a personality of such original force and magnetism that sometimes it has even obliterated his real stature as a player. He is, as Joe Trimble has called him, the Kid Ring Lardner Missed, and possibly more—the last of the glorious line of baseball's great characters.

In this age where ballplayers have kept growing taller and more statuesque until the breed is now in appearance a combination of the stroke on the college crew and the juvenile lead in summer stock, Berra adheres to the classic blocky dimensions of the oldtime catcher. He stands

5 feet 8 and weighs about 192 and looks even chunkier (especially in a baseball uniform) than these figures would augur, for he has the broad and wide-set shoulders of a much taller man, a barrel chest and enormous arms. Unlike most men of similar musculature, Berra is very lithe, very loose—in fact, there is such friskiness in his movements (except when he is catching the second game of a double-header) that, as he approaches 34, he still conjures up the picture of a beknickered boy of 13 or 14. Berra's build is quite deceptive in other ways, or at least it has led a number of observers into glib deductions that are strikingly wayward. For example, nearly everyone decided years ago that a man with his nonmissile dimensions would *ipso facto* have to be a slow runner. Only in recent years has it been generally appreciated that Yogi has always been extremely fast, one of the Yankees' best base runners, in fact. Even stranger is that ivied slice of myopia which depicts Berra as all awkwardness at bat, sort of a slightly more skillful Pat Seerey who busts the ball out of the park by sheer brute strength. This is simply not correct. While there is assuredly little esthetic splendor about the way Yogi bunches himself at the plate, he handles the bat beautifully, with a delicacy and finesse which few place hitters approach and which is rarer still, of course, for a power hitter. He has magnificent timing, releasing his wrist action at the last split second. This explains why when Berra is hitting, he can hit anybody or anything, including more bad balls than anyone since Joe Medwick. In the 1955 World Series—not the 1956 Series in which he hit three home runs and batted in 10 runs, but the 1955 Series in which he made 10 hits and batted .417—Yogi put on one of the finest demonstrations of straightaway hitting in modern times, meeting the ball right between the seams again and again and lining it like a shot over the infield, very much in the fashion of Paul Waner and Nap Lajoie. "There's no one more natural or more graceful than Yogi when he's watching the pitch and taking his cut," Phil Rizzuto said not long ago. "He's all rhythm up there, like Ted Williams."

Williams and Berra are alike in one other respect: they are talkative men. Splendidly endowed as Williams is in this department, he is simply not in Berra's class. In truth, no player in the annals of baseball has been, and those who potentially might have challenged his preeminence made the mistake of playing the wrong position. Stationed behind the plate, Berra has a steady flow of new faces to ask how things are going, and during lulls between batters there is always the umpire. Early this year Casey Stengel, a fairly articulate man himself, had a few words to say about Berra's verbosity. Asked if he considered Berra to be the best late-inning hitter in the game, a claim many have made for him, Casey replied that he didn't know about that. "I'd have to look into it," he said. "He could be the best late-inning hitter in baseball because he's got to hit sometime during a game, and he is a very bad early-inning hitter. Sometimes Mr. Berra allows himself to go careless. He forgets to start the game with the first inning. He's out there behind the plate saying hello to everybody in sight. Oh, Mr. Berra is a very sociable fellow. He acts like home plate is his room."

In all of Yogi's actions on the ball field, as these vignettes may suggest, there is a beguiling spontaneity and a total lack of affectation. Beyond this, a tide of friendliness comes pouring through, and it communicates itself in a wondrous way not only to the people within earshot of his gravelly banter but also to the outlanders perched in the deep recesses of the stadium. It is difficult to think of another performer in sports who possesses Berra's particular quality of empathy: you just sense you like that guy. Viewed at intimate range—and it is a pleasure to report this since it is all too seldom true of national figures who are irresistible in their public roles—Berra turns out to be the same guy he appears to be: friendly, full of unposy vitality, marvelously good-natured. There are times when Berra's exceptional energy gets worn down and responding to his fans becomes a nervous strain, but he has absorbed the niceties of applied public relations and employs them well at these moments. What is remarkable, though, is the genuine consideration which Berra, on most occasions, shows the countless strangers who yell to him wherever he may be or who come over to talk with him—he treats them as if they were neighbors he has known all his life. In this connection, the story of Yogi at Ruggeri's (first told by Bob Burnes of the *St. Louis Globe-Democrat*) comes to mind. One winter, not long after he had made his mark in the majors, Yogi took on the off-season job as head waiter at Ruggeri's restaurant on The Hill in St. Louis, his home town. One evening when he was catching up with two young couples who were walking toward their table, Yogi overheard one of the two men, awed by the high style of the restaurant, nervously confide to the other, "Gosh, I feel out of place." "Relax," Yogi interjected. "After you've been here 10 minutes you'll think it ain't any different than a hamburger joint."

There is, however, a lot more complication in Berra than meets the casual eye. When Sal Maglie joined the Yankees, a friend asked him what if anything was different about the players from what he had expected. "Yogi," Sal replied. "Yogi worries a great deal." These periods do not last too long, but when Yogi is troubled, it goes all through him; he is not only grave, he is gloomy. He is also quite a sensitive person, which many people miss, though they shouldn't. Moreover, there is considerable shyness in him. At social gatherings away from the park, he will on some occasions hang mutely on the edge of a group engaged in conversation, keeping his distance momentarily, but when he joins in, he arrives in force. All of this makes Yogi not one whit different from you or me—except that most of us lack his buoyant good nature and the grit and instinctive soundness which knit him together—but it is rather important to mention these things in Berra's case since he has been so invariably portrayed as a happy-go-lucky child of nature.

This distortion, to a considerable degree, stems from the incomparable Berraisms which he has produced since he first came up. They are the Sneadisms and Goldwynisms of baseball. The only qualifying point that need be made about Yogi's *authentic* Berraisms is that they are not the product of stupidity but rather of the pleasure he gets in participating on all fronts and expressing himself. He is anything but facile at translating his thoughts into words but, far from being a slow man on the bases upstairs, Berra has an essentially good mind and a very active one. If there is a fund of good will in Yogi, there is also a native shrewdness. He has, for instance, invested his money very soundly. He now represents himself capably in his salary symposiums with George Weiss, having matured tremendously over the years in his sense of values, his own included.

Berra's remarks can be incisive as well as comic; for example, after sitting in on a strategy conference before an All-Star Game, in which a long time was spent debating the best methods for pitching to Musial: "The trouble with you guys is you're trying to figure out in 15 minutes something no one has figured out in 15 years." He also has the gift of good taste, which he has demonstrated most markedly, perhaps, in his choice of Mrs. Berra (Carmen Short, also from Missouri), a fine-looking girl with a very crisp, perky personality. Thanks to Carmen and to his great friend Rizzuto, Yogi has long since abandoned his celebrated allegiance to comic books. It was slightly exaggerated anyhow. He never was able to rise higher than vice-president in the Ghoul Club, an organization made up of Yankees—Don Larsen, president—who feasted on horror comics until the books were banned as injurious to minors. Yogi made his debut as a hard-cover man with Robert Ruark's *Something of Value*, a suitable bridge. Halfway through the book, he lost it, suffered agonies at the thought of the money he would have to shell out for another copy, but eventually did. That was the turning point. He now reads a fair amount and enjoys it, his favorites being realistic novels like *The World of Suzie Wong*.

As far as baseball goes, Yogi, despite the camouflage of his mannerisms, thinks well and swiftly and has become a master of the hard art of talking shop and thinking baseball. While he is gabbing away with batters, another part of his mind is setting up a pitching pattern for instant use as well as filing away for future reference pertinent dope on each hitter. "On a number of occasions," Casey Stengel has opined, "I am aware I have held a meeting in the clubhouse before a game when there was some doubts among the coaches and myself on how we should pitch to particular hitters. If we don't agree on a decision, we have asked Berra what he thinks about it, and we have generally gone along with what he has suggested. He is a good studier of hitters." Stengel, who has been known to refer to Berra as "my assistant manager" because of his veteran catcher's ever-readiness to contribute his knowledge to the common cause, not long ago meandered into an oblique shaft of revelation which recalled his famed soliloquy on the short-fingered Japanese during his appearance before the United States Senate. "Berra," said Casey, "is alert because he's got very good hearing. He has better ears than any other catcher in the game. He hears everything that's said on the field and not only there but away from the field. He knows all the scandal. If Topping wasn't there, he'd run the business for him, or George Weiss, his business, or me, he'd take over my job."

Stengel has also long been struck by Berra's knowledge of sports in general. So is everyone who knows him. Yogi's old friend Joe Garagiola, the former Cardinal catcher who currently is a highly successful baseball broadcaster and after-dinner speaker, frequently tells his audience on the banquet trail that "funny as it will sound to many of you, Yogi could have been an A student in college." Joe then elaborates on this by stating that Yogi has an exceptionally good memory for anything he wants to remember, such as sports.

This is a very significant part of Berra—his abiding love of sports—and it explains the man directly. In a sports-oriented nation like ours there are literally hundreds of thousands of boys and grown-ups who are attached to sport before any other consideration, but it is really extraordinary to find an experienced professional athlete for whom agents have not withered nor customers staled his first youthful affection for his game and others. Here Berra is plainly exceptional. After all these bruising seasons he has somehow managed to retain a boy's full-hearted enthusiasm for the game of baseball. This has always been so obvious that it used to be said that he would probably be delighted to play for the Yankees even if they paid him nothing. Well, Yogi has seen to it for quite some time now that he is well rewarded for his services but, once he enters the dressing room, that spirit of the young boy, all eagerness for the game, clutches him wholly. He loves to play ball like other men like to make money or work in the garden. And this is what makes Berra the ballplayer he is.

Moreover, as Stengel's and Garagiola's remarks adduce, Yogi is infatuated not only with baseball but with all sports. For him they are practically the staff of life. They have always been.

The outline of Yogi's early years and his road to the top are fairly well known to sports fans, and to summarize them elliptically is probably enough for our purposes. He was born in St. Louis, May 12, 1925, the son of Paulina and Pietro Berra. Mr. Berra worked in the kilns in one of the local brick factories. The Berras lived on 5447 Elizabeth Avenue, the Garagiolas at 5446, on "Dago Hill." (At banquets Garagiola is at his drollest when he tells his audiences, with the air of someone explaining something quite abstruse, "A lot of Italian families live on that hill, you see, and that is the reason it is called Dago Hill.") Yogi left school at 14 after completing the seventh grade. After this he had a long series of small jobs in various plants. He lost one after another because sports came first; whenever it was a question of whether to play in a big game or pass it by and stay on the job, he chose the former. Deep within him he clung to the obscure hope that somehow or other he might be able to make a career in sports. As he has always been the first to admit, he owes the chance he had to pursue this hope to his older brothers, Tony, Mike and Johnny. All three were fine athletes, and two showed such talent for baseball that they were approached by big league clubs to join teams in their farm system. (Tony, the oldest brother, Yogi has always claimed, was the best ballplayer in the family.) The pressure to bring money into the hard-pressed family forced the older boys to forsake their ambitions in baseball and to knuckle down to wage-earning in local plants. However, when Yogi began to blossom out in American Legion Junior Baseball, his brothers insisted that he be given the chance they had never had, and they were so adamant about this that they eventually broke down the opposition of their parents. In 1942, when he was 17, Yogi was signed by John Schulte, a scout for the Yankee organization, for $500. This was the amount which Joe Garagiola, eight months younger than Yogi, had received from the St. Louis Cardinals after he and Yogi, both of them left-hand-hitting catchers, had been given a tryout the year before. The Cards had also wanted to sign Berra but had not offered him a bonus for signing. Though it almost killed him to do so, Yogi had turned down their contract, not because of envy of his pal—there is no envy in Berra—but because he felt he was worth $500 too. In 1943 the Yankees assigned him to Norfolk, their affiliate in the Class B Piedmont League.

The fact that two members of their gang had been signed by big league clubs was a towering feather in the hats of the kids on The Hill. Mulling over Yogi's chances of making good, they were positive he would, for they had known him as a superlative all-round athlete, a mainstay for their team, the Stags, in their organized league games as well as in their sand-lot games and street games. For instance, when as young kids they had played football on Elizabeth Avenue, Yogi always did the kicking not only for his side but on fourth down he was switched to the opposing side to kick for them. He was the only one in the bunch who could be counted on to control the ball so that it came down in the street and not through somebody's window. One autumn day when Yogi (then about 15) was watching a Southwest High practice scrimmage, an episode with all the hallmarks of one of those Hollywood "discovery scenes" took place: the kicker for the high school team got off a short wobbly punt which twisted over the sideline near where Yogi was standing. Picking the ball up, Yogi, wearing sneakers, casually boomed the ball back half the length of the field. Over to the sideline rushed the coach to find out who was the unknown star who could kick like that. On learning that Yogi had quit school and was working, the coach pleaded with him to "join" the high school, assuring him that he could arrange things so that he would have the lightest study load imaginable, but Yogi, ruining the perfect scenario, would have none of it.

Yogi was an average if clamorous basketball player, pretty fair at roller hockey and truly outstanding at soccer, a game that has long been big in St. Louis. He played halfback and was so fond of the sport that he went on playing it even after he had definitely arrived in professional baseball, and probably would have continued to play it had not the Yankees, fearful of injury, ordered him to retire. It was typical of him that he became an ardent pro football fan at a time when most St. Louisans were either uninformed or apathetic about the NFL, and so staunch a devotee of ice hockey, a game he had never played, that on the nights when the St. Louis Flyers' home games were scheduled he would take a two-hour nap late in the afternoon so that he would have the pep to stay awake. "The main thing about Yogi that impressed us as kids," Garagiola was remembering recently, "was how fast he picked up any sport. One time the Italian-American club wanted some kid to represent them in the city boxing matches. They got Yogi. If you wanted something done, you always got Yogi. He'd never boxed before, but he turned out to be darned good at it: I think he had five fights and won them all, two by knockouts, before his folks made him quit. Another time I remember we went up to the YMCA and found a ping-pong tournament going on. Yogi had never played the game before but he entered. In his first match he was just trying to return the ball across the net, but he got the hang of it quick and went all the way to the final." Garagiola paused a long moment. "Just talking about those old days," he resumed, "brings back to your mind what a wonderful guy Yogi was even as a kid. He was never one to come forward and try to stand out, but he was the fellow who got the other fellows together. He was a peacemaker kind of kid. More than that, he had a lot of strength and cheer in him. When you were troubled about something, there was no one like him. Why, just to see him come bouncing around the corner half solved your problem. 'Here comes Yogi,' you'd say to yourself. 'It isn't as bad as it looked.'"

As far as baseball went (and its close relatives, softball and cork-ball, an offshoot particular to St. Louis), Yogi as a youngster did some of the pitching for the Stags and played every position except first base. He did little or no catching until he was 14. "I got the job because no one else wanted it," he remembers. "You took quite a beating back there. You didn't have any shin guards or belly protector." He did the catching, when he was 16 and 17, for the Fred W. Stockton Post American Legion team, and was one of the chief reasons why the team in 1941 and 1942 was the class of its section and both seasons reached the final round of the national championship finals. Up with Norfolk in '43, Yogi blew hot and cold, batting a mild .253 for the season, but in 1946, following his wartime tour of duty with the Navy, he hit .314 with Newark, the Yankees' farm club in the AAA International League, and was considered ready to go up with the big club. In the Navy, incidentally, he had seen action of the roughest kind in the landings in Normandy and later in southern France. He was a rocketman on a Coast Guard boat, one of a group of 36-foot LCSSs (Landing Craft Support Small) which on D-day were disgorged from a larger vessel some 300 yards off Omaha Beach to help open the beach for the first wave.

During his first full year with the Yankees, 1947, Berra, a very young 22, was nervous and conspicuously unpolished behind the plate. Although he drove in 54 runs in 83 games that year and a thumping 98 runs in 125 games in 1948, he made many costly errors in judgment behind the plate as well as physical errors. Work as he did to correct them, he continued to make them and was frequently played in right field, where he could do far less damage. These were days of anguish for him, because on top of these concerns he was the target of some of the most brutal personal riding any newcomer to the majors has ever been subjected to. In the final analysis, it was his own hardy character that saw him through, but he was extremely fortunate in the men he was associated with. He was fortunate, for instance, that his idol, Joe DiMaggio, was around to support him in many critical moments. One typical example of DiMaggio's help occurred during one of those stretches when Yogi had been exiled to right field. Way down in the dumps after popping up his previous time at bat, Yogi shuffled dejectedly out to right at the beginning of the next inning. DiMaggio noticed this. An inning later, as Yogi was gallumping out to his position, Joe, instead of sprinting out to center as was his hustling habit, followed out after Yogi and yelled to him to get moving. "Always run out to your position, Yogi," Joe continued as they ran out together. "It doesn't look good when you walk. The other team may have gotten you down but don't let them know it."

Yogi has also been fortunate in playing under managers like Bucky Harris, a kindly man, and Casey Stengel, who has directed the Yankees since 1949. When Casey first took over he set about building up Berra's confidence in himself as a catcher, and here his most valuable contribution was his decision to turn Yogi over to Coach Bill Dickey, that most accomplished technician, for a full course of instruction. "There was a lot he had to be taught which he'd never been," Casey has said. "He squatted too far away from the hitter and was off balance and a poor target. Another thing, he didn't know how to block a bad pitch with his body. Dickey showed him how to drop down on his knees. Then, he didn't throw well because nobody had ever taught him how to take that step. He has a strong arm and he became a very accurate thrower. He'd throw runners out for us when you couldn't have blamed him if he didn't, for he was working with a poor pitching staff in that respect. Many of the pitchers we've had, I don't know if you know, have been no good at keeping the runners close to the base." Dickey not only instructed Berra in every facet of the mechanics of catching, he taught him how to call a game. "Yogi before Dickey and Yogi after Dickey—the difference was like night and day," Rizzuto has commented. "Before, he was never thinking ahead like a catcher must. He hesitated all through a game calling the pitches. He didn't know how to set a batter up for the curve with the fast ball, and so on. He was really shaky and the result was that the pitchers didn't have any confidence in him. After his schooling with Dickey, he started to think ahead automatically, he set up very good patterns and he began to study the hitters intelligently. Our pitchers began to lean on his judgment very quickly after this. Only Reynolds or Raschi ever shook him off and they didn't do it very often."

Above all Yogi was fortunate in having Phil Rizzuto as his roommate on the road trips and as a staunch friend at all times. Yogi was (and is) stoical by nature. Never one to moan or alibi, he prefers to keep his troubles to himself. During his first seasons in the majors he simply had too many troubles to absorb and sometimes they accumulated into a ponderous burden, and you cannot overestimate the good it did the young man, so distrustful of his ability to get across what he felt in words, to find himself understood when he opened himself to Rizzuto. Rizzuto showed Berra all the ropes, additionally, but he was beautifully unpaternalistic—he never forced his advice on Yogi, merely gave his opinion when asked and let Yogi make his own decisions, which were invariably quite logical. "Yogi is an iron man and it really works against him," Phil reflected recently. "All the fellows on the team know he's caught innumerable double-headers after only five hours of sleep. They know that over the last dozen years he's caught many more games than any other catcher, many more. He's gotten out there and done the job despite a staggering number of painful injuries, jammed thumbs and split fingers and the rest. That's why Yogi never gets any sympathy. No one thinks he needs it."

When Yogi is learning something new, he customarily gives the impression that his mind is wandering and that he isn't following his instructor. For instance, he never gives back a paraphrase of what the other person has been saying, which is the most common method by which students indicate that they understand a new thing. For all the ambiguity of his reactions, Yogi has a first-rate aptitude for learning. It is, in fact, hard to think of a man who has done as much for himself. Today he leads a rounded and enviably full life, at the core of which is his home in Tenafly. There is a lot of pep and sense in the Berra household. "Once in a while after we've lost a tough one or if I've played a lousy game," Yogi was saying not long ago, "I get angry and I'm still angry when I get home. My wife doesn't let me get very far with it. Carm will tell me, 'Don't get angry with me. You played badly. I didn't.'" The spirited Mrs. Berra has a lively interest in baseball, but her major pastime is antiques. She has acquired for the house some handsome pieces, both American and European, among them an old table of Italian walnut at which the Berras eat breakfast and their snack meals. All smiles at the shoe being on the other foot for a change, Yogi loves to tell about the morning Bill Skowron walked in the breakfast room, studied the table for a moment and then declared, "With all your money, Yogi, you can certainly afford to buy a new table."

While Yogi has indeed come a long way from St. Louis, the wonderful thing about him is that in many essential areas he has not changed a bit from the kid on The Hill. For him—and this is just one phase of that appealing immutability—anybody who can play sports a major part of his hours is still the most privileged of people. His zest for reading sports and watching sports and talking sports when he is not playing sports has diminished not at all. During the autumn, when many baseball players are tapering off from the season's grind by hunting, Berra gets his mind off baseball by traveling to some spot like Pinehurst for a therapeutic week of golf, and then indulges his passion for football by going not only to the New York Giants' games but to those of local high school teams. As the colder weather comes on, Berra becomes almost as regular in his attendance at the basketball and hockey games at Madison Square Garden as Gladys Goodding, the well-tempered organist. Mrs. Berra has now cut down on the number of events she attends, but still goes to a few with him. On other occasions Yogi takes his two oldest boys or goes with friends from the Yankees or friends in his neighborhood with whom he also plays golf. And sometimes Yogi just drives in alone, sure in the foreknowledge that at courtside or rinkside he will run into some fellows he knows.

At the half-time interval of the first game of a recent pro basketball double-header which he went to with a neighbor from Tenafly, Yogi, after getting in a few hands of klob in the Knickerbocker office with some newspapermen, returned to his seat just in time to be slapped on the back by a tall, athletic-looking fellow. "Hey, you character, where you been keeping yourself?" the tall man, who turned out to be Joe Black, the old Dodger pitcher, asked with obvious affection. Yogi's eyes lighted up with pleasure. "This guy's a no-good catcher," Black explained to the friend he was with. "Trouble with him is he can't hit." Yogi and Joe gabbed about old times and new jobs until the second half got under way. In the break before the start of the second game another tall, husky fellow, circulating in the courtside section, spotted Yogi and came over for a similar reunion. "That was Doby," Yogi later explained to his friend from New Jersey, exhibiting more than a little of the same pride an average fan would take at being on speaking terms with a real big-leaguer.

This high regard applies to all athletes Berra admires, not just to baseball players. They are "his people." A flavorful illustration of the kick he gets from knowing them took place last December when Berra was invited by Herb Goren, the Rangers' public relations director, to watch a game against the Montreal Canadiens from the press box. While the teams were whirling through their pregame warm-up drills, Berra was seized with the urge to say hello to Boom Boom Geoffrion, the Montreal star, whom he had got to know last April when the Stanley Cup playoffs and the baseball season overlapped. Berra shouted down to Boom Boom a couple of times but was unable to get his attention, not that this was too surprising considering that the press box hangs high above the ice and that Berra's foghorn voice has neither the penetration nor carrying power of, say, Maria Callas' or Leo Durocher's. Goren happened to pass at this moment and, when Berra made known his problem, Goren said he would telephone down to the Canadiens' bench and have them point out to Geoffrion where Berra was seated.

Berra sat with his eyes riveted on Geoffrion during the next five minutes. Nothing happened. He was still waiting watchfully when Goren returned. "I changed my mind, Yogi," he said dourly. "This is an important game for us. If Boom Boom knows you're watching him, he'll play harder than he might otherwise."

"All I want to do is wave hello," Yogi protested, a little downcast.

"I'm sorry, Yogi, but that is a thing not good for the Rangers," Goren said, slipping into an inexplicable Hemingway-type speech pattern. "We must forget it. Boom Boom would get full of courage if he knows you are here."

As a loyal Ranger fan, Berra agreed that Goren's psychology might be right. However, it was a full 10 minutes before he could shake off the glum mood that overtook him in his disappointment, and twice during the game, when the path of play brought Geoffrion to that part of the rink nearest Yogi's position in the press box, he suddenly stood up and yelled "Boom Boom" to Boom Boom, without success, however.

During the off season when Berra must endure the hardship of having no assured supply of conversational fodder presented to him in the shape of enemy batsmen, his encounters with old friends at athletic events help to provide his gregarious soul with the communication it constantly craves. On the other hand, unlike the modern sports pundit who views each event as a springboard for his trenchant, altogether Toynbean comments, Berra is a quiet, intent and excitable spectator, with what nowadays amounts to an old-fashioned point of view: he doesn't focus primarily on the stars, but on the team play and the winning and losing of a game. He roots for the New York teams but makes an exception when the Knickerbockers play the St. Louis Hawks. "I can't go back on my real home town, can I?" he explains in his most serious voice. "And Ed Macauley, he was a big hero of mine when he was playing college ball. I've got to be loyal to him."

Berra stays in shape during the off season by cutting down on his eating—he frequently skips lunch—and by fairly regular exercise. One of those men who are bored by calisthenics and point-to-point walks and for whom a workout has to be the unconscious byproduct of playing a game, he fools around with a basketball on the backyard court he has set up (for the kids, of course), bowls and golfs. When Yogi warily took up golf some 10 years ago, he merely used an adaptation of his baseball swing. Hitting from the left side he was a very wild and woolly golfer, and the few powerhouse blows he got off generally journeyed in the wrong direction. Three autumns ago when he was playing a round (and an anguishingly bad one) at White Beeches with Tommy DeSanto, one of the club's best players, DeSanto suggested on the 11th hole that Berra borrow one of his right-handed clubs and see how he made out. Berra proceeded to hit his best shot of the day. He played in the rest of the way with DeSanto's clubs and has played right-handed ever since, though, interestingly enough, he continues to play his wedge shots and to putt left-handed. Since switching over, Yogi's golf has shown steady improvement, and his club members now consider his 14 handicap about two shots too high. He has had an 88 on the awesome Pinehurst No. 2, an 81 at White Beeches and a 38 for nine at Miami Springs. Berra's long hitting is not the strong point of his golf. His approach to the

game is. He understands its fine fabric as only the natural games player
does. He is an intuitive appraiser of the strategy of holes and the demands
of individual shots. He has a proper seriousness about trying to play each
shot as well as possible and a proper humor about his failings—"Whatta
touch!" he continually berates himself whenever his putting stroke lets him
down; he is interested in the games of the people he plays with, he-chirps
good conversation and at the right times, he competes just hard enough and
without gamesmanship and, all in all, is almost the perfect golf companion.

There are few people who can match the bonhomie which emanates from
Berra when he is in an expansive mood, which he was one day last November
after he had finished a particularly satisfying round at White Beeches. He
had played with two friends from New York who wanted to round out their
safari into the hinterland by visiting the Berra-Rizzuto alleys, which lie a
complicated half-hour drive away from the course. It was arranged that
Berra would lead the way in his car and they would follow in theirs. "There
are two tolls," Berra informed them. "You'll need a quarter for the first and
a dime for the second. You got it?" They had, and the abbreviated caravan
rolled off.

Some minutes later Berra swung his Pontiac into an entrance to the
Garden State Parkway. He paid his toll and gabbed a moment with the toll
attendant. His friends then drove up to the attendant, and the driver held
his hand out with a quarter in it. The attendant waved it away. "Mr. Berra,"
he said, "has already taken care of it."

AUGUST 2, 2010

Cardinal Virtue

Once dubbed baseball's perfect knight, the greatest Cardinal of them all played his entire career with quiet brilliance and boundless good will. Today the man remains a vibrant, vital part of baseball in St. Louis and a model of grace for the game

BY JOE POSNANSKI

Stan Musial does this origami trick with a dollar bill. He folds the bill one way, then back. He folds it again and again, never looking at his hands. He smiles throughout. If he's in the right mood, Musial might offer a corny joke to keep the time moving. Horse walks into a bar. Or, How do you know that God is a baseball fan? That sort of thing. He will break into his particular brand of baseball chatter: "Whaddya say! Whaddya say! Whaddya say!" After a few seconds Musial holds up the dollar bill and, absurdly, it has transformed into a ring. The audience always oohs with surprise. Musial will look surprised too. *How did I do that?* Then Stan Musial, with the tenderness of a groom, will slip the dollar bill ring on someone's finger, wink and walk off to the happy murmur that he has inspired in people for most of his 90 or so years on Planet Earth.

It's a good little trick.

The question is, Why would a man learn such a trick?

And what does it say about Stan the Man that he's so good at it?

"Stan Musial," his teammate Bob Gibson says, "is the nicest man I ever met in baseball." Gibson smiles. "And, to be honest, I can't relate to that. I never knew that *nice* and *baseball* went together."

This is a story of little stories. Small kindnesses. Quiet dignity. These are at the heart of Stan Musial. His greatness is not made up of the bold stuff of action heroes. There is no rushing into burning buildings here. Even after all these years it is hard for people to explain exactly what Stan Musial means to them. Willie Mays, sure, that's easy: He means youth and a baseball cap flying off in a rush of wind and long-ago stickball games in Harlem. Mickey Mantle means tape-measure home runs and impossible promise and a body that could not hold up to the pounding and late nights. Hank Aaron means dignity and consistency, and a home run record pursued through pain. Sandy Koufax means high fastballs and low curves and a pause for Yom Kippur as the World Series began. Ted Williams means the never-ending quest for perfection and just the right pitch to hit.

But what of Stan Musial? There has never been a best-selling biography of the man. There has never been a movie about his life. There are few legendary stories about him. There are few baseball records he can call his own.

"Stan Musial didn't hit in 56 straight games," says Musial's friend Bob Costas, who began his broadcasting career with KMOX in St. Louis. "He didn't hit .400 for a season. He didn't get 4,000 hits. He didn't hit 500 home runs. He didn't hit a home run in his last at bat, just a single. He didn't marry Marilyn Monroe; he married his high school sweetheart. His excellence was a quiet excellence."

Too quiet, perhaps. ESPN recently called him the most underrated athlete ever. Fox did not even televise Musial throwing out the first pitch before last year's All-Star Game in St. Louis. A few years back, when Major League Baseball held a fan vote to name its All-Century Team, a special committee had to add Musial because the fans did not vote him as one of the 10 best outfielders ever. *Ten!* Only Aaron had more total bases. Only Tris Speaker and Pete Rose hit more doubles. Using Bill James's famous formula, only Babe Ruth and Barry Bonds created more runs. Still, Musial did not get America's vote. He is not forgotten, not exactly. It is more this: For most of the nation, Stan the Man is a name that has faded into the great American past like singers wearing tuxedoes, John Wayne movies and kids shooting marbles.

But not in St. Louis. No, here they shout out for Stan Musial. They hold a citywide campaign—Stand for Stan!—to encourage President Obama to award Musial the Presidential Medal of Freedom, something like an American knighthood, a medal that has already been given to Musial contemporaries Aaron, Williams, Joe DiMaggio and Frank Robinson. Fans are encouraged to have their photos taken with a paper Flat Stan the Man, a play off the children's book, *Flat Stanley*. People meet at the Musial statue in front of the new ballpark; the Musial statue has long been St. Louis's favorite meeting spot, even before it was moved from in front of the old Busch Stadium to the new one. And during spring training this year Cardinals players came back to the clubhouse to find a reading assignment, a story about Musial that manager Tony La Russa had printed out for them to read and discuss.

"To me," La Russa says, "Stan's spirit is very much a part of what we're trying to do here."

There is, perhaps, even a bit of desperation about it all. Stan Musial will turn 90 in November. He appears in public less and less often. And there's a feeling here in St. Louis, an unmistakable feeling, that when we lose Stan the Man Musial, we will lose something precious and wordless and irreplaceable.

There's a feeling here, an unmistakable feeling, that as a nation we already may have lost it.

Stan Musial was never thrown out of a game. This is a pretty remarkable thing if you think about it. He played ball in the majors from 1941 to '63 (with a year spent in the Navy in '45). He changed dramatically in those years; he was the fifth-youngest player in baseball when he began and the third oldest when he walked away. A quick count shows that Musial dealt with at least 40 different home plate umpires—from Augie Donatelli to Ziggy Sears—and he never got one of them on a bad day. Or, more to the point, they never got him on a bad day.

There's one Musial story that has been told many different ways... according to different versions it happened in Brooklyn or Philadelphia; it happened in the top of the ninth or in extra innings. It led to a grand slam or a heroic homer into the lights as in *The Natural.* The many versions of the story suggest that there were countless other incidents like it in Musial's career. But this is how the story really happened.

It was April 18, 1954, in Chicago. The Cardinals trailed 3–0 in the seventh, and lefty Paul Minner was on the mound. There was a man on first, one out, when Musial smacked a double down the rightfield line. Or, anyway, the Cardinals thought it was a double. Wally Moon, the man on first, ran around the bases to score. Musial stood happily at second. The Cardinals' bench cheered. And apparently nobody noticed that first base umpire Lee Ballanfant had called the ball foul.

No footage of the play remains, of course, so we only get what we can read in the newspaper reports: Apparently the ball was definitively fair. Cardinals players came racing out of the dugout to go after Ballanfant, starting with shortstop Solly Hemus. Donatelli, the crew chief, who was behind home plate (and who apparently realized that Ballanfant had blown the call), threw Hemus out of the game. Cardinals manager Eddie Stanky was right behind. Donatelli threw him out of the game too. Peanuts Lowrey rushed out, and Donatelli was telling him to get back or he would get tossed too. And it was about then that Musial, who apparently was not entirely sure why there was so much commotion, wandered over to Donatelli.

"What happened, Augie?" Musial asked. "It didn't count, huh?" Donatelli nodded and said the ball had been called foul.

"Well," Musial said, "there's nothing you can do about it."

And without saying another word, Musial stepped back into the batter's box and doubled to the same spot in right field. This time it was called fair. The Cardinals rallied and won the game.

Musial was famous for signing autographs. So many Musial stories revolve around his seemingly boundless willingness to give people his signature. The old Cardinals announcer Harry Caray used to tell a story of a Sunday doubleheader in the St. Louis heat and humidity. Musial played both games, of course—in the 11 seasons after he returned from World War II, Musial averaged 153.5 games per 154-game season. And after the nightcap, Caray said, Musial looked as if he had been through a prizefight. In those days they still called boxing matches prizefights.

When the second game ended, Musial stumbled out to the parking lot. He barely looked strong enough to stand. And there, at his car, he found dozens of fans waiting, hoping, shouting, "Stan! Stan the Man!" Caray turned to the person next to him and said, "Watch this." And together they watched Stan Musial walk up to the group and shout out his trademark "Whaddya say! Whaddya say! Whaddya say!" And he signed every single autograph.

Musial grew up the fifth of six kids in a five-room house in Donora, Pa., a hardscrabble town built around the U.S. Steel Zinc Works factory that pumped black smoke into the sky. Musial would always believe that that black smoke killed his father, Lukasz, a zinc worker who died in 1948. Stan himself worked at the Zinc Works one summer—just long enough to know he never wanted to work there again. Our games overflow with athletes who feel lucky and blessed because they escaped the hard destiny that seemed inescapable when they were young. But it's as though Musial felt luckier and more blessed, as though he spent every waking moment fully aware of the good fortune in his life. Sometimes when he was out with his wife, Lil, people would ask for autographs at inopportune times, and Lil would suggest he politely decline. "These are my fans," Stan would say, lovingly but firmly, and sign them all. Teammates used to bet each other how often they would hear Musial use the word *wonderful* on any given day.

Robin Roberts, the late Hall of Fame pitcher, was once talking about a modern-day player he saw walk past a young boy who desperately wanted an autograph. Roberts was too polite to name the player, but he did not hide his contempt.

"Now, to me, that's one thing that really has changed," Roberts said. "There's so much money in the game now.... Players don't see themselves as part of the crowd now. They're separated. They're big stars. I know it's more of a business now. But I'll tell you this: In our day you didn't walk by a kid who wanted an autograph."

Then, Roberts shrugged: "I probably shouldn't be so hard on the guy. I'm sure over the years I probably missed a few kids. I don't remember doing it, but I'm sure I disappointed someone. None of us are perfect. We all disappointed someone from time to time. I guess. Well, all of us except one."

"Who was that?" I asked. Roberts looked at me with surprise, as if he thought the answer was obvious. Finally he answered.

"Musial," he said.

Stan Musial never led the league in home runs. He came close once—that was in his epic 1948 season, when he was one home run short of becoming the only man in baseball history to lead his league in batting, runs, hits, doubles, triples, homers and RBIs. To this day, Musial fans will tell you he lost that home run in an August rainout in Brooklyn, though nobody knows for sure.

Anyway, that's just legend. And Musial's career was so defiantly about what is real. He never led the league in home runs, but he led the league in doubles eight times and triples five. That was real. Musial broke hard out of the batter's box day after day, game after game. Dodgers pitcher Carl Erskine often said that his strategy for pitching Musial was to throw his best stuff and then back up third base.

Musial never struck out 50 times in a season. That was real. "I could have rolled the ball up there to Musial," another Dodgers great, Don Newcombe, says, "and he would have pulled out a golf club and hit it out."

The Brooklyn Dodgers pitchers tend to have special memories of Musial because he always seemed to hit his best in New York City. The numbers at the baseball database Retrosheet are not quite complete, but they show that Musial hit .359 with power for his career at Ebbets Field in Brooklyn (and a similar .343 with power at the Polo Grounds against the Giants). It was supposedly Brooklyn fans—based on their griping "Here comes the man again," when Musial would come to the plate—who created the nickname Stan the Man. They held a Stan Musial Day in New York at a Mets game once. Chicago Cubs fans once voted him their favorite player, ahead of all the hometown stars, including their own lovable Ernie Banks. That was real.

"All you have to do to understand what Stan Musial means is watch him around other Hall of Famers," La Russa says. "You can fool fans sometimes.

You can fool the media sometimes. But you really can't fool other players. And when you see Musial in a group of Hall of Famers, they hold him in such high esteem.... It's like he's on another level."

La Russa then tells his own Musial story. He did not really get to know Musial until he became manager of the Cardinals in 1996. By then La Russa had won a World Series, two pennants and more than 1,000 games as a manager. But whenever he would find himself sitting in the office with Musial, he would call his father, Anthony, in Florida.

"Guess who I am in the office with, Pop," he would say.

And then Stan Musial would take the phone, and he would shout, "Whaddya say! Whaddya say! Whaddya say!" Then he would say, "Mr. La Russa, your son is doing a wonderful job here. Just wonderful."

And later in the day, almost without fail, Anthony would call his son and say, "Was that *really* Stan Musial?"

Anthony died in 2002. "I always had to tell him, 'Yeah, it was really Stan the Man,'" La Russa says, and, yes, there are tears in the eyes of the son.

Dick Zitzmann has been running Stan the Man Inc. for a long time now. He has seen the same scene again and again and again. Musial folds the dollar bill into a ring. Musial stops at a table in a restaurant and plays *Happy Birthday* on the harmonica. Musial reflexively hands out autographed cards to kids. Musial puts his hand on the shoulder of a teary-eyed fan and says, "No...thank *you*!" He has seen it all so many times that he has to remind himself that this is not how superstars normally act.

"Stan loves people," Zitzmann says. "He wants you to be a friend. It really is amazing. When he signs an autograph, he is as happy as the person who is getting the autograph. That's the essence of Stan Musial. He is happy when he's around people."

Another Brooklyn Dodgers pitcher, Joe Black, told me a story once. We were sitting next to each other on a plane when, without provocation, he simply started telling the story, one he has told many times. He was pitching against the St. Louis Cardinals—this was 1952, his rookie year, his best year. Black had come out of the Negro leagues, and he was young, and he pitched fearlessly. He thought this happened the first time he faced the Cardinals; Black pitched three scoreless innings that day. But he wasn't entirely sure that was the day. What he remembered clearly, though, was the voice booming from the Cardinals' dugout while he was pitching to Musial.

"Don't worry, Stan," that someone from the Cardinals dugout had yelled. "With that dark background on the mound, you shouldn't haven't any problem hitting the ball."

Musial did not show any reaction at all. He never did when he hit. He simply spat on the ground and got into his famous peekaboo batting stance—the one that Hall of Fame pitcher Ted Lyons said "looked like a small boy looking around a corner to see if the cops are coming"—and he flied out. It was after the game, when Black was in the clubhouse, that he looked up and saw Stan Musial.

"I'm sorry that happened," Black remembered Musial whispering. "But don't you worry about it. You're a great pitcher. You will win a lot of games."

Yes, Joe Black told the story often—and it's a good story. But what I remember about the way he told it on the plane that day was how proud Black was to be connected to Musial. This is the common theme when people tell their Musial stories. No one tries to make Musial larger than life—he was only as large as life. He didn't make a show. He didn't make speeches. He didn't try to change the world. He just believed that every man had the right to be treated with dignity.

Musial believed in being a role model. He thought that was part of his job, part of why he was being paid so much money. He thought it was the least he could do. Musial smoked for a long time—he even advertised Chesterfields when he was young. But when he realized how he might be influencing kids, he quit the Chesterfield job and, shortly after that, quit smoking. In the interim he would smoke under stairwells so nobody would see him.

He would never allow photographers to snap him in the clubhouse without his shirt. Teammates and opponents say they would occasionally hear him swear, but certainly not where fans could hear him. The same goes with drinking—he might have had a couple here and there, but Stan Musial would never allow himself to be seen tipsy in public. He has been married to that high school sweetheart, Lil, for 70 years now.

In 1958 he became the first player in National League history to make $100,000 in a year. The next year he had his worst season—he hit only .255 and missed 40 games with nagging injuries. He went to Cardinals management and insisted they cut his salary by the maximum 20% (which the Cardinals did). Years later, when asked about that move, Musial said simply, "There wasn't anything noble about it. I had a lousy year. I didn't deserve the money."

Stan Musial and Albert Pujols were having their photo taken together to lead into the All-Star Game at Busch last year. It was a monumental moment for a couple of reasons. One was obvious: Here were two generations coming together, two of the best hitters in baseball history in the same place at the same time. They even shared a nickname. They called Albert Pujols El Hombre—Spanish for The Man. The other reason was something more poignant. Stan the Man doesn't get around much anymore.

The conversation was halting at first. The two men had spoken before, of course, but that was usually at a ballpark, where the sounds of batting practice or infield drills filled the silences. Here there was nothing but silence in the silences, and the two great hitters who tended to do their talking at the plate groped for words to express their feelings.

In time, though, spurred by *St. Louis Post-Dispatch* baseball bard Rick Hummel, the conversation blossomed. Pujols and Musial talked about the weight of their bats, their golf games, umpiring and so on. Pujols asked Musial for his secret to hitting with two strikes. "Know the strike zone," Musial said.

And then Pujols was told about one of Musial's most amazing baseball feats. Musial has so many feats: At different points in his career he led the National League in batting, on-base percentage, slugging, hits, doubles, triples, runs, RBIs, walks, intentional walks and total bases. But if you had to define Musial with one number—the way 755 describes Aaron and .406 gets at Williams and 56 helps explain DiMaggio—then that number is probably 1,815. That is the number of hits that Musial had at home *and* on the road.

Pujols—who prides himself on consistency—was incredulous.

"I wonder if he meant to do that," Pujols said.

Not long after that, Pujols politely asked people to stop calling him El Hombre. He understood that his own nickname was an homage to Musial. But he still asked people to stop it. "There's only one Man," he said.

Speaking of Hummel—he has been covering sports for the *Post-Dispatch* since 1971 and has been covering baseball for almost 30 years. In baseball writing circles he is known simply as Commish. No *the* in front of Commish. That would be too formal.

Over that time he has grown close to Musial. Certainly no writer in America knows The Man better. Hummel has heard Musial play the harmonica enough times to know his entire repertoire. ("Four songs," Hummel says with a big smile. "He says he knows 50, but I've only heard four. *The Wabash Cannonball. Take Me Out to the Ballgame. Happy Birthday.* And the national anthem.") Hummel has heard all of Musial's jokes—he thinks there might be fewer than four. Hummel remembers well the first time Stan Musial called him by name and how good it made him feel.

One day during spring training last year Hummel was sitting in La Russa's office with the Cardinals manager, Hall of Famer Red Schoendienst and Musial, and he was listening to the stories when suddenly Musial did the oddest thing. He reached into a bucket next to La Russa's desk. And he pulled out a baseball. He wrote on it, TO RICK. STAN MUSIAL. And he handed the ball to Hummel.

"I didn't ask him for it or anything," Hummel says. "I just took the ball and looked at him and thanked him. And he went on like nothing happened."

Hummel smiles like a little kid. "I know exactly where that baseball is," he says.

In St. Louis they remember Musial daily. There probably is not an athlete in America more closely tied to a city than Musial is to St. Louis. And it isn't all nostalgia. He's still a very real part of Cardinals baseball. "In this modern era of baseball we emulate Stan's values and loyalty, not only to the Cardinals but also to our city and region," Cardinals general manager John Mozellak says, and player after player, fan after fan, reiterates the thought. St. Louis parents—themselves too young to remember Musial as a player—pass along the stories.

Musial still goes to the Stan the Man Inc. office daily to sign a few autographs. He doesn't show up in public much, though. "Stan is slowing down," a close friend says. He spends his time now helping Lil and having quiet lunches with his best friends. Nobody denies that he is not always himself, but they all say that when the baseball talk starts, the years will melt away, and Musial will look and sound like the old days.

He doesn't come around the ballpark much. He was there for Opening Day, of course—Musial will not miss Opening Day—and the hope around here is that the Cardinals will make the playoffs so that Musial might come around again. "I never worry about Stan when he's around baseball," Hummel says. "It's the off-season that makes me worry."

Even now, when a bit of his youth comes blowing through, Musial will pull out the harmonica and play one of his songs. He can still pull out one of his favorite jokes—like the one he told Pujols about how he has a three-handicap in golf, the three handicaps being his driving, his irons and his putting. He can still fold a dollar bill into a ring. What does it say about Stan Musial that he learned that particular trick, worked on it, perfected it?

"He loves making people happy," Zitzmann says. Yes. That's what it says. Maybe there have been a handful of better ballplayers. Maybe there have been a handful of more important baseball players. Maybe there have even been a handful of more memorable players. But no baseball player, none, worked so hard to make people happy. He hit the ball hard into the gaps, ran hard out of the box, signed every autograph, shook every hand and turned dollar bills into memories. And, all the while, he kept telling us that he was the lucky one. Whaddya say!

THE NEGRO LEAGUES

Baseball's Forgotten Pioneers

Former Negro league players gave too much
to the game to be left in obscurity

BY SHELLEY SMITH

Seventy-seven-year-old Bill Wright lives in a tiny, crumbling house in Aguascalientes, Mexico, barely able to walk because his feet are twisted with arthritis and he's unable to afford surgery. Things were different a half century ago, when he was a strapping young outfielder and gifted hitter for the Elite Giants of the old Negro leagues. In the 1930s and '40s, he dazzled the thousands of fans who crammed into parks to see him and teammates like Roy Campanella and hundreds of other black players.

One of those watching was Brooklyn Dodger president Branch Rickey, who saw the talent of those black players. He also saw how many fans paid to see them. The annual East-West Classic, the Negro league all-star game, filled Comiskey Park; the New York Black Yankees drew crowds of 30,000 and more to Yankee Stadium; and cities such as Kansas City supported the Negro league Monarchs on a par with major league teams in other cities. Rickey wanted those fans, too, so in 1945 he chose Jackie Robinson to be the man who would break major league baseball's color barrier.

The fact is, Wright, and many like him, had almost as much to do with the integration of baseball as did Robinson. Yet Wright now lives in poverty and obscurity, as do so many other former Negro league ballplayers. George Giles, a Negro league first baseman between 1927 and '38, spent his years after baseball living in the back of a convenience store in Manhattan, Kans. When I visited him there last June, he showed me his "Hall of Fame"—a cinder-block wall covered with clippings of himself and of his grandson, Brian Giles, a journeyman infielder who played in the major leagues in the 1980s. George Giles told me he was barely making ends meet, and he asked if I had heard whether baseball ever was going to "do something for us." He died on March 3.

Most of the 140 or so former Negro league players who are still alive played for $2 a week in meal money and $60 a month in salary, wages that sometimes went unpaid. They were called "nigger" as often as they were called by name. They often traveled by bus for days to get to the next game, and sometimes they played as many as four games in one day. They changed clothes in farmhouses, and they shared bathwater—when they could get it—with teammates.

By the time blacks were allowed to play in the major leagues, most of the Negro league stars were too old and road weary to be of interest to American and National league teams. And with the integration of the game, the Negro leagues died out. "We held no grudges," Wright says, "because we had so much fun."

Willie Grace, 73, a Negro league outfielder for nine years who now is nearly blind and living alone in Erie, Pa., says, "Heck, we would have played for nothing." Which is about all they are getting in return from the game—no pension or health insurance. What little baseball-related assistance they receive comes from the limited resources of two charities.

Baseball Assistance Team (BAT), an organization funded by contributions, with its expenses underwritten by Major League Baseball, has helped many down-and-out former ballplayers, including 24 ex-Negro league players, on the basis of need. One of BAT's vice-presidents is Joe Black, a former Negro league and Brooklyn Dodger pitcher. He visited training camps in Arizona last spring and approached over two dozen current black players and coaches, and he asked them for contributions to BAT. Seven players and coaches—Dusty Baker, Andre Dawson, Ken Griffey Sr., Ken Griffey Jr., Willie McGee, Kevin Mitchell and Dave Stewart—signed sizable checks. The rest had conveniently forgotten their wallets and checkbooks. What most of today's stars don't realize is that the efforts of people like Wright, Giles and Grace paved the way for the Dwight Goodens and the Bobby Bonillas to sign $5 million contracts.

The Negro League Baseball Players Association, established two years ago by two ardent baseball fans in New York, attorney Ed Schauder and music producer Richard Berg, has raised about $40,000, which has been distributed to some Negro league players through licensing royalties, honorariums for speaking engagements or direct grants. The association also arranges for former players to appear at memorabilia shows at which they sell their autographs on trading cards produced for them by the association. Still, the players often take home little money because most collectors have no idea who they are. Willie Mays once gave $100 handshakes to each of the Negro league players attending a show with him because he knew they hadn't made nearly enough to justify their 2½-hour appearance.

The best way to recognize the contributions made by the Negro league players would be for Major League Baseball to set up a special fund for them and to vigorously solicit contributions. After all, Rickey made his decision to sign a black player not only because it was morally correct, but also because it made financial sense. Last August, Southern Bell, Major League Baseball and the Atlanta Braves honored more than 70 former Negro league stars at a reception in Cooperstown. The pride these men felt that night at the Hall of Fame, and the camaraderie they shared, was remarkable. Baseball commissioner Fay Vincent thanked the men for having given so much of themselves to the game.

The start of another baseball season should remind us that it's time these players received something in return.

The Guiding Light

Buck O'Neil bears witness to the glory and not
just the shame of the Negro leagues

BY STEVE WULF

*There's nothing greater for a human being than to get his body to react to all
the things one does on a ball field. It's as good as sex; it's as good as music. It
fills you up. Waste no tears for me. I didn't come along too early. I was right
on time.*

—BUCK O'NEIL

Buck stuck, but he was Foots first. He has also been called Country and Cap
and just plain Jay, and while Satchel Paige was alive, he was a man called
Nancy.

John Jordan O'Neil, born Nov. 13, 1911, in Carrabelle, Fla., has collected
almost as many nicknames during his seven decades in the game as all of
the current major leaguers combined. But then he has led so many different
baseball lives, and with the exception of that month back in 1937 when he
played in a straw skirt for the Zulu Cannibal Giants, all of them have been
distinguished.

As a smooth-fielding first baseman for the Kansas City Monarchs from
1938 to '54, O'Neil won a Negro American League batting title (hitting .350 in
'46) and played in three Negro League East-West All-Star Games and three
Negro World Series. As the manager of the Monarchs from '48 until '55 he
won five half-season pennants and shepherded 14 of his players, including
Ernie Banks and Elston Howard, into the majors. As a scout for the Chicago

Cubs he signed four elected or near-certain Hall of Famers: Banks, Lou Brock, Lee Smith and Joe Carter. In 1962 the Cubs made him the first black coach in the major leagues.

At 82, the still-graceful, still-handsome O'Neil still scouts for the Kansas City Royals. When he's not doing that, or shooting his age over 18 holes, he champions the players and memories of the Negro leagues. But O'Neil is most impressive not for what he does or what he did, but for what he *is*. Banks, who knew O'Neil when, says, "He is a role model, a father, a mentor, a teacher, a *sensei*, a hero, a gentleman, a man. Who do you think I got my let's-play-two attitude from? From Buck O'Neil, that's who."

Hal McRae, the Royals' manager, says, "Buck just makes you feel good. You might be blue, you might be in a slump, but a few minutes with Buck and the world is a wonderful place. Do you know what he is? He's the guiding light."

It's a light that shines on the past as well as the present. The Negro leagues were born because organized baseball wanted nothing to do with integration, and O'Neil and his teammates encountered prejudice daily. But the Negro leagues were also a glorious enterprise well worth celebrating, and that's where O'Neil comes in. He takes particular pride in the Monarchs, and he harbors no bitterness over the fact that he was past his prime when Jackie Robinson finally broke the color line, in 1947. "Buck never curses his fate," says Banks. "He knows that what he did as a player and manager paved the way for the rest of us."

And O'Neil's light shines often in *Baseball*, the nine-inning, nine-night documentary that airs on PBS starting Sept. 18. The film, by Ken Burns of *Civil War* renown, presents a sweeping panorama of the national pastime, and while *Baseball* has much to recommend it, its best moments come while O'Neil is on the screen.

He is at the heart of *Baseball*'s "Fifth Inning," subtitled "Shadow Ball." On one level, shadow ball was the amazingly realistic pantomime of baseball—without the ball—often performed by Negro leaguers before their games. But it is also a metaphor for the black baseball that shadowed the segregated major leagues. O'Neil illuminates those shadows, bringing the Negro leagues to life in all their glory and pain, jazz and blues.

As an eyewitness he links Babe Ruth to Josh Gibson to Bo Jackson. As a confidant of Paige's he reveals a new side to the great pitcher. As a singer... well, if you can't watch all 18½ hours of the show, be sure to catch O'Neil during the "Seventh Inning Stretch." He'll take you out to the game.

Foots

"How old is this ballpark?" someone asks Jordan Kobritz, the principal owner of the Daytona Cubs.

"As near as anyone can document," says Kobritz, "it's 55 years old."

"Sixty," says Buck O'Neil. "It's at least 60 years old. I played here in 1934 for the Miami Giants, on our way up to face the Jacksonville Red Caps, a good team made up of railroad porters. Over there, that's where the Jim Crow section of the bleachers was."

The field in question is now known as Jackie Robinson Ballpark because this is where Robinson played his first integrated game in organized ball, as a member of the 1946 Montreal Royals. O'Neil has come to Daytona to rekindle some memories and visit his niece, Sally Griffin.

There's nobody on the field on this June afternoon, but O'Neil can still see the Giants: "That's me over there on first base. 22-year-old Foots O'Neil from Sarasota [Fla.]. On second, Winky James from Key West. Our shortstop is Bill Riggins, who played for the New York Black Yankees, and at third base is Oliver Marcelle. Ollie was a Creole from New Orleans, a fine-looking man. But he got part of his nose bit off in a fight in Cuba, and he had to play with a piece of tape on the nose. He'd been so proud of his looks, so he was never the same after that."

Griffin has brought along some mementos, one a 70-year-old report card from a school in Sarasota for sixth-grader John O'Neil. He earned excellent grades, including an A in personal hygiene, which will come as no surprise to people who know how meticulously he dresses.

Back then he was known as Foots because he had size-11 feet, pretty big dogs for a 12-year-old. He was also a pretty good first baseman, and one day the manager of the semipro Sarasota Tigers asked Emma Booker, the principal-teacher at Foots's small school, if he could borrow the kid for a game. She said yes, and soon Foots, not yet in his teens, was traveling all over the state playing baseball. He also got to see a lot of the white man's game during spring training: John McGraw's New York Giants trained in Sarasota. Babe Ruth and Lou Gehrig were based in Tampa, and Connie Mack's Philadelphia Athletics were in Fort Myers.

But there was work to be done, and because his father, John Sr., was a foreman in the celery fields, Foots became a box boy, carrying the crates of celery. "I was considered a good box boy because, while most of the box boys could only carry two crates at a time, I was big and strong enough to carry four," O'Neil says, "I did that for about three years, at $1.25 a day. One day I was having lunch by myself next to a big stack of boxes, and it was so hot, I said out loud, 'Damn, there has got to be something better than this.'

"It turns out my father and some of the older men were on the other side of the stack having their lunch. That night my father told me, 'I heard what you said today.' I thought he was going to reprimand me for swearing, but he said, 'You're right. There is something better than this. But you can't find it here. You're going to have to go out and get it.'"In those days there were no high schools for blacks in Sarasota, but thanks to the eighth-grade education Booker gave him, Foots was able to get an athletic scholarship to Edward Waters College, a Methodist school in Jacksonville. There they called him Country, and they made him the first baseman on the baseball team and a lineman on the football team. The baseball coach, Ox Clemons, schooled O'Neil so well that the Miami Giants, a Negro semipro team, stole him away in 1934, by which time O'Neil had earned his high school diploma but was still two years short of a college degree. It just so happened that one of the owners of the Giants was a man named Buck O'Neal, although it would be a while before Country became Buck.

In 1935 Marcelle, the third baseman with the taped-up nose, invited O'Neil to join him on a team he played for called the New York Tigers. "We started out in Sarasota, mind you, and we had nothing to do with New York," says O'Neil. "That was just a way to get the people to come to the games. Out where we were headed, nobody was going to know the difference." They were also headed into the Depression, and the Tigers spent the summer and fall chasing after ball games in Louisiana, Texas, Kansas and Colorado, living hand to mouth, hopping freight trains, sometimes relying on O'Neil's pool-playing abilities for money.

O'Neil and Doby Major, another player from Sarasota, decided to go home from Wichita, Kans., that October, and O'Neil's father wired them train tickets. But they had only 75 cents between them for the three-day trip, and used it to buy day-old bread in Chattanooga. By the time they got home, O'Neil says, "our day-old bread was two days gone. When I got home I ate so much, my mama cried."

Up in the stands at Jackie Robinson Ballpark, O'Neil recalls another adventure from that summer of '35: "One night we had to sneak out of a boardinghouse in Shreveport without paying our bills. But a few months after that, I sent the landlady a check for what we owed her, which wasn't much, maybe $50.

"Many years later I'm passing through Shreveport on my way to scout a player, and I decide to stay at this same boarding-house. I inquire after the landlady, and a woman says, 'That was my mother. She passed away a few years ago. Did you know her?' I tell the woman my name, and she smiles and leads me into one of the rooms. There on the wall, framed like a picture, is my check. I guess I had restored her mother's faith in us."

Buck
A hand comes down hard on the shoulder of Ken Burns.

"Can we have Buck back now?"

Burns, who is sitting in the press dining room at Kauffman Stadium on the night of Aug. 3, turns around to see that the hand belongs to the Kansas City vice president for baseball operations, George Brett. "Actually," says Brett, "we don't need him now that we've won 11 in a row. It's when we start losing that we'll need him."

The Royals have given O'Neil time off this summer to help promote *Baseball*, but don't think for a moment that his role with the club is ceremonial. "I depend on him," says McRae. "Whether it be for advice or for information, he's a big help around here." Indeed, when O'Neil walks into the Royals' clubhouse, the room gets a little warmer. He'll do ball tricks with one of the kids, swap stories with K.C. first base coach Lee May or quietly advise a player in a slump.

This night also happens to be Monarchs Night, and the Royals are about to play the Oakland A's while wearing replica uniforms of the 1924 Kansas City Monarchs, who were the first "world champions" of the Negro leagues. This unprecedented homage to a Negro league team by a major league team is a wonderful—albeit overdue—gesture that bridges time, culture, race and spirit.

On the mound to throw the ceremonial first pitch is Burns, dressed in a Monarch jersey. But as he goes into his windup, his catcher, every inch a Monarch, every inch a ballplayer, waves him off. Much to the delight of the crowd, O'Neil takes off his glasses and puts them on Bob Motley, a former Negro league umpire standing behind him. Only then does O'Neil signal for his batterymate to throw the ball.

O'Neil didn't actually become a Monarch until 1938, when he was 26. He had played the '36 season with the Shreveport Acme Giants and most of the '37 season with the Memphis Red Sox. He did spend one month in '37 playing in that straw skirt for the barnstorming Zulu Cannibal Giants. "I was making $100 a month with the Red Sox, and the Giants offered me a lot more, so I jumped," says O'Neil. "Abe Saperstein owned the team, and we didn't think that much about wearing the costume. This was *show* business. At least I didn't have to put on the war paint like some of the guys. Besides, we had trunks on underneath our skirts. A first baseman in a stretch would have been pretty vulnerable without those trunks."

His stay with the Cannibal Giants was memorable for another reason. The promoter for the team, Syd Pollock, had also worked for the Miami Giants when O'Neil played for them, and Pollock somehow confused this O'Neil with that club's co-owner, Buck O'Neal. So he started billing the Giants' first baseman as Buck O'Neil, and the name stuck.

The next year, J. Leslie Wilkinson brought O'Neil to Kansas City. Wilkie, who was the only white owner in the Negro leagues, had had his eye on

O'Neil for quite some time, and O'Neil immediately became the Monarchs' starting first baseman and number six hitter. "It hit me my first week with the Monarchs," says O'Neil. "I caught a routine throw from the second baseman, and as I was trotting off the field, I thought, Damn! I just caught a throw from Newt Allen. Newt was one of the greatest players in the Negro leagues back when I was a child."

From 1939 to '42 the Monarchs won four straight Negro American League pennants. They had a number of stars: pitcher Hilton Smith; shortstop and right-fielder Ted Strong, who also starred for the Harlem Globetrotters; and outfielder Turkey Stearnes, a peculiar man who liked to talk to his bats. And in '39 Paige joined them, but that's another two dozen stories.

"We were like the New York Yankees," says O'Neil. "We had that winning tradition, and we were *proud*. We had a strict dress code—coat and tie, no baseball jackets. We stayed in the best hotels in the world. They just *happened* to be owned by black people. We ate in the best restaurants in the world. They just *happened* to be run by blacks. And when we were in Kansas City, well, 18th and Vine was the center of the universe. We'd come to breakfast at Street's Hotel, and there might be Count Basic or Joe Louis or Billie Holiday or Lionel Hampton."

World War II broke up the Monarchs' dynasty, at least temporarily. One of O'Neil's few regrets is that he didn't get to play for Kansas City in 1945, the year Jackie Robinson was a Monarch. O'Neil was then in the Navy, stationed with a black stevedore battalion at Subic Bay in the Philippines. Recalls O'Neil, "We loaded and unloaded ships. I was a bosun with 18 or so men under me. One night at about 11 o'clock the commanding officer gets on the horn and says, 'John O'Neil, please report to my office immediately.'"I didn't know what he could want. But when I got to his office, this white man said to me, 'I just thought you should know that the Brooklyn Dodgers have just signed Jackie Robinson to a minor league contract.' Well. I got on the horn and said, 'Now hear this! Now hear this! The Dodgers have signed Jackie Robinson.' You should have heard the celebration. Halfway around the world from Brooklyn, we were hollering and firing our guns into the air."

After the war O'Neil returned home to Kansas City and married Ora Lee Owen, a schoolteacher from Memphis whom he had met a few years before.

As she did then, Ora is waiting patiently on this Aug. 3 night for John—as she calls him—to return. She is sitting in a private box at Kauffman Stadium while Buck and some of the other Monarch alumni sign autographs outside the stands. The demand for the signatures of these once-forgotten players has been so great that they are still signing an hour and a half after the first pitch of the game.

Finally, after about six innings, the men come back from their grueling autograph session. Rather than looking tired, however, the Monarchs, in their uniforms, actually seem younger than they did a few hours earlier. Is it possible, O'Neil is asked, that a little time spent in a baseball uniform can take years off your age?

"You got *that* right."

Nancy

Standin' in a corner, 18th and Vine.

Those aren't exactly the lyrics to *Kansas City*, but on the morning of Aug. 4 they're close enough. Standing in a corner of the Negro Leagues Museum at 18th and Vine are the now familiar team of Buck and Burns. In their own ways they arc eloquent preachers, and they are here to address the audience at a benefit breakfast for the museum. Burns introduces O'Neil as the most remarkable man he has ever interviewed and then adds, "Buck is 82. I'm 41. I guess that makes me half a Buck."

O'Neil tells a story about his 80th-birthday celebration at his church: "There was all this babbling about Buck O'Neil *this* and Buck O'Neil *that*. Just in case any of it went to my head, a young boy I knew came up and introduced his friend to me. He said, 'I want you to meet Buck O'Neil. He's an old *relic* from the Negro leagues.' I said, 'Son, you are *so* right.'"As he almost always does before such an audience. O'Neil tells a Satchel Paige story. He has a lot of them, always making sure that the absent Paige addresses him as Nancy. There was the time Paige heard an opposing player in Denver call him an "overrated darkie." He told Nancy to bring in the infielders and outfielders and had the seven of them kneel around him as he struck out the side on nine pitches.

But as O'Neil points out in the "Fifth Inning" of *Baseball*, Paige was more than a clown, more than a great pitcher. "A part of Satchel that no one ever hears about," says O'Neil, "is this part of Satchel. We're going up to Charleston, but the rooms weren't ready yet. So he says, 'Nancy, c'mon with me. We're gonna take a ride....' We went to Drum Island [S.C.]. Drum Island was where they had auctioned off the slaves.... We stood there, he and I, maybe 10 minutes, not saying a word, just thinking.

"'You know what, Nancy?' he says.

"'What's that, Satchel?'"'Seems like I been here before.'"I said, 'Me, too.'"At the breakfast at 18th and Vine, someone in the audience asks the question everybody wants O'Neil to be asked: "Why did Satchel call you Nancy?" O'Neil smiles the way he must have smiled at a hanging curveball in 1946.

"We were playing near an Indian reservation in Sioux Falls, South Dakota, on our way to Chicago to play the Chicago American Giants," he says. "Satchel met a beautiful Indian maiden named Nancy, and he asked her if she'd like to visit him in Chicago, and she said sure, so Satchel gave her the name of our hotel. Well, now we're in Chicago, and I'm sitting in the coffee shop of the hotel when I see a cab pull up, and out steps Nancy. I greet her and tell her that Satchel is upstairs, and the bellhop carries her bags to his room.

"A few minutes pass, and another cab pulls up, and out steps Satchel's fiancèe, Lahoma. I jump up and say, 'Lahoma, so good to see you. Satchel's not here right now, but he should be along shortly. Why don't you sit here with me, and I'll have the bellman take your bags up.' I go over to the bellman, explain the situation to him and tell him to move Nancy's bags into the room next to mine, which is next door to Satchel's. A few minutes later he comes down and gives me the sign that everything is O.K. In the meantime, Satchel has climbed down the fire escape, and lo and behold, here he comes walking down the street. I say, 'Look, Lahoma, here's old Satch now,' and Satchel gives her a big greeting and takes her upstairs.

"That should've ended the trouble, but when we were turning in that night I heard Satchel's door open and close. Then I heard him knock on Nancy's door. I know he wanted to give her some money and apologize. But while he's whispering kind of loud, 'Nancy! Nancy!' I hear *his* door open again, and I knew it was Lahoma coming out to see what was going on. I jumped out of bed, opened my door and said, 'Yeah, Satch. What do you want?' And he said, 'Oh, Nancy. There you are. I was looking for you.'

"And from that day on, Satchel called me Nancy."

Cap

"Hello, Cap," says the former first base coach for the Monarchs.

"Hello, Hamp," says O'Neil.

At a New York screening of the "Seventh Inning" of *Baseball*, the two octogenarians greet each other like long-lost friends. It has been a while since O'Neil has seen Lionel Hampton.

"I loved to watch the Monarchs play," says Hampton, the great bandleader and vibraphonist. "One day in 1948 Cap—that's what the players called Buck—said to me, 'You're around here so much, I might as well put you to work.' So Cap let me coach first base for one game, and then he gave me the jersey. It was one of the great thrills of my life."

As strong as jazz and black baseball were in Kansas City in the 1930s and '40s, by the early '50s they had begun to diminish. Nightclubs closed, and the Monarchs, like all the other Negro league franchises, began to suffer because of the integration of the big leagues. O'Neil's job as manager was no longer to win but rather to prepare young black players for their chance at the majors: Banks, Howard, Gene Baker, Pancho Herrera, Sweet Lou Johnson, Hank Thompson.

Before the day-old bread was two days gone again, O'Neil quit the Monarchs after the 1955 season to scout for the Cubs. His job was to find black players in the South, and he put 40,000 miles a year on his car. He discovered Brock when he was a skinny outfielder at Southern University. He tracked down 17-year-old Oscar Gamble in Montgomery, Ala. He also found trouble one night in Jackson, Miss.

O'Neil and Piper Davis, the black scout who signed Lee May, were in Jackson looking for a high school game. They saw the lights of a ballpark, pulled into the parking lot and asked the two men at the entrance if this was where the game was. "Oh, yeah, this is where it is, all right," said one. O'Neil and Davis got out of their car and walked to the field. On the mound, though, was not a pitcher but a member of the Ku Klux Klan. The ballpark was filled with men in sheets, and the two scouts made a hasty exit.

In May 1962 the Cubs made O'Neil the first black coach in the major leagues. Although *Ebony* did a big feature on him, the predominantly white media largely ignored his appointment. (SPORTS ILLUSTRATED did O'Neil as a "Face in the Crowd.") At the time, the Cubs were in their College of Coaches stage, rotating several different coaches as the head coach (i.e., manager), and John Holland, the Chicago general manager, paid lip service to the idea that O'Neil might one day be the manager.

But the Cubs were never serious about that; they didn't even want him on the coaching lines. Perhaps the one man in this world for whom O'Neil holds any animosity is Charlie (Jolly Cholly) Grimm, the old Chicago first baseman and manager who occupied a front-office position while the college was in session. During a 1962 game with the Houston Colt .45s, both head coach Charlie Metro and third base coach El Tappe were ejected. O'Neil was the logical choice to take over third base, but Fred Martin, the pitching coach, was brought in from the bullpen to man the box. "After 40 years in baseball and 10 years of managing, I was pretty sure I knew when to wave somebody home and when to have him put on the brakes," says O'Neil. "Later I found out that Grimm had ordered the other coaches never to let me coach on the lines."

It wasn't until 1975 that the Cleveland Indians made Frank Robinson the first black manager. In the meantime, O'Neil returned to scouting, signing Smith and Carter, among others. It's no coincidence that O'Neil's four Hall of Fame–quality players—Banks, Brock, Smith, Carter—all share his positive outlook on life. "The measure of a man," says Banks, "is in the lives he's touched."

And, in O'Neil's case, the lives he has preserved. "Sometimes," he says, "I think the Lord has kept me on this earth as long as He has so I can bear witness to the Negro leagues." As a member of the Baseball Hall of Fame veterans committee, O'Neil fulfills that responsibility. He says there are still 10 Negro Leaguers worthy of the Hall. For now, he will settle for just one: Leon Day, an outstanding pitcher and outfielder for the Newark Eagles who's still alive and well at 78 in Baltimore. O'Neil also wants to correct the impression of the Negro leagues left by the movie *The Bingo Long Traveling All-Stars & Motor Kings*. "We weren't a minstrel show," he says. "We didn't just pile into a Cadillac and pick up a game here and there. We had a schedule. We had spring training. We had an all-star game. Most years, we had a World Series. We were professional ballplayers."

Over the years, O'Neil has been a strong force behind many Negro league reunions. In fact, it was at such a reunion, in Ashland, Ky., in 1981, that he spoke those life-affirming, baseball-affirming words: *Waste no tears for me. I didn't come along too early. I was right on time.*

He has also been raising funds for an expanded Negro Leagues Museum, to be built across the street from the current one and next to a new Jazz Hall of Fame. "Wouldn't that be something?" he says. "To see folks flocking to the corner of 18th and Vine again."

John

O'Neil is leading a small caravan to Forest Hill Cemetery in South Kansas City. That's where Paige is buried. It's also where Confederate General John Shelby put up Shelby's Last Stand, and the irony certainly isn't lost on Burns, who visited the cemetery for his Civil War research: "One of the reasons I decided to do *Baseball* after *The Civil War* was that the first real progress in racial integration in this country after Reconstruction didn't come until the Dodgers signed Jackie Robinson."

Paige's gravesite, which he shares with Lahoma, whom he married in 1947, is extraordinary. For one thing, it's on an island of grass in the middle of the cemetery's main road. "Satchel was buried someplace else in the cemetery, but they moved him here so that more people could find him," says O'Neil. "Even after he died, Satchel was on the run."

For another thing, there are portraits of Satchel, who died on June 8, 1982, and Lahoma, who passed away four years later. And on the tombstone are inscribed his famous Rules for Longevity: AVOID FRIED MEATS WHICH ANGRY UP THE BLOOD, etc.

We have to know: "Did Lahoma know why Satchel called you Nancy?"

"Oh, yes," says O'Neil. "She loved the story. She *knew* Satchel. I never would have told the story if she hadn't heard it from him first."

When Paige was buried, O'Neil delivered the eulogy. "People say it's a shame he never pitched against the best," O'Neil said at the time. "But who's to say he didn't?"

It's funny that John Jordan O'Neil is only now being discovered, at the age of 82. But in an age when the racial divide seems to be widening, at a time when baseball is being torn apart, along comes this man to repair some of the damage.

Yes, Buck O'Neil is right on time.

JUNE 20, 1994

No Place in the Shade

Cool Papa Bell could play with the best of them, but
in this SI Classic from 1973 he tells why baseball
was a bittersweet gig for Negro leaguers

BY MARK KRAM

In the language of jazz, the word *gig* is an evening of work; sometimes sweet,
sometimes sour, take the gig as it comes, for who knows when the next will
be. It means bread and butter first, but a whole lot of things have always
seemed to ride with the word: drifting blue light, the bouquet from leftover
drinks, spells of odd dialogue and most of all a sense of pain and limbo. For
more than anything the word means black, down-and-out black, leavin'-
home black, gonna-find-me-a-place-in-the-shade black.

Big shade fell coolly only on a few. It never got to James Thomas Bell, or
Cool Papa Bell as he was known in Negro baseball, that lost caravan that
followed the sun. Other blacks, some of them musicians who worked jazz up
from the South, would feel the touch of fame, or once in a while have the
thought that their names meant something to people outside their own. But
if you were black and played baseball, well, look for your name only in the
lineup before each game, or else you might not even see it there if you kept
on dreamin'.

Black baseball was a stone-hard gig. It was three games a day, sometimes
in three different towns miles apart. It was the heat and fumes and bounces
from buses that moved your stomach up to your throat and it was greasy
meals at fly-papered diners at three a.m. and uniforms that were seldom

91

off your back. "We slept with 'em on sometimes," says Papa, "but there never was enough sleep. We got so we could sleep standin' up."

Only a half-mad seer—not any of the blacks who worked the open prairies and hidden ball yards in each big city—could have envisioned what would happen one day. The players knew a black man would cross the color line that was first drawn by the sudden hate of Cap Anson back in 1883, yet no one was fool enough to think that some bright, scented day way off among the gods of Cooperstown they would hear their past blared out across the field and would know that who they were and what they did would never be invisible again.

When that time comes for Papa Bell—quite possibly the next Hall of Fame vote [he was, in fact, inducted into the Hall in 1974]—few will comprehend what he did during all those gone summers. The mass audience will not be able to relate to him, to assemble an image of him, to measure him against his peers as they do the white player. The old ones like Papa have no past. They were minstrels, separated from record books, left as the flower in Thomas Gray's *Elegy* to "waste its sweetness on the desert air." Comparisons will have to do: Josh Gibson, the Babe Ruth of the blacks; Buck Leonard, the Lou Gehrig of his game; and Cool Papa Bell—who was he?

A comparison will be hard to find for Papa. His friend Tweed, whom Papa calls *the* Black Historian, a title most agreeable to Tweed, says that you have to go all the way back to Willie Keeler for Papa's likeness. Papa's way was cerebral, improvisational; he was a master of the little things, the nuances that are the ambrosia of baseball for those who care to understand the game. Power is stark, power shocks, it is the stuff of immortality, but Papa's jewellike skills were the object of shoptalk for 28 winters.

Arthritic and weary, Papa quit the circuit 23 years ago, at age 47, ending a career that began in 1922. During that time he had been the essence of black baseball, which had a panache all its own. It was an intimate game: the extra base, the drag bunt; a game of daring instinct, rather than one from the hidebound book. Some might say that it lacked discipline, but if so, it can also be said that never has baseball been played more artfully, or more joyously. "Before a game," says Papa, "one of our big old pitchers, he'd say, 'Just get me a coupla runs, that's all.' You see, we played tricky ball, thinkin' all the time: We get a run, they got to get two to beat ya. Right?"

The yellow pages of Tweed's scrapbooks don't tell much about the way it was, and they don't reveal much about Papa, either; box scores never explain. They can't chart the speed of Papa Bell. "Papa Bell," says Satchel Paige, "why he was so fast he could turn out the light and jump in bed before the room got dark!" Others also embellish: He could hit a hard ground ball through the box and get hit with the ball as he slid into second; he was so fast that he once stole two bases on the same pitch. "People can sure talk it, can't they?" says Papa.

Papa says he did steal two bases on one pitch, which was a pitchout. "The catcher was so surprised the way I was runnin' that he just held the ball," says Papa. "I asked him later what he doin' holdin' that ball, and he said he didn't know, 'cept he *never* seen a man run like that before in his life." It is also a reliable fact that once in Chicago, on a mushy field, he circled the bases in 13.1 seconds, two fifths faster than Evar Swanson's major league record. "On a dry field," he says, "I once done it in 12 flat."

Papa could run all right, and he could hit and field as well. He played a shallow centerfield, even more so than Willie Mays did when he broke in. "It doesn't matter where he plays," Pie Traynor once said. "He can go a country mile for a ball." As a hitter Bell had distance, but mainly he strove to hit the ball into holes; he could hit a ball through the hole in a fence, or drag a bunt as if it were on a string in his hand. Bell never hit below .308, and one time when he was hitting .390 on the last day of the season he purposely gave up his batting title; he was 43 at the time.

"Jackie Robinson had just signed with the Dodgers, and Monte Irvin was our best young player," says Papa. "I gave up my title so Monte would have a better chance at the majors. That was the way we thought then. We'd do anythin' to get a player up there. In the final two games of the season, a doubleheader, I still needed a few times at bat to qualify for the title. I got two hits in the first game and sat out the second. The fans were mad, but they didn't know what we were trying to do. After the season I was supposed to get the $200 for the title anyway, but my owner, he say, 'Well look, Cool, Irvin won it, didn't he?' They wouldn't give me the $200. Baseball was never much for me makin' money."

Papa Bell earned $90 a month his first year, back in 1922. He would never make more than $450 a month, although his ability was such that later he would be ranked on Jackie Robinson's all-time team in the same outfield with Henry Aaron and Mays. Bill Veeck, who also saw Bell play, puts him right up there with Tris Speaker, Joe DiMaggio and Mays. "Cool Papa was one of the most magical players I've ever seen," says Veeck.

The money never bothered Papa; it was a game, a summer away from the packinghouse. "'Cept one time," adds Papa, "when one team told me to pay my expenses from St. Louis to Memphis. They'd give it to me back, they said. I get there, and they say no. Owner of the club was a dentist. I say to 'em I didn't come down here 'cause I got a toothache. So I went back home. Owners are owners, whether they are blue or green."

Papa spent the winters in the packinghouse until he learned of places like Havana and Vera Cruz and Ciudad Trujillo that competitively sought players from the Negro leagues. He will never forget that winter in Ciudad Trujillo. It was in 1937, he thinks, when Dominican strongman Rafael Trujillo was in political trouble. He had to distract the people, and there was no better way than to give them a pennant. First, Trujillo had his agents all but kidnap Satchel Paige from a New Orleans hotel. Then he used Paige to recruit the edge in talent from the States: namely, Papa Bell and Gibson, who, along with Orlando Cepeda, the storied father of the current Cepeda, gave the dictator a pat hand.

The look of that lineup still did not ease Trujillo's anxiety. "He wanted us to stay in pajamas," says Papa, "and all our meals were served to us in our rooms, and guards circled our living quarters." Thousands would show up at the park just to watch Trujillo's club work out, and with each game tension grew. "We all knew the situation was serious, but it wasn't until later that we heard how bad it was," says Papa. "We found out that, as far as Trujillo was concerned, we either won or we were going to lose big. That means he was going to kill us." They never did meet Trujillo. They saw him only in his convertible in the streets, all cold and white in that suit of his that seemed to shimmer in the hot sun. "A very frightenin' man," says Papa.

Trujillo got his pennant and his election. A picture of Papa's, taken near a large stream, shows the team celebrating; the dictator had sent them out of the city—along with their fares home and many cases of beer. It had been a hard buck, but then again it had never been easy, whether it was down in Santo Domingo or back up with the St. Louis Stars or the Pittsburgh Crawfords or the Homestead Grays or the Chicago American Giants. East or west, north or south, it was always the same: no shade anywhere as the bus rattled along, way down in Egypt land.

Papa took the bumps better than most. Some, like Gibson, died too young; some got lost to the nights. *Coolpapa*, as his name is pronounced by those who came from the South, well, Coolpapa, he just "went on movin' on." That was the way his mother taught him back in Starkville, Miss., where he was born in 1903; look, listen and never pounce, those were her words, and all of them spelled survival. Work, too, was another word, and Papa says, "If I didn't know anythin', I knew how to work."

Long days in the sun and well after the night slipped across the cotton fields, all that Papa and his friends could talk about was "goin' off." Papa says, "One day some boy would be there along with us, and then he'd be gone. 'Where'd he go?' I'd ask. 'Why that boy, he done gone off!' someone'd say. Next you'd see that fella, why he'd be back home with a hat on and a big, bright suit and shiny shoes and a jingle in his pocket." They would talk of the great cities and what they would have when they, too, went off, and only sometimes would they hear about baseball. An old, well-traveled trainman used to sit under a tree with them on Sundays and tell them of the stars he had seen.

"Why, there's this here Walter Johnson," the trainman would say. "He can strike out anybody who picks up a bat!"

"Is that right?" Papa would ask.

"Sure enough, boy. You think I'd lie? Then there is two old boys named Ty Cobb and Honus Wagner. Well, they don't miss a ball, and they never strike out!"

"Never miss a ball?" gasped Papa. "Never strike out? Is that right?"

"I'm tellin' ya, boy. I've been to the cities and I know!"

"Well, mmm, mmm," Papa would shake his head. "Only one thing botherin' me. What happen when this here Walter Johnson is pitchin', and these other two boys are battin'?"

"Y'all go on!" the old man would yell, jumping up. "Y'all leave me alone. I'm not talkin' anymore. Don't none of ya believe. I should know. I've been to the cities!"

By the time he was 16, Papa was up north in St. Louis with several of his brothers and sisters, who were already in the packinghouse. "Didn't want to know 'bout ball then," says Papa. "Just wanted to work like a man." His brother suggested that he play ball on Sundays. "'James,' he said, 'you a natural. You throw that knuckleball, and there ain't nobody going to hit it.'" Soon he was facing the lethal St. Louis Stars of the Negro National League. "They were a tough club," says Papa. "And mean! They had a fella named Steel Arm Dicky. Used to make moonshine as mean as he was on the side. His boss killed him when he began to believe Steel Arm weren't turnin' in all the profits."

Bell impressed the Stars, and they asked him to join them. "All our players were major leaguers," says Papa. "Didn't have the bench to be as good as them for a whole season—we only carried 14, 15 players. But over a short series we could have taken the big leaguers. That October we played the Detroit Tigers three games and won two of them. But old Cobb wasn't with them, 'cause 12 years before a black team whipped him pretty good, and he wouldn't play against blacks anymore. Baseball was all you thought of then. Always thinkin' how to do things another way. Curve a ball on a 3-2, bunt and run in the first innin'. That's how we beat big league teams. Not that we had the best men, but we outguessed them in short series. It's a guessin' game. There's a lot of unwritten baseball, ya know."

The Stars folded under the Depression. Papa hit the road. An outfielder now, he was even more in demand. He finally began the last phase of his career, with the Washington Homestead Grays; with Gibson and Leonard and Bell, it was one of the most powerful clubs in the black leagues' history, or anybody's history for that matter. "I was 'bout 45 then," says Papa. "Had arthritis and was so stiff I couldn't run at times. They used to have to put me in a hot tub. I had to get good and warm before I could move." Yet, he had enough left to convince Jackie Robinson that he should never try to make it as a shortstop.

"It was all over the place that Jackie was going to sign with the Dodgers," says Papa. "All us old fellas didn't think he could make it at short. He couldn't go to his right too good. He'd give it a backhand and then plant his right leg and throw. He always had to take two extra steps. We was worried. He miss this chance, and who knows when we'd get another chance? You know they turned him down in Boston. So I made up my mind to show him he should try for another spot in the infield. One night I must've knocked couple hundred ground balls to his right, and I beat the throw to first every time. Jackie smiled. He got the message. He played a lot of games in the majors, only one of 'em at short."

Papa was named to manage the Kansas City Monarchs' B team in 1948, the agreement being that he would get one third of the sale price for any player who was developed by him and sold to the majors. He had two prospects in mind for the Browns. "But the Browns didn't want them," says Papa, shaking his head. "I then went to the Cardinals, and they say they don't care, either, and I think to myself, My, if they don't want these boys, they don't want *nobody*." The Monarchs eventually sold the pair: Ernie Banks and Elston Howard. "I didn't get anythin'," says Papa. "They said I didn't have a contract. They gave me a basket of fruit. A basket of fruit! Baseball was never much for me makin' money."

Life began all over for Papa. He took a job at the city hall in St. Louis as a custodian and then a night watchman. For the next 22 years the routine was the same, and only now and then could he go to a Cardinal game. He would pay his way in and sit there in the sun with his lunch long before the game began; to those around him who wondered about him, he was just a Mr. Bell, a watchman. He would watch those games intently, looking for tiny flaws like a diamond cutter. He never said much to anyone, but then one day he was asked by some Dodgers to help Maury Wills. "He could run," he says. "I wanted to help." He waited for Wills at the players' gate and introduced himself quietly.

"Maybe you heard of me," Papa said, "maybe not. It don't matter. But I'd like to help you."

Wills just looked at him, as Papa became uneasy.

"When you're on base," said Papa, "get those hitters of yours to stand deep in the box. That way the catcher, he got to back up. That way you goin' to get an extra step all the time."

"I hadn't thought of that," said Wills, who went on to steal 104 bases.

"Well," Papa smiled, "that's the kind of ball we played in our league. Be seein' you, Mr. Wills. Didn't mean to bother you."

After that year Papa seldom went to the ballpark anymore. He had become a sick man, and when he walked, his arthritic left side seemed to be frozen. There was just his job now. In the afternoons he would walk up to the corner and see what the people were up to, or sit silently in his living room turning the pages of his books of pictures: all the old faces with the blank eyes; all of those many different, baggy uniforms.

Nights were spent at city hall, making his rounds, listening to the sound of radio baseball by the big window, or just the sound of the hours when winter mornings moved across the window. When it was icy, he would wait for the old people to come, and he would help them up the steps. Often, say about three a.m., he would be looking out the window, out across to the park where the bums would be sleeping, their wine bottles as sentries, and he would wait for their march on the hall. They would come up those steps and place their faces up against the window, next to his face and beg to be let in where it was warm.

"We're citizens, old Bell, let us in," they would yell.

"I know," Papa would say.

"It's cold out here," they would say.

"I know," he would answer.

"No, you don't, you...." And Papa would just look away, thinking how cold it was outside, trying to think of all the things that would leave him indifferent to those wretched figures. Then it would be that he sometimes would think of baseball, the small things he missed about it, things that would pop into his mind for no reason: a certain glove, the feel of a ball and bat, a buttoning of a shirt, the sunlight. "You try to gel that game out of your mind," he says, "but it never leaves ya. Somethin' about it never leaves ya."

Papa Bell is 70 now [he died in 1991, at 87]. He lives on Dickson Street in North St. Louis, a neighborhood under siege: vacant, crumbling houses, bars where you could get your throat cut if you even walked in the wrong way, packs of sky-high dudes looking for a score. They have picked on Papa's house a couple of times, so now when he feels something in the air, hears a rustic outside of his door, he will go to the front window and sit there for long hours with a shotgun and a pistol in his lap. "They don't mess with Papa anymore," says his friend Tweed, looking over at Papa sitting in his city hall retirement chair. "It's a reclinin' one," says Tweed. "Show 'im how it reclines, Papa."

Now the two of them, Tweed and Papa, who sits in his chair like a busted old jazz musician, torn around the edges but straight with dignity, spend much time together in Papa's living room. They mull over old box scores, over all the clippings in Tweed's portable archives. They try to bring continuity of performance to a man's record that began when nobody cared. They assemble pictures to be signed for people who write and say that they hear he will be going into the Hall of Fame; the days are sweet.

"Can't believe it," says Tweed. "Can you, Papa? Papa Bell in the Hall of Fame. The fastest man who ever played the game."

"Ain't happened yet," cautions Papa, adjusting his tall and lean figure in his chair.

"Tell me, Papa," says Tweed. "How's it goin' to feel? The Hall of Fame... mmm, mmm."

"Knew a fella blowed the horn once," says Papa. "He told me. He say, 'Ya got to take the gigs as they come.'"

THE STORYTELLERS

JULY 30, 2001

The Sound of Summer

TV has the gimmicks, but for patter and word
pictures, you can't beat baseball on the radio

BY STEVE RUSHIN

You can keep your flat-screen, your high-definition, your plasma-projection TVs. All I need is my AM radio, with its 9-volt battery, its Doobie Brothers hits, its Casey Kasem dispensing wise counsel: "Keep your feet on the ground, and keep reachin' for the stars."

The first big league baseball game that I "saw" was described to me by Herb Carneal on WCCO-AM in Minneapolis. My AM radio seemed to me then, as it does now, a technological wonder beyond words, pulling in the 50,000-watt flagship stations that have forever been affiliated in my mind with a ball club: the Reds on WLW, the Cardinals on KMOX, the Indians on WWWE ("*Three* Double-yew *E*").

Indeed, the first baseball game ever broadcast was carried by KDKA in Pittsburgh 80 years ago next week, and the electronic revolution in the ensuing decades has done nothing to alter the fact that baseball is still best experienced on the radio. It isn't merely because of the game's memorable voices, though many of them remain a marvel. (Listen to Marty Brennaman, his vocal cords smoked like a couple of cured hams, punctuate a Cincinnati win with "And *this* one belongs to the Reds.") It's not simply that the soundtrack of summer in so many cities—the background vocals issuing from taxicabs, beach blankets and backyard barbecues—has been the play-by-play of Vin Scully or Mel Allen or Ernie Harwell (or Jack Buck or Harry Caray or Red Barber).

No, there are countless reasons that baseball, unlike children, should be heard and not seen. Every ballpark is beautiful on the radio, and the great players even better when imagined. Babe Ruth, in the days before television, was whatever you wanted him to be and no less authentic for existing largely in the mind's eye. "What the imagination seizes as Beauty," wrote Keats, "must be truth." Which is to say, if the Phillies radio broadcasters *tell* you that the Vet is architecturally exquisite—and you believe them—why, then, it is.

Of course, baseball's lumbering pace is perfectly supplemented by radio, which abhors dead air and fills it with ceaseless sponsorships, one for every mundane moment of a ball game. So, during Yankees games on WABC radio, "the umpire's lineup is brought to you by Weitz & Luxenberg, setting the standard in asbestos litigation for over a decade."

I am a connoisseur of such promotional pairings (umpires presented by lawyers, that seems about right) and all the other rituals of baseball on the radio. I enjoy pausing for station identification. I breathlessly await the inevitable admonishment not to rebroadcast or retransmit the accounts and descriptions of this game without the express written consent of Major League Baseball. I still love—when the announcers embark on a leisurely discussion of yesterday's lunch—removing the 9-volt battery from my radio and testing its potency with my tongue. (The resulting shock was, in an age before PlayStation, the greatest thrill a kid could have.)

Lately I've been listening to baseball games broadcast in Spanish on the radio. With a few exceptions—*pelota, Heineken, Chuckknoblauch*—I cannot understand a word, but each play is described with such urgent enthusiasm (you can almost see those upside-down and right-side-up exclamation marks bracketing every sentence) that I am enraptured. *This* is baseball the way it oughta be, in which even the laziest infield fly-out is reported in tones more appropriate to the crash of the Hindenburg.

What else do I like about baseball on the radio? Only everything: I like falling asleep to a night game on the West Coast and waking the next morning to Weather on the Ones and Traffic on the Twos. I like the impossibly cheap tokens of appreciation given to guests of the pregame shows. ("For stopping by the booth, His Holiness will receive a $25 gift certificate from Jiffy Lube, with 27 locations in the Tri-State.") And while I can't say I like them, I *have* come to accept the sponsor jingles that take root in the head of a regular listener by May and soon become unshakable even by exorcism.

Which is why the swingin' jingle of Foxwoods Casino (played relentlessly during Yankees broadcasts) has played relentlessly in my brain all summer: "Take a chance, make it happen/Pop the cork, fingers snappin'/Spin the wheel, 'round and 'round we go/Life is good, life is sweet/Grab yourself a front-row seat/And let's meet/And have a ball/Yeah, let's live/For the won-*der* of it all!"

There's a second verse, and I know that too, for baseball on the radio has taught me so much—new songs, the power of imagination, a new language. So I say to you, my fellow sports fans:

¡Pelota! ¡Heineken! ¡Chuckknoblauch!

JULY 1, 2013

The Endless Summer of Bob Uecker

A Brewers radio broadcast isn't just about the game (thank God).
It's a trip inside the beautiful mind of Milwaukee's first fan

BY LUKE WINN

Inning 1

Understand this about the Bob Uecker Experience: Even if you're observing him in his natural habitat, matching his radio voice with his vantage point, you're not sharing the same view. Here he is in the bottom of the first inning of the 53rd game of his 43rd season calling the Brewers on WTMJ, sitting in the visitors' booth at Citizens Bank Park, peering out into a hot haze at dusk. "Looking out at downtown Philadelphia here in the background," Uecker says to listeners on 36 stations in Wisconsin and one on Michigan's Upper Peninsula, as well as on MLB.com and Sirius XM. "Looking *alllll* the way up the shoreline. Atlantic City, people in the water up there. Boy, what a sight." Uecker's pitch recognition skills were such that he batted .200 in six seasons as a major league catcher, but at 78 he apparently is telescopic, able to spot details more than 60 miles away—or decades back in time. "500 Club in the background," Uecker says, name-checking the classic A.C. nightspot that burned down in 1973. "Boats. Sailfish.... Octopus."

Gonna have to take your word for it, Uke. "The pitch, swing and a bouncer hit to first. There's Betancourt. Yuni B. takes care of Ben Revere." I can confirm, from over Uecker's shoulder, that Milwaukee's Yuniesky Betancourt, undistracted by mollusks, logs the out 3-unassisted.

"Amazing," Uecker says, "what you can see when you want to."

Sometimes Uke makes you see things you'd prefer not to, such as on April 2, shortly after Rockies catcher Yorvit Torrealba required a repair tool for his busted mitt: "I think it's called an awl. It's a pointed tool with a hole at the top. And you can stick the leather thong in there. I wear a thong once in a while. Leather kinda gets—swing and a fly ball, foul—little testy sometimes." Uke can also pretend not to see what displeases him. On April 19, when shortstop Jean Segura committed one of the greater baserunning gaffes of all time—he went backward to first base in a rundown after thinking he had been picked off second, then was thrown out trying to steal the base he had just been occupying—Uecker, who does not as a rule make jokes at the expense of his employer's ballplayers, sighed and said, "And this one will be talked about for a long time. Not by me."

It's a shame that you can't see him talk, can't watch the ripple effect words have on his face, the creases and folds and that bulbous schnozz, the whole cartoony lot of it framed by a swept-back, polar-white mane. In the Philly booth Uecker is a festival of facial animation, while the rest of him is placid. His head stays level. His back and disproportionately broad shoulders stay tilted toward his tabletop microphone. He taps his black loafers slowly, soundlessly, as he speaks. Uecker wears an earpiece in his right ear, attached to a clear cord that curlicues behind his neck. He sits on the right side of the booth, with highlighted game notes and a scorebook. His 36-year-old broadcast partner, Joe Block, is on the left, a modern straight man juxtaposed with an irreverent treasure.

Block wears headphones with a wraparound mike, and the screen on his laptop rotates between Microsoft OneNote, a Twitter interface and browser windows with MLB GameCast, FanGraphs and Baseball Reference. Fact-checking is an occasional requirement of his job. Uecker has remarkable recall, particularly about the peculiarities of great ballparks, but will concoct alternate histories if he desires. On April 30, 2012, in Block's first regular-season month on the job, Brewers slugger Ryan Braun hit three home runs at the Padres' Petco Park, the second one reaching the upper balcony of the Western Metal Supply Co. warehouse beyond the leftfield wall. Uecker served listeners this backstory:

"They used to furnish rifles to the Union Army back in the 1800s. And automobile rims to the Henry Ford company for the first automobiles that were ever made. Western Metal Supply. None of that is true."

As odd as his on-air material can be, Uecker's off-air material is a source of greater intrigue, in part due to a story comedian Artie Lange spilled in 2009 on Letterman about a visit he and Norm Macdonald made to the Brewers' booth during spring training. With deep reverence, Lange described Uecker as a "jazz musician" alternating between game commentary and, with his cough button (a muting device for his mike) depressed, fantastically dirty subcommentary. Uecker, a staunch believer in the separation of public fun and private filth, was not pleased that it leaked. Block says that at least 10 broadcasters have prodded him for cough-button stories, assuming that a Dirtier Harry Doyle—the loutish Indians announcer Uecker played in the *Major League* movies—lurks beneath the surface.

"There's a lot of Uke in Harry Doyle, but that's clearly a character," Block says. "If Uke is being playful about something, Harry Doyle is bombastic about it. If Uke enjoys one Miller Lite, say six times a year before a game, Harry Doyle is drinking an entire bottle of Jack Daniels. Is Uke an everyman? Absolutely, but is he this crass drunk like Harry Doyle? Not from what I've seen."

I don't receive the Artie Lange treatment either, but Uecker also knows I'm there to write about him. I do hear him, between innings, express genuine excitement over Milwaukee bullpen catcher Marcus Hanel's having eaten seven cheesesteaks that day. ("The record," Uke says to Block, "is 15 for a three-game trip.") Uecker messes with his producer of 28 years, Kent Sommerfeld, by no-look chucking advertising script cards in his direction. Suspecting that he's been excluded from a pregame ice cream run, Uecker stands up and yells, in the loving way that men who've been working in close quarters together for decades are wont to address each other, "Kent, you had some, didn't you, you c————!" Uke then stomps out of the booth, returns with his own cup of ice cream and sits eating it while Block finishes a pregame spiel of lineups and out-of-town scores, building up to his big handoff: "Once again with you on the call, HERE'S BOB UECKER!"

Inning 2

Lately, I listen to get lost. It's preferable to just listening to the losing, something my Brewers, 31–43 through Sunday and tied for last place in the National League Central, have done often enough to make Uecker turn water-park ads into suicidal ramblings. "Enjoy Mt. Olympus in Wisconsin Dells," he says on April 14, while Milwaukee is in the midst of a 32-inning scoreless streak. "That's where I'm going—to jump off."

This is my 33rd year of existence and 27th of Uecker immersion, so I am familiar with his primary law of broadcasting: If the game merits locking in, he locks in. You hear every *bender down low for ball one* and *bouncer wide of third* and *fastball right down Wisconsin Avenue*. You get a golden-age baseball call with a few dollops of nonsense—an aside, perhaps, about sunscreen's potential as a condiment (on June 10: "It's good on chicken sausage—use the 30") or guidance on Mother's Day (May 4: "Give mom a gift that's brewed for her—a 24-pack of Miller").

If the cause is lost, Uke tries to get you lost in something else. Sometimes he starts early, such as on July 4, 2007, after Uecker stumbled upon a convention of animal-costume fetishists at the Pittsburgh Westin, where the Brewers were staying. Uecker, his then partner Jim Powell recalls, "was like a kid on Christmas morning." The game had barely begun when they went on a 15-minute digression:

"Furrier Society, I believe it is," Uecker said. After putting the topic on hold to call a Braun home run, he resumed: "That's no big deal, that's what they feel. They wear animal costumes because they feel a little animalish. And I've felt that way myself a couple of times. I haven't dressed up for it. I've worn a fig leaf or two." Later Uecker emitted a sort of bird whoop and directed Powell to provide listeners with a website for more information on the Furry movement. Presumably this is the first time "alt dot lifestyle dot furry" was said during a major league broadcast.

In the fifth inning on May 5 against St. Louis, the occasion of the Brewers' wearing throwback uniforms to honor their 1913 American Association predecessors led to a deep exploration of farm clubs in the Cream City: how Uecker, who grew up near the old Milwaukee Zoo in the '40s, would hound a first baseman named Heinz Becker for autographs, hanging on the bumper of his car, and how those Double A Brewers had a manager, Nick Cullop, who was known as Tomato Face, even in the newspapers. Then Uke was off to the Hollywood Stars and the Pacific Coast League in the '40s. He informed Block:

"They wore shorts, did you know that? They did. They wore like Bermuda shorts, knee-high. One ball, two strikes. Check 'em out. Some guys with some decent-looking legs." (Block: "I'll work on that.") "Yeah, take care of that, will ya?"

In the ninth, as part of the "Ask Uke" segment for which listeners submit questions, he told a story about rooming with Eddie Mathews on the Milwaukee Braves in the 1950s. He then dipped into the Uecker Self-Deprecation Collection, which accounts for about 75% of his shtick: "I think we led all roommates, in the National League only, in home runs. As a room. [Mathews] had like 430, and I had two." When the Ukeship landed and listeners were reacquainted with inning, score and reality, the Cardinals were up 10–1, about to complete a four-game sweep. It was rock bottom for the Brewers. It was my favorite Uecker game of the season.

Innings 3, 4 & 7

Uecker passes off every third, fourth and seventh inning to Block, and is rarely heard during those periods.* I ask Uke how he kills the time. "By changing my diaper," he says.

His wit remains sharp, but lines about getting old have been seeping into broadcasts. Uecker, twice divorced and a father of four, is still calling a full schedule, despite having endured three major heart surgeries (the most recent in 2010), the removal of three quarters of his pancreas, and three knee replacements. His first joke of spring training this year, in the bottom of the first on March 1, was about his prostate: "I spent most of my winter just following Joe Theismann's advice—easy flow." When Uecker addresses his own mortality, it's almost always with the phrase, "If I take a Dixie...."

I would learn that Uecker mostly stays in the booth. He texts during off-innings in the Phillies game. His tweeting potential is immense, but he seeks privacy when he's not at the mike. "I don't Twitter, tweet, t---," he says. "I don't do none of that stuff."

Inning 5

I'd always take a radio with me any place I went. I remember when I was taking a bath my sisters always used to throw a radio in the tub for me.

[They] hooked it up to a truck battery.

—UECKER, MAY 2, BREWERS VS. CARDINALS

That segment was notable less for the image of a nude, electrocuted Uecker than for the reminder to Milwaukee fans that baseball on the radio predated Bob. (He joined Merle Harmon and Tom Collins in the Brewers' booth in 1971 after spending '70, the team's first season in Milwaukee, as what then owner Bud Selig called "the worst scout I ever had.") The first king of Dairyland radio was Earl Gillespie, who called the 1950s Braves, the dynastic Packers and Wisconsin football, did TV sports news and even had his own fishing show. "You turned on anything in Milwaukee," Uecker says, "and there was Earl."

After the bathtub story, Block asks about the late Gillespie and his partner, Blaine Walsh: "Did they call games different back then? Was it a quicker pace, or—"

"No, I don't think so," Uecker says. "I think those guys were pretty relaxed. Earl Gillespie used to sit up in the broadcast booth with a big fishing net and try to catch foul balls." Gillespie was an unhurried former player—just a minor league first baseman, but that still lent him some cred—with a Miller High Life flag hanging outside his booth. When he called Uecker's lone homer as a Brave, in 1962, he began with, "Swung on and a drive INTO DEEP LEFT...." When Uecker sees a ball like that now, he tends to start with, "Swing and a driiiive to left and DEEP!"

Gillespie was a "Holy Cow" guy—he claimed he said it before Harry Caray became synonymous with the phrase as the Cardinals' play-by-play man in the 1950s and '60s. Uecker is no Holy Cow guy. But when he slipped one into his call of Dale Sveum's walk-off homer on Easter Sunday 1987, a shot that lifted the Brewers' record to 12–0–"GET UP! GET UP AND GET OUT OF HERE, *gawwwwne* for Sveum, and they've done it again! Twelve in a row on a two-run blast by Sveum to win it. Oh, my goodness. Holy Cow! Do you believe it?"–it seemed like an ode to Earl *and* Harry.

Uecker broke in with the Braves in 1962, then was traded to St. Louis in April '64, falling into a world championship as a backup to Tim McCarver and getting exposed to the KMOX radio team of precaricature Caray and Jack Buck. Uecker told me about an LP that KMOX put out after that season. It includes Caray's clubhouse interviews after the Cardinals clinched the pennant, and when he puts the mike in front of Uecker ("Hey, Uke! Uke!"), all Caray gets back is an imitation of himself: "Here we are in the Cardinal clubhouse, along with Jack Buck...."

Caray spawned a million mimics. But the earliest recording of Uecker's voice that I could find also happens to be the earliest recording of a Caray impression that I could find. Uecker can still do the voice that he honed as a Cardinals scrub. Sitting in the Brewers' dugout in Philly, he's listing announcers he reveres–including Vin Scully, the Dodgers' 85-year-old treasure and the poetic opposite of Uke's stand-up act; Bert Wilson and Milo Hamilton in Chicago; and Buck and Caray–when he slips into gravelly Harry: "*I don't believe it. Here's Boyer, he struck out three times tonight, and the Cardinals still without a run....*"

Inning 6

Uecker imitators must perfect a complex repertoire: his drawn-out vowels ("*heeeeeeee* struck him out"), his talent for sausage-ad improvs, his deftness at weaving balls and strikes into story time, his propensity for breaking into his home run call on balls that lack the sauerkraut to get over the fence. This sequence, from the bottom of the sixth on April 29 against the Pirates, is a fine template:

"Baseball being brought to you in part by Usinger's. People here in Wisconsin, and everywhere else for that matter, know fresh is best, like fresh crisp kraut, stacked high on a tasty Usinger's brat hot off the grill. And the pitch by Sanchez rides high and outside. All into a local-made Pretzilla soft pretzel bun, and you've got the perfect meal, folks. And if you're looking for tailgating par excellence, that's the way to do it. Outside on Segura, two and oh. Baseball season and Usinger's sausage: doesn't get much better than that, nope. I probably eat Usinger's sausage at least twice a day. And maybe five to six pounds. There's a strike on the outside corner."

(Block: "And now we know what you're doing during the third, fourth and seventh.")

"Two balls and a strike. I pack it and stack it. That's low on Segura, 3 and 1 now. Woodman's Food Market home run inning. Jenna Speltz from Independence. Woodman's gift card jackpot, 1,200 bucks now. Whoo. And the pitch to Segura, a drive to right, DEEP! GET UP, GET OUT OF HERE—OFF THE WALL! Just missed, Jenna. He's going for three now and he's going to be in there with a sliding triple."

Inning 8

Here's a true story about Uecker and sausage. He's friends with the Brewers' clubhouse guys—he appears in TV sausage ads with the director of clubhouse operations, Tony Migliaccio, and is the godfather to Migliaccio's son—and every year around Christmas, they get together for lunch in Milwaukee. Another regular attendee is Johnny Logan, who played shortstop for the Braves in the 1950s and likes to bring gag gifts to the lunch. Before they met up in 2005, when Logan was 78, he informed Migliaccio, "I got somethin' for Bobby. I'm gonna give him a big sausage." When Uecker, then 70, tore open the wrapping paper on a four-foot salami, he asked why he, of all people, would need more meat.

Later, while Logan was distracted in conversation at the other end of the table, Uecker asked a waiter for a big knife, cut the sausage in half and disappeared for a few minutes. When the lunch ended and the guests were wishing one another a Merry Christmas, Uecker encouraged Migliaccio and the other clubbies to hang back and watch Logan start his car. It sputtered and sputtered, and finally—boom!—two feet of salami rocketed out of the tailpipe and into the street. No one beats Uke in a septuagenarian prank war.

Here's a measure of Uecker's status as a Milwaukee icon. On June 6, Logan was inducted into the Miller Park Walk of Fame, which meant he got a granite plaque with his name on it outside the ballpark. Logan was a four-time All-Star and started on the Braves' 1957 championship team. Uecker played just two seasons with the Braves, appearing in 46 games, with that one home run. But due to his broadcasting prowess Uecker has been in the Walk of Fame since 2003...and last year he was honored with a statue outside Miller Park. The stadium's other statues are of Henry Aaron, Robin Yount and Bud Selig. The first two are Hall of Famers; the last brought baseball back to Milwaukee in 1970, hired Uecker, helped push through public funding for Miller Park in '95, and for the last 21 years has been commissioner of MLB. Yet when Selig dropped by the booth on March 1, Uecker got away with alluding to the used-car-dealer-turned-commish's being too cheap to serve liquor at a recent in-home medical school benefit.

"With your medical background," Selig said, "I thought that it was important that you be there, Bob."

"You know I found, that the drugs that I was looking for—and not in the sense of drugs, and drugs are drugs, I'm talking about things that could help me, cocktails—"

"Well, there's a question about what could help you."

"Cocktails, which you *didn't have*...."

When Uecker bid Bud adieu at the end of the inning, it was with these words: "CREAM PUFF! Allan H. Selig. AL!"

Inning 9

I've only felt sorry for Uecker once, and it was in the midst of a grand celebration. On Sept. 23, 2011, the Brewers clinched their first and only NL Central title at home. Uecker was locked in for their 4–1 win over the Marlins. His full-throated call of Braun's eighth-inning homer induced goose bumps. As nearly the entire crowd and all of the Brewers stuck around to watch the Cubs close out the second-place Cardinals on the jumbotron, sealing the division for Milwaukee, Uke called the conclusion of that game too. When the Brewers bolted for their clubhouse to pop corks, Uecker's four-decades-younger partner, Cory Provus, pulled the duty of chasing them down for interviews. Uecker fraternizes with the team as if he's still a player and has spent his life as the life of the party, so it seemed to be killing him that they were partying and he was stuck in the booth. I agonized for him right up until he cut away to a last batch of commercials by saying:

"And we'll come back with more here from Miller Park, but we'll take a break. How long we goin', Kent? Two-minute break. O.K., that's good enough for me. Change clothes, and get ready to go downstairs and get... annihilated."

That is the voice of a city where the baseball has fluctuated in quality, more bad than good, but the drinking has always been prodigious. Uke's act was polished on bigger stages; in the 1970s and '80s he took breaks for *The Tonight Show*, the WWF, *Mr. Belvedere*, *Saturday Night Live*, *Major League*, national Miller Lite ads and baseball broadcasts on ABC—enough projects that he considered, at times, leaving the WTMJ booth altogether. He is beloved for many reasons, but chief among them is his choice to always come home. "I don't think he ever wanted to do anything more," Powell says, "than be the voice of the Brewers."

On April 19, Uecker told Block a story about the constraints of going national: "When I first started doing color on network [TV] stuff, you know the guys in the truck are telling you—Rickie [Weeks] bluffed a move to second, back he goes headfirst—they would show something they wanted you to talk about, and I didn't think it was interesting, so I wouldn't say anything. And then they're all over you in the truck: 'Look, when we show something up there, start talking about it.' Well, I don't think it's interesting. 'It's not up to you, it's up to us.'"

With the Brewers, it's all up to Uke. Every ad is an improv opportunity, every laggard inning a launching pad. The material is his, and he can spin hours upon hours of it out into the night, stitching together the gaps between benders and drives, distracting a fan base from the misery of last place. It's amazing what you can see when you want to. It's amazing what you can do, when you decide what is interesting and what is true.

The Spirit of St. Louis

For generations of fans across the Midwest, Jack
Buck has been the soundtrack of summer

BY RICK REILLY

Promise me one thing. Promise that at the end of this you won't feel sorry
for Jack Buck.

As square as a pan of corn bread, as American as a red Corvette, Buck
has been doing what he loves in the St. Louis Cardinals' radio booth for
47 years, which makes him just about the exact center of this country. The
last thing he wants is sympathy.

Yeah, Buck has Parkinson's disease, which makes his hands tremble
and his arms flail. He also has diabetes, which means poking needles into
himself twice a day. He also has a pacemaker. And cataracts. And vertigo.
And excruciatingly painful sciatica. And a box of pills the size of a toaster.
But all that only gives him more material to work with.

"I wish I'd get Alzheimer's," he cracks. "Then I could forget I've got all
the other stuff."

Luckily, you can still find the 76-year-old Buck at the mike during
every St. Louis home game, broadcasting to the Cardinal Nation over more
than 100 radio stations in 11 states. Herking and jerking in his seat, his
face contorting this way and that, he still sends out the most wonderful
descriptions of games you've ever heard.

"I've given the Cardinals the best years of my life," Buck says. "Now I'm
giving them the worst."

That's a lie. Despite enough diseases to kill a moose, Buck has gotten even better lately. "I have no idea how," says his son and radio partner, Joe, "but his voice has been stronger lately. It's like he's pouring every ounce of energy God can give him into those three hours of the broadcast."

Yet Buck makes it all sound effortless, like talking baseball with the guy across the backyard fence. He's natural, simple and unforgettable. When Kirk Gibson hit his dramatic home run for the Los Angeles Dodgers and limped around the bases in the 1988 World Series, Buck, calling the game for CBS Radio, said, "I don't believe what I just saw!" When St. Louis's Ozzie Smith hit a rare lefthanded home run in Game 5 of the 1985 playoffs, Buck said, "Go crazy, folks! Go crazy!" When Mark McGwire hit No. 61 in 1998, Buck said, "Pardon me while I stand and applaud!"

Like thousands of other eight-year-old boys in Middle America in 1966, all I had of baseball most nights was Buck. If I fiddled enough with my mom's old radio in our kitchen in Boulder, Colo., I could pick up Buck doing the Cardinals' games on KMOX. Bob Gibson. Tim McCarver. Curt Flood. I worshiped Buck then. I respect him now.

He was a kid whose family couldn't afford toothpaste; who didn't go to the dentist until he was 15 (and immediately had five teeth pulled); who worked as a soda jerk, a newspaper hawk, a boat painter, a waiter, a factory hand; who was the first person in his family to own a car; who took shrapnel in an arm and a leg from the Germans in World War II; who danced in Paris on V-E Day.

This is a man who is coming up on his 10,000th game broadcast; who was in the stands the day that Joe DiMaggio's 56-game hitting streak ended; who called Stan Musial's five-home-run doubleheader; who ate dinner with Rocky Marciano in Havana; whom Jesse Owens called friend; who survived the Ice Bowl—and 16 years in the booth with Harry Caray.

I would eat a bathtub full of rubber chicken just to hear him emcee a banquet. He has more lines than the DMV. If an Italian woman wins the door prize, Buck says, "You know, I've always had a fondness for Italian women. In fact, during World War II an Italian woman hid me in her basement for three months. [Pause.] Of course, this was in Cleveland."

If anything, Parkinson's has given Buck more banquet material. "I shook hands with Muhammad Ali recently," he says. "It took them 30 minutes to get us untangled."

This may be Buck's last year behind the mike, so he's savoring every inning. So should we. "This is his victory lap," says Joe. "This is him circling the outfield."

That lousy day is coming, of course, when he opens his mouth and the Parkinson's won't let anything come out. But don't feel sorry for him. "Hell, I've touched so many bases," says Buck, "I've got no quarrel with these last few."

So, on the day he quits, he'll have to pardon us while we stand and applaud.

MAY 10, 2016

The Voice of Baseball

After 67 years as baseball fans' best friend, Vin Scully—the voice of summer—is in his final season in the booth. Want to know the man behind the mike? Pull up a chair...

BY TOM VERDUCCI

Rain lashed against the windows of Fordham's Rose Hill Gymnasium, a 3,400-seat basketball facility cloaked in the style and masonry of a Gothic Revival church. Finely dressed attendees filed past the three double doors at the main entrance under the soaring archway with a cross at its crest. The gym's gray Manhattan schist, the same stone that is bedrock to the city's skyscrapers, acquired a more serious tone without the sun to twinkle its mica.

The nation's oldest continuously used NCAA Division I basketball facility was built in 1925. Three years later, in the same neo-Gothic style and four miles away, the Church of the Incarnation rose on West 175th Street in Washington Heights. In between, in 1927, was born one of the most famous matriculates of both the university and the parish school, Vincent Edward Scully.

Scully, class of '49, returned to Fordham to give the commencement address to the class of 2000. It was the first time he had returned since he and the Dodgers left Brooklyn for Los Angeles in 1958.

"I'm not a military general, a business guru, not a philosopher or author," Scully told the graduates in the adjacent Vincent Lombardi Fieldhouse. "It's only me."

Only me? Vin Scully is only the finest, most-listened-to baseball broadcaster that ever lived, and even that honorific does not approach proper justice to the man. He ranks with Walter Cronkite among America's most-trusted media personalities, with Frank Sinatra and James Earl Jones among its most-iconic voices, and with Mark Twain, Garrison Keillor and Ken Burns among its preeminent storytellers.

His 67-year run as the voice of the Dodgers—no, wait: the voice of baseball, the voice of our grandparents, our parents, our kids, our summers and our hopes—ends this year. Scully is retiring come October, one month before he turns 89.

One day Dodgers president Stan Kasten mentioned to Scully that he learned the proper execution of a rundown play by reading a book written by Hall of Fame baseball executive Branch Rickey, who died in 1965. "I know it," Scully replied, "because Mr. Rickey told me." It suddenly hit Kasten that Scully has been conversing with players who broke into the major leagues between 1905 (Rickey) and 2016 (Dodgers rookie pitcher Ross Stripling). When Scully began his Dodgers broadcasting career, in 1950, the manager of the team was Burt Shotton, a man born in 1884.

It is as difficult to imagine baseball without Scully as it is without 90 feet between bases. To expand upon Red Smith's observation, both are as close as man has ever come to perfection.

"Los Angeles is a city of stars," says Charley Steiner, a fellow Dodgers broadcaster for the past dozen years and, at home games, a regular 5:30 p.m. dinner partner with Scully and Rick Monday, another colleague. "And Vin is the biggest star of them all. I don't care who it is—Arnold, Leo, Spielberg, Kobe, Magic—nobody is bigger than Vin, and I'll tell you why: With everybody else you can find some subset of people who don't like them. Nobody doesn't like Vin Scully.

"Vin is our Babe Ruth. The best there ever was."

Scully was named the most memorable personality in Dodgers history in a fan poll—beating all players—and that was 40 years ago. With Jerry Doggett, Scully formed the longest-running broadcast partnership in history—until his partner retired 29 years ago. Scully was inducted into the broadcaster's wing of the Hall of Fame—34 years ago.

I am not in search of more tributes to Scully, nor, as appreciative though he may be, is he. "Only me" is uncomfortable with the fuss about him. He blanches at the populist idea that he should drop in on the call of the All-Star Game or World Series.

"I guess my biggest fear ever since I started," he tells me, "besides the fear of making some big mistake, is I never wanted to get out ahead of the game. I always wanted to make sure I could push the game and the players rather than me. That's really been my goal ever since I started—plus, trying to survive. This year being my last year, the media, the ball club, they have a tendency to push me out before the game, and I'm uncomfortable with that."

Tributes are plentiful. What I am searching for is a rarity: Scully on Scully, especially how and why he does the incomparable—a man on top of his game and on top of his field for 67 years.

Vin is America's best friend. ("Pull up a chair....") He reached such an exalted position not by talking about himself, not by selling himself, or, in the smarmy terminology of today, by "branding" himself, but by subjugating his ego. The game, the story, the moment, the shared experience.... They all matter more. As I drive up Vin Scully Avenue toward the Vin Scully Press Box (more tributes) to meet with Vin Scully last month, I worry that getting Scully to turn his perspicacious observational skills on himself may be harder than Manhattan schist.

Scully's modesty makes me think back to Rose Hill Gymnasium on that rainy day in 2000. Michael T. Gillan, the dean of Fordham's College of Liberal Studies, presented Scully with an honorary doctorate of human letters. With just two Latin words Gillan defined what makes Scully: *eloquentia perfecta*. The literal translation is "perfect speech," but the words connote communication of the highest order.

The concept emerged from the rhetorical studies of the ancient Greeks, grew through Renaissance humanism and was codified in Ratio Studiorum, the 1599 document that standardized the Jesuit teaching tradition. All Fordham freshmen must take Eloquentia Perfecta, a seminar course taught by the school's most accomplished faculty. *Eloquentia perfecta* is the mastery of written and spoken expression guided by consistent principles. One of its core principles is humility. The speaker begins not with himself but with an understanding of the needs and concerns of his audience.

"Hello. I've meant to thank you."

This is how Scully greets me. The unmistakable honey-dipped voice of the Irish tenor is lyrical as ever at 88. He walks into a suite on the press box level looking like a red-crested bluebird on the first day of spring, the famous thatch of red hair topping a suit jacket, shirt and tie in pleasing complements of blue. As always, he is impeccably dressed. He is sucking on a Jolly Rancher, a workplace habit he picked up years ago when he found a huge bowl of the candies in his Colorado hotel room. Every third out of a broadcast Scully pops one into his mouth "just to keep the pipes a little fluid" and then removes it when the game resumes.

He brings up an award presentation I made more than a year ago at the annual dinner of the New York chapter of the Baseball Writers Association of America. The award honored Scully, Sandy Koufax and Bob Hendley on the 50th anniversary of a flawless night of baseball at Dodger Stadium: Koufax threw a perfect game, Hendley threw a one-hitter for the Cubs, and Scully called the broadcaster's equivalent of a perfect game.

More than a half century later, Scully's words from that game still float melodically, a conflation of Dylan Thomas and Bob Dylan that plays in your head like a favorite tune:

"Two and two to Harvey Kuenn.... One strike away....

I had forgotten about the dinner. Scully, who rarely travels long distances, did not attend. Yet here he was, not just reminding me of it but also thanking me. "You had some very lovely words to say," he told me.

I remind Vin about the home opener this year, when Koufax was among many former Dodgers greats who greeted him in a pregame ceremony on the mound."

"I thought, Oh, wow. That's nice," he says. "Sandy has always been one of my favorites. Of all the players on the mound, he and I threw our arms around each other."

Just then something magical happens.

I see it in his eyes. Vin is about to go on a trip. It's the kind of trip that is heaven for a baseball fan: Vin is about to tell a story. For a listener, it's like Vin inviting you to ride with him in a mid-century convertible, sun on your arms, breeze on your face, worries left at the curb. Destination? We're good with wherever Vin wants to take us.

"Because, oh, I'm sure I'm the only person alive who saw Sandy when he tried out."

And we're off....

"Ebbets Field. We had played a game on kind of a gray day. Not a lovely day. And I was single, and the game was over early. I had nowhere to go, and somebody said, 'They're going to try out a lefthander.' So I thought, Well, I'll go take a look, and went down to the clubhouse. I looked over and my first thought was, He can't be much of a player. The reason was he had a full body tan. Not what you call a truck driver's tan, you know? Full body.

"But I did notice his back, which was unusual. Unusually broad. So I thought, I'll go watch him, you know? And I had played ball at Fordham, so I saw some kids that could throw really hard and all of that. He threw hard and bounced some curveballs and...nice, but you know, I never thought, Wow, you're unbelievable. Nothing like that at all. So what a scout I am."

It's classic Vin. He never speeds when he drives. He takes his time. He stops to note details, such as the weather and the expanse of a teenage Koufax's back. The use of the word "so" to link his sentences, where most people use the sloppier "and," is warm and friendly. It is one of his trademarks. He includes himself in the story, but only as a self-deprecating observer.

"His timing is impeccable," Monday says. "He's never in a rush. It's like the game waits for him. We have a little joke among us. When Vin starts one of his stories, the batter is going to hit three foul balls in row, and he'll have plenty of time to get it in. When the rest of us start one, the next pitch is a ground ball double play to end the inning."

Jan. 22, 1958, was an unusually warm winter day in New York. Sometime after 6 p.m., a handful of men climbed on a freight car at the Sunnyside rail yards in Long Island City in order to access a second-floor window of the Delmonico International Corporation's five-story warehouse on Orchard Street. The men loaded 400 cartons onto wooden skids and broke four locks to get the merchandise to the ground floor loading platform, where a truck waited for them. The loss was noticed the next morning. Police questioned more than 50 possible witnesses but learned nothing.

What made the heist especially intriguing was that the thieves left untouched thousands of dollars' worth of electronic equipment. They targeted only cartons of one particular item. *The New York Times* broke the news with this headline above a story on page 17: 4,000 TINY RADIOS STOLEN IN QUEENS; BURGLARS MOVE $160,000 CARGO FROM BUILDING AT BUSY RAIL FREIGHT SPOT.

The target: the TR-63 transistor radio by Sony.

Sony was a new name in the U.S. market. Just months before, it had introduced the TR-63 and selected Delmonico as its sole U.S. distributor. The TR-63 wasn't the first transistor radio, but Sony's model was groundbreaking for its small size. The publicity given to the heist, complete with a description of these tiny $39.95 radios in "green, red, black and lemon," and especially because of the discerning eye of the burglars, caused a consumer sensation. One year later the U.S. market would be flooded with six million transistor radios made in Japan.

On the same day the thieves hit the Delmonico warehouse, three men walked onto the field of the cavernous Los Angeles Coliseum for a publicity event. Ed Davies, wearing a suit, and Morris DeConinck, sporting a fedora, both from the Del E. Webb Construction Company, stood behind a surveyor's theodolite in one corner of the stadium's field. Exactly 90 feet to their right, Michael Auria, another Webb employee, drove a stake in the ground. Shutters clicked. The men were laying out the baseball field for the new home of the Dodgers, who with the Giants had bolted New York City to bring major league baseball to California. Auria's stake marked the site of first base.

Only five days earlier the Coliseum Commission had granted Dodgers owner Walter O'Malley permission for his team to play in the stadium while its new home in Chavez Ravine was being built. The photo made obvious one of the many oddities of the Coliseum as a baseball venue: It was huge. Behind the Webb employees arose 79 rows of seats, reaching 106 feet above field level. One day Dodgers outfielder Duke Snider would try to heave a baseball out of the Coliseum. He could only reach row 60. He also hurt his arm in the attempt, which prompted manager Walter Alston to fine him $250.

"In the far reaches of the vast arena...the game resembled a pantomime," Al Wolf would write in the *Los Angeles Times* after the 1958 home opener. "You couldn't follow the ball, but the actions of the players told you what was happening."

Jan. 22, 1958—the day the transistor radio became a hot consumer item and the day the Coliseum became a baseball stadium—was the day Vin Scully became a Los Angeles icon. A fan base new to major league baseball needed help not just learning the nuances of the game but also simply following the action from hundreds of feet away. The portable transistor radio had arrived just in time. The voice coming through that punched aluminum speaker grill would be both their teacher and friend.

It nearly wasn't Scully. KMPC, the Dodgers' radio station, wanted to hire its own announcers rather than inherit Scully and Doggett. O'Malley insisted the two remain.

O'Malley, in the name of capitalism, created another force that contributed to the cultural phenomenon of Scully. In Brooklyn the owner had televised virtually every Dodgers home game from 1947 through '57. But in January of '58, O'Malley told SI that "subscription TV will offer a solution to the problems that are plaguing many major sports." The previous year he had entered into a relationship with a pay television company called Skiatron. Once in L.A., O'Malley no longer wanted to give away his product to viewers (even if technological and political hurdles would keep pay TV years away from being a viable option).

From 1958 to '68, with only a rare exception here or there, Dodgers fans in Los Angeles could see their team on television only in the nine to 11 annual games the team played in San Francisco. O'Malley blocked the national Game of the Week from the L.A. market, even when the Dodgers were on the road. Virtually the only way to "see" the Dodgers play was to hear Scully describe it—even if you were in the Coliseum. California's booming car culture, its beautiful weather that encouraged a mobile citizenry and the early local start times for most road games made Scully's voice ubiquitous.

After just two years in Los Angeles, the Dodgers left KMPC for KFI and a sponsorship deal with Union Oil and American Tobacco Company that paid the club $1 million annually, the game's second biggest local media package, even with virtually no television income, behind only the Yankees.

Scully was the driving force of the revenue. By 1964 the Dodgers were paying Scully more than most of their players—$50,000, which was more than three times the average player salary and almost half the earnings of Willie Mays, baseball's highest paid player at $105,000.

"I had played six years in the major leagues," says Monday, who grew up in Santa Monica and broke in with the Athletics in the American League. "It wasn't until my seventh year, when I was with the Cubs and we played the Dodgers, that my own mother finally thought of me as a major leaguer. Because it wasn't until then that she heard Vin Scully say my name during a broadcast."

Circumstances created an ideal audience for Scully. By tone, wordsmithing and sheer talent, Scully turned that audience into generations of votaries. He became not only a Southern California star but also a national treasure, branching out to call 25 World Series on radio and television when baseball was king. (In 1953, at age 25, he was the youngest ever to call the Series; in 1955 he called the first one televised in color; and in 1986 he called the highest-rated game in history, the Mets' Game 7 win over the Red Sox.) He was the lead announcer for CBS in the 1970s on football, golf and tennis; the lead announcer for NBC on baseball in the 1980s; and even a game-show host (*It Takes Two*) and afternoon talk show host (*The Vin Scully Show*) in the late '60s and early '70s. The man who called his first event, a 1949 Boston University–Maryland football game, from the roof of Fenway Park armed with a microphone, 50 yards of cable and a 60-watt bulb on a pole now can be heard worldwide by anyone with an Internet connection and an MLB.tv subscription (though, because of a cable carrier dispute, not in 70% of the Los Angeles viewing market).

"Many of the best announcers have *some* of the best qualities Vin may have," says MLB Network's Bob Costas. "The command of the English language, the terrific sense of drama, the ability to tell a story.... But it's as if you had a golfer who was the best off the tee, the best with the long irons, the best with the short irons, the best short game *and* the best putting game."

Time for another ride. Hop in...."We were in the back of the auditorium," Vin says. He is driving us back to Fordham Prep in the early 1940s. "I remember I said, 'Larry, when we get out of here, what do you want to do?' And he said, 'I'd love to be a big league ballplayer.'

"And I said, 'I wonder what those odds are.' And then I said, 'Well, you know, I'd like to be big league broadcaster. I wonder what those odds are.'

"And then I said, 'How about this one for a long shot: How about you play, I broadcast, you hit a home run?' And we said, 'The odds, no one would be able to calculate that!'"

Larry was his friend, Larry Miggins. A few years later, on May 13, 1952, playing for the Cardinals, Larry Miggins hit his first major league home run. It happened at Ebbets Field against the Dodgers. On the call that inning in the broadcast booth happened to be Larry's buddy from Fordham Prep, sharing duties with Red Barber and Connie Desmond.

"Incredible, isn't it?" Scully says. "I mean, really, absolutely incredible. And probably the toughest home run call that I ever had to call because I was a part of it. He hit the home run against Preacher Roe, I'm pretty sure. And I had to fight back tears. I called 'home run,' and then I just sat there with this big lump in my throat watching him run around the bases. I mean, how could that possibly happen?"

Scully has called roughly 9,000 big league games, from Brooklyn to Los Angeles to Canada to Australia and scores of places in between. He has called 20 no-hitters, three perfect games, 12 All-Star Games and almost half of all Dodgers games ever played—this for a franchise that was established in 1890. The home run by Miggins was and remains the closest Scully ever came to breaking down behind the microphone.

Scully was born in the Bronx. He and his mother, Irish-born Bridget Scully, moved a few miles away to a fifth-floor walk-up apartment in Washington Heights soon after his father, Vincent Aloysius, a traveling silk salesman, died when Vin was four. Scully's life path opened with clarity when he was eight years old. He crawled underneath the family's massive wooden radio console to hear broadcasts of college football games; he heard a crowd before he ever saw one. The sound, as he likes to tell it, washed over him like water from a showerhead. He was hooked. When one day Sister Virginia Maria of the Sisters of Charity at the Incarnation School assigned her grammar class to write an essay on what they wanted to be when they grew up, Scully wrote enthusiastically of his dream to be a sports announcer.

"So now, when I'm in the booth, Kirk Gibson hits a home run and the place goes bananas," he says. "I showed up, I sit there, and for that little moment I'm eight years old again."

Says Costas, "He never shouts, but he has a way within a range that he can capture the excitement. If you listen to the [1988 World Series] Gibson home run.... 'In a year that has been so improbable...' he's letting the crowd carry Gibson around the bases, but then he has a voice that has a tenor quality that cuts through the crowd."

Most every other great announcer is framed by singular calls—and Scully, from the 1955 Dodgers to Koufax to Aaron to Buckner to Gibson, has a plethora of them. Such a narrow view, however, sells short his greatness. Like listening to all of *Astral Weeks*, not just one track, Scully is best appreciated by the expanse of his craft.

"What he truly excels at," Costas says, "is framing moments like that and getting in all the particulars so the drama and anticipation builds. You don't always get the payoff, but he always sets the stage. Other announcers have great calls of special moments. What he's incredibly good at is leading up to those moments—all the surrounding details and all the little brushstrokes to go with the broad strokes."

Here is more of what sets Scully apart: his literate, cultured mind. Scully is a voracious reader with a fondness for Broadway musicals. He doesn't watch baseball games when he's not broadcasting them. "No, not at all," he says. He has too many other interests.

He once quoted from the 1843 opera *The Bohemian Girl* after watching a high-bouncing ball on the hard turf of the Astrodome: "I dreamt that I dwelt in marble halls." When he appeared with David Letterman in 1990 he quoted a line from *Mame*. He suggested a title if Hollywood wanted to turn the 1980s Pittsburgh drug trials into a movie: *From Here to Immunity*. Last week, during a game against the Padres, he offered a history on the evolution of beards throughout history that referenced Deuteronomy, Alexander the Great and Abraham Lincoln.

Barber, his mentor, majored in education and wanted to become an English professor. Lindsey Nelson taught English after he graduated from college. Mel Allen went to law school. Ernie Harwell wrote essays and popular music. Graham McNamee started out as an opera singer. When Scully calls his last game—either the Dodgers' regular-season finale on Oct. 2 in San Francisco or, if they advance, a postseason game—we lose not just the pleasure of his company with baseball but also the last vestige of the very roots of baseball broadcasting, when Renaissance men brought erudition to our listening pleasure.

"I really like to do the research," he says. "So, in a sense, that's a little bit in that renaissance area, the research of the game. Plus, I've always been—even in grammar school—always afraid to fail. So I always studied, not to be the bright guy but just to make sure that the good sisters didn't knock me sideways, you know?"

A story: At age 88, in preparing for his 67th home opener, Scully notices a player on the opposing Diamondbacks' roster with the name Socrates Brito. The minute he sees the name, Scully thinks, Oh, I can't let that go! Socrates Brito! Inspired in the way of a rookie broadcaster, Scully dives into his research. So when Brito comes to the plate, Scully tells the story of the imprisonment and death by hemlock of Socrates, the Greek philosopher. Good stuff, but *eloquentia perfecta* asks more:

"But what in the heck is hemlock?" Scully tells his listeners. "For those of you that care at all, it's of the parsley family, and the juice from that little flower, that poisonous plant, that's what took Socrates away."

It's a perfect example of a device Scully uses to inform without being pedantic. He engages listeners personally and politely with conditionals such as *For those of you that care...* and *In case you were wondering....* Immediately you do care and you do wonder.

Scully isn't done with Socrates. In the ninth inning, Brito drives in a run with a triple to put Arizona ahead 3–1.

"Socrates Brito feeds the Dodgers the hemlock."

Someone once asked Laurence Olivier what makes a great actor. Olivier responded, "The humility to prepare and the confidence to pull it off." When Scully heard the quote, he embraced it as a most apt description of his own work. So I asked Scully, because he pulls it off with such friendliness, if he had a listener in mind when he broadcasts games.

"Yes. I think when I first started, I tried to make believe I was in the ballpark, sitting next to somebody and just talking," he says. "And if you go to a ballgame and you sit there, you're not going to talk pitches for three hours. You might say, 'Wow, check out that girl over there walking up the aisle,' or, 'What do you think about who's going to run for president?' There's a running conversation, not necessarily the game. So, that's all part of what I'm trying to do—as if I'm talking to a friend, yes."

So, we are getting closer.

Time for another ride. This time we're going to the Polo Grounds. Oct. 3, 1951.

"First of all, Red Barber had said to me when I first started, 'I don't want you to get close to the players, because if you get too close to the players, it will change your descriptive powers. Suddenly you see your man make an error, and you'll try to make up for it and it would become a twisted broadcast.'

"The one fellow I got close to, despite Red's rulings, was Ralph Branca. And Ralph was going to marry after that game—the next week. And he and [his fiancée] Ann and I went around the world together, but that's another story. But I was closer to them, and I had a couple of dates with Ann's roommate, and so, we got closer.

"So when the ball was hit, there was a home run, and I instinctively looked down at the club box because my friend Ann was there. And I watched her very deliberately, carefully open up her purse, take out a handkerchief, close the purse, open the handkerchief and bring it up to her face. And I really felt sorry for her and for everybody.

"And then in those days, in order to get to the clubhouse, you had to walk all the way to centerfield, and you went up the stairs and went in the door. And then there were, like, three steps to go up to the next level. And there was my pal [Branca], sprawled on the steps, head down, arms extended. And I actually had to tiptoe over him. So, it was really tough.

"Anyway, it was deathly quiet and I thought, I can't hang out here. So I went up into a trainer's room, and there was Jackie [Robinson] and Pee Wee [Reese]. Just the two of them. Nobody else there. I walked over and didn't say a word—just sat down in a chair and it was silent.

"And then Pee Wee said, 'You know, Jack, the one thing I just don't understand?' And Jackie said, 'What, Pee Wee?' He said, 'Why this game hasn't driven me crazy.'"

The pitcher Branca relieved in that game to face Bobby Thomson with one out in the ninth inning was Don Newcombe, the same man who started the first major league game Scully ever broadcast, on April 18, 1950, at Shibe Park in Philadelphia. When the Dodgers feted Scully before the home opener this year, Newcombe was one of the greats to meet him on the mound.

There was a moment at the end of the ceremony when the former players retreated to give Scully his own space and his moment near home plate. Gazing up on the adoring Dodger Stadium, where he has worked 55 of his 67 years in the business, Scully stood alone with his thoughts.

"I looked at him," Monday says, "and I saw a look I never saw before. It was emotional. He never lost it, but it was wistful."

Ralph Waldo Emerson once said, "Nothing great was ever accomplished without enthusiasm." I remind Vin of this, and then I tell him, "You can't be this great for this long without enthusiasm. So, for Vin Scully, what are the points of enthusiasm?"

"Well, I guess the challenge to be prepared, number one," he says. "As soon as I have a little breakfast, I'm on the computer checking rosters to make sure that in that dramatic moment [I know if] somebody comes into the game who wasn't on the roster three days before. Again, the fear of failing.

"And then, there's the one thing that to me is the most important, and that's the crowd. The enthusiasm of the crowd is enough even on those days when I think, you know, I'd rather be home sitting under a tree and reading a book or something. I've been asked several times now already, 'What would you miss the most when you retire?' I said, 'The crowd. The roar of the crowd.'"

Finally, it's time for me to take Vin on a trip, to let him slip into the passenger side. We're going back to Fordham. Rose Hill Gymnasium, May 20, 2000.

"Oh, boy," Scully says. "What an honor that was, you know?"

Scully spoke for 19 minutes that day. It was as far as he ever pushed himself "out ahead of the game."

By then death had made too frequent a habit of visiting his otherwise dreamy life. The toll included that loss of his father to pneumonia when Vin was four; of his first wife, Joan, at 35, from an accidental overdose of medication when he was 44; of his broadcast partner and close friend Don Drysdale, at 56, of a heart attack on the road when Vin was 65; of his son Michael, 33, in a helicopter crash when he was 66; and of Doggett, 80, another broadcast partner and close friend, when he was 69. Through the sorrow, as through the joy, what carried him was his faith. The kid from Church of the Incarnation has long been a parishioner of St. Jude the Apostle Catholic Church in Westlake Village, Calif.

His words without baseball are even more beautiful and much more personal. His commencement address is as much the heart of *eloquentia perfecta* as its original definition in 1599.

The world "will try very hard to clutter your lives and minds," Scully told them, but the way forward was to simplify and clarify.

"Leave some pauses and some gaps so that you can do something spontaneously rather than just being led by the arm."

"Don't let the winds blow your dreams away...or steal your faith in God."

Drawing upon his own bouts of grief, "be a bobbed cork: When you are pushed down, bob up."

"It is written that somewhere in every childhood a door will open, and there is a quick glimpse of the future. When my door opened, I saw a large radio on four legs in the living room of my parents' home. Above all, don't ever stop dreaming. Sometimes even your wildest dreams can come true."

I ask him to imagine his younger self, Fordham class of '49, sitting in the same gym, hearing the same words from someone else: "How do you think those 'wildest dreams' turned out for a young Vin Scully?"

"Oh, for me, absolutely right on the money," he says. "I'm not only getting this job to do a sport that I love, but then God's charity allowing me to do it for 67 years.... It's overwhelming. I mean, I have a big debt to pay in heaven—I hope when I get there—because the Lord has been so gracious to me all my life."

Emerson also wrote, "The only way to have a friend is to be one." Because his voice reached so many, so far, so kindly and for so long, no one in baseball ever accrued more friends than Vin.

COLORFUL CHARACTERS

NOVEMBER 10, 1986

The Hub Hails Its Hobbling Hero

Even though Bill Buckner let Game 6 slip through his
injured legs, the fans in Boston showed last week how much
they admired his courageous play in the World Series

BY PETER GAMMONS

He awakened on the morning after the morning after, knowing that he had
two more rivers to cross. First, there was a parade in downtown Boston.
Then he would drive 40 miles to Worcester, check into the University
of Massachusetts Medical Center hospital and, after 10 years of ice,
acupuncture, DMSO and holy water, have an operation to clean out his
junkyard left ankle. As he started to get out of bed, he heard some mention
of the Mets' parade on the radio. "More than two and a half million people
honored the world champions yesterday in New York," said the announcer,
"and the parade finished with the Mets' team bus going through Bill
Buckner's legs."

"Here I just experienced the best year of my life with a team, and I feel
rotten," Bill Buckner said to his wife, Jody, as they drove down Route 93
toward Boston last Wednesday morning. "This whole city hates me. Is this
what I'm going to be remembered for? Is this what I've killed myself for
all these years? Is a whole season ruined because of a bad hop? I've got to
go through the humiliation of this parade, partly because I know I don't
deserve it. Oh well, there'll only be two or three players and about 50 people
who'll show up to boo us."

When Buckner got to the Red Sox clubhouse, he found at least 15 teammates and coaches waiting for the parade. It was a crystal-clear autumn morning as the Red Sox climbed aboard the flatbed truck that would take them to the rally. When the truck turned onto Boylston Street, Buckner heard the bells of the Arlington Street Church pealing, *Take Me Out to the Ballgame*, and when the truck neared Copley Square, he saw that the street was lined with faces and banners as far as he could see. Buckner had asked not to speak at the rally at City Hall Plaza, and so he stood at the end of the stage. But when he heard the ringing one-minute ovation that followed his name, Buckner stepped forward and thanked the crowd.

"That was the most incredible experience of my career," he said to Jody as they drove to Worcester, past a THANKS, RED SOX sign on the Mass Pike and a HOMETOWN OF HERO MARTY BARRETT sign at the city limits of Southborough. When the Buckners stopped at traffic lights in Worcester, people in other cars beeped their horns and waved at them.

While Buckner was checking into the hospital, the clubhouse kids were piling up his mail at Fenway Park. "He normally gets no more than one actual letter a week," said batboy Dean Lewis. "He's gotten almost twice as much World Series mail as anyone else." A New York City policeman told Buckner he was "a symbol of courage." A California polio victim called him "an inspiration," a New Jersey man said he was "a true model for all our children," and a 70-year-old lady in Illinois wrote, "because of you, I watched my first World Series." Among the hundreds of pieces of mail, the most negative was a letter from a Rhode Island doctor who chastised Buckner for risking permanent damage.

In an exhausting World Series that ended in New York with the Mets as world champions, the Red Sox became this generation's Brooklyn Dodgers. And former L.A. Dodger Bill Buckner, 36, with 2,464 hits and 16 major league seasons behind him, became baseball's Walter Brennan. He often looked as if he were running in galoshes, and after he staggered around third and belly flopped across home plate in Game 5, he admitted, "I didn't slide—I died." He crawled like an alligator into one base. He went after a pop-up, fell down and did a backstroke trying to make a catch in Game 4. He scurried on hands and knees to tag the first base bag with his glove. He limped out for the national anthem, bat in hand, just in case he needed a cane. He wore a high-topped right shoe for the Achilles tendon he pulled in the seventh game of the playoffs, but it was the pain in two parts of his left ankle that had created the original limp and had necessitated nine cortisone shots since April. Little wonder Buckner ended up hitting .188 for the Series, finished 18 innings, stranded 31 runners and made the error on Mookie

Wilson's ground ball that gave the Mets their dramatic 6–5 victory in the 10th inning of Game 6.

"I just want to tell you that you'll always be my inspiration," said a small boy who ducked into Buckner's hospital room Wednesday night. "Thanks for a great season." Then the boy disappeared.

"Today cleared a lot off my chest and my mind," said Buckner as he settled back in his hospital bed. "From my perspective, I didn't think the error was such a big deal. Letting them tie up the game was more important. There was no guarantee we would have won. Hell, there was no guarantee that Bob Stanley or I could have beaten Wilson to the bag if I had caught the ball. When Jody and I got back to the room that night, I watched the replay and I was right there, head down, glove down, completely relaxed.... It just took a funny sideways bounce between my legs. By the time I watched it, I wasn't bothered because I was completely geared towards the seventh game.

"Then Monday I agreed to do an interview for *The NBC Nightly News*, and all the guy kept asking me was, 'How can you look at yourself in the mirror? How can you face your teammates?' I went out for batting practice, and I thought one sign that said NICE LEGS was funny, but when I got the standing ovation from the Mets' fans during the introductions, it wasn't so funny." Neither was the Mets' management's decision to replay the error on the Shea Stadium message board before the bottom of the fifth inning. Nor were the post-seventh-game questions from the press about manager John McNamara's decision not to pinch-hit or bring in a defensive replacement for Buckner in Game 6.

"I hadn't been pinch-hit for all season, and the only time [Dave] Stapleton had gone in for me on defense was when the Achilles was killing me back at the start of the Series," Buckner said in the hospital. "The one thing anyone has ever said about me defensively is that I have good hands. And, while my average stunk, [hitting instructor] Walter Hriniak figured out that I hit the ball hard for outs 11 times in 32 at bats. When I hit the line drive to deep left center with the bases loaded that ended the second inning of the final game, I thought I had knocked in three runs. Ron Darling was pitching me inside, and Lenny Dykstra always played me to right center, but for some reason Mookie played me to left center. Dykstra never would have caught the ball. That's when we should have won the damn thing. Right now, that hurts more than anything."

That, even more than the ankle. Buckner has won a batting title (1980), hit .300 or better seven times and knocked in 212 runs in the last two seasons. He has a good shot at 3,000 hits, which means the Hall of Fame, and he has always had a big and justified reputation as a clutch hitter. And people who know him wonder what he might have been were it not for the ankle. "He could get down to first base with anyone when he was young," says Tom Lasorda, who signed Buckner, took him to the Rookie League and had him in Triple A. "Dick Vermeil, who recruited him for Stanford, was once asked which recruit he most regretted not coaching," says Lasorda. "And he answered, 'Wide receiver Bill Buckner.' He could *fly*."

Buckner batted .314 and stole 31 bases for the Dodgers in 1974. Then on April 18, 1975, when they were playing the Giants in Dodger Stadium, he tried to steal. "I remember it as if it were yesterday," Buckner says. "John Montefusco was pitching, Marc Hill catching. I'd just been trying to learn to slide from Davey Lopes, the way he barely hit the ground. I never did hit the ground, my foot caught under the bag and I flipped right over." He struggled through the season, had a tendon removed in September and bone chips taken out in October. After a .301 average and 28 stolen bases in '76, he went back in for yet another operation that winter. That surgery resulted in a staph infection. Then came the preseason trade to the Cubs in 1977 for Rick Monday, and when Buckner reported to the Cubs' training camp hobbling on a cane, Chicago asked the National League to annul the deal on the grounds that he was damaged goods. "I *was* damaged goods," he says. "But I wanted to prove them wrong, so I played the first half of the season. It was a painful mistake. I never walked right again."

Says Buckner, "I always said that I'd wait until after I retired to have the cleanup operation because I learned to cope with it, and it didn't get any worse. This year it got worse." For the last eight seasons, Buckner has soaked his feet in ice for an hour before—and 30 minutes after—every game. In 1978, he began working in Chicago with bodybuilder Bob Gadja and chiropractor George Ruggerio, who created a series of machines and exercises for the ankle. "They saved me," Buckner says. Buckner has tried vitamins, acupuncture, DMSO and, before Game 5, holy water from a fan.

His diet helped. He is the same 185 pounds he was when Vermeil sought him for Stanford in 1968, and he and Jody are health food nuts. Buckner, who owns a 1,000-acre, 300-head cattle ranch in Star, Idaho—it's run by his brother, Bob—says, "I may be the only cattle rancher in America who doesn't eat red meat."

But then, as his closest baseball friend, Bobby Valentine, says, "Buck is unique, thank goodness. When we were freshmen at USC, he would challenge me to a race every day. Every day I beat him, and as soon as we had finished, he would swear that he'd beat me the next day. Every day." Says Buckner, with a laugh, "There are a lot of Bill Buckner stories."

His brother, Bob, says, "Bill gets his mind set on something, and won't accept that it doesn't work out the way he wants. One Christmas he thought he was going to get a shotgun. He didn't, and he stayed in the bathroom for five hours."

The Buckners grew up in a small California town called Rancho del Mar, halfway between Napa and Vallejo, where, Bob says, "All there was to do was play baseball and hunt." Bill was both an exceptional athlete and student whose college choices came down to USC and Stanford. When he went to visit Southern Cal, he met Valentine, who was another football/baseball recruit. A week later, Valentine was selected in the first round of the 1968 June draft by the Dodgers, who then made Buckner their second pick. Though Buckner attended USC, he never played sports there.

After the draft, Lasorda, who had scouted in the spring and was going to manage the Dodgers' Rookie League club in Ogden, Utah, went to sign the 17-year-old Buckner at a doubleheader in San Rafael. Buckner had seven hits in the two games, and afterward Lasorda asked him, "Do you like to fight?" Buckner nodded. "Then you're coming with me to Ogden, where we're going to fight and we're going to win."

"We fought," says Buckner, "and we won." Lasorda and his players developed a special camaraderie in Ogden, so special, in fact, that it is not inconceivable that someday the Dodgers will have Lasorda as the general manager, Valentine as the manager, and Buckner, Tom Paciorek, Joe Ferguson and Charlie Hough as coaches. Ogden was also the place where the legend of Bill Buckner, with an assist from Lasorda, was established. The manager wrote letters to then Dodgers Wes Parker, Willie Davis and Ron Fairly, promising to take those players' jobs away, and signed the names of Buckner, Valentine and Paciorek, respectively. "I visited the clubhouse after the season," Buckner recalls, "and you should have seen the look I got from Parker."

"Buck was always getting thrown out of games," says Lasorda. "Throw helmets? He broke one a night. Finally I told him I'd fine him if he ever did it again. He made an out and I heard this banging. I look over and he was smashing his head against the wall so hard he was bleeding. One night in Triple A [1970], he and Valentine collided going for a pop fly. Buck broke his jaw, and the front office told me to sit him out for five weeks. Buckner missed only one game and wound up hitting .335 and learned to spit and swear with his jaw wired shut."

Buckner didn't stop battling all the way to Boston. He once fought Cubs manager Lee Elia on the top step of their dugout. His fight with Gary Carter is legend. Buckner got so mad at popping up in a 1980 game in Montreal that he smashed his bat down, accidentally breaking Carter's mask. The next week in Wrigley Field, after Buckner got a hit, Carter picked up Buckner's bat and broke it over home plate. So after Carter rounded the bag after a hit, the two of them ended up rolling on the ground, swinging.

Buckner would never be accused of being California mellow. He still yells at the wind, the hitting background or line drives that get caught. But ever since his first winter in Boston in 1984–85 when Hriniak told him, "If you'll shift your weight, you can hit homers," his fire has been devoted to hitting. In his 14 seasons before 1985, Buckner never hit more than 16 homers and only once did he drive in more than 75 runs, but in the last two years, he has hit 16 and 18 homers and knocked in 110 and 102 runs. Last year, when his ankle didn't bother him as much, he stole 18 bases, played 162 games and amassed 201 hits.

In 1986, Buckner's body finally broke down, and after hitting in the low .200s for two months, he limped to a low .267. It wasn't unusual to see him before games with ice taped to his ankle, Achilles tendon, lower back, elbow and shoulder. "This is weird," he said last Friday, 24 hours after the operation. "I hardly hurt. I won't know what it's like."

After Dr. Arthur Pappas removed a large chunk of bone from the top of the left foot and cleared bone chips and other debris from the ankle, he told Buckner that he should feel better than at any time since 1976. "I used to think, 'One year at a time,'" said Buckner, his left ankle in a cast and his right foot in a bandage. "Now I'm thinking three years and 3,000 hits. There's no reason I can't do it now if I'm healthy. Not only that, but I'll be wearing the high tops. Maybe they'll do for me what they did for Y.A. Tittle."

Maybe he can even get people to forget about a certain ground ball.

JULY 2, 2007

What's in a Name?

The shortstop synonymous with big league futility—
Mendoza Line, anyone?—maintains a reputation well
north of respectability in his native country

BY ALEXANDER WOLFF

The Mendoza line rings. It's Mario Mendoza's wife, Irma Beatriz, calling to check on her husband. Not an hour earlier he had been fired as manager of Piratas de Campeche of the Mexican League. Mired in seventh place in the eight-team Southern Division, chronically unable to come up with a timely hit, Campeche felt it had no choice but to release a member of Salón de la Fama, Mexican baseball's Hall of Fame.

Mendoza nonetheless keeps an appointment with a writer and a photographer from the U.S. who have assured him that they're not interested solely in his other claim to immortality: the so-called Mendoza Line, major league lingo for a .200 average, above which all hitters are at pains to stay. In fact, these *norteamericanos* reassure Mendoza, they've come to the Yucatàn as much to document his life today. And today...he got fired.

"It doesn't do any good to be at my apartment feeling sorry for myself," Mendoza says, sitting in a restaurant in Campeche in mid-May. "My philosophy has always been to enjoy life while you can. Now, I don't really know what will happen. But I've been through something like this a few times before."

Mendoza is 56, with knees brittle from patrolling ball fields as an infielder, coach or manager in the majors and minors, throughout the U.S. and Mexico, summer upon winter for 37 nearly unbroken years. He actually fared better in the big leagues than his Line would indicate, batting .215 over nine seasons with the Pirates, Mariners and Rangers. For seven summers after that, as a shortstop in the Mexican League, he hit a robust .291 and became known as Manos des Seda, or Silk Hands.

The knack for picking grounders is what prompted the Pirates to purchase the contract of the Chihuahua native from the Mexico City Reds in 1970. "There've been 100 Mexican players in the big leagues," Mendoza recalls. "I was number 28." It wasn't easy negotiating the Pittsburgh farm system, what with Dominican players snapping towels at him in the shower and an African-American teammate telling him, "You're not black, you're not white—you're orange." By 1974 he was a part-time starter at shortstop, but with the better-hitting, lesser-fielding Frank Taveras gaining playing time over the next few years, Mendoza asked to be traded following the '78 season. The Pirates obliged, sending him to the Mariners in a six-player deal that brought Enrique Romo to Pittsburgh. "I still remember [Pirates manager] Chuck Tanner telling me they made the trade because they believed Romo could help them win a World Series," Mendoza says. "And the next year that's what happened."

Meanwhile, in Seattle, Mendoza started at short but hit only .198—the fourth major leaguer ever to play as many as 148 games in a season and fail to break .200. (Of course, he wouldn't have earned that distinction if he weren't doing some serious compensating in the field.) Though technically he was an every-day player, Mendoza would often be removed for a pinch hitter, once getting called back to the dugout in the second inning. "It made it hard," Mendoza recalls. "If I could have gotten to the plate three or four times a game, I could have made better adjustments."

The Mariners of the '70s were no powerhouse, but their locker room was surely one of the loosest. Outfielder Tom (Wimpy) Paciorek always had a joke to share or a ruse to spring, and veteran DH Willie Horton enjoyed the way Mendoza teased him for his decrepit body and inept fielding. Before every game in the Kingdome, Horton would summon Mendoza to his locker. "Mex, get me loose!" he'd bellow, whereupon Mendoza would punch Horton in the upper body. After an interval Horton would say, "O.K., I'm ready now," and the game could begin.

It was this very clubhouse back-and-forth that forged the expression. As Mendoza remembers it, Paciorek coined the Mendoza Line in the late '70s. Paciorek has always shifted credit to first baseman Bruce Bochte but doesn't dispute spreading word of the Mendoza Line to Royals third baseman George Brett. "At the beginning of the 1980 season Brett was struggling and made a comment about being around the Mendoza Line," Mario says. "Once Brett made that remark, [*SportsCenter* impresario] Chris

Berman picked it up." And once he did, it hurtled with escape velocity into the culture at large.

"That," Mendoza says dolefully, "is all people remember me for."

The Mendoza line rings. It's former big league starter Ted Higuera, Campeche's pitching coach, calling with condolences. Mendoza urges Higuera to accept the club's offer to replace him as manager. "Mario is an awesome guy, a family guy, a gentleman," Campeche G.M. Gabriel Lozano will say. "That's why this was so hard to do. But it's easier to get rid of one guy than 28. And if we had lost a couple of more games, people were going to start calling him names."

A few stray catcalls would be preferable to the dubious status posterity has conferred upon Mendoza. It's not that his name is synonymous with offensive fecklessness. That distinction surely belongs to utilityman Tony Suck, who in two seasons during the late 19th century hit .151. Nor does baseball lack other phrases to indicate at-the-plate incompetence—to be "on the Interstate" is to hit .170, .180 or .190. (Imagine a road sign reading I-70, I-80 or I-90.) But the Mendoza Line has entered everyday usage, perhaps because of its Mexican tang, which conjures up a border and all that lies south of it.

Since Mendoza retired as a player, the Mendoza Line has been appropriated by an indie rock band from Athens, Ga., and invoked by Brandon on *Beverly Hills, 90210* in reference to marginal grades. It has also spread to pro football, where NFL wags sometimes refer to the Kordoza Line, after Kordell Stewart's career passer rating of approximately 70, another minimally acceptable mark. The phrase is widely known even in Mendoza's native land, where ESPN Deportes baseball personalities make routine use of it.

Mendoza did get back at Paciorek, occasionally subjecting him to practical jokes like novelty exploding cigarettes or a faceful of cake. And in his own way, Mendoza also got back at Brett. In late September 1980, with Brett trying to surmount the Williams Line of .400, the Royals star came into a three-game series with Seattle, hitting .394. Brett went 2 for 11, largely because Mendoza robbed him of three hits on plays up the middle. Brett finished the year at .390.

The Mendoza line rings. It's his eldest son, 28-year-old Mario Jr. "I was once let go by major league baseball," father tells son. "How hard can this be?"

Mario Jr. can relate. Once a pitching prospect with the Anaheim Angels, he shared several spring trainings with his dad, who managed him at Class

A Lake Elsinore in 2000. But that season, young Mario suffered a stress fracture in a vertebra, causing major league clubs to lose interest in him, and he now pitches for Saltillo of the Mexican League.

The elder Mendoza's return to Mexico as a player took place after two seasons with the Rangers and one in the minors. In spring training in 1981 manager Don Zimmer told him, "Hey, Mex, you hit .220, and I'll be satisfied." He batted .250 over the first two months of the season, and in mid-June the Rangers lurked just a few games behind the A's in the AL West. Then the strike hit, wiping out two months of the season. After play resumed, Texas faded and so did Mendoza, who finished at .231. The Rangers released him early the next season. Failing to hook on with the Pirates in spring training in '83, Mendoza joined the Triple A Hawaii Islanders as a player-coach for a season, then returned to Mexico for the remainder of his playing career. Since turning 45, he has collected a major league pension. But by failing to squeeze one more season out of the bigs he is just short of qualifying for the maximum amount.

The Mendoza line rings. It's Roque Sanchez, Campeche's first baseman. "We failed you," he says, speaking on behalf of his fellow Piratas. "I'd always dreamed of playing for a manager just like you."

Mendoza's style is light-tempered. "It keeps guys, especially young guys, relaxed," he explains. Indeed, his embrace of conviviality helped launch his managerial career. On the Pirates' visits to San Diego, Mendoza enjoyed clowning with the grounds crew. "I'd tug at the hose when they watered the third base side," he says, "or roll balls out of the dugout at them." One of those groundskeepers was a college kid named Bill Bavasi, son of Padres president Buzzie Bavasi. By the early '90s, when Mendoza's Mexican League career was winding down, the younger Bavasi had moved into the Angels' front office. He figured the shortstop who related so easily to all types would make a good manager in the minors, where Latinos in particular can thrive or flail depending on their support system.

In '92, Mendoza began managing at Class A Palm Springs. He spent 10 seasons in the Angels' system, then one more with the Giants. Since 2003 he has been the Mexican Dave Bristol, managing four teams including, until a few hours ago, Campeche.

Piratas have offered to keep him on as a roving instructor, but already there have been feelers from another Mexican League club. Mendoza holds a ticket for an early-morning trip home to Navojoa, 40 miles from the Sea of Cortez, where he and Irma Beatriz like to invite neighbors over for evenings of cerveza and conversation in the "bleachers," the steps that lead to the door of their home. (In addition to Mario Jr., the couple have two other children, Irma Maria, 25, and Manolo, 17.) If a job offer comes, he'll rearrange his plans.

Mendoza has packed his bags. He holes up in a cantina, watching on TV as Higuera leads Campeche to a victory over Leones de Yucatàn. His cellphone lies on the table before him. The Mendoza line is open.

The Passing of a Counterfeit Bill

The reported death of Bill Henry
came as a surprise to Bill Henry

BY RICK REILLY

Former major league pitcher Bill Henry died a couple of weeks ago. He found out about it while sitting in his favorite chair.

What happened was, the phone rang in his Deer Park, Texas, home and his wife, Betty Lou, picked it up. A baseball historian named David Lambert was calling to offer his condolences on the passing of her husband in Lakeland, Fla., of a heart attack, at 83.

This was news to Betty Lou.

"Bill didn't pass away in Florida," she said. "He's sittin' right next to me."

Turns out the Bill Henry who died had been passing himself off as the one still alive for some 20 years. The counterfeit Bill Henry's wife believed he'd been a big leaguer. His family believed it. Their friends did too.

Hard not to, really. Both men were 6'2", lefthanded, square-jawed and squinty-eyed. "I look at their pictures and think, Dad looks more like the real Bill Henry [did in his playing days] than the real Bill Henry does," says the dead man's stepdaughter-in-law, Jeanine Hill-Cole.

Besides, counterfeit Bill's stories sounded so *real*, all about his 16-year career as an All-Star reliever with six major league teams in the 1950s and '60s. Twice a year he would even address a Baseball, Humor and Society class at Florida Southern College and tickle the students with stories about barnstorming with Satchel Paige. "Heck, I'd make more money with Satchel than I ever did in the regular season!" he'd chuckle. "Most I ever made in the big leagues was $17,000."

The man had cojones the size of pumpkins. When the Detroit Tigers were in Lakeland for spring training, he'd go to the games and mingle with the old-timers. He'd even get the big backslap from former Tigers managers Sparky Anderson and Ralph Houk. "Tells you how dumb baseball people are," says Anderson.

Sure, every now and then somebody would ask counterfeit Bill why the birth date on his baseball card, Oct. 15, 1927, was different from the one he told people, Feb. 1, 1922. He'd laugh and say he did it to make scouts think he was younger. The truth was, "Bill was just a good town-team pitcher," says Charles Carter, counterfeit Bill's childhood friend from back in Moberly, Mo.

Anyway, after he died, the Lakeland *Ledger* did a nice obit, and the AP picked it up and it ran all over the country. That's when the real Bill's phone started howling.

Betty Lou's sister called from Houston, distraught. "I'm still kickin'," the live Bill insisted. "Honest!" His daughter-in-law called from Seattle. Her dad had read her the obit, and she was shocked. She thought Bill had been doing fine.

If they were shocked, you should've seen counterfeit Bill's wife of 19 years, Jean. She wondered what else he'd lied about. She soon found out when she went into the basement and found Army records that showed Bill fibbed about the year he was born—1924 instead of 1922—and even about his name. He'd always said he had no middle name. Turns out he was actually Clarence William Henry Jr. "Now I'm not sure *who* I was married to," she says.

How did he fool all the people all the time? Maybe because there weren't that many people left to call him on it. Jean was counterfeit Bill's third wife; they married in Michigan, where he was a salesman. Both his kids and both ex-wives were dead, and he'd been an only child. There was a cousin Jean met, named Bill Nicholson, but he was never around.

"It's amazing a guy could pull a hoax for that long, isn't it?" says the real Bill, now a 79-year-old Houston ship dispatcher. "I'd congratulate him. If that's what the guy needed to do to help his career, it don't bother me.... I just hope they don't stop my Social Security."

Ever meet Satchel? "Nope." Do better than $17,000 a year? "Yep."

The real puzzler is *why*? Why would a handsome man with a lot of friends, a great wife and a six handicap create such an elaborate and exhausting lie? Not for love. Jean didn't know a bunt from a banana. Did he say it once as a lark and then get caught in it? Did he yearn for a ballplayer's life instead of a salesman's? Did he thrill to the con?

"What does it matter?" asks one of his best friends, Bob McHenry. "Bill was a good man. He hurt nobody. He never tried to make money off it.... Look, we live in God's waiting room here. Bill probably made a lot of old guys happy. All of a sudden they knew a major leaguer!"

Last week came the topper. Jean went to the funeral parlor, and the folks there couldn't find his ashes. Now she wonders if she's got the right ones.

You gotta hand it to him. The guy never quits.

JULY 2, 2018

Kid Glove

Famed for his precocious achievements behind the plate five
decades ago, the 70-year-old former leader of the Big Red
Machine is now devoting himself to molding children—his own.

BY L. JON WERTHEIM

The scene is so familiar that it borders on cliché. Two brothers, ages 12
and eight, sit in the backseat of a white SUV, headed to school, this one in
South Florida. Their father is at the wheel. He was up early to make omelets
and pour cereal, but at 6:40 he had to resort to bribery to roust the little
guy—"he's the sleeper"—by promising to make a Dunkin' Donuts stop before
drop-off.

They've barely pulled out of the driveway when they start arguing over
the SiriusXM offerings. The kids want Top 40. The father wants Brooks &
Dunn or Toby Keith or...basically anything that *isn't* Top 40 or hip-hop. But
the kids outnumber him.

So with the same grimace he flashed pitchers when they shook off his
signs, the greatest catcher in history turns the dial and the three males in
the SUV start singing along to 21 Pilots and Imagine Dragons. Dad messes up
the words, as he often does.

Johnny Bench is 70. He doesn't *look* 70; his physique, tanned by the
Florida sun, hasn't swollen significantly from his playing weight of 221
pounds, with muscles still discernible. He says he doesn't feel 70.

And Lord knows, he isn't living the life of a 70-year-old. A single dad
to Justin, a sixth-grader, and Josh, a third-grader, he rises at 5:30 to do
laundry and lay out his kids' clothes. He spends nights checking homework

145

("both are on the honor roll," he brags) and uses his iCalendar less to keep track of tee times than to schedule after-school activities and pediatrician appointments.

The backstory is complex but, Bench says, ultimately quite simple. Johnny and his fourth wife, Lauren Baiocchi, who's 45, had been living in Palm Springs with their two sons. Johnny wasn't loving the California desert; he had the urge to return to South Florida, where he lived from 2014 to '17, and it was closer to Lauren's parents, who live there. So the family scouted homes in Palm Beach Gardens. But when it came time to move, Lauren decided she wasn't going. And Johnny wasn't staying. Lauren and Johnny divorced. And while the matter wends its way through family court, Johnny has primary custody of the boys.

Almost 30 years after his Hall of Fame induction, Bench did not envision this life, solo parent trying to get his kids to expand their tastes beyond chicken fingers, limiting screen time and coordinating sleepovers. He looks around on parents' nights and the generation gap is clear. Says Bench, "Not too many of my boys' friends' parents are saying, 'Hey, I remember watching you play.'"

If life at 70 is different than the way he'd imagined, Bench points out that it is irrelevant. "What matters is *now*," he says. "I want those boys to be well-raised and well-behaved and well-educated. It's a commitment, but I've made that commitment to them. Happy to have."

As if on cue, he receives a text. "That's right," he says, his voice dropping an octave. "Josh asked me last night if Nick could sleep over..."

Back to his original train of thought: "When people say, 'You have two wonderful boys and you're a great father...'" Bench's voice trails off, and as he restarts, it catches. "I don't have a ring for that, but I'll tell you: If I can be considered a Hall of Fame dad, then, well, that's more important than anything else I may have achieved."

As the tears form in the corners of his eyes, Bench quotes a country song—as he often does. "Ever heard 'Mr. Mom' by the band Lonestar?" he asks. Bench grabs his phone, toggles through iTunes and there in the middle of an Italian restaurant sings along in a pleasant, rumbling voice:

Well, Pampers melt in a Maytag dryer
Crayons go up one drawer higher
Rewind Barney for the fifteenth time
Breakfast at six, naps at nine
There's bubblegum in the baby's hair
Sweet potatoes in my lazy chair
Been crazy all day long
And it's only Monday, Mr. Mom

Understatement: Johnny Bench's childhood bore little resemblance to Justin's and Josh's. He grew up in Binger, Okla., where the population, then and now, has hung around 600. His father, Ted, worked for a propane company, rising early and driving an oil truck, and his mom, Katy, kept order for their four kids.

Johnny—never John—was one of those sports omnivores who excelled at everything. But Ted had been a semi-pro baseball player, and as Johnny was growing up, Mickey Mantle was proving that Oklahoma boys could become luminous stars on the diamond. So baseball took precedence in the Bench home. By elementary school, Johnny was listing his future profession as "major leaguer" and practicing his autograph. He chose catching because— an early bit of analytics—his father thought it was the position that offered the greatest probability for making the majors.

In Binger his ambition engendered giggles and suggestions that the Bench boy manage his expectations. But Johnny never required the validation of others. At 17, in 1965, he was a second-round draft pick of the Reds. While playing for Class A Tampa that year, he caught the attention of no less than Yogi Berra. "He can do it all—now," Berra said.

In Bench's first game with Triple A Buffalo, in 1966, he broke his right thumb. During his recovery he sat in the stands at Crosley Field above the Reds' bullpen and yelled down, "If any of you guys are catchers, you'd better remember me. I'm gonna take your job."

Which he did. In 1968, Bench played his first full season and was named National League Rookie of the Year. That offseason, SPORTS ILLUSTRATED ran a feature on "The Big Zinger from Binger."

In 1970, Bench continued his ascent, hitting 45 home runs and driving in 148 runs. Yet when he won the NL MVP award that fall, it was as much for his defense as for his offense. Bench's right arm was worthy of U.N. weapons inspecting; he took as much pride in throwing out base runners as he did in launching balls over fences. He led the major leagues in caught-stealing percentage in 1969 and '72. "Man, did he know how to call a game," says Tom Seaver, a teammate from 1977 to '82. And before it was an occupational requirement, Bench had perfected the dark art of framing pitches.

By 1972 the Big Red Machine was humming. Bench was NL MVP again, hitting 40 home runs and knocking in 125 runs. In the bottom of the ninth inning of the definitive Game 5 of the NLCS, with the Reds trailing the Pirates by a run, Bench came to bat. "As I went to the plate," he later recalled, "I heard my mom hollering my name: 'Hit me a home run.' I thought, I wish it were that easy!" He did it anyway, tying the game. The Reds scored another run to win the game and the pennant before falling to the A's in seven games in the World Series.

Though barely in his 20s, Bench comported himself like a veteran. During just his second season in the majors, he reckoned that the arm of his pitcher, Gerry Arrigo, was tiring. So Bench called for a curveball. Six years older than Bench, Arrigo declined. When Arrigo reared back and threw a fastball, Bench caught the pitch barehanded. Point made. As Bench once recalled to SPORTS ILLUSTRATED, "I didn't want to show him up, but...." For a 1972 *Time* magazine story headlined "Baseball's Best Catcher," Cincinnati pitcher Jim Maloney, eight years Bench's senior, said, "He'll come out to the mound and chew me out as if I were a two-year-old. And I like it."

Though he came from rural Oklahoma—"two miles beyond RESUME SPEED," he likes to say—Bench projected an air of sophistication. A bon vivant, he knew the best restaurants in every NL city. He subscribed to *Time* and made it a point to know the landed gentry of Cincinnati. He began producing and hosting a daily morning show on local television, interviewing Bob Hope and Gerald Ford, among others. He hired his team's young radio announcer as his sidekick. "I gave Al Michaels his first job in television," he says.

Confident and self-possessed, Bench was a wallflower compared with the team's shaggy-haired outfielder. For a time Bench and Pete Rose were cast as contrasts: the graceful, polished, socially ambitious catcher versus the gritty, dirt-on-the-uniform, what-you-see-is-what-you-get grinder. While that was an oversimplification, an unmistakable chill passed between them. "Bench and Rose were never bosom buddies, not even close," says Michaels. "There was a healthy rivalry. Who was the alpha dog? But this was never to the detriment of the team." (Bench points out: He and Rose were civil enough to share several business ventures, including a car dealership and a bowling alley.)

The Reds of the '70s were an extraordinarily close unit; many of the players lived in the same apartment complex. The team's core—Bench, Rose, infielders Joe Morgan and Tony Pérez—could scarcely have been more different in background, playing style and personality. It didn't matter. Bench recalls that Ted Marchibroda, the NFL coach, once asked him what made the Reds so successful. "We're called the Reds, which is funny because we don't see color," Bench explained. "We have black leadership, white leadership, Spanish leadership. None of it makes a difference. You could go to a bar after a game and take a team picture because we all hung out together."

Nor was the team destabilized by the social stresses of the late '60s and '70s. While some teams were questioning and challenging convention— the A's presented themselves as a mustachioed band of rebels—Cincinnati players offered little push back to team strictures banning facial hair, decreeing that the white-and-red uniforms show only a certain amount of stocking and demanding that players "show proper posture" in the dugout. The team's manager from 1970 through '78, Sparky Anderson, was a revered figure whose decisions went largely unquestioned by his minions. "We respected him, but he respected us, to the point that he would ask for our input," says Bench. "Your reaction: My God, he thinks I have a *brain*. He made you feel like a professional."

Bench jokes that he dates himself when discussing his salary. He made $11,000 his rookie season and $85,000 his first MVP season, less than today's MVPs make per game. For another signifier of how times have changed, he talks about the basketball team he and his teammates—including Rose— formed during the offseason. They'd barnstorm Ohio, playing games mostly for charity. According to Rose, the team went 47–4, losing only to the alumni teams of the 1961 and '62 NCAA champion University of Cincinnati squads. Eventually Reds management forced the team to dissolve after centerfielder Bobby Tolan ruptured his Achilles tendon in one game. "Imagine that today," says Bench, laughing. "Not too many front offices would go for that, huh?"

In 1975, Cincinnati returned to the World Series and won, beating the Red Sox in seven. A year later the Reds swept the Yankees. The Big Red Machine's bill of particulars: five seasons, four division crowns, three pennants, two World Series titles. Bench is reluctant to make "best ever" pronouncements, but others will. Suffice to say that when "Sports Dynasties" is a *Jeopardy!* category, the mid-'70s Reds are invariably mentioned.

Bench had, by '75, cemented his status as the finest practitioner of his position. He made 14 All-Star teams, and he won 10 Gold Gloves, every year from 1968 through '77. (For the sake of comparison, Buster Posey has one.) Over his career Bench threw out 43% of the risk-tolerant base runners who chose to test his arm.

Midway through his career, his body launched an insurrection. His hips ached constantly, the legacy of a car accident Bench endured as a teenager. His knees were inflamed from infinite home plate collisions. He had back trouble, surgery to remove a lesion on his lung in 1972, and he broke his left ankle in 1981. Half a lifetime later he still recalls the rough treatment he received from unsympathetic fans. "They say, 'Don't let the boos get you down.' But do this: Walk into your office tomorrow and have two people boo you. Then, when you walk out of your office, they boo you again. The next thing you know, you're back in your office, you're not coming out."

Bench took solace in some advice he received from two men. Bobby Knight, legendary basketball coach and longtime friend, told him, "A critic is a legless man who teaches running." Bobby Richardson, the former Yankees second baseman, said, "This crowd on Earth, they soon forget the heroes of the past. They cheer like mad until you fall."

Over the final three seasons of his career, Bench caught only 13 total games. He retired in 1983, having played his entire career in Cincinnati, and did not agonize over the decision. Years later John Elway asked him, "How did you know when to retire?"

Bench had a simple answer: "When you can't be John Elway anymore." He says now, "I came to a realization that I couldn't be Johnny Bench anymore. I walked away from a $900,000 contract. I wasn't earning it." Then he laughs. "Of course, Elway won two more Super Bowls [after our conversation], then retired on his own terms."

After baseball Bench was host of the classic children's show *The Baseball Bunch,* which ran for six years. He was a regular on the motivational-speaking circuit and the spokesperson for a Cincinnati bank. He'd go hunting with his pal Knight and golfing with any of his innumerable celebrity friends. He lent his name to charities and scholarship drives and golf classics, raising millions. "The great thing about it," he says, "is I knew I had a life. You feel bad, some of these guys, they walk away, and they didn't save a dime."

It was often suggested that Bench had the temperament to be a good manager. But, he says, "I don't want to deal with incompetence. I played on a team that was the level of what it was. Really, it's hard for me to accept people who don't make an effort, are not professional. The great thing in my life is, I don't have to deal with them."

As for his old teammates, they remain kindred spirits. Bench sees Pérez, who lives nearby, in Miami. He goes fishing with Seaver. He runs into Rose at card shows, and they text each other on their birthdays.

Then there's Morgan, of whom Bench says, "Couldn't find a better ballplayer anywhere, ever." Morgan flirted with death several years ago, following complications from knee surgery. When he turned a corner, "First thing Joe did was send me a video of him walking around the room without a cane. I said, 'It looks like you got two canes, the way those legs are shaped.' But he's doing better now, and it makes me so happy."

Talk of Morgan's recovery has Bench taking full inventory of his life. "I'm blessed by a lot of things," he says. "Blessed with who I've had in my life, where I've got."

By the metrics of friends, experiences, net worth, Bench's life has been a full one. But, by his own admission, he's been considerably less successful in his personal life. Naturally, he has lyrics from a country music song ready for that. Two songs, in fact: Tammy Wynette's "Till I Get It Right" and "The Dance" by Garth Brooks. "So I'll just keep on fallin' in love till I get it right." Moments later he sings, "I could have missed the pain, but I'd of had to miss the dance."

Early in his career, Bench was hailed as "baseball's most-eligible bachelor," a distinction he shed before the 1975 season when he married Vickie Chesser, a toothpaste model who'd previously dated Joe Namath. Four days after they met, Bench proposed; 13 months after they married, they were divorced. ("I tried. I even hand-squeezed orange juice," she told Phil Donahue in December 1975. "I don't think either of us had any idea what marriage was really like.")

Before Christmas 1987, Bench married Laura Cwikowski, an Oklahoma City model and aerobics instructor. They had a son, Bobby Binger (named for Hope and Knight, and Bench's hometown), before divorcing in '95. They shared custody of the boy. "He was—is—a great dad," says Bobby, who works in Cincinnati as a production operator on Reds broadcasts. "Definitely firm. I remember him making me wear slacks and a button-down for my 12th birthday. But he did a lot of things you later appreciated."

Bench took his third at bat in 1997, marrying Elizabeth Benton, and his fourth marriage came in 2004, to Baiocchi, the daughter of pro golfer Hugh Baiocchi. Bench chooses his words cautiously talking about their recent breakup, in part because it involves his sons' mother and in part because there are matters still in court. One point he makes without hesitation though: Primary custody suits him fine.

"Being a dad can be challenging, sure. But even when it's not fun, it's enjoyable—if that makes sense," he says. "I don't mind the work. I mean, how can you complain about doing *laundry*? You throw it in, put some soap in, push the button and come back when it's done."

Bench has help, too. The two daughters of Gary Carter—another great catcher of Bench's era—live nearby, and they've helped line up babysitters and housekeepers. Lauren's parents (who are Bench's contemporaries) live a few miles away and are happy to pinch-hit when Johnny travels. Bobby flies to Florida once a month or so, helping out with his half-brothers. "Sometimes I'm good cop, sometimes bad cop," he says. "Dad tells them to put down the XBox, and they'll say, 'In a minute.' Then I say, 'I know you started a new game. You can fool your dad, but you can't fool me!'"

Justin and Josh both play sports, but they feel little pressure being the sons of a Hall of Famer. Neither plays baseball, but Johnny would like both to be involved in the game. The boys' friends have scarcely heard of Johnny Bench. And Bench is fine if the boys prefer soccer or music or whatever.

Like any father—especially one of a certain age—Bench imparts lessons by recounting gauzy stories. He tells stories of fishing trips and cross-country flights and USO tours, and cautionary tales of celebrities he knew who went broke or never grew up. "If what you did yesterday is big to you now," he says, "then you haven't done much today."

Most of the stories don't involve baseball, but there's one, set in the late '60s: Bench was 18 and playing in Buffalo. A pair of older pitchers, Dom Zanni and Jim Duffalo, pulled him aside. They noticed that for all his natural talent, he was flailing at breaking pitches. The next afternoon they met at the park. "They threw me curveball after curveball after curveball," Bench recalls. "Two games later I hit two home runs off curveballs. The pitcher was Sam Jones, supposedly *the* curveball guy."

The moral of the story is obvious, but the 70-year-old single dad of preteens, smiles and takes his swing. "I tell the boys: You have to know how to deal with curveballs."

FEBRUARY 6, 1989

The Hit Man Hits Back

After his most trying year as a Yankee, Don Mattingly is now back
home in Indiana, preparing to attack the upcoming season

BY PETER GAMMONS

It was 1:30 on a Sunday morning in Mattinglys' 23 restaurant, and some guy
they say came from across the river, from Owensboro, Ky., had just hit 17 of
20 in the free throw court next to the bar. Now it was the restaurateur's turn,
and Don Mattingly, wearing blue Levi's cords, a polo shirt and Converse
basketball shoes, stepped past a locker containing a Larry Bird Celtics
uniform and took his place at the foul line.

"This is the way an Indiana boy shoots free throws," Mattingly said,
bouncing the ball four times as he squared his shoulders to the basket.
Few of the people in the bar stopped to watch the most famous person in
Evansville, Ind., an Ohio River city of 130,000, shoot hoops. Most everyone
has known Artie—Donald Arthur Mattingly is Artie to some of the boys back
home—since high school. Chip Wire was the baseball team's student manager
when Artie was a three-sport hero at Evansville's Reitz Memorial High, and
he was in the bar. So was Larry Bitter, Memorial's second baseman. And Karl
Ralph, whom Mattingly calls Fast Eddie and whom he credits with teaching
him the low-rider style of wearing baseball pants that Mattingly brought
with him to the big leagues; Ralph was the centerfielder on the American
Legion team—Funkhouser Post #8—for which Mattingly played outfield and
first base. Bob Durchholz, a high school friend, was sitting at the bar next
to Michael Mattingly, the third of the four Mattingly brothers. "Watch," said
Michael, nudging Durchholz. "Donnie'll refuse to lose."

After missing his first shot, Mattingly made the next six and then missed again. When he reached 10 shots, he had made eight.

Bartender Doug Mattingly—who's no relation to Don but will become Bird's brother-in-law when his sister Dinah marries Larry Legend in July—was watching when someone flipped off the lights in the basketball court. Unruffled, Don unerringly hit one shot, then another, then another, until he had finished his 20. Twelve in a row, 18 of 20. "Indiana boy," he said, and walked away.

Mattinglys' 23 (named for his uniform number) stands at the crossroads of the public and private lives of its proprietor, who—and this is hard to believe—is just 27 years old. When Mike Pagliarulo, the New York Yankee third baseman and Mattingly's closest friend on the team, came into the restaurant last winter, one of the first things he said was, "Donnie, your prices are too low."

"This isn't New York," Pagliarulo was told by Mattingly's father-in-law, Dennis Sexton, who is co-owner and manager of the place. "This is Evansville—German and conservative—where the portions had better be large and the prices small."

This is also where Mattingly wanted his restaurant, not New York, where "it would be mine in name only," he says. "This is me." And it is, right down to the eye black he's wearing in the picture on the sign outside the restaurant.

Mattingly stops by three or four nights a week during the off-season to chat with customers, sign autographs and generally help out. There are sweatshirts and posters for sale at the souvenir stand—a portion of the profits go to charity—and kids can have their picture taken with Mattingly. One guy who lives in Staten Island, N.Y., has flown in two years in a row to celebrate New Year's Eve at Mattinglys' 23, and parents have come all the way from Chicago to make a child's birthday something special. But the patrons are mainly just the good people of Evansville. The menu ranges from $15 filet mignon to hamburgers or fried chicken for about $5, and the character of the place bears Mattingly's unmistakable stamp: unpretentiousness. He and his wife, Kim, sometimes peel potatoes, bus tables or tend bar.

"What I always wanted was a small neighborhood honky-tonk, with down-home cooking and Hank Williams Jr. on the jukebox," says Mattingly. "But even though we went to something larger, I wanted to run it like it was a honky-tonk."

Late one midweek afternoon in January, a young boy sidled up to Mattingly, who was standing outside the kitchen. The kid stared up shyly, saying nothing. "Would you like me to sign something?" asked Mattingly. The boy nodded, and Mattingly grabbed a menu and asked his name. "Kyle Murphy," he answered, still bashful. "It's my ninth birthday." Mattingly signed the menu and told Kyle how to get his picture taken wearing a Yankee cap, then noted that the boy's sneaker was untied. Nervously, Kyle bent down, but when he stood up, the laces were still untied. Mattingly dropped down on one knee, tied the sneaker and, when he stood up, said, "Hey, thanks for coming."

Mattinglys' 23 has sports memorabilia throughout its hallways, three dining areas and bar. Walk in the door to the first dining room and you see DiMaggio and Ruth. There's a legends area—with tributes to Ruth, Gehrig, Rose, DiMaggio, Thurman Munson and others. There's a boxing ring with tables inside the ropes (Pags's favorite dining spot). There's a Hoosier Room, with tributes to local sports figures, such as Don's late brother, Jerry, the oldest of the Mattingly boys, who was a basketball guard at Evansville College (now the University of Evansville); Andy Benes, a former U of Evansville pitcher, an Olympic star and the first player taken in the 1988 baseball draft; and Bobby Knight. Over the bar are portraits, four feet high, of the two hitters Mattingly most reveres, Rod Carew and Ted Williams, and in a glass case is a pair of the hightop shoes Bill Buckner wore in the 1986 World Series. There's a Louisville Slugger display about the making of a Don Mattingly model bat, a scoreboard with up-to-date standings—this winter it gives those of four major college basketball conferences (ACC, Big East, Big Ten, SEC)—and an array of menus and pictures signed by noted guests, including George Steinbrenner. Only one small wall, just inside the entrance, is devoted solely to Mattingly pictures—photos that take him from his signing with the Yankees in June 1979 to his Class A days in Oneonta, N.Y., to '85 American League MVP. "Don wanted this to be a restaurant, not a monument to himself," says Sexton.

Before Don and Kim headed home the night he buried those 10 free throws in the dark, he went into the kitchen and made two pizzas—from scratch—for some friends who were still in the bar. Then he went back to the free throw court.

"This is really my game," he said. After four running strides he took off and tried to dunk. He stands a shade under six feet, and his flight was easily a foot short. The ball banged off the wall, as did Mattingly. "Problem was, the other kids got bigger and quicker—and I stayed short and slow," he said. Then he put on his lined denim jacket, the one that has a signature in ink above the left breast pocket: MELLENCAMP. "Another Indiana boy," Mattingly said.

It's about a 15-minute ride from the restaurant to the Mattinglys' house, north of Evansville in Darmstadt, a farming community of 1,200. Don and Kim bought the house in 1984 after he signed a one-year contract with the Yankees for $130,000. It's a six-room redbrick, with three bedrooms and a play loft for their two boys, three-year-old Taylor and 18-month-old Preston. The house sits on top of a hill on four acres, which are also home to deer and to a huge pileated woodpecker that fascinates Don. In the driveway a small tractor is parked beside a backboard with a rim that's only about 9½ feet high. "Guys like me got to have a chance," he says.

Mattingly may well be the best player in baseball, but he is coming off his worst big league season—a year marked by subpar numbers, a public spat with George Steinbrenner and the inevitable trade rumors that followed—which is why he's sticking close to his home and family this winter while he works hard to prepare for the season ahead. Except for one quick visit to New York (and their in-season house in Tenafly, N.J.), a couple of days in Vegas for the Ray Leonard–Donny Lalonde fight and a few more in Hawaii for the player reps' meetings, this is where the Mattinglys are spending their time until spring training. "That's the only change in Don since he married my daughter in '79—he's more protective of his time with his family," says Sexton.

Ray Schulte, Mattingly's business manager, says, "Even during the season, when [his agent] Jim Krivacs or I want to do business, we have to go on the road with the Yankees so we don't infringe on Don's time with Kim and the kids." Mattingly is equally jealous of his time in the off-season. He no longer hunts or plays golf, and he caught his first fish at the union meetings in Hawaii (a 210-pound marlin). "He hasn't done a card show since 1984. and I was offered a minimum of $100,000 to do a special one," Schulte says. "I could get him a speaking engagement every night of the winter for $10,000 to $20,000 a pop, but he doesn't do them. He only goes to one or two dinners a winter, and they're either for charity or as favors."

Mattingly's winter days begin at 6:30, when the boys wake up, and tend to end early, around 10:30. He usually fixes the kids' breakfast. "I'm an early-morning person," he says. "Anyway, Kim has to be both mother and father for much of the season."

Don and Kim met in 1976 when her father coached his American Legion team. He went to the Yankee farm at Oneonta right out of Memorial High in '79 and, a month later, called and asked her to join him. They were married on Sept. 8 of that year and spent their five-day honeymoon at the Regal 8 Inn on Highway 41, a few hundred yards from the Evansville airport. Then they immediately headed for Florida and the start of Instructional League play. "Unlike a lot of baseball couples who met when the player was already famous, Kim has been beside me all the way," says Don. "She's slept on floors, she's slept in rooms that didn't have doors, from Oneonta to Greensboro to Puerto Rico."

"Who loves you, babe?" she asks him a couple of times a day. "Who *really* loves you?" It's a standing line in the Mattingly household. "He dogs me and

I dog him," Kim says. "In this business, you need all the dogging someone can give you." When her husband is showered with praise or adulation at the restaurant, for instance, she'll sidle up to him and whisper, "Oh, Don, you're the greatest—but who *really* loves you?" During the season she'll tell him, "Don't come home unless you get two hits."

And home, after all, is what Mattingly is all about. "I don't find that I've changed the way I live in Evansville," he says. Apart from Mattinglys' 23, Don and Kim's favorite restaurants are the Log Inn and the Darmstadt Inn (where, legend has it, Abe Lincoln once ate), both hearty family establishments. Don enjoys going to University of Evansville basketball games, especially now that the Aces are coached by Jim Crews, a former assistant under Knight, whom Mattingly calls "the one person I'd really like to meet."

So what's a big-time night out in Evansville? This winter Mattingly sat ringside for Hulk Hogan and the World Wrestling Federation show at Roberts Memorial Stadium, and when he went backstage last month before a Joan Jett and the Blackhearts concert at the same arena and mentioned to someone in the band that he played the harmonica, he was handed a blues harp that once belonged to rock 'n' roller Robert Plant and asked to show his chops. Mattingly blew a few notes and the band was soon jamming behind him. Could Artie Mattingly be the next Paul Butterfield? "Less likely than my being the next Gehrig," he says, "and there's no chance of that."

Although he may live much the same way he always has, Mattingly finds that people back home assume he has been changed by all the money he's making, which is now close to $3 million a year in salary, investments and endorsements. "In 1985, when I won the MVP, I started hearing how I didn't sign an autograph, or I didn't care as much, and it gets worse every year," he says. "Supposedly, the better a player I become, the worse a person I become. I know people don't really mean it. I know I have to get used to it. But I don't think I've changed. Evansville hasn't changed, and Evansville is me."

Evansville is also his parents and his brothers, and they "get a lot of enjoyment out of what I do, but they don't treat me any differently than they did when I was at Memorial." Don says. But then, these are the people who know that Mattingly is now, as he always was and ever shall be, a ketchup man. He loads ketchup on eggs, potatoes and steak. In Mattinglys' 23, the waitresses bring him a bottle without asking. Not so on the Upper East Side of Manhattan. "Sometimes the waiters look away as they hand me the bottle," Mattingly says, "or, more often, they put it in a small dish so no one in the restaurant will think that anyone who'd use ketchup would eat in the place. But if I'm paying $30 for a steak, I'll put whatever I want on it. In my house, we didn't have steak, we had hamburger steaks."

That house is a white cracker box on a quarter-acre lot in a working-class neighborhood two miles across town from the restaurant. Bill and Mary Mattingly have lived in that house for 48 years. "It's hard to believe that we could have raised four athletic sons and a daughter in a house this small," says Mary. Bill, now retired, rode the mail trains between Nashville and Chicago, and Don says his father's passion for trains is still burning, which explains why, when Bill goes to see Don play, he likes to ride the rails to Yankee Stadium, Comiskey Park and Fenway Park.

The Mattinglys' English ancestors settled in Virginia in the 17th century, but Bill isn't sure when they reached Evansville. What's certain is that they did—there are 88 Mattinglys in the local phone book, not including Don, who is unlisted. All of Bill and Mary's children, as well as Bill's sister and two brothers, live within five miles of the little house on Van Dusen Avenue.

"It seems as if all the kids did in our neighborhood was play sports from sunup to sundown," says Randy, the second of the Mattingly boys, who's now 37. "My dad coached Jerry and me in Little League, but even when he stopped, he always took time off from work to see our games. He never said much, but he and Mom went to all our games, and since there were four brothers all spaced five years apart, that was some task. He also made it easy for us. When each one got to high school age. he'd tell us not to bother getting a job, but to play sports, and he'd find a way to keep us in a little pocket change. Donnie was the youngest boy, and he didn't have any choice. He had to play with us."

"There's no substitute for learning to play from older brothers," Don says. "Anyway, the whole neighborhood was lined with jocks."

Before Don was three, he was the mascot for Jerry's basketball team at Rex Mundi High. (Jerry was also a wide receiver on the football team—where his quarterback was a fellow named Bob Griese.) Jerry grew into a 6'2" star guard for Evansville College, and he played baseball well enough to receive three pro contract offers. While working on a highway construction crew in 1969, at the age of 23, he was killed in an accident.

Randy, 6'4", a starting quarterback for the Aces, was a passer who was the Division II leader in total offense in 1971 and was selected by Cleveland in the fourth round of the '73 NFL draft. After spending one season bouncing from the Browns to the Chicago Bears to the Buffalo Bills to the Cincinnati Bengals, Randy returned a $1,500 check the Dallas Cowboys had sent without stipulation when they asked him to come for a tryout. Instead, he opted for Canada, where he thought he would play more and where he lasted four seasons as a backup for Saskatchewan, Hamilton and British Columbia of the CFL.

Next in line was Michael, a good enough athlete to earn a scholarship to Indiana State University–Evansville, where he played a year of basketball and three years of baseball. "All the rest of us grew to six-two or six-four," Michael says, "and if Donnie had gotten to our height, he'd probably have stuck with basketball. But he was the one kid in the family who had our father's special quality–perseverance. Anything either one of them set their minds to, they do."

Don always played with the older boys, especially in basketball, because his brothers could hoist him through a window at Rex Mundi High so that he could open the doors after the building was locked. But, of course, the Mattinglys didn't play only basketball. In the backyard of their house was the Wiffle Ball field. "Just look at the yard, and you'll see how I developed my hitting style," says Don. If he pulled, he would hit a big tree. If he went to left center, he could clear two garages and put it into an alley for a home run.

One of Mattingly's considerable natural athletic talents was his ambidexterity. Back in Little League, he switch-pitched on occasion, going three innings righthanded and three innings lefthanded. And in Legion ball, Sexton had Mattingly–who then as now threw and hit lefthanded– play second base in the conventional righthanded manner. (As late as 1980, Mattingly's first full year in the Yankee farm system, "The organization was worried about his lack of speed and power," according to Bob Schaefer, who managed him that year in Greensboro, N.C. "And because he could throw righthanded, serious consideration was given to moving him to second base.") Mattingly still takes ground balls at shortstop righthanded, but when he played three games at third in '86, he did so lefty.

By his junior year at Memorial, Mattingly knew "my running and jumping ability and size dictated that baseball was going to be my sport." Long before that–by the age of 10, in fact–he had figured out how to make baseball pay off. He would go to Garvin Park (where there's now a sign that reads EVANSVILLE YOUTH BASEBALL: NORTHSIDE HOME OF DON MATTINGLY), take a position in the parking lot outside Bosse Field–home of the minor league Evansville Triplets–and retrieve foul balls, which he would sell back to the club for 50 cents apiece.

Later, after he became a local hero, "Don refused to ever wear his letter sweater or jacket because he didn't like to draw attention to himself," his mother recalls.

"I preferred to play ball, not talk about it," he says. Being an Indiana boy, he knew a lot about Bird, and some of his reticence may have followed Bird's example. Unquestionably he copied Carew's every mannerism at the plate. But one thing was plainly his own: his tenacity. "I was lucky because I had a high school coach [Quentin Merkel] who is just like Bobby Knight," he says. "He'd stay out until dark, working with us, pushing us."

In Mattingly's senior year, Merkel draped netting in the gym as a makeshift batting cage. "I couldn't believe it—I could hit all day, all winter, and never have to chase the balls," says Mattingly. "I was up there in lunch hours, recess, free periods, after school...."

"He was a ballaholic," says Kim, whom he had begun dating by then. "Actually, he was a nerd."

The nerd hit .500 as a junior and .552 as a senior, and Memorial won 59 in a row those two seasons before losing the state finals in his last high school game. Those seasons landed him in SI's "Faces in the Crowd," and Steinbrenner likes to say he saw the item and told his scouts to draft Mattingly. "That sounds good, but there were two Yankee scouts who'd been on me all year," says Mattingly.

Because Bill Mattingly had told every scout that his son would honor his commitment to attend Indiana State on a baseball scholarship, the Yankees waited until the 19th round of the June '79 draft to select Don. A week later, Yankee scout Jax Robertson visited the little white house on Van Dusen Avenue, and Don, who wasn't as sold on college as his father had hoped, blurted out, "I want to play ball." Robertson offered him $23,000, a high figure for a low-round selection, and Don was on his way to Oneonta— and his first "slump." Says Mattingly, "I thought I was going to hit .500 in Oneonta like I did at Memorial, so I was down because I thought I was really struggling." At his low point, he was hitting .340. He finished his first minor league season at .349.

After the Instructional League that winter, 18-year-old Don and 17-year-old Kim moved in with her parents. "He wore the same woolen shirt every day and hardly ever showered or shaved," says Kim. "He just hit and worked out, hit and worked out. He was a maniac." She pauses. "No. Not was—is."

Mattingly's garage is his baseball laboratory, and he reserves his mad-scientist hours for the time he spends there. There are cardboard cartons and a few odd trophies, but there's barely room for one compact in the three-car garage because of the batting cage and the pitching machine. Besides these tools of the hitter's art, there's also a boxer's speed bag. "I watched Sugar Ray Leonard work on this thing and figured it had to help me," says Mattingly. "It's great for my hands, my hand-eye coordination." He puts on a pair of light gloves, takes a stance in front of the bag and bears down on it as if he were facing Frank Viola.

Then he hits. Some days he's in the garage before sunrise. Sometimes he waits until Taylor and Preston have gone to sleep at night. But every day since New Year's, Mattingly has been in the cage, hitting off the pitching machine. "He gets locked in there the way he gets locked in during the season," says Pagliarulo. "I've never seen any other baseball player like him."

Almost every day during the off-season, Mattingly runs, racing against a clock, competing with himself. And on Mondays, Wednesdays and Fridays he also does heavy-duty lifting at The Pit, an Evansville gym where the motto is NO CARPET, NO SAUNA, JUST IRON. He works on his legs, back and upper body. He's aiming to go into this season at 185 pounds, five less than his playing weight of the past three years.

Mattingly's contract stipulates that he can't play basketball or racquetball, his two favorite off-season sports. "I understand why they forbid them," he says, "but I'm not sure it's right. I can do other activities for the physical conditioning I need, but I think it's good mentally to compete year-round. I try to do that with my running. I try to compete in my lifting by pushing myself to the point of failure. But there's nothing like competition. That's what baseball—all sports—is all about: willpower, beating someone, winning."

"Check Donnie's eyes during a game," says former Yankee pitcher Bob Tewksbury. "They're right out of a horror movie. He yells at opposing players. He paces in the dugout. I've never seen anyone compete with that kind of passion."

"Don and I believe that playing every game at breakneck speed is *fun*," says Pagliarulo. "He'll holler, 'Nothing gets through this infield...everyone's uniform had better be dirty.' If Don were miked at the plate, you'd hear him let out a kind of ninja scream every time he swings. That's the way he is."

Says Mattingly: "I don't actually dislike any opposing players, but I hate them when I play against them. Especially pitchers. I'm competing with them, every at bat, 162 games a season. You have to hate the guy. You have to get your mind into a sort of rage. I try to think of all the things the guy has done to irk me over the years; fortunately, I seldom forget things. Take [Orioles pitcher] Mike Flanagan, for instance. He may be one of the nicest people in the game, but when I go up against him, I remember that he drilled me in the side after I hit a grand slam off him in spring training in 1986. Then I think, Yeah, drop down and throw that weak sidearm junk... don't challenge me, you son of a bitch. You have to push yourself like that every at bat, constantly striving for another level."

"In high school they used to kid him about all the grunting noises he made on the basketball court," says Wire. "It doesn't matter if it's Wiffle Ball or chess, Don hates losing," says his brother Michael. "I taught him to play chess when he was five. I wasn't bad for a 10-year-old, but he kept playing and playing and playing until he could beat me. He simply refuses to lose."

He certainly wouldn't on the final day of the 1984 season, when he was battling teammate Dave Winfield for the American League batting title. Mattingly, who went into the game trailing by two points, went 4 for 5 to finish at .343, three points ahead of Winfield, who went 1 for 4. "Anyone who knows Donnie knows that the fact that the Yankees haven't won eats at him," says Pagliarulo. "He doesn't want to say it publicly because he feels he had a bad year last year, but not winning got to him. One night he told me, 'Michael, I haven't won since A ball. It's killing me.' And I'll tell you something: Until you see Don Mattingly in a pennant race, you won't have seen the real Don Mattingly. He doesn't care about stats. He wants to win."

Back in Greensboro, in Class A ball, Mattingly was involved in a pennant race. "He was like Carl Yastrzemski in 1967," says Schaefer. "If we needed a single, he singled. A double, he doubled. Two runs, he knocked them in. He locked himself in for a two-week period that was almost scary."

Last winter, Mattingly guaranteed that the Yankees would win a pennant in '88. But the season turned out to be the worst of his career—even if he did hit .311 with 18 homers, 37 doubles and 88 RBIs. He had a pulled muscle in his rib cage. He had a war of words with the Boss. "One of the reasons I decided to spend the whole winter here is that no matter where I went in New York—a Knicks game, out to dinner—I'd be asked the same questions about George," says Mattingly. "I just want to let it cool down and remain a Yankee."

There were also questions about a back injury that was diagnosed in June 1987 as a protruding disk. "When I was on the disabled list with the disk, the doctors thought it was serious," Mattingly says. "But later they told me that there's an abnormal space in my spine, so the protruding disk doesn't affect the nerve. And while it looks bad on X-rays, it's not that serious. It's something I have to live with."

A pain in the back is one thing. Steinbrenner is another. "When all those rumors surfaced late last season that George was going to get rid of me, people back home asked me about being traded to St. Louis or Cincinnati. That might be easier, less pressure. I like Toronto a lot. But I don't want to leave New York. Yeah, I'm a small-town Indiana person, but I love the excitement and pressure of playing in New York. When I was growing up, I was a Reds fan. I didn't know much about the Yankee uniform and what Ruth and Gehrig and DiMaggio and Mantle had done. Now I do, and I'd like to play my whole career there.

"When I realize what Gehrig did and think that no matter what I do the rest of my career, that I'll never approach him, I find that neat. When I signed my [three-year, $6.7 million] contract before last season, I didn't ask for a no-trade clause because I'd always figured that if they didn't want me,

I didn't want to be there. I didn't think I'd be traded so soon, but I guess—for a while there, at least—I was gone."

The Steinbrenner Wars began on Aug. 21, after a loss to Seattle. All the anger and frustration came pouring out of Mattingly. "I never wanted to let it get to me, but it had been building up for three years," he says. "It wasn't just 1988, far from it. For years, I'd let George take his little shots." In '85, for instance, the Boss refused to let Mattingly's arrest in Kansas City for urinating outside a restaurant be forgotten (although the charges were dropped). That same year Mattingly said the Yankees could use the mental rest of an off day, and Steinbrenner responded by saying Mattingly should get a "real job" as a taxi driver or steelworker and find out what life and hard work are all about. In 1987, when Mattingly won a record $1.975 million arbitration award, Steinbrenner said, "The monkey is clearly on his back. He has to deliver a championship like Reggie Jackson did. [Mattingly's] like all the rest of 'em now. He can't play little Jack Armstrong of Evansville, Indiana, anymore." Finally, last year, Steinbrenner called Mattingly "the most unproductive .300 hitter in baseball."

After that defeat by the Mariners, Mattingly said, "They think money is respect.... They don't want us to win games.... We have a lot of unhappy players.... It's hard to come to the ballpark. It's not fun to play here. The game should be fun."

A week later, Blue Jay general manager Pat Gillick told Toronto reporters that Mattingly was on the trading block. At the time, Steinbrenner denied it, but at the same time he was pressing Krivacs, Mattingly's agent, for an apology. Mattingly couldn't apologize. Among other things, Kim had told him not to come home if he did.

"After I let out things that had built up inside me, I felt great the rest of the season," Mattingly says. "I was like a new kid. I didn't want trouble with Mr. Steinbrenner. You know, I really do like him and respect him, and I know that he's helped my career by challenging and motivating me. Despite what he says sometimes, I believe he likes and respects me. But that whole thing wasn't about money. I *know* I had a bad year. I got into a rut early. I swung at too many bad pitches. It was the most inconsistent performance of my life. He can criticize my ability or my production or my numbers. But don't question my intensity, my effort, my integrity. Two million dollars is a lot of money, but two million dollars isn't respect or integrity."

On the final day of the season, in Detroit, several players came up and wished Mattingly well. "I felt like I'd died, or I was retiring," he says. Then, when he went back to close his New Jersey house, clubhouse man Nick Priore hugged him and gave him a kiss. "I'm told that's the Italian kiss of death," says Mattingly. "So I cleared out my locker."

Mattingly was told during the World Series by sources outside the Yankees that Steinbrenner had made a deal with the Giants that would have sent Mattingly and pitcher Rick Rhoden to San Francisco for first baseman Will Clark and pitchers Atlee Hammaker and Craig Lefferts. But the Giants had backed off trading the two lefthanded pitchers when they learned that another San Francisco southpaw, Dave Dravecky, had a tumor on his pitching arm.

Later in October, Mattingly got calls from a couple of members of the Yankee organization—including new manager Dallas Green—urging him to try to settle his differences with Steinbrenner. Otherwise, he would be traded—and never mind that Mattingly's statistics over the past four years, including his relatively modest ones for 1988, put him in a class far above any other player in the game, as Murray Chass noted in *The New York Times*.

Mattingly made the call to the Boss. Kim could hear Steinbrenner's voice a room away from where her husband was holding the receiver. The conversation, often animated on Don's end as well, lasted close to an hour. "If I wasn't gone before, I'm gone now," Don told Kim. The next day, he got a call from a well-placed Yankee source. "Whatever you did, George has changed his mind," he was told. "You won't be traded."

"If they still trade me," he told his brother Michael a few days later, "they'll find out it was the biggest mistake they ever made. If they keep me, I'll make it the smartest move they ever made."

"Don started getting that look in his eye," Michael remembers. "All of a sudden, he was locked in, obsessed with 1989."

On another winter night at the restaurant, Mattingly was asked about the approaching season. "I don't set numerical goals," he said. "But why can't a player hit the ball hard four times a game—sometimes five times—162 games a year? Why not? Can you imagine what that season would be like? Every morning I'm out there running, every day that I pump iron, every day I hit the speed bag, every day I hit—that's what I get locked in on. No, not 162 games. More than that. The playoffs, the Series...."

"Can I interrupt for a second for an autograph?" asked a young woman. "You probably don't remember me, but I was a grade ahead of you and used to ride the bus to parochial school with you every day. I was real fat then."

"Did he pick on you?" the girl was asked.

"Not little Donnie," she said. "He wasn't like other kids. He was always polite and nice. A real Indiana boy."

MAY 23, 2011

Randy (Macho Man) Savage's Dream Was to Make It to the Majors

Before he entered the squared circle, a legend of professional wrestling pursued a career on the diamond

BY JEFF PEARLMAN

The boy had a dream, after all. From the time he was 7 or 8 years old, the one thing Randall Mario Poffo wanted to do was play baseball. He was the kid who carried his mitt and bat everywhere; who begged his little brother Lanny to get off the couch and come to the back yard for some extra BP; who pinched himself every time his father, Angelo, took the boys to Wrigley Field or Comiskey Park to catch Hank Aaron or Roger Maris or Willie Mays as they came through town.

Was Randy Poffo the greatest athlete Downers Grove (Ill.) North High had ever produced? Probably not. But when it came to determination and drive, well, he was in his own league.

Once, while he was matriculating at Herrick Junior High, a physical education teacher questioned whether any of the students could do 100 sit-ups without stopping. Randy exceeded 1,000. Another time, John Guarnaccia, a longtime childhood friend, spotted the right-handed Randy throwing balls with his left hand. "Uh, what are you doing?" he asked.

"Well, a coach might want me to pitch," Randy replied. "But I don't wanna burn out my arm. So I'll learn to do it lefty, and I'll save my right for the important things."

Guarnaccia laughed and walked away.

"No exaggeration," he says now. "Randy became fully ambidextrous."

As a junior at Downers Grove North, Poffo batted .500 for the Trojans, leading them to a West Suburban Conference title. The next year, he improved to .525 and Downers Grove North repeated. With the local reputation as a winner, a player with power to all fields and a cannon of an arm from behind the plate, a future in pro ball seemed all but inevitable. A handful of scouts had come to suburban Illinois to watch him play, and while he didn't perform particularly well in their presence (a 102-degree fever rendered him useless), the interest was undeniable.

"We all assumed Randy would be welcomed into professional baseball," says his brother Lanny. "It was more than his dream. It was his destiny."

On June 8, 1971, Randy Poffo—handsome, polite, clean cut—sat inside his house at 3909 Venard Road and waited for the phone to ring. At approximately 10 a.m., the Chicago White Sox opened baseball's amateur draft by selecting Danny Goodwin, a catcher out of nearby Peoria Central High. Roughly three hours later, with the 40th pick, the Chicago Cubs took catcher Steve Haug, also from Illinois. One spot later, the Oakland A's tabbed catcher Ron Williamson. Four picks after that, Michael Uremovich, another catcher, went to the Twins. Then Steve Hergenrader to the White Sox. And David Christiansen to the Angels. And Michael Frazier to the Dodgers. And...and...by the time two days and 48 rounds had passed a whopping 66 catchers were selected.

None by the name of Randy Poffo.

"That was the darkest of dark times for us," says Lanny. "To describe it simply as sad does the pain no justice. Randy was ignored. Completely ignored. I assure you, he never forgot that feeling.

"Never."

Randy Poffo died last Friday.

Before we go on, you should probably be told as much. Randy Poffo, the kid who dreamed of playing baseball, was driving his Jeep Wrangler in Pinellas County, Fla., when, at approximately 9:25 a.m., he suffered a massive heart attack. The Jeep veered over the raised concrete median divider, crossed over several lanes and crashed head-on into a tree.

When police arrived, they found Poffo's wife, Lynn, hurt but stable. Beside her, slumped forward in the driver's seat, was the lifeless body of a thickly built man with a white beard and a familiar face. He was 58. "I believe Randy was already gone when it hit," says Lanny, who wrestled in the WWF under the sobriquet, The Genius. "Which is the better way, I suppose."

If the accident sounds familiar but the name does not, that's probably because Randy Poffo was better known—actually, universally known—as Randy (Macho Man) Savage, one of the most accomplished and beloved professional wrestlers of all time. A former champion in both Vince McMahon's World Wrestling Federation and Ted Turner's World Championship Wrestling, the Macho Man became something of an iconic figure, what with his distinctive "Oooh Yeah!" growl, his bright, flamboyant duds, his outrageous appearances in Slim Jim commercials ("Snap into a Slim Jim!") and his cameo role as Bone Saw McGraw in the movie *Spiderman*.

Yet to a small handful of people, Macho Man Savage was merely a role, a funny-yet-foreign character that defined but a tiny sliver of a person's life. To them, Randy Poffo was not a wrestler; not a pitchman, not an actor, not a comic book character.

He was a ballplayer.

"That was his love," says Barry Cernoch, a high school teammate. "That's what Randy was all about."

Back in the 1960s, Downers Grove, Ill., was the model of suburban bliss. Located 30 miles west of Chicago, the village served as the perfect outpost for commuters who worked in the Windy City, but didn't desire to live there. It boasted a high-achieving school district, shops and restaurants and a nonexistent crime rate. In other words, it was the ideal place for Angelo and Judy Poffo to start a family. In particular, Angelo—who was born and raised in Downers Grove—loved the low-key simplicity of things. By night, he was "the Masked Miser" and "the Carpet Bagger," a loathed villain of professional wrestling whose infamous Italian Neckbreaker move shut down opponents. By day, however, he was merely a (albeit large) suburban dad, a proud graduate of DePaul University who stressed academics above all else.

Randy was born on Nov. 15, 1952, and before long he was walking, talking and breathing all things baseball. Though his preferred team was the Cubs, his two favorite players were Cincinnati's Pete Rose (for the hustle) and Johnny Bench (for his status as the game's elite catcher). In 1962, when her oldest son was 10, Judy Poffo signed Randy up for Downers Grove Little League. He was assigned to a team called, oddly, the Moose, which was sponsored by a local VFW lodge. From the very first day, he was a catcher.

"What was immediately noteworthy was that Randy threw the ball back to the pitcher with more velocity than the pitcher pitched the ball to Randy," says Guarnaccia, his childhood friend. "He was definitely the best player in town for his age. There was no doubt about it."

In order to help Randy (and, later, Lanny) develop, his parents built a winterized batting cage (with a pitching machine) beside the house. A one-time catcher at DePaul, Angelo filled Randy's mind with strategies and ideas: how to call a game, how to block the plate, how to see the field, how to emulate players like Bench and Randy Hundley.

Following his sophomore year at Downers Grove High, Randy was shocked to learn that his parents were planning on uprooting the family for 11 months to Hawaii. Angelo had a lucrative opportunity to wrestle on the big island, as well as in Japan, and he also saw it as a chance for his kids to focus solely on baseball. So in 1968–69, the Poffos lived in a small apartment on Kanekapolei Street in Honolulu, and the boys—to their delight—simply missed a year of school. "We were home schooled, where we had to write reports for my mother," says Lanny. "But it was nothing formal."

During the time away, Randy and Lanny played baseball nonstop. There were never-ending games of catch, followed by more never-ending games of catch. Though only 16 at the time, Randy made his semipro debut, starting at catcher for the Gouvea's Sausage Phillies. One of his teammates was John Matias, who, two years later, would play outfield for the White Sox. "That time in Hawaii made Randy a different level player," says Lanny. "It helped us both develop in big ways."

The Poffos returned to Illinois, and Randy spent his final two seasons starring for one of the state's better prep teams. But when the 1971 draft came and went, his heart sank. Sure, he could probably follow his father into the family business. But the goal wasn't to become a professional wrestler. It was to play ball.

Which is why, the day after the Los Angeles Dodgers used the 794th and final pick to take Don Stackpole, a (what else?) catcher from Wildomar, Calif., Angelo Poffo forced his son into the car and drove 283 miles to St. Louis, where the Cardinals were holding a two-day open-call tryout camp. In his first at-bat during hitting drills, Randy laced a line drive into the right-center gap that bounced over the wall for a ground-rule double. When the session ended, he was brought into the executive offices and offered a $500-per-month contract and an invitation to join the organization's rookie league club in Tampa. Of the approximately 300 players in attendance, he was the only one to catch the franchise's eye. "No bonus whatsoever," says Lanny. "Randy signed the same day as Keith Hernandez. He was elated. It wasn't about the money. It was so much bigger than that."

"You know what's funny about Randy?" says Jim Walthour. "He was quiet. You wouldn't think that from someone who went on to wrestle like he did. But he really was. A quiet, nice young man."

Walthour is on the other end of the phone. Randy Poffo has been dead for less than 48 hours, and the memories—inspired by sadness and nostalgia—come flowing. Long ago, in the blissful summer of '71, the two ballplayers shared a dingy hotel room off Tamiami Trail in Sarasota, Fla. They were mere boys at the time—Randy not yet 19, Jim just north of 20—assigned to the Cardinals' Gulf Coast League team. "We actually signed our contracts at Busch Stadium on the same day," says Walthour, who batted .205 that first season and was out of the game within two years. "Randy was a great guy. A really hard worker, and a kid with a lot of pride."

Unlike the major leagues, where special athletes rule the landscape, rookie ball is a place where baseball players come in all shapes, sizes and skill levels. It's the spot where organizations first figure out which guys can play, which guys might be able to play and couldn't. A whopping 46 men suited up for the GCL Cards in 1971, and only six reached the major leagues. Of those, only three—outfielders Jerry Mumphrey, Mike Vail and Larry Herndon—had lengthy careers.

The take on Poffo was mixed. In 35 games, he batted .286 (best for any regular), with a team-high two home runs (the ballparks were enormous) and a .492 slugging percentage. He worked his rear off, usually staying late after workouts and games to run the outfield and practice throwing down to second. He also possessed unusually strong forearms—not overly muscular, but thick and tight.

"He used to do, like, 1,500 sit-ups every morning," says Jethro Mills, a pitcher with the team. "That says something." (Angelo Poffo actually held the world record for sit-ups, once completing 6,033 in four hours and 10 minutes). Yet Poffo was also as slow as mud, and his swing—while dynamic when he made contact—was long and twitchy. "He was average in a lot of areas," says Mike Moore, who served as a longtime minor league general manager in the 1970s and later became the president of Minor League Baseball. "Didn't run fast, average bat, average defensively. But a super individual."

Because the days of summer baseball are long and the minds of young players are often devilish, the intense Poffo proved a great mark. Teammates loved the kid, but also laughed at his never-say-die approach to everything. Though he was anything but obnoxiously competitive, Poffo found motivation in proving others wrong. If someone said he couldn't throw a baseball from the outfield to home on one hop, he did it. If someone said he couldn't hit the tree behind the leftfield wall, he did it, too. Hence, one day, while Poffo sat alone in the clubhouse, a gaggle of Cardinals spoke loudly of the atomic sit-up, and how nobody—absolutely nobody—could successfully unleash one.

"What's the atomic sit-up?" Poffo asked.

"What," replied a teammate, "you think you can do it?"

"Hell," he said, "if it's a sit-up, I sure can."

Poffo was told to get on the floor in sit-up position. One teammate would line up behind him, place a towel over Poffo's eyes and try and hold his arms down. "And Randy had to break free and do a sit-up," says Mills, laughing. "So it was up to him to fight and fight and put up a full effort." Someone shouted Go!, and Poffo—eyes covered—struggled forward, trying to sit up. "While this is happening, another guy pulls down his pants and stands in front of Randy, his ass hanging in front of Randy's face. Randy's fighting, fighting, fighting, and suddenly the guy holding his arms just let's go."

With that, the future WWF heavyweight champion found his face in another man's anus.

"Maybe the funniest thing I saw all year," says Mills. "But Randy could laugh about it. He was a good sport."

Despite a productive rookie run, Poffo wasn't promoted. He returned to Sarasota for the 1972 season and continued his path as a marginal prospect with good pop but only so-so potential. Though his three home runs (in 52 games) led the team, there was nothing about his game—save for his throwing arm—that suggested he possessed genuine major league talent.

He did, however, possess genuine major league smarts.

As highly touted teammates like Mumphrey and Vail made comfortable salaries, Poffo battled to survive on $500 a month. Yet while he lacked the natural baseball ability to make it big, his ability in another area came in handy. "You wouldn't believe how much money Randy made in the minors from playing cards," says Lanny. "He'd make sure to play with all the bonus babies, and he'd take them to the cleaners. Was he the best baseball player? No. But he had a brain like a razor blade—very sharp. I always said, Randy belonged on ESPN with the poker players."

Once again, Poffo began 1973 in the Gulf Coast League. But then, just when he appeared to be on his way out, something amazing happened: His bat came alive. Poffo batted .344 in 25 games, and midway through the season was euphoric when the organization promoted him to Class A Orangeburg of the Western Carolinas League.

He was assigned to room with a young outfielder named Tito Landrum, who would go on to play nine major league seasons. "Every time we saw each other, we'd always in front of friends, make a big deal about who owed who for the last month's rent," Landrum recently told the *Baseball History Examiner*. "To be honest with you, right down to this day I couldn't tell you if I owed the last month's rent or he owed the last month's rent."

If professional baseball was the dream, Orangeburg, S.C., proved nightmarish. The Cardinals played in dilapidated Mirmow Field, often swimming through cheesecake-thick layers of humidity. The surface was a rock-and-mud salad, the stands were 70 percent empty; the team finished 50–72. Plus, the ball club was managed by Jimmy Piersall, the one-time Red Sox slugger whose mental stability was often in question. "Man, was he ever crazy," says Bill Lorillard, a lefthanded reliever with the team. "On Opening Day in Orangeburg that season, he was standing on the third base side and the umpire was brushing off the plate. Jimmy slid down the line and took out the umpire for no apparent reason."

Poffo had started in the Gulf Coast League, but upon being promoted he found himself either on the bench or spelling others at catcher or first. He hit .250 in 116 at-bats, and showed little. A highlight came late in the season when Guarnaccia, a fourth-round draft pick of the Phillies now playing for Spartanburg, stepped up to the plate while Poffo was catching. The two smiled at each other—a couple of kids from suburban Illinois, reunited in a gnat-infested minor league stadium. "When I got up there Randy looked at me and said, 'I'll tell you what pitches are coming.' And he did," Guarnaccia says. "That was just loyalty to a friend. Nothing more."

Poffo's season concluded shortly thereafter, when he separated his right shoulder in a home plate collision. At season's end, the Cardinals released him.

"That was hard for Randy," says Lanny. "I don't think he took it well, because he saw it as perhaps the end of the road."

There was one last chance. With a vacant spot on their Class A Florida State League club, the Cincinnati Reds signed Poffo and assigned him to the Tampa Tarpons. Though he batted only .232, he paced the team with 131 games, 461 at-bats, nine home runs and 66 RBIs. "Honestly, he didn't have the talent to go any farther," says Moore, who was the Tarpons' general manager. "He just didn't. But I'll never forget this—one day [manager] Russ Nixon and I got to the stadium at 1 in the afternoon, and I peeked out onto the field and saw these baseballs flying across the diamond. It was Randy, all alone, with a bucket of balls, standing in center and throwing them one by one to home plate, all with his left hand. I said, 'Randy, what are you doing?' He looked at me and said, 'Trying to make myself more valuable.' He was that type of guy."

With the season and, as it turned out, his baseball career coming to a completion, Poffo seemed resigned to the fact that he'd never crouch behind the plate at Busch Stadium and hear the roar of the crowd as a Bob Gibson fastball slammed into his glove. It just wasn't realistic, and no matter how hard he worked it was never quite enough.

There was, however, a neon sign of things to come. Midway through a game against the Winter Haven Red Sox, Poffo was preparing to bat when

Rac Slider, the opposing manager, signaled for a pitching change. As the opposing lefthander warmed up, Poffo walked up to the plate and timed the pitches. "So the pitcher just rears back and drills Randy in the helmet," says Don Werner, a Tampa catcher. "Randy charged the mound and started fighting the guy. We were all wondering what in the world he was doing."

Little did anyone know, Randy Poffo's baseball career was days away from completion.

Little did anyone know, Randy (Macho Man) Savage's wrestling career had just begun.

JULY 19, 2018

Tamed Fury

A boiling intensity fueled Kirk Gibson on the field, and in his
prime it often sparked loathsome behavior. With help, he is
now a changed man, even as his body faces a new challenge

BY S.L. PRICE

The first time I saw Kirk Gibson in the flesh, he was rampaging toward me,
near-naked and jeering; the second time, he limped to the plate and hit
one of the most dramatic home runs in history. One moment was heinous,
the other heroic. In each he seemed unbound by humanity's usual norms
and limits, bigger than life, incomprehensible. Both events occurred three
decades ago. Now it was a late-March morning in 2018, and as I approached
a dugout, I recognized the broad back of Gibson, sitting alone.

This was at a practice field in the Detroit Tigers' spring training
complex in Lakeland, Fla. A coach throwing batting practice grunted, an
equipment cart clattered: Gibson waited for his youngest son to take his
cuts. A passing staffer, startled by the famous face staring out at the field,
stopped long enough to venture a polite, "How you doin'?"

"Oh," Gibson said warmly, arms opening wide, "just listening to the
sounds of baseball."

That was my first direct proof that, maybe, the man's jagged edges had
worn smooth. *The sounds of baseball?* In his prime with the Tigers and the
Dodgers, in the 1980s, Gibson was hardly your *Let's play two!* romantic; his
vibe was about as pastoral as a punch in the face. He smashed titanic home
runs. He ran the bases like a mustang. Shrewd, profane, honest and cruel,
he leveled any opponent, umpire, teammate or, yes, manager fool enough

to get in his way. Tigers catcher Lance Parrish once described Gibson in the clubhouse as "a caged animal." Detroit owner Tom Monaghan, miffed by Gibson's unkempt Viking look, bid his one-time ALCS MVP good riddance in '88 by declaring him "a disgrace to the Tiger uniform."

In other words, you couldn't take your eyes off Kirk Gibson. In other words, they increasingly miss his like in Motown and in L.A.—where, snarling at the steepest of odds, he delivered the signature blow in each city's last triumphant World Series run. Yes, three decades have passed; nothing remains the same. Why should he? I had heard about Gibson's calmer demeanor first as a coach with the Diamondbacks and then as their manager, about his 2015 diagnosis of Parkinson's disease and the endearing way he calls his new opponent Parky. I'd read sympathetic takes on his ongoing—though reduced—performance as a color analyst on TV, seen the startlingly sweet graduation speech he gave at Michigan State in May 2017, weeks before turning 60.

"Remain humble, and always treat others with kindness and respect," a berobed Gibson advised the crowd at his alma mater. "A harsh comment can hurt another person, but a kind word can produce amazing things."

Amazing, all right. To hear Mr. Rogers pieties trip from the mouth that once dumped f-bomb abuse on reporters and autograph seekers won't ever lose its novelty, but the world has taken note of Gibson's olive branch and returned it in kind. He got an honorary doctorate and cheers on that East Lansing stage and, after a 39-year wait, was inducted last December into the College Football Hall of Fame. If not the metamorphosis of his fellow 1980s celebs—Trump? Schwarzenegger?—it's a second act unmatched by the rest of that era's baseball churls.

Part of this recalibration, of course, stems from the $13.5 million that Gibson has raised for Michigan State and the more than $2 million for Parkinson's research. Part arises from the sympathy sparked anytime someone struggles publicly with a disease. But part also lies in what the disease has done to him specifically: Parky, an incurable, progressive brain disorder that attacks motor function, has made Kirk Gibson *smaller*.

I noticed this instantly in Tigertown. Left arm wedged close to his side, head slightly ducked, Gibson now takes up less space than a 6'3", 220-pound alpha male ever should. I saw it more clearly a few weeks later, when he appeared at Dodger Stadium on Opening Day for a 30th-anniversary celebration of his epic World Series home run. The waiting media didn't know what to expect; one radio hand recounted being scorched by a Gibson tirade in 1989. "If you had a microphone," Gibson's onetime fellow Dodgers employee said, "*you* were a jerk, and out to get him."

Then Gibson walked in, slowly, and sat. He wore a comfy gray cardigan and took all questions, face displaying a Parkinson's-induced blankness, voice higher and flattened, also related to Parkinson's. He joked, detailed yet again the torn left hamstring and sprained right knee of 1988 and the events leading to A's closer Dennis Eckersley's infamous backdoor slider, praised teammates, appreciated fans. After 15 minutes came a pause for water, the room silent as Gibson brought the bottle to his mouth, shaking.

Later, before 53,595 fans, Gibson dutifully reenacted his '88 triumph—the halting walk to the bat rack, the practice swings—but this time there was no Eckersley and it wasn't nighttime; he looked pale in the afternoon sun. The crowd stood as one, saluting him with the same double fist pump that Gibson had unleashed rounding second to end Game One. After lofting a ceremonial first pitch, he answered with two last labored pumps, relieved that it was done.

The next day Gibson went back to Chavez Ravine, warier but still game; the weekend figured to raise $200,000 for Parkinson's. (The Kirk Gibson Foundation is dedicated to fighting the disease.) So he held court in a luxury box and told the stories, weathered the smiling faces and found himself reduced further. That night, the first 40,000 fans received a 30th-anniversary Gibson bobblehead, seven inches tall with fist held high—the most tangible signifier yet of his new, softer image. You might even call it cute.

The winning home run? All that love pouring from the stands? That's the kid's dream of sports. No one envisions the drudgery—17 years of games, 10,000 dirty hours of practice, the aching legs, long bus rides and late flights—that go into forging a revered place in baseball history. Or that all the hard work would lead, on a dull March Saturday, to a half-empty mall in California's San Gabriel Valley.

But here is Gibson now, on glory's flip side. No grass, no scoreboard: just the windowless confines of what was once a Kay Jewelers, and a charge to sign all manner of baseball paraphernalia until his hand gives out. He sits at a table with his 31-year-old son, Kirk Robert, hovering, surrounded by reminders of his younger self: armies of Kirk Gibson bobbleheads (standard and special edition gold), piles of pictures and cards and gloves and batting helmets and jerseys, stacks of programs and balls and bats. Even some bottles of Cabernet.

Earlier, a crowd of 450 had surged into a nearby storefront to pay for a glimpse, a handshake, a signature. Former Dodgers manager Tommy Lasorda and ace Orel Hershiser were also there, but, says memorabilia dealer Jim Honabach, Gibson was the main draw. "The home run," he says.

"Biggest sports moment in L.A. history." And in such brevity lies the key to Gibson's unique place in the baseball firmament. He never once finished a full season above .300, never mind with 30 home runs or 100 RBIs or 40 stolen bases; the lone time he won a league MVP award, in '88, he batted .290 with 25 homers.

No, Gibson's appeal always centered on clutch at bats, fearsome competitiveness, maximum testosterone. In 1983, the same day he hit a ball 540 feet out of Tiger Stadium and into a lumberyard, Gibson lashed a drive to deep centerfield, all but caught teammate Lou Whitaker racing home and then sent Whitaker, the catcher, the umpire and the five spare baseballs in the ump's pocket sprawling. Whitaker was tagged out, Gibson scored. In '85 he took a fastball to the jaw that would require a hospital run and 17 stitches; Gibson angrily, bloodily, waved off the trainer and took first base, demanded to play the next day and clubbed a homer in his first at bat.

"A man's man," says former Tigers teammate Alan Trammell. "I've never met anybody like him."

Indeed, Gibson's fierceness created its own category—"That's just Gibby"—with leeway and expectations unfamiliar to most. Maybe other pro athletes have flown themselves to home games, but who else has been excused from spring training to break (at 25,200 feet) a Cessna altitude record? Who else but Gibson—then 55—would turn a late-night trade talk at the 2012 winter meetings into a WWE tussle by head-butting and pinning Rangers general manager Jon Daniels to the ground? Who but Gibby—just to show Parky that he won't go gently—would grind himself to exhaustion on a five-day, 800-mile snowmobiling trek in January across northern Michigan?

"I was lying on the floor bawling, and just kept repeating, 'He's always been Superman,'" says Tigers minor leaguer leftfielder Cameron Gibson, 24, Kirk's youngest son, of the day he learned of his father's illness. "He's not supposed to be hurt. It's impossible."

Putting a price on such mystique isn't easy; that doesn't mean you can't try. This morning's base rate was $99 per signed item, $49 more for personalization. After scratching away for hours, Gibson suddenly raises his head and calls out, "Look." I walk over. "This is one of my favorite photos," he says. "From your magazine."

The shot is from the July 17, 1995, issue, during his last season: A 38-year-old Gibson, back with the Tigers, in a collision at home plate, bulldozing Royals catcher Pat Borders. Two days before, Borders had not blocked the plate on a similar play and, Gibson says, before his next at bat admitted to Gibson that he'd lost sleep over it. "Because," Kirk Robert chimes in, "he had wimped out."

Reliving all this, his dad's eyes gleam with that old mean delight. You can feel it as Gibson describes the next time he charged home: how both men knew what was coming, how Borders planted and Gibson unleashed his favorite football trick, learned at MSU, the Flipper, driving his right forearm into the catcher's neck. Borders crumpled. (Borders, now managing at Class A Williamsport, didn't respond to requests for comment.) "How're you going to hold on to the ball when a truck runs over you?" Gibson crows. He points to the photo's key reveal—the clinical way he's going for Borders's throat.

"Eyes on the target," Gibson says.

Just as Dad taught him. Kirk grew up the son of public school teachers, Bob and Barb, in Waterford, an hour northwest of Detroit, with two protective older sisters. It's puzzling, at first, when an athlete from bland circumstance competes as if sprung from hell; his parents saw Kirk's restless intensity early and thought it innate. Still, tinder needs a spark. And before the teaching career and an earlier stint auditing taxes for the state, before serving on the USS *Missouri* in World War II, Bob was strong, fast, poor—and sure that the Depression had stolen his chance to play organized sports. He channeled his remaining ambition into his only son.

"He was real hard on me, very structured," Kirk says. "Lunchtime in elementary school he made me run home, maybe a mile, had lunch ready, and we'd eat fast so we could practice before I ran back. If it was football, we'd be out in the backyard and he'd teach me how to carry it. *Catch the ball! Catch it with your fingertips!* Basketball, I'd be out shoveling the snow so we could go out and shoot."

"He used to hate that, because Kirk wanted to play," Barb says. "But, no, it was, 'You get out there, and do that.'"

Kirk's lone rebellion was the stray fastball he'd fire at his dad's shins in junior high, but Bob liked that. Raw aggression and speed would carry his son until his athletic skills jelled as a Waterford Kettering High senior, enough to earn a football scholarship from the only big school that came calling. And Kirk hit the ground sprinting at Michigan State in 1975, alienating seniors by turning practice jogs into races of humiliation, shuddering the Spartans' toughest defender with a crackback block, earning the starting flanker spot as a freshman.

Fourth game that year, the Spartans went to South Bend and beat Notre Dame 10–3; Gibson contributed only a message. Lined up opposite All-America cornerback Luther Bradley, he broke and never stopped. "Bradley starts backing up," says teammate Mark Tapling. "Gibby speeds up and Bradley's still backing up, and it was like, 'Holy smokes, he's not stopping!'"

Ran right over the top of him, making his point: *Here's how it's going to be today.*"

Even then it was clear: He reveled in his mastery, especially one-on-one. That's why football was Gibson's true calling; unlike most people—and certainly most baseball players—he took elemental pleasure in physical menace, in breaking a man's will by making him hurt. The fact that such ferocity came in an imposing package with soft hands and—as clocked by the Patriots in his senior year—4.2 speed made Gibson an outlier. "So big and strong, so fast, and his strides were so long that he tore up the ground: CARRRGGGH! CARRRGGGH!," says Trammell, hands clawing air. "Literally, you could *hear* him running."

"Gibby would sweep into a room, O.K.?" Tapling says. "He was big, had a big stride, long and purposeful. He never sauntered. And that creates a force field."

His aura grew during junior year, when Gibson took up baseball for the first time since high school. The initial plan was to skip spring football and maybe gain leverage in negotiations with NFL teams. Then he batted .390 with 16 homers and 21 stolen bases. The Tigers drafted him with the 12th pick of the 1978 June draft (the NFL Cardinals drafted him in the seventh round a year later), and he spent that summer with Class A Lakeland, keelhauled daily by manager Jim Leyland. "I don't give a f--- if you're an All-American football player!" Leyland boomed in the car from the airport. "You want to drink all night and chase women? Go ahead. But you'll be on that field with me every day at 8:30 a.m. until I send you to the big leagues. Understand?"

Gibson's response? "I said, 'Bring it on, *bitch*,'" he recalls. "My mentality was really crazy at that time."

Crazy had its upside. Leyland tutored him mercilessly for six hours every day—outfield, baserunning and throwing drills, cuts in the batting cage—and then, at 2:30 p.m., began the team's prep for that night's game. Gibson only thrived. During one steamy BP in their second summer, Leyland finally barked, "That's enough," but Gibson shook him off. "I had this big incinerator full of baseballs and fed him every one," Leyland says. "He's the only guy that could hit the whole incinerator—and still take more."

The downside? Gibson got kicked out of his last college football game for fighting the entire Iowa Hawkeyes bench in East Lansing, and he had no clue how to reset his motor for baseball's daily grind. Three days after he was called up to Detroit in the fall of 1979, Gibson demanded to pinch-hit against Yankees flamethrower Goose Gossage ("I want him!") and struck out flailing on three pitches. When pitcher Jack Billingham began hazing him the next spring, Gibson sent him flying through the training room doors, leaped on his chest and vowed to kill him. "Go ahead!" Gibson screamed. "Say one more word!"

Manager Sparky Anderson didn't help matters by dubbing Gibson the next Mickey Mantle; for every booming homer and stolen base, there was a weak throw from rightfield, a fly ball bouncing off his head or some new injury. At best a Gibson at bat resembled a man hacking through a jungle: He hit under .200 in May, July and August in 1983, looked lost on the field and off, batted .227 for the season and was booed regularly. He boasted of slapping an abusive fan in a Detroit bar. Anderson busted Gibson down to part-time, skittering just out of reach when Gibson lunged at him. But Sparky couldn't run forever.

One afternoon in Seattle, with Gibson sprinting in the outfield, the 49-year-old Anderson lined up like a cornerback and challenged him to run a route. The manager apparently hadn't seen what happened to Luther Bradley. "Ran his ass over," Trammell says.

"It hurt him: He was an old man," Gibson says. "He got up and had tears in his eyes, hat was off, hair was all f----- up. He's like, 'You sonuvabitch! You're crazy!' I said, 'Get your f------ ass out of here because I'll do it again.' I just couldn't contain it."

Gibson isn't speaking only about competition. He approached too many interactions—especially once the failures began to mount—with a nasty edge. His parents' breakup in the early 1980s couldn't have helped matters, but Gibson remained close to both; he's certain that his problem rose from within. "I enjoyed dominating people," he says. "When I played football? You dominated, you hurt people and you didn't care. I couldn't separate that off the field."

By 1984, Gibson had begun trying to do just that—but the process would take years. I knew nothing about it then. All I could see from afar, with *SportsCenter* in its infancy and the Internet a dream, was that the Tigers had catapulted to one of the greatest starts ever and that Gibson, en route to 91 RBIs, 27 homers and 29 stolen bases, was realizing his promise. Me, too: I began the season waiting tables—fresh out of college, baseball besotted—and it seemed wondrous when, come summer, I landed a newspaper gig covering weekend games in the Bay Area. Getting to glimpse the first-place Tigers in early September felt like a gift.

It was a Sunday, late afternoon. Detroit had won 6–3, and after interviewing the A's, I wanted a close-up look at everybody's pick to win the Series. I pushed open the door to the visitors' clubhouse. A young woman, interning with *The Detroit News* and soon to return to college, hurtled by, in tears. I looked up, and here came Gibson on the chase: bare-chested with a hand on his crotch, gleefully shouting the woman's name and the words, "You want to f--- me."

In the years since, covering athletes at all levels, I've never seen an act more vile.

What happened next? A more obvious question today. If what Kirk Gibson did that Sunday in Oakland happened in this age of cellphone cameras, social media and #MeToo, his season—if not career—would be over by the time the team landed the next day in Detroit.

But then? Nothing happened next. Like every other reporter present, I wrote nothing about it. The young woman herself never reported it, and she has turned down every request to discuss it publicly (and requested that SI not use her name now). I heard that she received private apologies from a couple of players, the private support of scribes near and far. The incident became a staple of Detroit media lore, and her own paper reported it—with one witness describing it as "the most vulgar personal attack imaginable"— but only six years later, and buried deep in a piece on the increasingly volatile relations between the press and pro athletes.

Not that Gibson's bullying wasn't considered, at the time, odious. It just seemed typical then, especially in baseball. Yes, some courteous players occupied every clubhouse. But I didn't even cover the beat full-time, and within three years of witnessing Gibson's abusive behavior, Reds pitcher John Denny went after my best friend, the *Cincinnati Post*'s Bruce Schoenfeld (Denny was assigned to six months in a rehab program, and charges were erased); A's slugger Dave Kingman sent my *Sacramento Bee* colleague, Susan Fornoff, a live rat in the Oakland press box; and Jim Rice of the Red Sox tore up the shirt of another close friend of mine, Steve Fainaru of *The Boston Globe*, in a clubhouse scuffle.

Some of this was due to personal grudge or the impulse to protect imagined turf. Some was by design. "We'd lose six or eight in a row, and Sparky would say to me, 'The boys are a little tight, why don't you take a little pressure off 'em? Pick out a media member,'" Gibson says today. "[Detroit beat writer] Brian Bragg came in one day between games of a doubleheader, and he'd written something about Lance Parrish—and it wasn't bad. But I made the biggest scene: 'Don't you come by my f------ locker!' I was way out of line. You know what, though? The team started winning ball games."

One reason the intern didn't report her clash with Gibson is because, she told *The Detroit News* in 1990, the abuse heaped on women reporters seemed no worse—just different—than what her male colleagues endured. Perhaps. But in the '80s women in clubhouses were grossly outnumbered and subjected to sexually tinged verbiage. Jockstraps were tossed.

Players thrust their hips back and forth. Any chance to embarrass female journalists was seized upon.

"Every time I went into a clubhouse, my stomach was in knots because I didn't know what I would face," says Lisa Nehus Saxon, who covered the Angels and the Dodgers from 1979 to 2000 for various papers and now teaches media at Santa Monica College.

But one team was particularly brutal. "The Detroit Tigers, without a doubt," pioneering Toronto scribe Alison Gordon told a Michigan newspaper, in 1982, when asked to name baseball's worst clubhouse. "They're babies... the last time I went into their locker room for a post-game interview, one of the players shouted out, 'Look out! Here comes the old whore!'"

Indeed, even with stand-up presences like Trammell, Parrish, Dan Petry and hitting coach Gates Brown, the Tigers seemed particularly vexed by the incursion of women reporters into the clubhouse. The staff ace, Jack Morris, later gained infamy for telling the *Detroit Free Press*'s Jennifer Frey, "I don't talk to people, especially women, unless they're on top of me or I'm on top of them."

And the front office didn't seem to care. General manager Bill Lajoie, who died in 2010, was given to playing down Gibson's off-field behavior so long as the outfielder remained a galvanizing force. Three weeks after the display in Oakland, Gibson mooned one woman during a pennant-clinching celebration in the clubhouse and, as *Free Press* columnist Mike Downey wrote then, joined pitcher Dave Rozema, Gibson's future brother-in-law, "to make a sandwich out of another one."

"Rude, crude and misogynistic," Downey says of Gibson in those days. "He would say and do things, particularly about and toward women, that were unimaginably awful. One time [first baseman] Darrell Evans turned to me—quietly, because he didn't want to cause trouble—and said, 'Class act, Kirk.' Several teammates found his behavior appalling but didn't want to disrupt team harmony by calling him out. Because that was a magical season in Detroit."

It was, but I had lost interest. Which is to say, I was young and brimming with self-righteousness, figured Gibson a cancer and baseball an accelerant, and found myself backing away from the sport just as his apotheosis arrived. After batting .417 against the Royals in the 1984 AL Championship Series, he single-handedly dismantled the Padres in Game 5 of the World Series: crunching a first-inning homer into the upper deck of Tiger Stadium; impulsively tagging up on an infield pop-up to score in the fifth; exacting storybook revenge upon his first and best tormentor, Goose Gossage.

That came in the eighth inning, Tigers leading by one. With first base open, Gossage refused the intentional walk; in his career he had faced Gibson 11 times and fanned him in seven of them. Standing at the plate, Gibson turned and bet Anderson $10 that his time had come. The three-run homer he lashed was framed nationwide as pure baseball payback; few were aware that it was also the most dramatic reinforcement of a new mindset.

Ten months earlier, embarrassed by his anemic performance in 1983 and poised to quit, disgusted by his negativity and scared by deteriorating relations with family, team and the public, Gibson phoned his agent, Doug Baldwin. "I can't handle this anymore," he recalled in his autobiography, *Bottom of the Ninth*. "I've got to get some help." Baldwin recommended Seattle's Pacific Institute, a self-styled high-performance clinic for strivers in politics, business and sports. Gibson flew there and over four days worked on adjusting his attitude through "a common-sense approach to becoming a better human being," says Frank Bartenetti, the staffer who took Gibson in hand. How? "Let me see if I can say this right: I'm a genius."

In their talks, Bartenetti urged Gibson to wield his mind as a tool, envisioning success, drawing on previous victories to bolster confidence. Gibson spent the entire 1984 season layering all that onto his game and took his spectacular turnaround as the clearest result. He returned to the institute that offseason—this time with his mother—and checked in often with Bartenetti by phone. Soon, subjects were expanding beyond the field.

For example, at 27, Gibson had to re-learn how to be nice. It was a homework assignment. Next time you're in a grocery store, Bartenetti told him, ask the cashier how she is; tell her to have a great day today and an even better tomorrow. Gibson's first attempt was nerve-racking.

"I'm standing there in the line, my grumpy-ass self, and thinking, *God-dang, I got to do it*," he says. "It was *that* hard for me."

But Gibson survived, and Bartenetti's wider lessons began to take. "Things don't just blow by me; I always analyze them," Gibson says. "I started to appreciate. At some point you realize that it gets lonely. You're going to be lonely if you keep going on that way, if you keep dominating people away."

Gibson became a family man in 1985, marrying longtime girlfriend JoAnn Sklarski and helping raise her eight-year-old daughter, Colleen; the next year Kirk Robert was born. Former drinking buddies speak in awe, still, about Gibson's transformation to devoted husband and dad, but the public heard something even more stunning. Alone among his contemporaries, unlike, say, Kingman and Denny and Rice, Gibson began dissecting his flaws. Always capable of being insightful and self-aware—with those willing to navigate his moods—Gibson repeatedly termed his younger self "a self-centered, egotistical jerk." Over the ensuing years he conceded "personality defects" (or, as he says now, "a social disorder"), and when it came to Monaghan's comment, he said, "Let's be honest: I was a jerk. He was half right. I wasn't a disgrace to the uniform, but I was crazy."

His progress had limits. Even Bartenetti, who loves Gibson like a son, calls him a "bad listener"; he never fully shed his prickliness, and those who irked Gibson during his first stint as a Tigers TV analyst, from 1998 to 2002, may still be shellshocked by his thunderingly profane responses. "Gibby's complicated, but I'm definitely in that camp defending him to the hilt," says Mets play-by-play man Josh Lewin, who paired with Gibson in the booth. "He's not the best. He's not perfect. He's a very kindhearted guy who's tortured in ways that we'll never understand. I don't know what makes this guy tick. No one seems to know. But he's fiercely loyal to the people he decides to give a s--- about."

And many reporters of that era say that when Gibson arrived in L.A. in 1988, his harassment of women journalists had all but ceased. "He never said anything crude to me that he wouldn't have said to a man," says Nehus Saxon. "By the time he got out here, he was much tamer."

"He clearly began to mellow," says Downey, who joined the *Los Angeles Times* in 1985. "He wasn't pulling that stuff anymore, as far as I know. He was cocky and couldn't quite get rid of that, but his teammates loved his competitiveness. I believe he had definitely matured."

As far as I knew, Gibson never spoke publicly about lewdly running that *Detroit News* writer out of the clubhouse; he never addressed the matter with her. But when I mentioned, in Lakeland, that I had seen him at his worst, in Oakland in 1984, he cut in: "Chick was there? A chick?" Then Gibson instantly recalled the intern's name, called her "a great person." Neither she nor he would say what led to the harassment, but Gibson said, "It was a weird time in the locker room, would you agree with that? We're so far down the line from that. She probably doesn't like me. I feel bad about that. Being reflective, it was wrong. That was wrong. I could've handled it better."

He went on to say that having been raised by a loving mom and two strong sisters, he is "very respectful of women." He calls himself a strong proponent of Title IX and points to his 22-year history of raising funds for Michigan State that benefit women's sports. "I try to undo things," Gibson says. "I'm certainly not a guy who says, 'I'm never going to apologize.'" Some believe that his Parkinson's has fostered, as Tapling says, "a kinder, gentler Gibby." Gibson doesn't think it's that simple.

"I hope so, but when I was a jerk, I did a lot of good things, too," he says. "I don't care what anybody says: In my heart there's always been a good person, but just as I did some good things in baseball, I did some bad things, too. As a person, I try to get better every day.

"Does it still happen? I try not to engage in a negative way, but it does. You've had negative engagements in the last week; you might be in your car, and one day feel like flipping a guy off and the next you might say, 'Hey, man, sorry.' It's not just me. All the s--- we've been talking about? I'm just like everybody else. I'm not a freak, O.K.? To be fair, you can examine me all you want about my negative traits. We've all got that to deal with. I want to be the best person I can be. I hope that I can help people."

Revisiting old public figures is a journalism chestnut. SI has its "Where Are They Now?" issue, of course, and I'm one of countless writers who have caught up with some actor, politician or athlete from the past. The obvious theme is change—the fade from the spotlight, the loss of physical or mental skills, the move to a new career—and how the star is navigating it. But in truth we're also taking stock of the personality we remember, seeing how it copes with the real world, all the while wondering (sometimes in hope, sometimes in fear) if anyone truly changes at all.

That question feels even more pointed in the case of Kirk Gibson. With athletic gifts and a headlong style geared for football, his baseball career became marked less by conventional achievement than by a series of private wars—Gibby vs. his body, Gibby vs. fame, Gibby vs. himself—and the victories won by his untamable will.

He's the first to admit: The same impulsivity that led a gimpy Gibson to growl, "My ass!" after hearing Vin Scully announce that he wouldn't be able to pinch-hit during Game 1 of the '88 World Series also led him to assail an intern. No, as a player and a man, Gibson wasn't like you or me. He didn't plan; he was too much id, a puzzle even to himself, and if part of us insists on seeing that repaired—or, as Gibson puts it, "channeled in the proper fashion"—another hopes that the most winning part, at least, survives.

For now, anyway, that seems likely. I first allowed that Gibson might well have evolved after the four hours I spent with him in Florida; after interviewing former teammates, his mother, wife and sons, some 30 people who have loved, respected or loathed him over the years; after hearing how he had ratcheted back his presence, becoming a voice of positivity *and* reason, for 11 years as a coach in Detroit and Arizona; after seeing how he, in 2011, his first full-time season in charge, won the NL West title and Manager of the Year with the Diamondbacks.

Gibson's intensity rekindled during his first years at the helm in Arizona, but it was measured; staff and media in Arizona reported no sign of bad Gibby. Yes, he ordered a pair of old-school, retaliatory beanings during a June 2013 game at Dodger Stadium, touching off two bench-clearing brawls that resulted in suspensions and fines on both sides. But it's notable that during the on-field chaos—with usually placid Dodgers manager Don Mattingly hurling the usually placid Trammell to the ground, and usually placid Dodgers coach Mark McGwire shoving and grabbing a fistful of Gibson's shirt—it was Gibson, of all people, who seemed the most composed.

By then, he was also the most fragile man on the field. Surgeries on his neck and left shoulder had left him stiff, sapped his energy and masked symptoms that turned out to be Parkinson's. In 2014 the bottom fell out. The D-Backs' roster, built in his hard-nosed image, mirrored Gibson's physical decline and went 63–96; Tony La Russa was hired to clean house, and fired general manager Kevin Towers and also Gibson with three games to play. Current team president Derrick Hall says the club retains "enormously positive feelings" for Gibson, not least because he demanded that his team engage daily with fans.

"Some players said, 'Gibby, you *never* would've,'" says Hall. "He said, 'You're exactly right—and I wish I had. The things I missed out on because I was so selfish and angry and upset, you need to do.' And he practiced what he preached—did anything we asked, always signing autographs, taking fan pictures: tremendous. He's one of my favorite guys of all time, and one of my favorite managers I've ever worked with."

I softened a bit more on him in Los Angeles last March, during Gibson's press conference to start the 30th-anniversary tribute. Up popped a softball question about his emotions during that limp around the bases, a chance to brag about his grit. Instead Gibson spoke again of how he had long been "a jerk headed in the wrong direction" and how, just before famously pumping his fist, he said, "I immediately thought about my parents because [my behavior] had hurt them."

Bob, who died in 1999, and Barb, 88, who still lives in Waterford, were there that night, behind home plate.

"I had hurt them," Gibson went on. "And I had told them, 'Don't worry, we'll get it straight, we'll have our day.' So my first thought when I put my arm out, obviously was 'We won the game,' and secondly my parents. I was just past first base. There's a saying: It all evens out—which, we know, it doesn't. But you know what? For a second, I believed that again."

Then, his third day in L.A. for the anniversary, something else happened. It was near the end of the autograph signing at the mall in the

San Gabriel Valley. Earlier, when some ailing faces had come through the line, Gibson told one woman in a wheelchair, "You can't give up, you know!" and I dismissed it as little more than a nicety. But I was chatting with Kirk Robert when a man in his late 40s approached and said, "I'm sorry: You're Kirk's son?"

And he began talking about his mother's dozen years with Parkinson's—the first ones manageable, the last few brutal—and I recalled Gibson's telling me that his symptoms had been misdiagnosed for years, that he had slurred and limped so often during his last years in Arizona, as far back as 2012, that a friend worried that he was having mini-strokes. I recalled Gibson saying how Parkinson's robbed his sleep, made it tough to defecate or punch in a phone number; how he'd been out on Figueroa Street the night before and had to fight to stay balanced while walking on a curb.

And now the man, Art Yoon, was saying that Gibson, earlier, had wanted him to wait so that he could try again to call Yoon's mom, Choon, but fans were still surging in and now Yoon had to leave for work. "Tell him thanks," Yoon said, and he walked away. Two minutes later, I chased him down outside, and told him I was a reporter.

Choon, 77, had also been at Dodger Stadium, with her husband, three decades before, when Gibson homered off Eckersley. She had planned to come today, on a mother-son outing to meet her hero at last, but her Parkinson's flared and she could barely stand. When Gibson heard that, he said, "Let's get her on the phone now," and pulled Art into a back room to try. The call kicked to voice mail.

Art began edging away then, but Gibson urged him to "hang tight." A bit later, while sitting and signing, Gibson searched the room for Art, caught his eye, and pantomimed tapping out a phone number. Art nodded and tried again: voice mail. He shrugged; Gibson nodded. And at a point in their brief exchange Art welled up, nearly lost it entirely from a combination of frustration, sadness, the lost chance to give his mom a surprise lift—and something that took months for him to put into words.

The moment passed. When I caught up with Art again in June, he said that he'd left his mom's number with Kirk Robert, but can't say if Gibson ever got through. Choon can barely cross the room now; there are days when her English is unintelligible; she doesn't know how to retrieve voice mails. But in Gibson's small efforts—the kind of dismissible niceness that once seemed beyond him—her son witnessed an act as indelible for him as some 34-year-old ugliness remains for me.

"He's a legend here in Los Angeles," Art says. "He probably can't walk 10 feet without someone wanting to buy him a drink. Despite that? He heard my mom's story and tried—twice—to talk to a woman who is seriously deteriorated. Though that was a very meaningful moment for her in 1988, I don't know if she'd even know who he is right now, and he took the time anyway. That level of humanity is uncommon, and Kirk isn't the only Dodger, the only celebrity, I've met. That is rare."

Later that evening, Art made it to Choon's house in Irvine for dinner. As they were setting the table, he told her the whole story, beginning with a coy, "Hey, you get a call from Kirk Gibson today?"

"The baseball player?" she asked.

A bit more than that, it seems. After all.

The Many Lives of Slammin' Sammy

Twenty years ago he and Mark McGwire juiced
baseball with their home run chase—and while we
view that era differently now, time has largely healed
baseball's PED wounds. Sammy Sosa, though, has been
mostly absent from the public eye and is persona
non grata at Wrigley Field. Where have you gone,
Slammin' Sammy? Let's start in Dubai...

BY JASON BUCKLAND AND BEN REITER

Inside the cool, hushed second-floor lounge of Dubai's grandest hotel, a waiter carefully prepares a shallow glass of 12-year Macallan. A familiar figure smiles, observing the meticulous way that his drink—nearly $100 for a double portion—is prepared. Three ice cubes, so symmetrical they could have been laser cut, gleam as they're tongued into the scotch without a splash or even a clink.

He leans back, arms wide, into a plush sofa trimmed in blue leather. A crisp blue suit clings to his shoulders and chest, still broad from 500 push-ups each day, even as he's set to turn 50 in November. His golden eyeglasses are stamped MAYBACH across each temple. A monogram peeks from under the left sleeve of his jacket: S.S. He gazes up into the majestic atrium of the 56-story Burj Al Arab Jumeriah, self-billed as "the Most Luxurious Hotel in the World" and famously shaped like a sail swelling above the azure waters of the Persian Gulf. "Now," he says, "you see why it's seven stars."

Twenty summers after he and Mark McGwire chased the ghost of Roger Maris—and saved a sport, as they both contend—this is the life of Sammy Sosa. Or at least the one he wants you to see. His are the curated days of an Instagram influencer, even if Sosa isn't much for social media. "I never watch Facebook, Instagram, some of that B.S. s---," he says. "I don't have time for that."

But those are the places we've glimpsed Sosa since he took his last MLB swing, in 2007. He looks different from the man whose every plate appearance late in the summer of 1998 was a public spectacle as he slugged his way to 66 homers, just behind McGwire's 70. His skin tone is lighter, the source of much confusion, speculation and ugly rubbernecking. (Deadspin: SAMMY SOSA IS A TERRIFYING VAMPIRE.) Sosa professes not to care. "Look at what I am today," he says, motioning a hand toward the opulence around him. "This is my life, and I don't take garbage from nobody. I do whatever I want."

It is, in some ways, his *third* life. In this one he's a devoted husband— he has been married to Sonia, the mother of his six children, for 26 years—and an international man of commerce. Although he won't provide many verifiable details, he says he has interests in his home country, the Dominican Republic (oil); as well as in Panama (stormproof housing); the U.K. (beverages and hospitality); and the United Arab Emirates (real estate).

He officially established residency in the UAE a few years ago, for business reasons but also for pleasure, which explains his twice-yearly trips to Dubai from his homes in Miami and Santo Domingo. Here, Sosa rubs elbows with the elite, laughing and cajoling his way through a chance encounter with two well-appointed Dominican businessmen, catching up with them in rapid Spanish outside an upscale restaurant and commemorating the occasion with a photo. Sosa says he knows the men from home, from years ago. "How about that?" he shrugs, grinning wide.

This is all a long way from his *first* life, which he spent sleeping on the dirt floor of his family's two-room house in San Pedro de Macorís, where he'd shine shoes in the park for a quarter. He attended school through seventh grade and didn't play baseball until he was 14. "When I made my first contact, I hit the ball very hard," he says. "My friend told my brother, 'We have a chance.'"

That led to his *second* life—the public one and, for many people, the one that continues to be problematic. When Sosa was 20, after his first season in the majors, he brought $40,000 in cash back to the D.R. and laid it out on a bed so his family could take turns jumping into the lush pile of green. Nearly a decade later the guy who as a rookie hit four home runs and was described in one early scouting report as 150 pounds and "malnourished," had transformed into Slammin' Sammy, a chiseled, joyous 225-pounder who delighted the world with his trademarks: sprinting from the Cubs' dugout to rightfield; hopping sideways toward first base as his homers rocketed into the night; touching two fingers to his lips, then to his heart, then back again to each.

How had he done it? Everyone thinks they know. The Cubs, the franchise Sosa shook from an 80-year snooze, certainly think they do. "Players of that era owe us a little bit of honesty," owner Tom Ricketts (whose family bought the team in 2009) told fans in January. "The only way to turn that page is to put everything on the table."

In fact, that's not necessarily the case. Most of the players tainted by accusations of steroid use have never apologized for, much less admitted to, any transgressions. And yet: The Giants will retire the jersey number of Barry Bonds (who never apologized) in August. Roger Clemens (never apologized) is a special assistant to Astros general manager Jeff Luhnow. Even Alex Rodriguez (sort of apologized) has returned as an adviser to the Yankees.

Sosa, though, remains in exile. The Cubs' view is that the power to change this situation is Sosa's alone. "It's never been our position that we want Sammy to wear a hair shirt and sit in front of Wrigley and be punished for weeks on end," says a team source. "This is simply, 'I messed up, and there's something to learn from it, and I'd love to get back in the fold.' It would take one sentence."

It's the one sentence Sosa won't say. "I never failed a drug test," he says today. "So why are you asking me about that, when they don't have nothing on Sosa?"

After Dubai, Sosa's travel plans include visits to Monaco, London and Paris. He'll go to cities all over the globe—except one. It's been 11 years since he set foot in Chicago.

Mark McGwire sits on an allegedly leather couch in a windowless office next to the visitors' clubhouse at Nationals Park in Washington, bathed in a sickly, fluorescent-green light. He wears a Lycra gaiter on his head, and a sleeveless Padres T-shirt reveals 54-year-old biceps—still considerable if no longer the 19 inches in circumference they were two decades ago. He's exactly where he wants to be. "I love it," he says of his nine-year career as an MLB coach. "I absolutely love passing on what I learned as a player."

The great home run race of 1998 started out between two American heroes, the Cardinals' McGwire and the Mariners' Ken Griffey Jr. Through May, McGwire had 27 and Griffey had 19. Then, in June, Sosa went nuts. He entered the month with 13 homers and ended it with 33, the most ever in a single calendar page. The tormented fans in Wrigley Field's bleachers suddenly had something to celebrate. And a demoralized country found a positive sports story to counterbalance a political scandal about a president and an intern. "We were bringing the game back," says McGwire. "People had a really bad taste in their mouths after the '94 strike; a lot of people didn't watch baseball. But '98 brought those fans back. I'm very proud of that. I still get people thanking me."

The enthusiasm over the chase meant that even loose suspicions about all the long balls were met quickly with qualifiers. When the AP's Steve Wilstein wrote in August that there was a bottle of Androstenedione in McGwire's locker—the substance produces testosterone in the body, and its use was banned in many sports but not by MLB—his third paragraph began with this: "No one suggests that McGwire wouldn't be closing in on Roger Maris' home run record without the over-the-counter drug...."

The chase felt good. America was falling in love, especially with McGwire's unlikely Dominican challenger. And as the two separated themselves from Griffey, Sosa became the soul of the summer.

While Sosa embraced the attention, McGwire bristled at times. He was often colder with the press than his spirited Chicago counterpart was. "If I didn't help the club win, and somebody else did, I felt really bad that the media was asking about me and not my teammates," McGwire says. "That's the thing I would get irritated about."

Sosa never seemed annoyed. He was thrilled to be chasing Maris with the 6'5" McGwire. "Coming from a different country, fighting with Goliath, me and him, *boom-boom-boom*," Sosa says. "I was already a winner just to compete with Mark." (It helped too that Sosa would receive news that his every home run triggered a party in the streets of the D.R.)

To accommodate a growing horde of reporters, special press conferences had to be called whenever the Cubs played the Cardinals. But the reality was that the two men at the center of it all rarely interacted. They'd say hello at first base or outside media rooms. When McGwire broke Maris's 37-year-old record with blast number 62 on Sept. 8, it was against the Cubs in St. Louis—the highest-rated regular-season game since 1982. As Sosa arrived from rightfield to throw his arms around McGwire—"You're the man!" Sosa shouted, over and over—you would have thought these two were great friends, united by more than their shared pursuit of history. The truth was something different. "We don't know each other that well," McGwire says.

As the NL Central rivals approached the last weekend of the regular season, even the team-first McGwire felt as if he were competing against one man—a man who had just tied him at 65 homers. The Cardinals were playing the Expos in St. Louis, the Cubs were in Houston. On Sept. 25, McGwire heard the Busch Stadium crowd gasp. "I knew Sammy had hit a home run," he says. "I had to put it into another gear: I'm not allowing him to pass me, to take over this record." McGwire homered in his next at bat, and then twice in each of his remaining two games. Sosa didn't go yard again. Still, if the record was McGwire's, history belonged to both of them, strangers paired forever.

Seven years later they were together again, subpoenaed to appear before Congress for hearings about doping. McGwire was tearful and opaque. "I'm not here to discuss the past," he said. "I'm here to be positive about this subject."

Sosa, at the time, seemed to have a modest grasp of the English with which he'd once chopped it up with Jay Leno. But the language was his second, and the stage in Washington, D.C., more stressful than the set of *The Tonight Show*. To lasting public opprobrium, he largely relied on someone else to speak for him in front of Congress. "I have never taken illegal performance-enhancing drugs," his attorney said on his behalf. "I have never injected myself or had anyone inject me with anything. I've not broken the laws of the United States or the laws of the Dominican Republic." It did not take seasoned lawyering to identify the gray areas, such as the possibility that he had taken PEDs orally or used substances that might have been banned from baseball but not illegal.

McGwire was then four years into his own exile from baseball, during which he remarried and started a second family. Yet his time away from the game was self-imposed; Cardinals manager Tony La Russa kept encouraging him to return as a coach. And he finally agreed to do so before the 2010 season, following a short apology tour in which he conceded, "I wish I had never touched steroids. It was a mistake. I truly apologize."

"I had to go through what I had to go through," McGwire says now. "But it wasn't easy." He has since worked steadily in the game, spending three seasons as the Cardinals' hitting coach, three in the same role with the Dodgers and three as the bench coach for the Padres.

When Sosa stood before Congress, he still had two seasons left to play: one with the Orioles and one, after a year away from baseball in 2006, with the Rangers. He hit his final homer—number 609, still the ninth-most ever—on Sept. 26, 2007, but no team has invited him back in any role since.

Perhaps that has something to do with the way his 13-year tenure with the Cubs ended, in 2004. The shine of 1998 had long before worn away, thanks in part to his being caught using a corked bat in 2003. He had his critics, those who felt Selfish Sammy only cared about the cameras and his stats, or that he took advantage of privileges granted him by his team. Thirteen minutes into a meaningless game on the last day of the '04 season, with Chicago miles from playoff contention and Sosa out of the lineup, the team's all-time home run (and strikeout) leader departed Wrigley for what would prove to be the last time. After the final pitch, a teammate approached Sosa's double locker with a bat. He stood over the rightfielder's boom box, the stereo that some felt he had used to exert his musical taste—and influence—over the clubhouse, and smashed it to pieces.

The attack, now the stuff of Cubs legend, seems to suggest that Sosa had turned off many with whom he'd shared the clubhouse. But not everyone remembers him that way. Whenever Jim Riggleman, who managed the Cubs from 1995 through '99, would chew him out for chasing steals or being sloppy in the field, Sosa always had the same reply: "You're right, skip." Says Riggleman, "He never fought me on anything."

When first baseman Derrek Lee joined the Cubs in 2004, Sosa often offered him a chauffeured ride home from games. "I would have a hard time thinking of one negative thing about him as a teammate," Lee says.

"He was a role model," says Aramis Ramírez, who became the Cubs' third baseman in 2003. "As a Dominican player, you wanted to be like him."

The Cubs no longer seem to wish that anyone be like him, but Sosa is not begging for the team's endorsement, either; he relishes the comforts of his new life. In Dubai, under the relentless desert sun, Sosa, in his blue suit, sits in the back of a black SUV as it weaves through traffic, stealing glances at this new world. Luxury car showrooms with tall glass windows line the freeway. Billboards rise high above the streets, advertising haute couture or exclusive real estate, or bearing the unsmiling likeness of Sheikh Mohammed bin Rashid Al Maktoum, prime minister of the UAE and ruler of Dubai.

As the shadow of the towering Burj Khalifa approaches, Sosa casts his eyes upward. He looks the part of a cosmopolitan dealmaker, black iPhone pressed to his ear. But he is not on some high-stakes conference call, discussing a deal. He's listening to Bible verses in Spanish. Often with Sosa, things are not what they seem.

Take his feelings about the Cubs. Sometimes he says he doesn't need them. But he also says, "I miss the game. I miss the fans. The people lifted me up for so many years. I would like to come back and say, 'Hey, I'm here.' Time will heal everything. Sooner or later—could be now, or 20 years—they have to open the door."

Time heals. It also does something else. "You're here one day," McGwire says. Then, "You're gone." Many young Padres have no memory of their burly coach as a player. Sometimes they'll watch videos of the summer of 1998 on the Internet. "Damn, Mac," they'll tell him, "you could *swing*." On the night before McGwire sat in the clubhouse at Nationals Park, a rookie phenom for

Washington, leftfielder Juan Soto, hit his first career homer. Soto was born one month after the '98 regular season ended.

McGwire has six children, including triplet eight-year-old daughters, and they too have to resort to YouTube to see their father at the peak of his powers. Only Matthew, a 10-year-old Cardinals bat boy in 1998 who now works for a golf apparel company, remembers. McGwire didn't keep a single artifact from his most famous summer; he distributed them to people who helped him along the way. "Not one item," he says. "I wanted everybody that was a part of '98 to have those pieces—my batting gloves, my shoes. They're in my mind. My heart. I didn't need them." Now, 20 years on, part of him wishes he'd saved something for his kids.

Sosa's oldest son, Sammy Jr., was just one in the summer of 1998. He's 21 now, tall and lean, a music engineer, the spitting image of his father as a younger man. Junior, as his dad calls him, helps him with his enterprises.

At one point during dinner on the 122nd floor of the Burj Khalifa, Junior, who has accompanied his father to Dubai, excuses himself to take a business call. Years ago he was an elite prospect in his own right. At 12 he was playing with boys five or six years his elder, traveling to the D.R. for summer camps alongside some of the country's best young stars. Even then, there was no escaping his father's shadow. "Steroid baby," people would call him. Junior quit baseball as a teenager, in part because the wisecracks grew to be too much. He never did tell his father what people had said about him.

Junior also doesn't discuss with his dad the things people say online. Sosa's appearance has changed, the result of a skin cream that he years ago began applying daily. "It doesn't affect him, but I'm sure he feels a certain way," Junior says. "Like, 'Man, I gave so many years and so much hard work for you guys, and now you want to undermine all that because of some decisions I'm making—some personal decisions that don't affect you at all?'"

When Junior was young, he resented the outsiders who clamored for his dad's attention, seeking photos at the mall or autographs at the movies. *I don't spend enough time with him,* he thought to himself. *And the little time I have with him, you're trying to take from me?*

But when Sosa left baseball—or when baseball left Sosa—he had more time to devote to his children. On the diamond he'd been all smiles, but at home he'd carried a hardened exterior, molded by the burden of a superstar's responsibilities. That softened with retirement. Now "he listens a lot more," says Junior.

Still, there are parts of Sammy Sosa that remain a mystery to his family. "He's a really closed-off person, even with me," Junior says. "He doesn't mean to be. There are some things I don't know about my dad that I wonder about."

Among them may be a fuller understanding of the summer of 1998—what it meant then and what it means now. "It feels like yesterday, 'cause that was the year that I shocked the world—that we shocked the world," Sosa says. Most remember that it was McGwire who hit 70 home runs, a record broken three years later by Bonds. But it was Sosa who batted .308 and led all of baseball in runs, total bases and RBIs. Sosa was the NL MVP.

That was a magical year for Sosa, but it may be only to him that it feels like yesterday. Most of his children (and his granddaughter Kira, born in April to his oldest daughter, Keysha) have had no opportunity to feel for themselves the way he was once revered. That is one reason why today, after a decade of reclusiveness, he is cautiously reemerging during this anniversary year.

The Cubs have allowed Sosa's number 21 to be worn by nine players since he left town. The only real sign of him at Wrigley these days is on a small flag that flutters among the dozens that ring the ballpark. It reads SAMMY on one side, 66 on the other. That's it.

While relaxing in Dubai—which generally means avoiding the 111° heat—Sosa will sometimes open up about his feelings toward his former team. On his last night, after nine hours of sightseeing and photo shoots, he changes into a white polo shirt and dark blue jeans. He's gripping another double 12-year Macallan when his pique emerges. "I passed Ernie Banks for most home runs in Chicago Cubs history," he says. "He has a statue, and I don't have nothing. So, what the f---?"

He expresses frustration, too, with the Ricketts family, who insist that they run a values-driven organization and who have publicly maintained a hard line toward Sosa—harder than any other owner of a club that once employed a legend of the steroid era. "They come in and buy the team and they have a mark on me, and I don't know why," Sosa says. Of chairman Tom Ricketts, Sosa says, "This guy never was there when I was there." (Ricketts declined to be interviewed for this story.)

The Cubs' mark on Sosa, though, hasn't always been indelible. According to a source close to the club, representatives of the Cubs met with Sosa in 2014, at the behest of Dominican government officials, to discuss a possible homecoming. According to the source, Sosa agreed that he would issue an apology—that is, something to acknowledge malfeasance, but short of a total confession. The next day, Sosa backed out.

Through an email from a spokesperson, Sosa confirms this account: *In an effort to put the past behind us I agreed to meet with a PR firm representing the Cubs. Everyone signed confidentiality agreements, so I do not bring this up in interviews. All I will say is that after meeting with this group, I agreed to make a statement that would heal things. Both sides agreed upon this statement. When the time came, I felt like I was being swept up in a PR machine that was moving way too fast and not adhering to the spirit of our agreement, so I pulled out. I never met with anyone from the Cubs and do not hold anything against them. I always wish them well.* —Sammy

Tom Ricketts has always said that the only way for Sosa to be welcomed back to Wrigley would be for him to admit his transgressions. Sosa acknowledges that he was willing (four years ago, anyway) to concede them in such a way that he could return to the place he still calls "my house." Semantic gymnastics typically accompany the topic of steroids in baseball, but it doesn't require an expert to come to a judgment as to what Sosa is really saying.

It is still fair, though, to wonder about a few other things. Such as why a billionaire who has never been anything but spectacularly wealthy—Ricketts's father, Joe, founded the brokerage firm TD Ameritrade—insists that a man who grew up sleeping on Caribbean dirt accede fully to his terms. Keep in mind, these values-oriented Cubs traded in 2016 for closer Aroldis Chapman, who had months earlier been suspended 30 games for allegedly choking his girlfriend and firing eight gunshots in her vicinity. (Chicago considered Chapman to have sufficiently apologized and to have paid his penalty by serving his suspension.)

Would the Cubs be more receptive to a reconciliation if not for a few twists of fate? For instance: What if a memorably bespectacled fan hadn't helped them wash out of the 2003 NLCS? What if they hadn't ended their 108-year curse in '16, with Chapman aboard and Sosa watching from Paris? Now, says Michael Wilbon, the ESPN personality and Cubs superfan, "I go to a lot of stuff in Chicago—cocktail parties, receptions, games. We don't ever talk about Sammy Sosa."

Or might things have played out differently had Sosa been more conclusively linked to steroids? His name wasn't, in fact, one of the 89 included in 2007's canonical Mitchell Report. Though he was fingered in '09 by *The New York Times* as appearing on a list of players who failed what was supposed to be an anonymous round of PED testing in '03, Commissioner Rob Manfred cautioned in '16 against drawing conclusions from that. ("It was hard to distinguish between certain substances that were legal, available over the counter, and not banned under our program," Manfred said of the testing round, which also named the Red Sox' wholly beloved slugger David Ortiz. "There were legitimate scientific questions about whether or not those were truly positives.") Had Sosa been more directly implicated, might that have forced some resolution?

Of course, Sosa could always just admit to something and be done with the matter, but that may not comport with the self-sculpted man he continues to show himself to be. So time moves on and Sosa remains in limbo, sartorially splendid and yet nowhere near the city or sport that made him famous. "You're from the Dominican, and you come to the States because this is the best place to play," says Lance Johnson, a longtime teammate who insists he never saw any evidence that Sosa used steroids. "You leave when you're done, and then you feel like you're not respected for what you did when you were here. Now, couldn't that make pretty much anybody into a recluse?"

Sosa isn't in hiding; he's just not where anyone expected him to be. Eventually, as midnight nears in the desert, he grows tired of answering questions about his second life. "One second," he interrupts, a cloud of shisha smoke hanging over the patio bar of yet another luxury hotel, a rare moment outdoors. "We're in *Dubai*. Look at the view."

Out in the darkness is the bright skyline of this once dusty outpost, home to fewer than 60,000 people when Sosa was born five decades ago half a world away, but since transformed by oil-rich sheikhs and slave labor into a gleaming metropolis of three million. It is the most artificial city in the world, but it is also undeniably real. It dazzles in the distance.

PERSONAL REFLECTIONS

MARCH 27, 1978

A Time for All Us Children

A spring training idyll in which a father takes his
son to meet that perplexing figure, his idol

BY FRANK DEFORD

"The regulars are on the other diamond," I told him.

He is eight years old, and he nodded, but only blankly, as I led him in
that direction. Then it occurred to me. "You don't know what *regulars* are,
do you?"

"No," he said.

That hurt a little. Regular has always been a classic spring training term.
The regulars have always reported after everyone else. The regulars have
always been given time to get in shape. Everyone else has to struggle in
spring training, bringing their arms around, scratching to make the squad.
The regulars are in Florida at their leisure.

In the days when I was growing up, a regular anything was sufficient
unto itself. There was no higher compliment than to be acclaimed a regular
guy. A regular fellow! The regular Army was such a standard that men knew
its members simply by initials: "He's R.A."

"Well," I said, "we are going to see Munson, Jackson, Chambliss, Rivers,
Nettles—what do you call them?"

"Oh," he said, with instant recognition, "the stars." Verbal inflation is
such that regulars have become stars, and mere stars are now superstars.
Regular, such a proud, honest word, has been taken from us, appropriated
by laxative ads. But never mind. That aside, little else of spring training

201

has been modified. In a world in flux it remains downright immutable; also, pleasant and gracious.

So a couple of weeks ago I took my son, whose name is Christian, with me to visit a few camps. Baseball, more than any other, is a generational game. It speaks best across the years. There are so few things you can show children to illustrate the way it was. But the timelessness of spring training endures and should be shared—can be shared.

Bill Veeck, his good leg crossed over his peg leg, a fresh cigarette in his chops, stared across the sunny fields. To be sure, his White Sox were in sporty new-fangled uniforms, and only a few of them spit tobacco juice upon the greensward. "But it can never change," Veeck allowed. "The same atmosphere must always prevail, because spring training is first and always a time of dreams, of wishful thinking." I introduced my child to Veeck; it is a time for all us children.

Any kid who takes an interest in sports immediately designates a favorite player. The choice is often irrational, as in other affairs of the heart, but it requires neither apology nor explanation. A favorite player holds that estate because...he's my favorite player.

Bill Russell, the great Boston Celtic center, used to argue with me that children had no business idolizing players; they should reserve such esteem for their own fathers, he said. I contended that it was a healthy sign for a kid to venerate some stranger who excels in the public arena. Somehow this extends a child, providing him with his first attachment to the larger family of the community.

Like most boys, I had a favorite player. His name was Bob Repass, and he played shortstop for the old minor league Baltimore Orioles. While I lived and died with Bob Repass ("Hey, Bob-a-re-pass!" we shouted), I do not recollect that he seriously diminished my devotion to my father. On the other hand, the heritage of Bob Repass still resides with me. He wore No. 6. To this day it is my firm belief that six is my lucky number. Why? Because it is my lucky number, that's why. Because Bob Repass wore it when I was eight years old.

Chris Chambliss of the Yankees is my son's favorite player. Why? Because. And if you are to examine spring training through the eyes of a child, you must begin with the favorite player. Chambliss is an auspicious choice. He is a Navy chaplain's son, guarded, well spoken, a respite from the pinstripe turbulence all about him—"class," in sports parlance.

Chambliss was tired from practice, but he greeted us at his locker and, with time, warmed to the unusual task of addressing a shy child instead of a badgering journalist. "Spring training is always the fun time of the year," he told Christian. "Maybe we should keep that in our minds. Baseball is still a game, whether or not you're making money—and no matter how much. If you're not having fun, you miss the point of everything and it will hurt you, too, because eventually your performance will decline."

It has always been my impression that few top athletes are avid sports fans. These fellows succeed so easily at games—and from such an early age—that they have no need to transfer any of their sporting interest to the performances of others. This is the reason, I think, why so few of them can comprehend the manic affection in which they are held. Chambliss is something of an exception. He collected baseball cards when he was a kid and rooted for his favorites, the Yankees and White Sox.

"Listen, there's nothing wrong with having an idol," he told Christian. "The mistake is trying to copy the idol. That's no good. Try to be as good as your idol, try to be better, but don't ever try to imitate him. That's where an idol is wrong. Be yourself."

Before we spoke to Chambliss, we had watched the regulars (stars) practice. We had come into a piece of luck, because on this morning the regulars worked out on a distant diamond, hidden from all the world by armed security officers and banks of high green Australian pines. Probably on no other day all season would the world champions play together in such glorious seclusion. What might the regulars reveal in their rare privacy?

For the most part, they proceeded with professional dispatch. But there were diversions. Cliff Johnson, the monstrous slugger, was the most engaging presence, ever bantering, razzing his teammates—an amiable figure utterly in contrast to his huge, forbidding form. Otherwise, even a man from outer space would have recognized the two ascendant personalities: 15 and 44, Thurman Munson and Reggie Jackson.

Forty-four had not been on the premises 10 minutes when he informed everyone that he would not be his usual self today because of a sore shoulder. The less his fellows responded with concern to this bulletin, the greater emphasis Jackson placed upon the next recitation. He alone of all the Yankees paid any sort of undue attention to Christian. In a lull, Jackson suddenly bellowed, "We gotta get this —— kid outta here so we can talk some ——."

The remark was addressed at large, with a smile, and Christian was rather pleased that the great man had paid him notice. Yet, while Jackson's comments were not offensive, they were consistent with the generally insecure posturing that he exhibited. In the end, I came away oddly embarrassed for 44.

By contrast, 15 seemed to move about confidently—tough, almost belligerent. And then came the moment. Jackson was standing behind the third-base side of the batting cage, telling yet another listener about his shoulder. Munson was 15 to 20 feet distant, walking away from Jackson toward the first-base line. I didn't hear precisely what Jackson said to the player next to him, but suddenly Munson tossed a ball in a high hook-shot arc that fell upon the netting in front of where 44 stood. "Some of us gotta work for a living, Jackson," Munson hollered.

The remark was gratuitous—rude, if not mean. Jackson hadn't even said anything to Munson. Jackson looked over at him, more hurt and baffled than angry. Munson smiled back at him, pleased. Christian tugged at me. "Why did he do that?" he whispered, confused.

This July, when I read the latest exclusive about how 15 and 44 really do admire and respect each other deep down inside, I will remember again this uneasy confrontation around the cage in Fort Lauderdale early in March. As petty as it was, it was starkly revealing.

Minutes later, Munson was catching batting practice. Johnson was hitting, Jackson was resting against the cage (his shoulder hurt him, he told the fellow next to him). Suddenly, to fill a vacuum, Jackson loudly called Johnson a familiar dirty name. Johnson called Jackson the same thing back. The other Yankees laughed. Christian snickered at the vulgarity, thrilled with being included in this coarse adult male society.

Then Johnson and Jackson started using the dirty word in meaningless ways, topping each other. With every repetition, the players would hoot and holler. Louder and louder, Jackson and Johnson. Saying a dirty word for no reason but to hear it. And the others laughing. Regular knee-slapping. Munson was beside himself. They were just like a bunch of little kids. Whatever these men thought of each other, whatever the travails of last summer, they had been away from one another for five months. They had been with people in suits and ties, with women and children, in the real grown-up world. And now it was spring training, the fun time, and they were children again, teasing and laughing at forbidden words said right out loud. I will remember that in July, too. "If you're not having fun in baseball, you miss the point of everything," Chambliss said.

Of all players, none ended the 1977 season more forlornly than Fred Patek, the shortstop for Kansas City. Because he is only 5'4", by far the smallest player in baseball, there is a natural disposition to care about Patek, and so it was all the sadder when television showed him slumped alone in his dugout, in pain, beaten, anguished. He had been spiked and then had hit into a double play in the last inning of the last game of the playoffs, when the Royals had the pennant taken from them by the Yankees.

"Oh, it's all behind me now," he said. "The pain was gone after a few hours, the deep involvement after a few days. You have to start again. What hurt was wondering if I had done everything I could possibly do, and when I finally satisfied myself that I had, I was O.K."

It was a hot day in Fort Myers, and Patek sat sweating and shirtless in the clubhouse, sipping a lunch of bean soup and Tab (alternately, that is, though could it really be any worse mixed?). He went on. "The thing that stays with you, though, is wondering whether you ever will get another opportunity to play on a world championship team. Someday, when I'm an old guy, will I look back in dissatisfaction and say, 'Well, I almost made it,' or will I be able to think that for one year I was one of the best players on the best team."

He asked Christian if he would like some Tab or bean soup. Christian declined; he was saving himself for franchise fare on the Tamiami Trail. But then Christian had a question for Patek. When we prepared for this adventure, I urged him to think up some questions he would like to ask, because sportswriters know too much (or think they do) and therefore ask only sportswriter-type questions. I was right. Christian's naive question was to elicit the most original explanation I have ever heard of slumps.

He asked Patek, "Do you ever get scared?"

Patek took a spoonful of bean soup and a swig of Tab and replied, "No, I've never been scared of other players, of spikes, of the ball." Pause. End of answer, it seemed. But then, "I'll tell you something. None of us ever understands why a player goes into a slump. I think that, all of a sudden, the player is scared of the ball. You need a lot of confidence to step up there against a pitcher, and it doesn't take much to shake that. It doesn't necessarily have to have anything to do with baseball. Our lives are too complicated to separate the game from the rest of it. Maybe you're having a fight with your wife. You lose just enough confidence so that you get scared of the ball. You shy away from it. I've found that the best thing you can do in a slump is admit that you're scared."

Patek is the ultimate regular. Because of his size he had more to overcome. To many kids, he is not just a hero but also a patron saint. And that goes not only for short kids, but also for fat kids, skinny kids, nearsighted kids. He has shown what you can do. "When I was a kid your age growing up in Texas," he went on, "I'd listen to all the games I could get on the radio. I was a Yankee fan. I still feel strange about them when we play. But I didn't have an idol. Every player was my hero. I thought baseball players were some kind of superior beings.

"When I finally got a chance to come to a camp, I was so grateful. To get ready, I ran five miles every day. I did sprints, I ran up and down the steps at a stadium. I thought everybody with a chance would do that. I thought, that's the way baseball players are. And then I got there, to the camp, and a lot of these kids with a chance weren't in shape. I couldn't believe these people could actually think they were professional baseball players and be like that. I was really disappointed. I was really hurt...for baseball."

One of the larger delights of spring training is its informality. In some places, like Sarasota, where the Pale Hose train, it positively resembles a garden party. Bill Veeck sits in the middle, entertaining visitors. Fans wander about, examining unknowns with strange uniform numbers in the 50s, 60s and 70s. Fundamentals are in bloom. On one diamond, the players practice relays from the outfield to third, over and over. On another, pitchers are fielding and firing simulated bunts to third, trying to learn by rote in March how to handle a situation they may not encounter until June or July.

Christian and I drifted over to the batting cages, where sophisticated machines were whirling in hard sliders. The kid was standing there awaiting his turn. His name is Thad Bosley, a tall and thin outfielder with a handsome baby face. Everybody thinks he can be a star, although he might require more seasoning. ("Seasoning" is the best spring training noun. The best verb is "find," always employed by the manager, who declares, "I don't want to go north before we find a centerfielder"–or long reliever, left-handed DH, whatever–as if this desired entity has merely been misplaced over the winter and will be discovered tucked away in the coat closet or the garage.)

Bosley is a thoughtful young man of 21. He had just taught himself to play the piano and was now beginning to master the flute. It was all a matter of regimen, of applying oneself, just like baseball. He referred to spring training, academically, as a time of "refining technique," but he also observed, philosophically, "You are foolish if you don't take the opportunity here to learn a great deal about yourself, too."

Bosley has played professional ball for five years and he has been up to the bigs briefly before, but this spring training is his real start. So, to be perverse, I asked him what he hoped to have at the end. He looked out thoughtfully toward the other players. "When I leave baseball," he said at last, "I would just like people to say, 'Thad Bosley, he could play the game.'"

Oddly enough, Bosley's spring training and the Hall of Fame, the shrine to the players who have completed the most glorious careers–the alpha and omega of major league baseball–share the same tempo and tenor. In between, where the score is kept, it is all big-city hurly-burly, but at Sarasota and the Hall the setting is tranquil. Dust to dust: spring training to Cooperstown, N.Y.

Every year, on a weekday in August, the new members are welcomed into the Hall of Fame in a ceremony conducted on a lawn adjacent to the place. Then, following a hot lunch, two major league clubs play an exhibition at the little stadium down the street. The fans spill over onto the field, which occasions a great many ground-rule doubles. Nobody minds a bit.

Last year the Twins and Phillies played (the Phils blew that one, too), and Ernie Banks led some oldtimers, dead and alive, into the hallowed diamond abbey. A number of the incumbent saints came back, and I directed Christian to them. It is his view that ballplayers are hands that write autographs; only incidentally are those hands attached to a body that plays baseball. "You ought to get that guy," I said, pointing him toward Musial or Feller, Campanella or Marquard. He didn't have the foggiest notion who they were. But what the hell, he didn't know who Ernie Banks was either. "Why are there so many Cub fans here?" he inquired.

The sun came through the clouds just as the mayor of Cooperstown began his welcoming address. There was red, white and blue bunting and the playing of *The Star-Spangled Banner*. On the platform, where the legends-in-their-own-time sat, the only artifacts were a huge plastic baseball and an American flag. That covered just about everything.

The commissioner read off Banks' name, and the place went up for grabs. He was proud and gracious, in a navy blue three-piece suit and a red, white and blue tie, and he concluded his remarks with this thought, "We got the sun out now, we got the fresh air, we got the teams behind us...so let's play two!"

I remembered all this as I watched the sun cross Thad Bosley's countenance. He had so far to go...and yet, it was all so much the same. Lay the first two down, Bosley, then take your cuts and run the last one out.

Here's to Opening Day, and a Kid's Belief That Anything Can Happen

On a cold day in April, Cleveland's baseball team had one young fan planning for the playoffs

BY JOE POSNANSKI

I only went to one Opening Day game as a boy. That was April 8, 1978. It was a Saturday. I was 11 years old. I remember it for a few reasons, one being that it was approximately 23 degrees below zero in Cleveland Municipal Stadium. I have often written about how cold Cleveland Municipal would get, even in the middle of July. The wind would howl off Lake Erie. The roof would cast this frigid shade—there were places in the Stadium where the sun never shined, puddles that would not dry until the place was imploded. I'm not sure it ever felt colder in there than that day in '78. Wayne Garland, who started the game for Cleveland, would say that the baseball felt like a piece of glass in his hands.

The Indians were playing the Kansas City Royals, and the Royals may have been the best team in baseball the year before. It's always tricky to make those sorts of pronouncements about a team that did not win the World Series (and in this case did not even *reach* the World Series), but the Royals won 102 games, most in baseball, and more to the point they were about as close to unbeatable as a team can be late that season. From Aug. 17 through Sept. 25 they went 35–4, something no Yankees team ever did, something no Cardinals team ever did, a feat that (I think) you have to go back to the 1906 Cubs to find previously. That Royals team lost to the Yankees in a five-game series, and you can take from that what you want, but the general point is that that was a great Royals team.

And I was 11, which means that I put a preposterous amount of meaning into that Opening Day. I was too young—I often still feel too young—to appreciate the length of a baseball season, the drone of 162 games, the numbing effects of tomorrow after tomorrow. To me, Opening Day would provide all the answers. The Indians were playing the Royals. If they could just win, they would prove what I knew in my heart to be true: That this was the year.

I have never fully recovered from this. And I never want to recover from this. I still put way too much stock into Opening Day. I take entirely too much joy out of looking at the standings on Day 2—with all those 1–0 and 0–1 records. I am an early season "Leaders" watcher...I can't help it. Hey, if Tuffy Rhodes had maintained that pace, he would have hit 486 home runs. Maybe you could not expect him to keep that pace...but even if he slowed, hey, 200 home runs would be pretty good.

My father was not especially happy to go to Opening Day, I remember...I now know why. I have inherited his hypersensitive frustration with not being able to find a place to park. I know this is not unusual, but I feel this unhealthy rage build up inside me—and I don't really have much rage—when I cannot find a place to leave the car. All I want to do is *leave the car.* Please? Just any place? Some place? Just give me a little bit of earth where I can leave this hunk of metal while I go do what I must do. Is that too much to ask? Earth may not be a large planet in the universal scope of things, but there is enough room out there for golf courses and baseball stadiums and state parks and planes to land and so on...there should be one more tiny hunk of dirt so I can get the hell out of my car. And so on.

So, my father more or less preferred to go to Cleveland Indians games *any other* day of the season (except July 4th) when there was plenty of space and very little traffic and friendly parking lot attendants who, shoot, would *park your car for you* as long as you just would agree to go into the game. There were more than 50,000 people at Cleveland Municipal that day because Cleveland, even in its darkest baseball moments, respected Opening Day. Though 50,000 people made Cleveland Municipal look barely half full, it was more than enough to shut down the traffic flow, especially because my father did not know any secrets about how to get in and out. I remember we were in the car for a long time, my father's face burning redder and redder as the time passed.

In fact, I don't know that we made it for opening pitch—Wayne Garland vs. a 22-year-old rookie blazer named Willie Wilson. I'm pretty sure we did not. I remember a long walk to the stadium. A long walk. I do remember being in our seats when my hero Duane Kuiper singled in the bottom of the first—I would have been devastated if I had missed that. Kuiper would come around to score when Willie Horton singled him in. And the Indians would go on to score three unearned runs off Dennis Leonard, the big blow being a rocket double to center by Buddy Bell. I seem to remember Bell's hit—I can see the ball flying over the center fielder's head—though that's probably just what I would call a "Retrosheet Memory"—when you see something on Retrosheet and think "Oh yeah, I remember that." If tomorrow, Retrosheet printed a retraction and said that, no, Buddy Bell did not get a double, it was actually Rick Manning, I would probably nod and remember it the new way.

The Indians led 4–0 for approximately 48 seconds—the Royals then scored four runs in the second to tie the game—Freddie Patek homered, which I remember pretty clearly, and Hal McRae homered, which I don't remember at all. I remember the Patek home run because I was the shortest kid in my class. I probably don't need to spell out the connection, but:

1. I was the shortest boy in my class.
2. Fred Patek was the shortest player in baseball at 5-foot-5.
3. The shortest boy in class needs inspiration.
4. Fred Patek was my inspiration.
5. When Fred Patek homered, even though it was against my Indians, I felt happy and strangely vindicated.

The Indians, in a rather unlikely way, came right back in the bottom of the second. And this is the part I remember most because it may just be the greatest live baseball-watching moment of my childhood. The Indians hit back-to-back home runs. That was titanic. Back-to-back home runs? Well, this is one thing that is absolutely true about 1970s baseball—you appreciated home runs, because, they didn't come along very often.

Look: I consider my Cleveland Indians childhood to be 1975–1981—from 8 to 14—and in those years, the Indians played 532 home games. They hit home runs in 263 of those games, did not hit a homer in 269 of them. So, basically, I had less than a 50-50 shot of seeing an Indians home run when I went to a game. And I had about an 18% chance of seeing the Indians hit *more* than one home run in a game. And the odds of seeing back-to-back home runs...staggering.

But there it was, and on Opening Day, with the crowd loud enough to linger in my imagination for a lifetime. Ron Pruitt hit the first. He was a backup catcher from Michigan who was close to my heart because, for some reason, Cleveland was flush with athletes named Pruitt at the time. Greg Pruitt was the superstar runner for the Browns, the brilliant little back with the tear-away jersey who, while at Oklahoma, had finished second in the Heisman Trophy voting to Johnny Rodgers in 1972. Mike Pruitt, who we were *constantly* reminded was of no relation, was Greg's bruising fullback then, and he would gain 1,000 yards himself in four of the next five seasons. Ron Pruitt, who was of no relation to either (though nobody made the point), hit the first home run in that memorable back-to-back, one of the highlights of my Indians childhood and, undoubtedly, one of the highlights of his Indians career.

Also, this is awesome.

Paul Dade hit the second home run. Dade had been a pretty good young player for the Indians in 1977, or anyway it sure seemed that way. He hit .291, though looking back it was just about the lightest .291 a player could hit (his slugging percentage was .356). He could run a little bit and he had killed the ball in June the year before, leading us to believe that the best was yet to come. Indians players always led us to believe that way—or at least me. I seem to remember that one of the themes of spring training that year was the emerging power of Paul Dade. And then he followed Ron Pruitt's bomb with one of his own.* And it was thrilling.

*He would hit three more home runs as a member of the Cleveland Indians.

The Indians maintained that 6–4 lead into the fifth when Andre Thornton, probably the most overpowering baseball presence of my Cleveland childhood, hit a two-run blast of his own (THREE HOMERS IN ONE GAME!) and gave the Indians an insurmountable 8–4 lead. The Royals tacked on a run, but Cleveland's Mike Paxton pitched three flawless innings to record his first major league save. Cleveland's Mike Paxton pitched three flawless innings to record his last major league save. Both true.

And I remember leaving the park shivering and utterly convinced that, yes, this was the year. The Indians had not just beaten the Royals, they had dominated them with a major power display on a freezing day in early April. As we walked and walked to the car, which of course we could not find right away, my mind was abuzz with possibility. Did you see that power? Just imagine how many home runs they would hit once the weather warmed up! Just imagine what they would do when they were not facing Dennis Leonard and the Royals! I was overcome with hope...I can remember, distinctly remember, wondering how to gently ask my father if we could afford to go to Indians playoff games.

Of course, the Indians would not hit three home runs in a game at home again until late September—when they were 25½ games back. Those three were Andre Thornton (of course), Dan Briggs and Wayne Cage. I was not there. The Indians lost 90 games. Anyway, I had long given up hope by then. I had grown disgusted with myself—I was getting to that age when I was putting away childish thoughts, when I realized that the Yankees won a lot, and that hope doesn't always lead to triumph, and that the Indians might never win no matter how much I believed. Of course, six months later, next Opening Day, I believed with all my heart all over again.

JULY 15, 2002

Farewell, Teddy Ballgame

With the death of Ted Williams, the author reflects on
encounters with the splendid splinter over half a century

BY LEIGH MONTVILLE

*If you grew up watching Ted Williams hit a baseball, well, you simply kept
watching, even after he stopped hitting. That was the way it was. From the
day he arrived at Fenway Park in Boston in 1939 as a slender 20-year-old
outfielder with a swing for the ages until last Friday, when he died of cardiac
arrest in Inverness, Fla., at age 83, he was part of your life.*

*As years passed, he might have changed, and you might have changed,
and times might have changed, but he always was a fascinating character.
He was a superstar before the word was invented. He was a man's man, icon
of all icons. Watch? You had to watch.*

At least I did....

Ted 1

The postcard from Ted Williams came to 80 Howe Street, New Haven, Conn., on
a late summer day in 1953. That's the best I can figure. I tried, just now, to pull
the card carefully from the lined, loose-leaf notebook page on which I had
glued it apparently 49 years ago, but the postmark was lost in the process.

I say the late summer of 1953 because that was when I was an autograph
demon. Most of the other cards in my old notebook—George Kell, Maurice
(Mickey) McDermott, Jimmy Piersall, a bunch of forgotten Boston Red Sox
names—have postmarks from the summer of 1953. I was on the case in 1953.
I was 10 years old.

I lived in a six-story apartment house, an only child, and I somehow discovered, alone in my bedroom, that if you wrote to your athletic idols, they sometimes wrote back. I was a writing fool. My basic message on a penny postcard was "Dear So-and-So, I am your biggest fan! You are great! Please send me your autograph!" I finished with my name and address, sent out the card and waited with the anticipation and faith of a trout fisherman on the banks of a fast-running brook on a Sunday morn.

The arrival of the mail every day became true adventure. I would riffle through the bills and the circulars, the grown-up and the mundane, looking and looking until one magical day...a postcard from Ted Williams.

He was the biggest fish of all. I might not remember the exact date his postcard arrived, but I remember the feeling. Even now I can't think of another piece of mail that has made me feel happier, not college acceptances nor good reports from doctors, nothing. The Ted Williams postcard was unadulterated bliss, wholly equivalent to a letter straight from heaven. Better. Straight from Fenway Park.

I had never seen a major league player in person, had never been to a major league stadium, had never seen a major league game. Television hadn't arrived at my house. Williams was a mythical figure, a creation of radio words and black-and-white newspaper pictures. He had the purity of Sir Lancelot, the strength of Paul Bunyan, the tenacity of, say, Mighty Mouse. Distance, to be sure, made heroes much more heroic than they ever can be today.

Williams had returned from the Korean War that July. He was almost 35 years old. He had been flying F-9 Panther jets for a year in Korea, fighting the Communists in their sneaky MiGs. He was back, and he was hitting as well as ever: a .407 average in the final 37 games of the season, 13 homers, a .901 slugging percentage. He could do anything, everything. He was number 9. He was the Kid, Teddy Ballgame, the Splendid Splinter. He hated to wear a tie! (I hated to wear a tie!) He was invincible.

I remember staring at the postcard for hours. Had he actually signed it? No doubt. The blue ink was a different color from the rest of the black-and-white card. On the front of the card was a black-and-white picture of Williams finishing a swing. His eyes seemed to be following a baseball he had just hit, probably into the bullpen in right. He seemed focused, serious, divine. I imagined him reading my own card by his locker, thinking about me. Should he reply? He could tell by my writing that I was an honest kid, a hard worker in school, obeyed my parents. Of course he should reply. I could see him pulling out this postcard from a special place, taking out his pen.

"Capital T," he wrote, with a big flourish, "e-d. Capital W," another flourish, "i-l-l-i-a-m-s." He dotted the i's high.

"You know," an older sportswriter told me a number of years later, "he never signed any of that stuff. The clubhouse guy, Johnny Orlando, his buddy, signed everything. Johnny Orlando could sign Ted Williams's name better than Ted Williams could."

I look at the postcard now. I somehow have kept it through college, through marriage, divorce, changes of jobs, changes of residence. Forty-nine years.

I don't know. Johnny Orlando?

I think Ted might have made an exception. Just once.

Ted 2

The sound of his voice preceded him. Or at least that's what I remember.

The year must have been 1978. Or maybe '79. The Red Sox clubhouse at Chain O' Lakes Park in Winter Haven, Fla., was divided into two rooms. The smaller room was reserved for selected veterans and the coaching staff. They shared the space with a pair of enormous washing machines. The machines were at work, taking out the stains from another spring training day. I was a sportswriter now, working for a Boston newspaper.

"Tell me this," the new voice said, loud, very loud. "What detergent do you use to clean these uniforms?"

Everybody turned toward the noise because there was no alternative. There he was, Ted, himself, huge, instantly dominating his surroundings. He was wearing a Hawaiian shirt. He would have been 59 years old. Maybe 60. He was tanned and robust, looking as if he had just returned from the high seas or the deep woods. A pair of sunglasses hung from his neck on a piece of fishing line.

"Tide," an equipment man said. "We use Tide."

"Now why do you use Tide?" the voice boomed. "Is it better than all the other detergents? Is it cheaper? Is there some secret ingredient? Why do you use Tide?"

The fun began. Somehow I had never been in the same room with Ted Williams, never had talked to him, never had been around him. Would he fill out the picture I'd had in my head for so long? Or would he—like so many famous figures encountered without their press agents and handlers—be a mean-spirited disappointment? What? At first glance I had to say he looked like John Wayne. He talked like John Wayne. He was John Wayne.

He was on the scene as a hitting instructor. For a number of years he had skipped the rituals of the baseball spring and gone off to fish for salmon or bonefish or do whatever he did, but for some reason he'd decided to return for this season. He would show up every morning in his old Ford station wagon, identifiable by the IF GUNS ARE OUTLAWED, ONLY OUTLAWS WILL HAVE GUNS sticker on the rusty bumper. He would change into his uniform and head to the minor league complex.

"What's your name?" he would ask some kid in a batting cage. "Get over here. Where are you from? Mississippi? Let's see what you're doing here."

He would jump from the cart, adjust the kid's stance. He would take the bat, squeeze it hard, swing with emphasis. See? *Pow!* He would talk baseball, baseball, more baseball, laying out hypothetical confrontations between pitcher and batter, each ball and strike forcing the pitcher to alter his strategy, so that at 3 and 2 he had to come in with a fastball, and, oh, brother, here it comes. Pow! The kid from Mississippi would return to work looking slightly dazed.

I stood with other members of the new generation of the Knights of the Keyboard, Williams's term for his longtime adversaries in the press box. I listened to his declarations. (If you were anywhere in the state of Florida, you couldn't avoid them.) I did the obligatory Ted-is-here column.

He was charming and frank. He actually listened to the questions, actually thought out the answers. He laughed easily in large sonic booms. The writers who had tormented him during his career, Colonel Dave Egan and Mel Webb and the rest, were dead. The torment also was dead. The uncomfortable star, sensitive to all criticism, spitting in the direction of the clacking typewriters, was long gone. Williams wore his advancing age as if it were a bathrobe and slippers. He couldn't care less what anyone wrote.

He would pose for pictures with a daily stream of worshipers, penitents, strangers. ("You gonna take that lens cap off before ya take the shot?" he would bellow. "Here, let me do it.") He would argue with anyone about politics, sports, detergents, anything. He would question. He would tell stories. He would interact, hour after hour. There was a liveliness about him that was different from the ordinary. He was larger than larger-than-life, if that makes any sense. He was Ted Williams, and he knew who he was. He played his own role. Himself.

The highlight of the spring came when he set up a public tennis match against Carl Yastrzemski, then the Red Sox' elder statesman. He didn't just challenge Yastrzemski to the match, he promoted it for an entire week. He told the world. Time, date, place, probable outcome (a huge Williams win). When the great day came—Yastrzemski, 21 years Williams's junior, won easily, making the big man move too much and lurch for shots—there must have been 1,000 people surrounding one of those apartment-complex courts, all to see an event that Williams simply invented.

"Is he always like this?" I asked Joe Lindia, a guy from Providence who was Williams's driver, old friend and roommate for the three weeks of spring training. "Is he always...Ted?"

"Always," Lindia said. "You go with Ted, anything can happen."

Lindia told a story: In one of Williams's last seasons as a player, the Red Sox trained in Scottsdale, Ariz. Lindia went out to visit. One day, an off day, Williams said they should take a ride. They drove to the far edge of the town and went to a seedy motel. Williams directed Lindia to a certain room at the back. Lindia had no idea what was happening. Williams knocked on the door. An old man, looking as seedy as the motel itself, answered. "Joe," Williams said. "Say hello to Ty Cobb."

They went into the room with Cobb. A bottle of whiskey was opened. Cobb and Williams talked baseball for a number of hours. Cobb, it seemed, had one theory about hitting. It was directly opposite to Williams's theory. The argument became intense. The two men were shouting at each other. They looked as if they might come to blows. "Look, I know how we can settle this," Williams finally said. "Ty, you say one thing. I say another. Joe, what do you say?"

"Funny, huh?" Lindia said. "The two greatest hitters in the history of baseball. I'm the one who's supposed to break the tie. I couldn't hit a baseball for a million dollars."

On one of the last days of training camp, I went to dinner with my young family at one of those steak houses with an all-you-can-eat salad bar. My son was five years old. Maybe six. I guided him to the salad bar to fill up his plate. On the way back to the table, I noticed Williams was in a booth with four or five people. Lindia was one of them. I was going to keep going, but Lindia waved and said hello. I waved back. Williams looked and saw my son.

"Hey," he said in that loud voice, "that's a great-looking kid."

My son had no idea who the man was. He smiled.

"I mean he's exceptional," Williams said, even louder now. "A great-looking kid."

I could feel the eyes of everyone in the restaurant turning in my direction. It was like one of those "My broker says..." commercials. People were looking at Williams, then staring at my son. People were nodding their heads in agreement. Yes, a great-looking kid. My son.

"Looks like he'd be a pretty good hitter," someone at the table suggested.

"I don't give a s--- about that," Williams said, loudest voice yet. "I'm just saying he's a great-looking kid. Look at him."

It was a moment. My son is 30 years old, and I still talk to him, maybe once a year, about what happened. He rolls his eyes.

Ted 3

The idea was that Ted was going to be dead pretty soon. That was what the producer said. Ted was going to hit his 80th birthday in a couple of weeks, he'd had the three strokes, he was half blind, and he didn't get around much, didn't submit to many interviews. Anything could happen, you know. This might be the last television interview he ever would do.

This was the summer of 1998. I was the interviewer. I showed up with two cameramen and the producer around noon on the appointed day at Williams's house in Hernando, Fla. The house was relatively new, part of the Citrus Hills development, which featured a bunch of streets named after former Red Sox players and officials. It wasn't the kind of house you would imagine for Williams. There was a commercial aspect here, a lack of dignity.

Buzz Hamon, then the director at the Ted Williams Museum and Hitters Hall of Fame, also located on the Citrus Hills property, briefed us on what to expect. There would be 30 minutes, no more than 45, with Williams. His attention would wander after that. He would be ready for his afternoon nap. He had a cook and an aide who helped him. Hamon said it had been a tough stretch for Williams. Not only had the strokes affected him, virtually all his friends had died. Joe Lindia had died. Williams's longtime companion, Louise Kaufman, had died. His dog had died. He pretty much had outlasted his generation.

I feared the worst. When Williams came into the den, where we had set up our lights, he was using a walker and was helped by the aide. He was shrunken, frail. The robust character of 20 years earlier was gone. The baseball god of 40, 50 years ago was long gone. He was helped into the easy chair and landed with a grateful thud. And he was wonderful.

I have a copy of the tape. From the core of that besieged and worn-out body, Ted Williams emerges. The voice is still loud, challenging, authoritative. It's him. His right hand might wander, almost out of control, and he might dab now and then at a little saliva coming from the side of his mouth, but he's funny and definitive and in charge.

I have my little list of questions, but they are mere starting points. He drives the conversation wherever he wants it to go. I'm only along for the ride. "Oh, brother.... Now here's something interesting! Glad you brought that up!...Oh, that's in all the books. Go read about it.... Where are you from? This is inside stuff you're getting, buddy."

He talks about fishing with Bobby Knight in Russia. He talks about how he thinks George Will knows a lot politically but not too much "baseballically." He talks about Joe Jackson and how he should be in the Hall of Fame, damn it! He talks about Mark McGwire, *loves* Mark McGwire, talks about Nomar Garciaparra, *loves* Nomar, talks about Joe DiMaggio and Willie Mays and Ken Griffey Jr., *loves* Ken Griffey Jr.

He takes a myth and deflates it. Remember the old story about the final doubleheader in 1941, when he could have finished with a .400 average simply by sitting out? The story is that manager Joe Cronin gave him the option, and Williams scoffed. Sit it out? He played the two games, went six for eight, finished at .406. He upheld the sanctity of the game, something no one would do in modern, stat-conscious times. Wasn't that how it went? Yes, but....

"I never thought about sitting out," he says. "Not once. But I gotta say this. I didn't realize how much .400 would mean to my life. I mean it had happened only 11 years before I did it, and I thought someone else would do it pretty soon. I felt there certainly would be other .400 hitters. I said that. Always said that. Now here it is, 50, 60 years later."

He talks about hitting the slider, invented during the middle of his career. That new pitch. He talks about hitting against the Williams shift, stepping back an inch or two from the plate to be able to punch the inside pitch to left. He talks about flying in Korea in the squadron of future astronaut John Glenn. He talks...and then he stops.

"You've got enough," he says. "Bye."

Just like that. Fifty-one minutes, 22 seconds. Exactly.

The tape doesn't show the conversation after the interview was finished. He talked informally for another 10 or 15 minutes. He was lively, friendly. He was funny. He took out the needle. "This isn't a paid interview, is it?" he said. "There's no money for this. Right?"

I said there wasn't. No.

"Well, I enjoyed it, and I'd do it again," Williams said, "but the next time there should be a little remuneration. Do you know what I mean? Remuneration. Some compensation."

"Maybe we could send you a hat," I suggested.

"You know where you could put that hat," Williams said.

He asked me who my boss was. I said I had a lot of them. He asked who was the biggest boss, the boss of all the bosses. I said I guessed Ted Turner was the biggest boss. This was a CNN deal.

"Well, you tell Ted Turner that Ted Ballgame would like some remuneration, O.K.?" Williams said. "Tell Ted that Ted would like something he could fold and put in his pocket. You know?"

I said that since this was an interview to celebrate his 80th birthday, maybe we could work something out, come back for his 100th. He laughed. He said, Ha, if we were back for that, he would do that interview for free. Ha. For sure.

The good news was that he didn't die soon after that day. The interview was far from his last. Within a year he seemed to be everywhere. He was the lead character in all celebrations for the Team of the Century. He was at the 1999 All-Star Game at Fenway. He was at Cooperstown. He was at the Yogi

Berra Museum in Montclair, N.J. He was with Ted Koppel late at night, with the *Today* show in the morning. He talked cooking with Molly O'Neill in the pages of *The New York Times Sunday Magazine*. He had a last triumphant tour.

I remember him going to his bedroom with the walker for his afternoon nap at the end of the interview. Final picture. The big event at night was going to be a Red Sox game on television, off the satellite. He wanted to rest. The cameramen were breaking down the equipment. Suddenly chimes rang out from the bedroom. They played the tune, *Hail, Hail, the Gang's All Here*. They were a signal that Williams required assistance. The aide hurried to the room. A minute later he returned. He was laughing.

"Ted just wanted me to tell you one thing," he said. "Don't forget the part about the remuneration."

Not a disappointment. No. Never.

Mets Autographs

Thirty is the age after which one should never be trusted,
or so it was said during the era when this tale begins.
But I'm not yet 30—not quite, anyway—and though
it's preposterous that I should still covet a certain
big league ballplayer's autograph at this point in
my life, I'm to be trusted when I say I do. Join me
in my metal box, and you'll understand why

BY ALEXANDER WOLFF

It's a drab olive file box with traces of rust, like the one on the kitchen windowsill in which my mother vouchsafed her recipe for ratatouille. On the front I affixed a brightly colored Mets decal, three inches in diameter, that is chipped and peeling now; across the lid I stuck a label, ammo from one of those dial-a-letter label guns, reading NY METS AUTOGRAPHS. Inside I keep the autographs of (almost) every member of the 1969 world champion New York Mets, all sequestered alphabetically by tabbed dividers. I throw that parenthetical "almost" in because with it lies a story, one that bears telling this summer, as the Mets celebrate their silver anniversary by sitting atop the game once again.

I flip the lid and inhale an archival mustiness. Some other aromas in the box are only implied. That of pickle brine, for instance.

Nolan Ryan had soaked a blistered finger in pickle brine during the late '60s, at the urging of Gus Mauch, the Mets' trainer. It was to the tonic powers of pickle brine that the kid from Alvin, Texas, could attribute the continued verve of his already legendary fastball.

I take a 3 x 5 file card signed by Nolan Ryan out of the box and smell it to see if it smells of pickle brine.

"Gus, get me some brine for soakin'," I imagine Ryan saying a few hours before a game that sceptered summer. "Think I'll knock off some of this fan mail between dips."

I can't recall exactly when I took up autographs, but it coincided roughly with my giving up baseball cards. In the sports memorabilia collecting community there has always been a tension between devotees of cards on the one hand and autographs on the other. I ultimately came to believe that cards were too impersonal and regenerative: Once you had acquired your 1966 Willie Mays, there would be a '67 Mays to collect and soon a '68 Mays, along with the 600-odd other cards that the Topps bubble gum people put out each year. Autographs, by contrast, were little concessions that players made directly to their public, without a corporate middleman. There was one per life, not one per year.

I had no idea what the '69 Mets would accomplish as I began writing to them for their signatures early that season. But one imperative lingered from my baseball card days, and that was to complete the set. I had to get every Met, no matter how inconsequential.

It would be a thrill to petition such stars as Tom Seaver, Cleon Jones and Tommie Agee for their autographs. But it would be an altogether different sort of challenge to get the scrubs: Duffy Dyer, third-string catcher; Amos Otis (some scrub he would turn out to be); Rod Gaspar—or Ron Gaspar, or Rod Stupid. (Baltimore's Frank Robinson, on the eve of the World Series supposedly said, "Bring on Ron Gaspar!" A teammate told him, "Not Ron—Rod, stupid!" Said Robinson, "O.K., bring on Rod Stupid!")

I would never trade my Kevin Collins, though the Mets did—had to, that June, to the Expos, along with Steve Renko and a couple of minor league pitchers—for Donn Clendenon, the righthanded power hitter they so desperately needed.

I had to have the coaches, too: From Rube Walker, the pitching coach, to Joe Pignatano, cultivator of tomato plants in the bullpen.

Card collecting had also alerted me to a problem attending the task of set completion. The cards in Topps' sixth and seventh series always appeared on store shelves in my area in late summer, when they would barely get in circulation before being chased from the shelves by football cards. The analogous hurdle for the autograph collector came when the Triple A season ended and farmhands came up. There was little time to collect those September call-ups from Tidewater and Memphis, but they belonged in the metal box, too. I had to scramble to get Bob Johnson's autograph, as well as Jim Gosger's. The signatures of Bob Heise and Jesse Hudson. And Les Rohr. Les Rohr is right in front of Nolan Ryan in the metal box. Though he appeared in only one game that season, giving up five hits, a walk and three earned runs in 1⅓ innings (an ERA of 20.25), Rohr is just as essential to me as Ryan. His is a minimalist name—Les is Rohr—and a rendering of that name is all he sent me. Some of the other September Mets, new to the majors and likely intrigued by fans' solicitations, seemed to want to do more than merely sign. They wanted to engage in dialogue.

"I don't have any photo," Jesse Hudson scrawled on the back of his file card. I must have asked Jesse for one, to use as trade bait.

Bob Heise had added, "Best Wishes." And Bob Johnson, inexplicably, wrote "Thanks."

Whatever for? Thank *you*.

To the extent that one can control such things, I modeled my handwriting after Jerry Grote's. A very slight leftward slant; prominent initial letter; much smaller subordinate ones.

Grote was my absolute favorite, and nothing about him seemed unworthy of emulation. I would glow while reading encomiums about him in *The Sporting News*—Lou Brock once called him the toughest catcher to steal against, tougher even than Johnny Bench. I had seen Grote hit his first major league home run on TV; had coerced my dad into taking me to a particular pregame promotion at Shea Stadium, where Grote met with and signed for his public; had even, through the willful titration of prepubescent hormones, developed a crush on Grote's lovely wife.

Only later would I learn that Grote was considered one of the game's great sour-tempered sonsofbitches. He left baseball briefly in 1979 with the *soi-disant* goal of spending more time with his family, but his wife soon left him.

Yogi Berra's *Berra* is a matter-of-fact scrawl, over when it's over. But his *Yogi* has some surprisingly baroque touches. The styles of those first and last names coexist stubbornly, not unlike Yogi's subway series of stints as a player, a coach and a manager with both of New York's baseball clubs.

Yogi's dual allegiances raise the age-old and profound question: Why follow the Mets and not the Yankees? Today it's easy to answer: One ball club is owned by a book publisher, the other by a convicted felon. But back then, it was much more complicated. I think I ended up with the Mets because 1) I had no older brothers and 2) both of my parents were overwhelmingly apathetic toward baseball. There was no hand-me-down prejudice toward excellence, of the sort that might be imparted with indoctrination into the game from an elder—I had no kin critiquing my swing with, "You have to watch Mickey Mantle. Now there's a stroke," or "If you'd been around in '27 you'd have seen the greatest team of all time, the Yankees."

The Mets, like me, were green and still learning.

Like other fringe groups of that era, sports memorabilia collectors of the '60s communicated with one another through a crude, almost underground press. The hobby's *samizdats* were cranked out in towns with names that seemed to have been lifted from a Kerouac itinerary: Yarmouth, Maine; Coffeeville, Miss.; Lake Ronkonkoma, N.Y. My favorite was *Sports Collector's News* (the exact pluralization and positioning of the apostrophe I can't quite remember), a dittoed journal produced in some Wisconsin backwater by a man with a Ukranian surname. *SCN* wended its way to most of its readers via third-class mail, so by the time each copy reached our mailbox it had (fortunately) long lost the clammy scent of duplicating spirit that I had learned to fear in grade school as heralding a pop quiz. It had (unfortunately) also long lost much of its legibility.

It indulged every idiosyncrasy. Nominally a monthly, but in fact a maddening occasional, *SCN* helped galvanize the farflung collectors of cards and books and autographs who, but for the *News*, would have been oblivious to one another's existence. Oh, there were other publications: *The Sports Trader*, published by a Mississippian who feuded openly with *SCN*'s editor, was a spare shopper, packed with ads from card collectors. But *SCN* ran more articles than ads, and its editor favored autographs over cards. In *SCN*'s many pages of blurred purple I learned how to store signatures, how to assess them for authenticity and—this was crucial, for we lived in upstate New York, hours from the nearest big league park—how to write away for them.

Collectors were implored to follow the strictest canons of etiquette when requesting an autograph through the mails, so as not to besmirch the hobby's good name. We were to enclose a fan letter, with an obligatory line or two about how we hoped that his sore shoulder would mend, or that he could avoid getting optioned to Memphis. We had to provide the courtesy of a stamped self-addressed envelope. And, for signing, we were to include a couple of 3 x 5s—more than one if we were bold, so as to have duplicates with which to trade.

Once, in a gala Christmas issue or some such, *SCN* even published a short story. The plot centered around a fictitious collector who tried everything to get the signature of a certain star. This star, alas, had a policy of not signing. Ultimately our hero wrote his hero a check; to cash it, the player had to endorse the check's backside, and the protagonist got the coveted signature with his next bank statement. To a kid innocent of the ways of commerce, the tale was bewildering. But it did provide me with a reassuring trump card, for several Mets were proving to be recalcitrant.

The story's very publication confirmed for me that readers of *SCN* were the humanists of the collecting world. They tended to favor the article over the advertisement, the warm signature over the cold card. It was a fellow humanist, whose *SCN* ad I had answered, who would turn my collecting life around.

To this day I'm not certain where Seminole, Fla., is, though I suspect one could hit fungoes from its center to St. Petersburg, where the Mets trained each spring. Mark Jordan lived in Seminole, and with day trips to St. Pete he came naturally to obtain all sorts of arcane Mets memorabilia, for which I sent him large chunks of my pocket money. As I sift through some of those items, it occurs to me that Mark must have pillaged Al Lang Field after every spring game. Here's a 15¢ Grapefruit League scorecard; a mimeographed radio script detailing what the Mets' play-by-play men would drop into their broadcasts back to New York; even a green-tinted lineup card, filled out in Gil Hodges's hand and signed by him, surname only.

Most of all, Mark Jordan had autographs. He would get them in person, in black felt-tip (as the hobby papers recommended), and on the reverse of each file card he would fastidiously type the date and circumstances of acquisition. As we began exchanging letters, I savored my good fortune. I made my Mets affections clear. Mark sold me some signatures, while I, dipping into my modest cache of programs, yearbooks and media guides, bartered for others.

Mark and I weren't pen pals, exactly, and to this day I know almost nothing about him. I imagined him to be tow-headed and living with his father in a house with a two-swamp-buggy garage, for my only exposure to young male Floridians came from the TV series *Flipper*. In one letter Mark referred offhandedly to an autograph as a "John Henry," and I was impressed that he could make such a worldly allusion. At that point, neither of us had undergone enough schooling to nail down the difference between John Henry and John Hancock.

Flipping through the box, it's obvious which John Henrys I got from Mark. They have his inscriptions on their backs: JIM MCANDREW IN PERSON 3/20/69, for instance.

I had resolved to get as many Mets as possible without Mark's help—on my own, through the mails—and snap up the occasional one I could in person. We lived near the upstanding minor league town of Rochester, N.Y., home to the Triple A Red Wings, Baltimore's top farm club. Rochester had the liability of breeding Orioles' stepfans, whose presence would later cause me great aggravation. But it also permitted me to corner Met-to-be Jim Bibby during one of the Tidewater Tides' swings through town. Bibby signed the back of a Wings' program for me, and I carefully cut out his autograph and taped it to a file card.

Steadily the metal box filled up. In retrospect, I'm amazed at the alacrity with which most Mets answered. But Tommie Agee could have wallpapered his locker with all the envelopes and file cards I plied him with over the rest of that summer; he could have featherbedded his ego with all the letters, each more fawning, I enclosed. September delivered to me a strange ambivalence: giddiness as the Mets conjured up one victory after another, and despair as nothing from Agee came in the mail. I had long since checked with Mark, who confirmed that he had somehow missed Agee during the spring. Oh, to have been one of those Game 3 outfield drives off the bat of Elrod Hendricks or Paul Blair, and meet up with Tommie Agee.

I considered the canceled-check solution. Back in 1969 a major leaguer just might have found tribute from an adoring fan something other than mere chump change, and gone through the trouble of cashing that check. Yet at age 12 I was at an interstice of personal finance, between my last piggy bank and first passbook savings. I had no check to write, no account on which to draw.

I pleaded my case to my parents, but to no avail. They didn't believe we had any business paying for Tommie Agee's lawn furniture.

Ever so gradually, the Rochester *Democrat & Chronicle* that crossed our doorstep each morning began to tell of the most extraordinary occurrences. The Mets seemed to have forgotten how to lose. By noon the mailman would have retraced the paperboy's steps, and I would have begun to consider each incoming autograph a sort of personalized notarization of whatever the Mets had done the night before. A few of our red-letter days, both mine and the Mets':

- May 28. Bud Harrelson's 11th-inning single beats the Padres, beginning an 11-game winning streak that causes much consternation around the NL. (On Sept. 23 Harrelson would hit another 11th-inning single to allow the Mets to clinch a tie for the Eastern Division title.)
- June 3. At the midpoint of the Mets' streak, Tom Seaver pitches New York past the Dodgers and past .500. Of course, these being the Mets, there is the strong likelihood that they will lose the next night and fall back to .500. But Jack DiLauro, some Tidewater flotsam, keeps them afloat. He shuts out L.A. for nine innings, and New York wins 1–0 in the 15th.

- June 13. Al Jackson, the last original Met, is sold to the Reds. A shame, for he has creditable penmanship. His sale must be a requisite act of exorcism.

- July 9. In the midst of winning the first "crucial series" in their history, the Mets watch a cub, Jimmy Quails, spoil Seaver's bid for a perfect game with a one-out, ninth-inning single. Does this look like the signature of a man obsessed with perfection? Seaver later calls his biography *The Perfect Game* and writes therein of that night: "I wanted that perfect game more than I'd ever wanted anything in my baseball life."

   I felt the same way about Tommie Agee's autograph.

- July 15. The Rematch at Wrigley. Today, Mets manager Gil Hodges delivers the riposte of the ages. Consider please Tug McGraw's signature: The whimsical loops to the capital "T" and "G"; the irrepressible flourish on that final "w." Now, recall Cubs third baseman Ron Santo, who had taken to clicking his heels to celebrate Chicago victories. And picture Santo exchanging lineup cards with Hodges at home plate before the game, protesting that he had to perform his fancy footwork, or the Bleacher Bums would boo him.

   "You remind me of Tug McGraw," Hodges tells Santo. "When he was young and immature and nervous, he used to jump up and down. But he doesn't do it anymore."

   The Mets take two of three again, including a 9–5 win the next day, which is assured for reliever Cal Koonce by a late double play. Koonce makes bold strokes with his capitals, getting all he can out of that hard-consonant alliteration. He had irony and scansion down pretty well, too; after the game Koonce pens these lines in his infield's honor:

   The Cubs have Kessinger to Beckert to Banks.

   Their ability carries no shame.

   But for general purposes

   I would just as soon have

   From [Al] Weis to [Ken]

   Boswell to [Ed] Krane[pool].

   In fact, Donn Clendenon had entered the game, replacing Kranepool in the fourth inning. But even relief pitchers are entitled to poetic license.

- August 13. Only 24 hours earlier the Mets were 9½ games behind the Cubs. But Jerry Koosman and Don Cardwell win, to finish back-to-back doubleheader sweeps of the Padres. The stretch drive has begun.

   Here, I hoped.

- September 12. Koosman and Cardwell win both ends of another doubleheader. But this time, with Art Shamsky out in observance of Rosh Hashanah, the Mets sweep the Pirates by twin 1–0 scores—and the pitchers single home each run.

  Here, I knew.

- September 24. The demipennant is clinched 6–0 over the Cards at Shea. Gary Gentry throws the shutout, and the next morning's New York *Daily News* carries this headline: THE MOON: ASTRONAUTS TOOK 9 YEARS, METS 8.

- October 6. The pennant is won 7–4, as the Mets take their third straight from the Braves. The Mets don't normally make shrewd moves. They once drafted someone named Steve Chilcott when they could have chosen Reggie Jackson. But homers from Wayne Garrett, whom Atlanta had pawned to New York for $25,000 over the winter, and Boswell finish off the Braves.

- October 15. Handwriting analysts believe that the closer the dot of an i is to its base, the more attentive to detail the writer is. Thank goodness for J.C. Martin's lack of attention to detail. Martin's dot over the "i" is the graphological equivalent of a passed ball, which reminds us that if the Mets backup catcher had tended to the detail of staying outside the first baseline while running out his notorious bunt in Game 4, Oriole reliever Pete Richert's throw wouldn't have struck Martin's left wrist, and Rod Stupid might never have scurried around from second with the winning run.

  Graphoanalysis can tell us more. Seeing that "T" crossed well above the stem, one would suspect Ron Taylor of being a dreamer. But a stopper out of the bullpen, as Taylor was, *should* believe that nothing is impossible. So should a doctor, which Taylor is today, for the Toronto Blue Jays.

  For contrast, look at third base coach Eddie Yost's autograph. The "t" is crossed squarely in the middle, suggesting practicality— exactly what you'd expect from a guy who drew 1,614 career walks, and what you would want in the coach's box at third. Today Yost lives in semiretirement in Wellesley, Mass., repairing antique clocks.

  A far-forward slant indicates a willingness to reach out to others. Good thing that, after his retirement from baseball, Ed Charles worked as a talent scout for the Mets.

  Those who underscore their signature envision themselves on a line of movement. They are self-reliant, it is said, and sometimes unusually motivated. Hodges was the only Met who underscored his.

  If there was only one, best that it was the manager.

I have always thought of strikeouts and Ron Swoboda together, as a sort of hand-in-hand, bat-in-hand-back-to-the-dugout couple. That may stem from Swoboda cracking a pair of two-run homers off the Cards' Steve Carlton on Sept. 15, obviating Carlton's 19 strikeouts and giving the Mets a 4–3 victory. Or from my being at Shea with my grandfather on a day Swoboda chose to whiff four times. Baseball normally passed my grandfather by, but this was so prodigious an exhibition of ineptitude that even he was impressed. Soon afterward he sent me a clipping from *The New York Times* about some Czechoslovakian politico named Svoboda, and a note suggesting that an Eastern European exile awaited the failed slugger. I was duly amused.

Two years ago I had the chance to conclude that Ron Swoboda might have been amused, too. I was in Phoenix, covering a meaningless early season basketball game between the Suns and the Cleveland Cavaliers. Soon after tipoff, as I sat in the press tribune above halfcourt, another foot soldier of the Fourth Estate slid into the seat beside me. We began chatting. He was full of gossip and spoke with a cynical edge—about the travails of the Arizona State athletic department, and Phoenix's prospects for a pro football team, and a particular Suns rookie who looked good out on the floor.

He introduced himself as Ron Swoboda, sports anchor for KTVK-TV in Phoenix.

The man who had sprawled his form blindly across Shea's rightfield greensward to preempt Brooks Robinson's liner in Game 4 was now my peer. I couldn't permit us to talk merely sports; we had to address transcendent things.

"You know, I lived and died with you guys then," I said. "Skipped metal shop to see your catch."

Swoboda looked as if someone had just jarred the ball loose. Quickly he steered conversation back to the Sun Devils' dirty laundry and NFL expansion franchises and Jay Humphries.

If I ever meet Tommie Agee, I resolved, I'll approach him differently. I won't let him know.

The "C" in his autograph comes right off of Cleon Jones's face.

The man with the fishhook scar caught the final out of the Series, an ironic fly ball off the bat of current Mets manager Davey Johnson. Then he genuflected on the warning track. Not long after the Mets gave Jones his release in 1975, a friend of mine, vagabonding through the Deep South, found himself in Mobile and decided to look him up. Cleon and his wife, Angela, received him graciously in their rambling ranch house, which sat on a manicured lawn surrounded by shotgun shacks.

"I'll never forget that scar," my friend recalls. "You could be standing right in front of him, yet when he spoke to you, he'd position his shoulders and face so you couldn't see it at all. It was obviously a learned behavior. The only time I'd seen anything like it was when I was once introduced to Bob Dole [the senator from Kansas, whose right arm is disabled from a war injury]. Dole locks you in with his eyes and sticks out his left hand, and he waits for you to make the necessary adjustment."

Cleon told my friend that he had shed most of his bitterness over the Mets' handling of the incident from the previous year, in which St. Petersburg police (perhaps patrolman Mark Jordan?) found him sleeping nude in the back of a station wagon at 5:00 a.m. with a woman who was not Angela. Mets president M. Donald Grant summoned Jones to New York and forced him to read a public apology. Cleon did just that, in a scene that Red Smith described as "an exercise in medieval torture."

It was so wrong for Cleon Jones, a man who had lived his life behind a scar, to be humiliated by M. Donald Grant, a man who had lived his behind an initial.

I swung a deal during the 1969–70 hot stove season. I sent several NFL media guides to a collector in Jim Thorpe, Pa., for a '68 Mets program (cover mottled during a rain delay) and a '67 Tommie Agee autographed bubble gum card that, in theory, completed my set.

But I have always had misgivings about that card. Agee is posed heretically in a White Sox uniform. The autograph doesn't resemble to my satisfaction the facsimile signature on the card's face. And, as a card, it's somehow violate in and of itself. So from time to time over the past decade and a half I have cast about for a purer and more persuasive Tommie Agee.

Several years ago I contacted R.J. (Jack) Smalling, an Ames, Iowa, insurance salesman, to enlist him in my search. Smalling is to autograph collecting what Ted Williams is to hitting, both fount and exemplar. In addition to having one of the largest collections of baseball autographs extant, Smalling has for years compiled *The Sport Americana Baseball Address List*, which includes a mailing address, or date and place of death, for nearly everyone who has ever played in the majors. Hobbyists use the addresses to obtain signatures and the necrology to fix their value. Like undertakers and lawyers, autograph collectors profit from death, and Smalling relies on a nationwide network of sources to track down death certificates for the most obscure ex-ballplayers. (Only one '69 Met player, Daniel Vincent Frisella, is dead. He was killed on New Year's Day, 1977, in a dune-buggy accident near Phoenix.)

Soon enough Smalling wrote me to confess that he was similarly bamboozled in *his* search, for Agee's current address. Yet he did have a 3 x 5 Tommie Agee kicking around the house, which he enclosed, gratis.

The "T" up front is vaguely J-like, and there's a healthy loop in the "o," both features that match Tommie Agee facsimile autographs.

But the first name has been spelled Tommy.

And so I'm in a metal box filled with autographs, bound for Queens. This box is a graffiti-defaced subway car on the A train, though I'm not taking it in the direction that Duke Ellington had in mind. Smalling's latest *Address List* has only an old entry for Agee, at 112-08 Astoria Boulevard in East Elmhurst, not far from Shea. But I have heard that he keeps a saloon called The Outfielder's Lounge, and there's just such an establishment in the phone book, at 114-12 Van Wyck Expressway in Ozone Park.

Just into Queens the A burrows above ground, before bending abruptly south toward Kennedy Airport and the Rockaways. I alight at that elbow, descend from the trestle and begin walking east along Rockaway Boulevard through the land of hyphenated house numbers: past Aqueduct Race Track, past storefronts of Italian-American fraternal organizations, and finally into a tidy neighborhood that straddles the Van Wyck Expressway.

At 114-12 there's no sign of an Outfielder's Lounge—only a brick building with a corrugated steel grate over its facade, and a sign reading SUPPER CLUB/CATERING/DISCO. I duck into the Car Clinic next door and tell the mechanic I'm looking for Tommie Agee. Agee and his bar have been gone for a few months, he says, and suggests that I try a spot up near Shea, hard by the Grand Central Parkway on-ramp.

"On Astoria Boulevard?" The site he describes sounds much like the address listed in Jack Smalling's book. "Is that the place he used to own?"

"That's it. It's not his place anymore, but that's where you'll find him."

A cabbie takes me to 112-08 Astoria, a restaurant called the Stadium Inn. It's early on a Saturday evening in July, and there's a small group around the bar—black, well dressed, middle-aged. I take a stool and ask the barmaid whether Tommie Agee ever stops by.

"All the time," she says. "He was in here Thursday night. He usually comes by Saturdays, too."

I show her my Agee bubble gum card. She laughs at his callow face, then passes the card among the other patrons, who all seem to know him.

I feel good. Soon the Temptations come on the jukebox, singing *Silent Night*, and I feel even better. A '60s group crooning a timeless hymn to a festival of gift giving: This would be the perfect fanfare to accompany Tommie Agee striding through the door.

But this is another season, and I sit, and sit some more, and he doesn't walk in. After I've tippled a little and felt the hours pass, the barmaid—by now I know her as Janice—offers to tell Tommie I've been by. I write out my address and hand her a 3 x 5, and ask if she might ask Agee to sign it and forward it to me. She agrees to, and I settle my account, tipping her handsomely.

"Tell him," I say to her on my way out, "it's for a 12-year-old I know."

DECEMBER 3, 2012

Tinker to Evers
to Chance...to Me

After years of boasting that he was related to Hall of Fame second baseman Johnny Evers, the author set out to explore—for better and worse—the century-old myth of the double-play artist

BY TIM LAYDEN

The cemetery spreads across a green hillside above the small upstate city of Troy, N.Y., where shirt collars and steel were once manufactured along the east bank of the Hudson River, but where neither is made anymore. At the entrance to the graveyard there is a three-story brick building that holds musty plot maps spread out on creaky tables. Nobody is inside, and it feels as if the structure has been empty for a very long time. It is a sunny autumn morning; the leaves have just begun to change color. A few cars are parked along the roadway that bisects the cemetery, one set of wheels on grass and the other on pavement, so that other vehicles can pass.

A tall man in a baseball cap speaks with a woman in sunglasses and then points in the distance. His name is Danny Catlin, and if you want to find a gravesite in St. Mary's Cemetery, he is your guy. "You give me the name and a date of birth or death," says Danny, "I call it in, and they give me the location." He is unabashedly cheerful, which feels vaguely at odds with his surroundings. Cemeteries have always left me uneasy. When I was a Catholic altar boy, I would stare off in the distance during burial services, unnerved by the ceremony and even more by the surroundings, silently counting down the minutes until I could leave all that death behind.

"Name?" Danny is holding his pen at the ready.

"You might know this one without calling," I say. "Johnny Evers?"

"The baseball player?" says Danny. "Oh, I know where he is." He speaks as if those laid to rest here are living people who have moved to new addresses. We walk down to the southeast corner of the property and stop at a Mini Cooper–sized hunk of light-gray stone. Five people are buried beneath this earth, the first since 1885 and the most recent since 1974. On the eastern face of the large tombstone are five raised capital letters: EVERS. Names and dates are etched into the other three sides of the rock, including:

JOHN J EVERS 1881–1947

Nowhere does it say that Evers (who pronounced his name *EE-vers*, not *EV-ers*, as widely assumed) was a major league baseball player in the early 20th century, a brainy Dead Ball era infielder who was voted into the Hall of Fame in 1946. Nowhere does it say that he and two of his teammates were featured in a piece of baseball doggerel that's familiar to many a century later. Nowhere does it say that he was a central figure in one of the most controversial plays in baseball history. And nowhere does it mention the failed marriage, the nervous breakdowns or the bankruptcies (though there are two infants buried in the plot and named on the stone, hinting at a deep unexplained sadness). Nor does it mention the feeling of emptiness, the lifelong struggle to find traction after baseball, because baseball had been such a perfect vessel for his consuming drive, and life was simply messy and complex and couldn't be defeated with scrappy want-to.

There's just a whisper of a breeze in the clear morning air, and seemingly not a sound on earth. Minutes pass before Danny asks, "He's a relative?"

"My uncle," I answer, and then I pull it back, awkwardly qualifying the relationship. "My mother's uncle. My great-uncle. He died nine years before I was born. Uncle Johnny."

These are the saddest of possible words:
"Tinker to Evers to Chance."
Trio of bear cubs, and fleeter than birds,
Tinker and Evers and Chance.
Ruthlessly pricking our gonfalon bubble,
Making a Giant hit into a double—
Words that are heavy with nothing but trouble:
"Tinker to Evers to Chance."
—FRANKLIN P. ADAMS, "Baseball's Sad Lexicon," *New York Evening Mail*, 1910

For most of my life my uncle Johnny was a parlor trick I would spring on unsuspecting peers. He was related to me, and he was verifiably famous;

this is a powerful social tool. Whether in the high school locker room or at the college keg party or at the bar with fellow sportswriters deep in the postdeadline night, somebody would always boast about an accomplished family member or close friend. This guy's cousin played at Boston College and had a tryout with the Falcons—made it to the last cut. (Half of these are wild exaggerations or straight-up b.s.) But when your hole card is the middleman in Tinker to Evers to Chance, and he's got a plaque in the Hall of Fame? I won a lot of one-upmanship games by matter-of-factly dropping Uncle Johnny's name and awaiting the reaction: *Whoa, what?* Not because a guy who played for the Cubs a century ago is equivalent to a modern celebrity, but because he embodies an odd combination of the familiar and the strange, cloaked in a thick mist of history.

Most of it was a lie. Not the genealogical part: John Joseph Evers was my maternal grandfather's brother. Not the baseball part, either: He was, indeed, the guy in the poem and the guy in the Hall of Fame. Those are the bold-line items I co-opted for the purpose of shutting down discussions and even impressing my own children with their heritage, slicing off a piece of another man's legacy and taking it for my own just because we share a little bit of DNA. But I knew far less about Uncle Johnny than I did about the many athletes I've interviewed and profiled. The last time I dropped his name was less than a year ago, at a party with a small group of sports journalists. I got the usual cred, but this time one of the guys followed up. "Did you ever think of writing a story about him?" asked my SPORTS ILLUSTRATED colleague Alex Wolff. And there it was, so obvious that I was embarrassed to have missed it all these years.

Of course I would write a story. I would go searching for Uncle Johnny, give myself a long-overdue history lesson and remind the world of the great man who had once borne my blood on big league diamonds. It would make us even, Uncle Johnny and me, make good on all those empty boasts I had delivered just for effect. And I can say now that it was a profound journey, one that left me staring for long hours into the eyes of men long dead, photographed when they were much younger than my 56 years; that left me sitting alongside my 81-year-old mother (one of the few people still alive who knew Johnny Evers and remembers him) talking about things that we had never talked about before; that left me holding in my hand one of the most famous baseballs in history, my fingers shaking because I knew where it had been and who had touched it.

But most of all, it was a journey that reminded me of what every reporter knows: Disturbing the dust of mythology almost always damages the myth.

Some truths: Johnny Evers was born in Troy on July 21, 1881, the fourth of six sons, nine children in all, to John Joseph Evers Sr. and Ellen Keating Evers. The family lived at 437 Third Street, three blocks from the Hudson in South Troy. My great-grandfather is described in city records as a "clerk," but he was also the president of the school board, a position with political clout. His son Johnny, like all of the Evers boys, was educated in Catholic schools with other Irish kids. And like all of the Evers boys, he played sandlot baseball hour upon hour. Their uncle, Tom Evers, had been a pro ballplayer in the 1880s. Johnny graduated from St. Joseph's Christian Brothers School in 1898, just shy of 17 years old. And it is here that his story vanishes briefly in the fog.

Nearly four years would pass before Johnny became a professional baseball player. It has been written with some authority for more than a century that he spent much of those four years working in a Troy collar factory, earning $4 per week dispensed in an envelope in four $1 bills. It is a plausible story because the collar trade was a thriving sector of Troy's economy, but there is no hard evidence for it. Troy city directories from 1899 to 1901 list John J. Evers, like his father, as a "clerk," although the 1901 edition also lists him as the coproprietor, with his older brother Mike, of Evers Brothers Saloon, in the building next to the family's home on Third Street. Several other published sources suggest that Johnny spent time as a sign painter's apprentice. So at 19 he was a bar owner, a civil servant of some sort and perhaps a factory worker. Given the stubbornness and drive that would characterize his major league career, it's probable that he was also playing baseball endlessly. He had his own amateur team, the Cheerups, and probably played for others as well.

A few more truths: In 1902 Johnny was signed to play shortstop for the Troy team in the New York State League, a minor circuit from which players occasionally ascended straight to the majors. He made his debut on May 9 at Laureate Field in North Troy, a small stadium along the Hudson. He batted leadoff and went hitless in three at bats against Ilion. The *Troy Times* made note of him in the final paragraph of its game story: "Young Evers played shortstop for the local team and is said to show much promise."

At 20 Johnny Evers was a small man; he would grow to be only 5'9", and at the peak of his major league career he weighed 135 pounds. In photographs he swims in his baggy flannel uniform. His most distinguishing facial characteristic was a protruding jaw, which would come to represent the tenacity and combativeness he displayed as a professional. "The spidery little fellow with the pugnacious jaw and the flaming spirit," Arthur Daley of *The New York Times* described Evers after he died.

On Aug. 21, 1902, Johnny's father died at age 54. Just eight days later the following item appeared on the sports page of the Chicago *Daily Tribune*: "Troy's clever shortstop, Evers, have [sic] been sold to the Chicago National League club and will report to that club in Philadelphia." That team, which was called the Orphans and in 1903 would become the Cubs, had lost infielder Bobby (Link) Lowe to an injury. An article published in *Baseball Magazine* in 1953 under the byline of Hugh Fullerton Sr. told the story of Evers's elevation. Fullerton wrote that George Huff, a football and baseball coach at Illinois who scouted for the Cubs in the summer, was watching a series of games between Albany and Troy when he received word that Lowe was injured. Fullerton, a prolific reporter whose suspicions played a role in uncovering the 1919 Black Sox scandal, wrote, "Huff...switched his attention to one of the second basemen in the game...a wiry little bunch of nerves and muscle. The kid was only a few months out of school.... But he gave unmistakable signs of possessing a baseball 'brain' in his head."

There is a probably a little fact and a little fiction in this tale, but this much is true: One month past his 21st birthday, having lost his father only days earlier, Evers took a train ride from Troy to Philadelphia. The next afternoon he started for Chicago, and he never again played in the minor leagues except ceremonially at the end of his career. Joe Tinker, an infielder from Kansas, was a rookie with the Orphans; Frank Chance, a big first baseman from California, was in his fifth major league season. Evers started that game at shortstop, but he was soon moved to second base, between Tinker and Chance. They turned their first double play on Sept. 15, with 10 games remaining in the 143-game season.

Over the next seven years the trio developed into a notorious DP combination. It was on July 12, 1910, according to baseball historians Tim Wiles and Jack Bales, that Franklin Pierce Adams mythologized the Cubs infielders with his poem. Adams was not a sportswriter but rather a respected columnist (he later would be a founding member of the famed Algonquin Round Table) who occasionally watched Giants games at the Polo Grounds. On that afternoon his editor asked him for eight lines of copy to complete a column, and "Baseball's Sad Lexicon" was the result. Tinker, Evers and Chance had turned a double play against the Giants the previous day, though in fact they never led the National League in that category; Uncle Johnny would be part of only 270 double plays in the six years from 1905 to '10, less than one every three games. Yet this is misleading. The Cubs were a Dead Ball era dynasty with excellent pitching. Opponents had few base runners; hence there were few opportunities for double plays. That Tinker, Evers and Chance were excellent fielders was taken for granted and easy fodder for Adams's rhyme. (In 1949 the MGM musical *Take Me Out to the Ballgame* would feature a DP combination called O'Brien, Ryan and Goldberg, patterned after Tinker, Evers and Chance. Frank Sinatra played Ryan, the Uncle Johnny role.)

Evers, meanwhile, was a vital part of Cubs teams that went to four World Series and won two championships. His rise is reliably told in the statistics of the era. Again, truths: From 1903 to '08 he averaged 134 games and was among the top five in the league in stolen bases three times. By the end of his career he had been first or second in most at bats per strikeout six times. The guy did not whiff.

There are practical differences between major league baseball in the first two decades of the 20th century and the game as it is played today. All of the players were white. (Uncle Johnny was born 16 years after the abolition of slavery.) Fielders wore tiny gloves, barely larger than modern ski mittens. The fields were much more uneven than today's. The period from 1900 (or earlier) to approximately 1919 was called the Dead Ball era for good reason: Baseballs were kept in play, and over the course of games they were beaten to a pulp.

In this world Evers was an exceptionally effective fielder. He was nicknamed the Crab. Some writings attribute the name to his manner of scooting low along the dirt to dig out ground balls, but many more ascribe it to his willingness to argue any point with anybody. Evers would stay up at night reading the rule book, looking for loopholes to exploit—time that would one day prove very useful.

The Cubs had 116 victories in 1906, tied with the 2001 Mariners for the most in major league history even though those Cubs played seven fewer games. Evers played 154 of the 155 games, more than any other member of that team. The Cubs were upset in the World Series by the crosstown White Sox, but in '07 they won 107 games and swept the Tigers and 20-year-old Ty Cobb for the championship. Evers hit .350 in the Series and had two doubles and three stolen bases. It wasn't until a year later, though, that his name would be indelibly written in the pages of baseball history.

The 1908 National League pennant race has been the subject of at least two nonfiction books—Cait Murphy's *Crazy '08* and G.H. Fleming's *The Unforgettable Season*—and a significant part of Eric Rolfe Greenberg's novel, *The Celebrant*, a fictional account of the life of Hall of Fame pitcher Christy Mathewson. The novel refers to Evers as "that hard, pitiless man, beloved everywhere in Chicago save his own team's clubhouse." This was surely informed by the fact that Evers, angered over a ball thrown too hard from too close, didn't speak to Tinker from '07 to at least '09.

The '08 season reached a climax on Wednesday, Sept. 23, at the Polo Grounds in New York, in a game between the Cubs and the Giants. The two teams were tied in the standings with another 10 games to play after that one, in which the score was tied 1–1 going into the bottom of the ninth. Mathewson had held the Cubs to five hits, while Uncle Johnny was "the criminal of the afternoon," the *New York Herald* wrote, "doing some highway robbing of a serious nature. He stole a single from [Moose] McCormick in the fourth inning by jumping up in the air and stabbing one that looked good for two sacks." There were two outs and McCormick was on first when 19-year-old rookie first baseman Fred Merkle—who was making his first career start because Fred Tenney had an attack of lumbago—lined a single to right. Then, with Merkle on first and McCormick on third, shortstop Al Bridwell singled to center. McCormick trotted home from third, and a celebration began. "Perfect ladies are screaming like a batch of Coney barkers," wrote *The New York Times*. Fans rushed the field.

Precisely what took place next will never be known, though this much seems certain: Merkle began running toward second base, but when it became apparent that McCormick would score easily, and fans swarmed the field, Merkle veered off and ran toward the Giants' clubhouse in centerfield. This was common practice. Some seconds—or minutes—later, Evers stood on second base with the ball. Home plate umpire Hank O'Day called Merkle out, disallowed McCormick's run, leaving the score tied, and called the game because of darkness. "In a moment, the scene became one of the wildest confusion," wrote the *New York Tribune*. "A dozen fights started."

It's not clear—and will never be clear—how the baseball wound up in Evers's hands on second base, or even if it was the baseball that Bridwell hit into centerfield. That is part of the fascination with what came to be known, cruelly, as Merkle's Boner. The ball might have been thrown in from center by the Cubs' Solly Hofman. Once it was thrown in, it might have been intercepted by Giants pitcher Joe (Iron Man) McGinnity, who was coaching third base that day, and McGinnity might have lost it to charging Cubs players or thrown it into the stands, where Cubs retrieved it, possibly by decking a fan in a bowler hat. Then again, the recovered ball might not have been the one that Bridwell struck. All of these scenarios have been described in reporting of the day and in subsequent books and articles. But one thing rings true: The impetus for the force-out was "the quick-witted Evers, ever on the alert to gain a point," wrote the *New York Press*.

Nineteen days earlier, during a game in Pittsburgh, Evers had similarly tried to annul the Pirates' winning run in the 10th inning. The umpire was O'Day, and the player on first base was Warren Gill. But O'Day claimed not to have seen either Gill leave the field early or Evers touch second base.

The run counted. The Cubs protested to National League president Harry Pulliam, who did not overrule the call, allowing Pittsburgh's victory to stand. But Evers had planted a seed in O'Day's head (and in those of his own teammates), and on Sept. 23 O'Day was surely watching when Merkle left the field and Uncle Johnny touched second base.

Again Pulliam did not overrule O'Day, though Pulliam was so shaken by the controversy that it was one of the reasons he shot himself dead 10 months later. The Cubs and the Giants finished the season tied for first. Chicago won a one-game playoff at the packed Polo Grounds on Oct. 8 and went on to defeat Detroit again in the Series.

Evers was at the pinnacle of his baseball career. He had batted .300 for the season (fifth in the NL), and his OPS was .777 (third). He again hit .350 in the World Series, and when it was over he went home to Troy and, in January 1909, married Helen Fitzgibbons, described by *The Sporting News* as "one of Troy's prettiest and most charming girls." Their son, John Jr., was born before the end of the year. Johnny was 27, and he must have been very happy. He was nervous and driven, but at that age and in that place, he couldn't have anticipated the troubles that lay ahead.

The 1910 season was 26 games old on May 20 when the Cubs' game against the Brooklyn Dodgers was rained out at Chicago's West Side Grounds. Johnny Evers left the ballpark in his new car along with his 18-year-old brother, Joe, my grandfather, who was living with Johnny in Chicago after the death of their mother. Also in the car was George A. Macdonald, 31, a writer for the *Chicago Journal* and a friend of Johnny's. A fourth passenger was described by the Chicago *Daily Tribune* as "a negro boy, who usually acts a mechanician," helping to drive the vehicle whenever Johnny, who was new to driving, needed assistance.

Moments after leaving the field, the automobile was struck by a trolley car and tossed onto its side. The Everses and the young mechanic were not hurt, but Macdonald was thrown partially out of the vehicle, and his head was wedged between the front fender and the body of the car, crushing his skull. He died that night in a hospital.

Evers was overwhelmed with grief. A wire-service story published three days after the crash was headlined JOHNNY EVERS IS NERVOUS WRECK and said Evers might miss the rest of the season. In 1913, in a reflective story in *Baseball Magazine*, Evers told author F.C. Lane, "The shock of sudden death was more than I could stand. I had my first touch of nervous prostration and was laid up for five weeks.... I felt a good deal, I imagine, the way a murderer feels."

Years later, when Evers was retired and living in Albany, N.Y., across the river from Troy, he would tell people that he could never shake the image of Macdonald's death. "That man's head," he would say, "it was just hanging out of the car."

He returned for 125 games in 1910 but broke his leg in a late-season game against Cincinnati and didn't play in the Cubs' five-game World Series loss to the Philadelphia Athletics. That December came another blow. Evers had bought the Emerson Shoe Company, on River Street in Troy, after the '03 season and given his brothers part of the business. He had begun the process of opening a second store in Chicago when he received news—by telegram—that his original partner in Troy had run that business into the ground. Evers told Lane, "I figured that I had lost about $25,000, all that I had in the world. Furthermore, I was suffering from complete nervous breakdown." Johnny was earning only $4,000 a year; it was like Peyton Manning losing $150 million. He filed for bankruptcy. (Remarkably, in the midst of all this turmoil Evers published a book with Fullerton called *Touching Second: The Science of Baseball*, a densely detailed work that is part handbook and part memoir and reveals Johnny's sharp baseball intellect.)

Evers played only 46 games in 1911. Lane met him at the Copley Square Hotel in Boston that summer and wrote of his "haggard face, his trembling hand and air of nervous tension.... He was but a wasted shadow of the grand second baseman whose work had been the marvel of the generation." Evers later told Lane that before the summer of '11 ended, Chance sent him home to Troy, where a car was waiting to drive him 175 miles to a remote hunting camp at the northern edge of the Adirondack Mountains. There Johnny slept outdoors for days and cut his cigar intake from "many" per day to just one. This was therapy in '11.

And it turns out that Evers had one more baseball life in him. He returned to the Cubs in 1912 and hit a career-best .341 with a career-high OPS of .873. In '13 he took over from Chance as manager of the team but was fired after the season. He leveraged a contract offer from the upstart Federal League into a $25,000 deal with the Boston Braves, which made him one of the highest-paid players in baseball history to date. In Boston, at 32, he teamed with Hall of Fame shortstop Rabbit Maranville to form the backbone of the 1914 Miracle Braves, a team that roared from last place on July 4 to win the pennant and defeat the favored Athletics in the World Series. Evers batted .438 in the Series and was named NL MVP for the season.

It had been a remarkable career: In a dozen years Evers had played on the winningest team in history, engineered one of the game's most controversial plays, used a nascent form of free agency and led a legendary comeback.

But tragedy followed him relentlessly, and it would eventually crush him. During that triumphant 1914 season, Johnny and Helen's five-year-old son, John Jr. (called Jack), became ill with scarlet fever and was quarantined at home in Troy. My cousin John T. Evers interviewed numerous family members in the 1990s, and they told this story: A doctor granted Helen, who was known as Nellie, permission to allow the couple's three-year-old daughter, Helen, to visit her ailing brother. Jack would get better, but little Helen became ill and died in less than two weeks. She is buried with her parents on the rectangular plot in Troy. Johnny's and Helen's marriage had been uncertain because he lived in Chicago and she in Troy; their daughter's death ended it. They separated, and many in the family assumed mistakenly that the couple had quietly divorced, something that was rare among Irish Catholics at the time.

In the late 1940s, after Johnny was gone, Nellie was a patient at St. Peter's Hospital in Albany after breaking her hip. A young nursing student was on duty that night when one of her friends told her, "There's a patient downstairs named Evers." That nursing student was Kathryn Isabel Evers. Everyone called her Kay, and she is my mother. She was torn because of a longstanding family mandate to avoid the woman who had brought disgrace upon her famous uncle's marriage. But my mother chose to talk with Nellie, and found her very sweet. They didn't talk about Johnny. When Helen Fitzgibbons Evers died in 1974, the obituary listed her as the widow of baseball great Johnny Evers. They are buried as husband and wife.

After 1914, Johnny played parts of three more seasons in the major leagues, but never effectively. He lost his temper ever more frequently and was suspended on multiple occasions; newspaper stories increasingly portrayed him as less a gifted and tenacious player than a loose cannon. Johnny's byline appeared on a 1917 story in *Baseball Magazine* in which he said, "I have never felt wholly right since I had that severe nervous breakdown some years ago." He promised a comeback that never materialized. He had two more unsuccessful stints as a manager, and by 1924 he was gone from the game.

On another fall day, far from the cemetery, I sat looking at a yellowed and creased 8-by-10 photo of a young baseball player from a long time ago. Research can lead down long, strange alleys. Joe Evers, 10 years younger than his brother Johnny and unharmed in that automobile crash that killed George Macdonald in 1910, made it to the major leagues too. This was never mentioned in family conversation. Like Archibald (Moonlight) Graham in *Field of Dreams*, my grandfather played a single game in the major leagues, for the Giants on April 24, 1913. One of his teammates that day was Fred Merkle, and their manager was John J. McGraw, who had managed the Giants in 1908. In the *New York Times* account of a 7–1 victory over Philadelphia, the last paragraph reads: "Joe Evers, Johnny's young brother, got into the game for the first time in the third inning, when he ran for Chief Meyers and was tagged out at third base on an attempted double steal."

And that was it. McGraw released Joe in mid-May, and Joe spent the next 12 years—with a two-year break to serve in the Navy during World War I—playing for eight minor league teams, mostly in the Midwest. My grandmother Isabel Maxwell Evers was with him the entire time. I would know her as a kind elderly woman who served me poached eggs on toast and sweet milky tea for breakfast. Throughout her 20s she was a baseball wife. Even now, it's unimaginable to me.

In the photo, which I had never seen until a relative gave it to me, Joe Evers is wearing flannel pinstripes, and his hat is tipped to the left. He has the light skin and freckles that are prominent in our family, and he seems to be looking at something far off in the distance. He could be in Peoria, Ill., or Muskegon, Mich., or Cedar Rapids, Iowa, all places where he was employed. He could be full of dreams or beaten hopeless. There's no one to ask and no way to know, no matter how endlessly I stare.

By the mid-1920s Johnny Evers was permanently back home, living in Troy with his married older sister, Anna Evers Kennedy. He opened a sporting goods store with his brother Joe; it bore Johnny's name, but Joe did most of the work. Johnny settled into a *Glory Days* life, frequently re-creating the Merkle play for newspaper reporters, spinning tales at smokers and other gatherings, and ingratiating himself with the Democratic pols who ran Albany and for a time gave him a patronage job in the city's recreation department. When he would visit my mother's family in Troy, she would be told to wear a dress, as if preparing for Sunday Mass. Once Johnny brought her a stuffed replica of Popeye's pet dog, Jeep, and one summer day he took her to a local stadium to meet Connie Mack, who was passing through.

In 1936 Johnny declared bankruptcy again, with no assets and with liabilities of $10,499, yet the store remained in business. Pictures from this era show a man, once thin, puffed up to more than 180 pounds, his famous jaw scarcely prominent. He suffered his first stroke in 1940 at age 59 and had two more in '42 and '43. By this time he had moved to a first-floor apartment on State Street in Albany, where he was cared for by a longtime friend whom the family knew only as Mrs. Spoor. My mother and her siblings would visit, and Johnny would sit in a chair by the window, squeezing a rubber ball to recover some strength in his left side.

On April 23, 1946, Johnny was elected to the Baseball Hall of Fame—along with Tinker and Chance—by the Old-Timers' Committee. Eleven men were elected that year, and it remains a uniquely controversial moment in the history of the Hall, having occurred during a period in which there was a wide gulf in admission standards between the Baseball Writers Association of America and the Old-Timers' Committee. (The year Uncle Johnny went in with Tinker and Chance, the BBWAA had still not voted in Lefty Grove and Jimmie Foxx.) "From that moment on," Bill James writes in his 1994 book, *Whatever Happened to the Hall of Fame*, "the argument that the Hall of Fame should be only for the greatest of the great was irretrievably lost." On Tinker, Evers and Chance, James writes, "They stand out as being among the least qualified players in the Hall of Fame." James compares Evers to pre-1900 second baseman Bid McPhee and concludes that McPhee, who was not yet in the Hall, was a better player. James does not say unequivocally that Evers does not belong, but that is the undertone of his argument. He spends more time on Tinker, who he says "was a fine player, and is not the worst player in the Hall of Fame." (In a long *Baseball America* feature in 1913, dozens of experts concluded that Evers was the best second baseman in the National League. Sabermetrician Jay Jaffe's JAWS system rates Evers the 16th best of the 19 second basemen in the Hall but behind four excluded second basemen, including Lou Whitaker and Bobby Grich.)

But on that day in 1946, James was three years from being born, and the selections of Tinker, Evers and Chance were celebrated by many baseball enthusiasts, especially Cubs fans. Joe ran up State Street from the store to deliver the news, and my mother remembers a family celebration. A wire service photographer took an inappropriate picture of Johnny, bedridden and wearing wrinkled pajamas, his facial nerves ravaged by his multiple strokes, with old photos spread out on his lap. Less than a year later he died of a cerebral hemorrhage at 65. Thousands attended his funeral in Albany before he was interred at the base of that grassy hillside in his native Troy.

Johnny Evers Sporting Goods survived long after its founders passed away (Joe Evers died of diverticulitis at 57 in January 1949), flourishing in the energetic hands of Joe's son, my uncle Joe Jr., who was left in charge at age 25 and built it into one of the most successful independent stores in the region. As a teenage athlete I would revel in making the 90-minute pilgrimage with friends to Uncle Joe's store to buy the latest gear: Adidas sneakers, white football cleats, track spikes as light as air.

When my uncle retired in 1988, operation of the store passed to his three sons, my first cousins Joe, Jack and Terry Evers. Roughly two years later, John T. Evers, the same cousin who did research and interviews that are used in this story, found a cardboard box in the back of the store labeled HISTORIC BASEBALLS. On one of the them was clearly written MERKLE SEPT. 23, 1908.

"The Holy Grail," John remembers thinking. "I'm holding the Merkle ball in my hands. I'm thinking, I don't believe this."

John took the ball home and put it in a plastic case on the desk where he did homework as a commuting student at Siena College in nearby Loudonville. Within another two years the store had begun to struggle against the rising tide of big-box competitors, and my cousins made a decision to auction the ball to raise money. "We were in trouble with the business," says my cousin Joe. "There wasn't much discussion." Experts authenticated the ball. There was no time to digest the painful symmetry: The most significant baseball in Johnny Evers's long career was being sold in an attempt to save the business that bore his name. In February 1993 the Merkle ball was purchased at auction for $30,250 by Charlie Sheen. A year later the business went under.

Five years after that, as Sheen was divesting himself of his baseball memorabilia collection, he sold the Merkle ball privately to Connecticut hedge fund manager Paul Reiferson, and in 2010, Reiferson offered the ball at auction. That May it was sold for $76,375 to an unnamed buyer. Having chased Uncle Johnny across more than a century, I felt a need to find the baseball. I asked the auctioneer if he would ask the buyer to allow me to see the ball. He agreed, and two minutes later I received an e-mail:

You rang?

Olbermann

Erstwhile ESPN sportscaster and liberal MSNBC and Current TV commentator Keith Olbermann has made an avocation of vigorously defending Fred Merkle's actions on Sept. 23, 1908, and absolving him of the nickname, Bonehead, that followed him through his life and deep into the hereafter. Olbermann has written, blogged and broadcast his support for the rookie who was hoodwinked by Uncle Johnny—whom Olbermann calls a "dark genius"—while doing only what had always been done. Olbermann bought the ball not only because he is an avid memorabilia collector but also because the Merkle ball holds a singular significance. "It's the Rosetta Stone," he says. "This is the time-travel node that puts you on the middle of this swirling dust storm with 10,000 fans on a Wednesday afternoon at the Polo Grounds 104 years ago."

I sat on a couch in Olbermann's New York City apartment on a rainy autumn afternoon and held the ball in my right hand. It is soiled to a dark brown and slick to the touch, as if it had been preserved with a thick coat of lacquer. The writing remains clear: MERKLE SEPT. 23, 1908. The National League stamp is visible and has been authenticated multiple times. Olbermann sees a cosmic significance in the ball. Merkle was haunted. Pulliam killed himself. Evers struggled with life. The Cubs have never won another World

Series. "It's almost a spirit-filled object," says Olbermann. "It took a little of the souls of everyone who touched it."

Maybe. But my attachment is more personal. As rain pounds against the glass, I roll my fingers over the seams, and Uncle Johnny comes to life. I know him now. He is scooping up ground balls on the Troy sandlot and then turning two in the National League, full of youth. He is forcing out poor Merkle because he knows no other way to play but ruthlessly. And then, so suddenly, he is sitting by a streetside window in a simple Albany apartment, old and weak, wondering where the games have gone.

OCTOBER 12, 2015

Penitence Race

For the 82nd straight year, there's no World Series
in our nation's capital. But there's reason to believe, D.C:
after decades in the desert, one fan has
done his part to turn the fates in your favor

BY DAVID SIMON

The static of the broadcast, the AM-band crackle that the cheap transistor spit up every time it swung or bounced—even this I remember. Just as I recall the heat from the water in the hallway fountain, its cooling mechanism never quite functional. And the godawful smell of the secondary wing boys' room.

It is 1971, and I am new to the fifth grade at Rock Creek Forest Elementary School, a few hundred yards north of the D.C. line in suburban Maryland, where everything is perfectly Proustian, perfectly preserved in memory.

I have been on the playground, playing strikeout with Firestone and Bjellos. It is an April afternoon, after school hours, yet unseasonably hot in my memory. I am wishing the water cooler actually worked, stumbling into the boys' room to take a leak before drifting back to the game.

On my little Sanyo, Frank Howard launches a grand slam off the Oakland A's starter, some fella with the improbable name of Blue. It is Opening Day. And though this is Washington Senators baseball, all things are still possible.

Two years earlier, in fact, my Nats, managed by the great Ted Williams, finished above the hated Yankees for the first time in my short life in a season when both played better than .500 ball. These guys are due. They have always been due. This, perhaps, is the year they pay out.

247

Mike Epstein follows Howard to the plate, and I rest the radio on the boys' sink. Epstein, my favorite. Superjew—and yes, that is his actual nickname. Thirty home runs in '69 hitting behind Howard, who had 48 jacks that year. And in '70, Epstein added 20 more.

Is there a hero more tailored to my existence? Is it possible to overstate the sociocultural and psychological import of a power-hitting Hebrew playing first base for the Washington Senators, the hometown team of a skinny, slap-hitting Jewish runt from Silver Spring, Md.? Surely, Mike Epstein, standing astride my childhood like a colossus for all the Chosen, is a personalized gift from the god of my fathers. To whom I now pray:

"Dear God," I offer aloud, my words echoing against the drab brown walls of the bathroom. "If you let Mike Epstein hit a home run right now, I will never, ever skip Hebrew school again."

Whereupon the very next pitch is launched into the rightfield upper deck of Robert F. Kennedy Stadium. Back-to-back with Howard. The Opening Day crowd cheering wildly because maybe, just maybe, this is the year, with the Nats embarrassing this Blue fella and shutting out Oakland to begin the great exodus from Egypt and bondage.

And here, now, comes the worst and most frightening image in this sequence of memory: That of a mop-headed boychild, arms above him, cheering wildly, his image reflected back from the old oxidized mirror above the school bathroom sink. I can still see that fool kid. Right now, in my mind's eye, I am looking at him as his moment of delirious joy evaporates into near Biblical loathing and terror.

What did I just promise God?

Oh.

No.

I'm not an idiot, or a fundamentalist. A sentient grown-up cannot take seriously the notion of petitional prayer in any sporting contest. Any modernist knows that a divine entity who would intervene in human affairs to hang a curveball or block a field goal is a deity with too much time on His hands. Any god who actually exists has to be playing for larger stakes than a playoff win or, worse, a five-year contract with built-in incentives. The sight of a wide receiver falling to one knee and crossing himself in the end zone is an affront to any theology that can matter. And we must concede that a serious god in whom real purposes abide cannot possibly give himself over to punishing the random collective of northside Chicago baseball enthusiasts merely because they don't live in St. Louis.

So, O.K., no worries. I made a vow and I broke it. Within three weeks I was again cutting out of Hebrew school on Tuesday and Thursday afternoons, hanging with friends, creeping down Beach Drive to play basketball in Rock Creek Park. But so what?

God, if He even exists, is good, or at least noninterventionist—an Unmoved Mover, as Aristotle would say, who rules from a heaven with high walls and leaves small matters of athleticism to men. A child's vow over such nonsense is unheard.

Except a little more than a month after that long-ago Opening Day, Mike Epstein, my favorite player, was traded to the Athletics. And by the following season my entire hometown baseball franchise, the Senators, was shipped to Texas to become the Rangers.

I did the rest of my growing up in Washington without baseball. And when I moved to Baltimore in late 1983, I could in no way enjoy the Orioles' victory in the World Series that year. The O's of old were Canaanites, a savage crew of Moloch-worshippers who routinely marched south against my tribe, with the Robinsons and Palmer and McNally and Boog smiting and martyring the Nats at will.

I rooted for Philly in that Series, and only embraced the Orioles when they began the '88 season with 21 straight losses. As only a Senators fan will, I came to my second franchise when it was in the basement, and for a long time the elevator did not move.

So note:

It is now nearly half a century since a small boy asked his god to hang a Vida Blue pitch for his hero, and neither team with which he has allied himself has to this moment returned to a World Series.

Lo, the Orioles have wandered like Israelites through Sinai since I took a mortgage in Baltimore, teased from New York by Jeffrey Maier's mitt and mocked from Chicago by Jake Arrieta's fastball. And the new Nats, reconstituted a decade ago, have touched the hem of greatness only to collapse at the very edge of every playoff opportunity. They ended the present season, literally, at each others' throats.

My vow, I have come to believe, was heard. And now I am Jonah, fleeing from my God and Nineveh, unwilling to address my sin. And the Nationals and the Orioles are both ships on a storm-tossed sea, their sickened, seasick fans unwitting victims of the outcast who walks among them.

Every season since 1971, the gaping maw of the whale awaits me. I am to be swallowed, along with the hopes of any baseball team I care about, into the belly of the beast and spit up in time to do it all again when pitchers and catchers report.

I gotta get right with God.

"Never happened," says Mike Epstein.

The phone line goes silent.

"No way," he adds.

Finally, I say something clever: "What?"

"I never hit a home run off Vida Blue, and I never hit a home run on Opening Day. You got it wrong."

"But I remember it."

"Never happened," he repeats.

I sit there on the other end of the phone, stunned like a cow with a sledgehammer. Me. In the boys' bathroom mirror. My promise. My sin.

"Listen," Epstein says finally. "You're not serious about this, are you? Because, I gotta just say, you realize this whole thing is a bit, ah, egocentric."

You think? Isn't everything that constitutes the theology of fandom egocentric? Believers who won't change their shirts for 16 Sundays if their team is winning? Acolytes who have to walk out of the room on a full count with loaded bases because if they stare at the television screen, the Fates will bring bad juju to the moment? Pilgrims who eat the same thing in the same inning in the same number of bites because the ritual assures the outcome?

Surely a direct appeal to Yahweh, the god of our forefathers, carries more gravitas than mere fate?

And no, I still don't believe a just god intervenes in professional sports. He does not care if Mike Epstein goes deep against Vida Blue, or whoever threw that pitch on whatever day he threw it. But does He care if a Jewish kid two years shy of his bar mitzvah promises to stop cutting out on Hebrew school?

Think on that for a moment, Mr. Epstein. Maybe this vow wasn't about baseball. Maybe it was about theology and spirituality and the 6,000-year-old faith of our ancestors.

"You're serious," Epstein says wearily.

"You and me, we gotta bury this together."

And somehow, I get this man to agree. Somehow, I convince him that the two of us hold the future of the Nationals, and possibly the Orioles as well, in our sin-stained hands.

He will come east from his home outside Denver, back to Washington. We will taste the bread of affliction together, share a Passover seder and use the Jewish holiday of liberation to commemorate the long years of wandering in baseball wilderness, to dream anew on a Promised Land flowing with milk, honey and freshly printed playoff tickets. Then, on Opening Day of the 2005 season, we will go to the old RFK Stadium, where the Montreal Expos have just relocated, and we will watch a ball game together.

I know I have Mike Epstein aboard when I can hear him laughing at me through the telephone.

"O.K.," he says. "You're nuts, but O.K."

All that is left for me, other than buying his plane tickets and reserving a hotel room, is to figure out my broken memory. Back-to-back home runs with Howard. Vida Blue. Opening Day. The upper-wing boys' room at Rock Creek Forest Elementary.

"I'll work on that," I tell my childhood hero. "And I'll see you next April for Passover."

Except the Old Testament god, He is not so easily appeased.

A few months before Passover in 2005, my brother-in-law, a sailing enthusiast, was caught in a storm off the Florida coast and, when a metal coupling fell from the mast, suffered an injury that would eventually prove fatal. That year's family gathering was no time to trifle with anything as obscure as baseball voodoo. And by the following season, my father had become invalided; our Passover seders became, for several years, private affairs. I couldn't follow through with Epstein.

Season followed season. The Orioles slowly improved and made a couple decent runs toward a Series, but last year's rollover to Kansas City seemed like a high wall. The Nats, for their part, looked weak-willed the year they sat Strasburg, and last season's playoff performance was so devoid of heart that some supernatural element could be plausibly suspected. In the back of my mind, totaling up the cumulative seasons of Series-less baseball in my wake, I piled up a weight of guilt that only Jews and Roman Catholics can carry.

Verily, my God was still an angry God. So, a decade after I first contacted Mike Epstein, I called him again. He didn't return the message. Not right away. Who calls a goof like me back a second time in a single life?

I had an editor from SPORTS ILLUSTRATED follow up, if only to make my pitch more plausible. And I called the Nationals' front office, asking about the possibility of honoring one of Washington's former baseball stars. And in July I flew to Denver, where, finally, seated across from an aging but still athletic man, in a breakfast spot south of the city, I did all I could to assure my boyhood hero of both my sincerity and my sanity. I also told him I had solved the false manufacture of memory, and it was a telling corruption at that:

"When you make a promise to God, a promise that you don't keep, a promise that you then secretly blame for the trade of your favorite player and then the loss of your entire baseball team, well, you kind of want the home run to matter. And for the Senators, the only way a home run could matter was to have it as close to Opening Day as possible because by May...."

"By April, you mean," laughed Epstein, remembering. "Those teams were so bad."

"By April," I agreed, "the Washington Senators were usually out of contention."

Mike Epstein and Frank Howard hit back-to-back home runs on Aug. 17, 1970, in the first inning of a 7–0 home win over the Kansas City Royals, off a pitcher named Bob Johnson.

It was summer. A hot day in D.C. My fifth-grade year hadn't started yet, but the school building would have been open as the staff was preparing for the start of school. In August, we were routinely allowed to use the bathrooms while we hung on the blacktop and played ball. That explained why my memory had no one else in the hallway or bathroom, why I was even allowed to have a transistor radio in school that day.

Ridiculously, I had offered up a vow to God over a single at bat in the first inning of a late-season game for a sixth-place team—that was last in the old American League East—that was in no way contending for anything. Not even pride. Biblically, this is the equivalent of Esau trading his birthright to his brother for a bowl of soup. Yet over the years, as the baseball fortunes of two cities fell and as I bricked a personal prison cell using mortared blocks of Judaic guilt, I imbued that useless home run with more and more meaning.

The Senators had in fact shut out the A's on Opening Day in 1971, beating Blue in the same convincing fashion that they had shut out Johnson and the Royals. That, too, was a warm memory, one that I happily conflated with Epstein's prayed-for homer if for no other reason than to make my plea for divine intervention more purposed and romantic.

"Do you remember what pitch you hit off Johnson?"

Epstein had some memorable dingers in his career. Three in one game. Four in consecutive at bats. And some astonishing artillery salvos to the upper deck of RFK, where they painted the seats blue in Superjew's honor. But an August home run in a game that meant nothing?

Epstein didn't remember the at bat, much less the pitch on which he turned.

Only I did. Kinda.

Never meet your heroes, it has been famously said, and as an old newspaperman, I've generally been inclined to credit the adage. A hero is someone far enough away so as not to reveal himself completely.

But the Michael Peter Epstein who has put up with my on-again, off-again courtship these many years, upon our first meeting in Denver, revealed himself to be a fine, if somewhat skeptical, soul.

Now 72, he has shaped a life with successes and pleasures beyond baseball. His wife, Barbara, is a nice Jewish girl he spotted in the stands of a minor league game in Stockton, Calif., and the marriage is now a half-century strong. Three children are grown, successful and happy.

A professional ballplayer from 1964 until he retired 10 years later—just before the rise of free agency and a seller's market—Epstein was obliged to turn on a dime and embark on a second career as a businessman.

A native of the Bronx, he nonetheless learned about the cattle market, of all things, and would own and operate ranches in Oregon and Wyoming. It is probably safe to say that in meeting the man, you are shaking hands with the only lefthanded Jewish power-hitting cattleman to ever stride this planet.

And for a third act, Epstein returned to the baseball world, developing batting techniques and drills that he describes as rotational hitting—an influential and level-swinging counter-revolution to the Lau-Hriniak school that dominated the game a couple generations ago.

Asked the ageless Talmudic question—"Which is harder: hitting or preventing hitting?"—Epstein doesn't hesitate before offering his own rabbinical dissent: "Teaching hitting. That's the hardest."

It was not something that he particularly wanted to do in life, but when the greatest hitter in modern baseball history prods and pushes repeatedly, you eventually give way. And Ted Williams, having managed Epstein for two-plus seasons with the Senators, had kept a friendship with his former player.

Williams knew hitting as a precise science, of course, but teaching it? He had no patience or vocabulary for explaining himself or his skill. But he would talk hitting with Epstein.

"You gotta do this," Williams told him on one hunting trip together.

"Why me?"

"Because you're a smart sonofabitch. I can do it, but you can figure out how to explain it."

Beginning with a series of 42 articles in the *Collegiate Baseball Newspaper* in the early 2000s, Epstein codified what Williams believed about smacking a baseball with a bat into a coherent, teachable methodology. Today, Epstein Online Hitting Academy—now a second-generation enterprise with Mike's son, Jake, at the helm—has become an influential font of batting analysis and coaching, based in Littleton, Colo., with 650 certified instructors operating nationally. It is the only hitting curriculum Ted Williams ever endorsed.

For Epstein—successful as a player, as a cattleman and businessman, as a hitting guru—life has been a series of pragmatic, goal-oriented paths and pivots. You show up, you do the work, you wait on the proper result. Stray prayers and divine interventions are not currencies in which such a man generally traffics.

But the Old Testament God, the jealous God, the unforgiving God of some improbably chosen tribe of ancient desert wanderers—maybe He's not interested in your modernist sensibilities, or in your hard-won rationalism. Maybe He's keeping different stats on this world, and judging mortals by different sabermetrics altogether. And maybe this God is not in the business of cheap forgiveness, either.

Because this ball season, on Sept. 21, the night before Yom Kippur, the sundown commencement of the Jewish Day of Atonement, I arrange to bring Mike Epstein—who remains politely dubious about the entire enterprise—to a stadium in the city of Washington, where the third and present incarnation of professional baseball in D.C. resides. There, just a mile or two down the Anacostia riverbank from the hollowed-out hulk in which Epstein once played, we stand in the Nationals dugout, waiting out a rain delay.

"God," Epstein assures me, staring at the infield tarp, "is really angry at you."

It's an hour past the game's scheduled start, and Epstein, having done all his interviews for local radio and pregame broadcasts, stands with a team escort at his side. In the escort's hand are a Nationals jersey with Epstein's name and number 6 adorning it, and a red ballcap with NATIONALS spelled out phonetically in Hebrew letters. But the rain is unrelenting, and there will be no pregame honorifics for Epstein or anyone else. In the end, a little after 9 p.m., this Monday game between the Nats and the Orioles—yes, my plan was to exorcise the demons from both franchises at once—is called for weather. It will be rescheduled as part of a Thursday doubleheader, a day which will find Epstein back in Colorado.

God will have no apologies from me.

Yea, as it shall ever be written: Man plans, grabs a bat and walks to the plate. God plunks him in the ribs with a nasty slider, and then, two pitches later, picks him off with an omnipotent little move toward first.

At sundown the next day, Mike Epstein and I find ourselves at Har Shalom Synagogue in the Potomac suburbs of Washington. We are side by side as the congregation rises for the Kol Nidre, the All Vows prayer, in which Jews ask God to forgive them for all of the promises that they, being human and foolish and fallible, will fail to honor in the coming year. Kol Nidre is so elemental to the Jewish ritual of forgiveness that we chant the prayer thrice, slowly, so that the words are given all possible attention and clarity.

As I gather my prayer shawl on my shoulders and turn the page of my prayer book, Epstein shoots me a look and actually smiles. "O.K., you're up," he says. "It's on you now."

Kol Nidre applies to the unkept vows of the coming year, but I'm asking for a retroactive dispensation. My great sin dates to my 10th year of life, and I know I didn't even learn the Yom Kippur liturgy until I was 12 or 13. Hey, with all those unexplained absences, I wasn't the brightest bulb in the Solomon Schechter Hebrew Academy. Sue me.

Yet on this night, I bend to the task. Beside me, I can hear my companion muttering the Hebrew as well; neither of us is particularly observant, but Epstein too has knowledge of the liturgy. But walking out of temple an hour and a half later, he only partially concedes the validity of our mission together:

"I get why you're here, but explain to me exactly why I had to make this trip? I did my job. I hit a home run. And God, he did his job, right? You're the only one here who still owes."

I do my best:

"You're part of the sin, too," I say. "I prayed for a home run in a meaningless August ball game, and I got it. But maybe you got something too. Maybe you benefited from the sin."

He looks at me, ever more dubious.

"Look," I say, "that year you hit 20 home runs, and early the next season you get traded to Oakland to play on a winning team. The year after that, you win a World Series, right?"

He nods.

"Maybe if you finish 1970 with only 19 home runs, maybe that's not such a clean, round number. Maybe when the Oakland front office is looking around for a lefty to hit behind Reggie Jackson and play first base, maybe they don't bite on Mike Epstein. Maybe if I don't ask God to have that Royals pitcher hang a curveball, you don't get traded, you don't hit 26 jacks in '72 and go to the World Series and get a ring."

Epstein considers my theories on man and fate for only a moment.

"Weak. Very weak," he says, laughing.

I drop him at his hotel and we say our goodbyes. And then, before getting back in my car, I shoot a look up at the dark Washington sky.

"C'mon, big guy," I actually say aloud. "What's done is done. Let my people go."

At that moment, the O's 2015 wild-card run is history, and with some irony, their last series with the Nats will fire the last torpedo into Washington's hopes as well. But next year might be different. I tell this to myself and drive home with hope in my heart.

Five days later, the Nationals' closer tries to choke the team's best hitter in the dugout, for all the world to see.

Oh, God.

THE GAME
WITHIN THE GAME

APRIL 16, 1990

The First to Be Free

In 1976, baseball's first free agents landed the big, big money. Lucky guys. They were set for life. Or were they?

BY LEIGH MONTVILLE

The day is no different from all the other days. Bobby Grich has options. This is no blue Monday. This is no hump-day Wednesday, not even a Thank-God-It's Friday. For Grich, this is a Saturday. The calendar does not exist. No matter that the rest of the world is at work. No matter that the rush-hour report on traffic from the Action Eye says that all freeways are clogged, everywhere. Saturday. Every day is Saturday.

"People are going to just hate me when they read this," the 41-year-old former second baseman says in his house in Long Beach, Calif., "but there are days when my biggest decision is about which coffee shop I'm going to visit for breakfast. There are a lot of days like that."

Golf today? Perhaps. His handicap is down to a three. He is going to play in the State Amateur. Skiing? He has become quite good at skiing. He travels every year to the Canadian Rockies to take a helicopter to those hard-to-reach virgin slopes. He also skis the celebrity circuit, head-to-head with those sitcom actors and Vegas voices. Fishing? He could catch another marlin, but where would he put it? On the rec-room wall? It would have to be a big one to replace the marlin that's already there. Travel is always a possibility, but—let's see—he has already been to Europe five times, Hawaii seven times, the Caribbean four times, Australia and New Zealand.... What to do?

"You know what's good?" he asks. "I have a houseboat in Lake Powell, in Utah," he answers. "You hitch up a little water-ski boat, maybe bring along a couple of jet skis. Throw in some food, some beer and a bikini. Just pull up the anchor, go to a cove somewhere and disappear for a week."

He is free. Isn't that the proper descriptive word? He is a free man, and every day is an ultimate 24-hour stretch of free time. He does not work. He does not think he ever will work another day in his life. Free. He does have an office, a little home office with a desk. The most prominent object on the desk is a book entitled *The Short Way to Lower Scoring*, by golfer Paul Runyan and Dick Aultman. Free.

For 17 years, Grich played major league baseball. When he began, in 1970, he had only the fuzziest ideas about lives of luxury, lives of leisure. After all, who made that kind of money from baseball? Maybe a Joe DiMaggio or a Ted Williams moved along to a comfortable retirement, but the rest of the players on the field eventually went back into their communities and found the time clock along with everyone else. In 1970, nobody had an agent. Oh, maybe a few big stars did, mostly to handle endorsements, but the ordinary players did their own simple haggling with management over their five-figure contracts—mostly low-five-figure contracts.

In 1976, the sky opened and money started to fall in a rain that has become heavier and heavier with each passing season. In the fall of that year, the first 24 free agents hit the market, freed by the 1976 court decision in the case of pitchers Andy Messersmith and Dave McNally. Each free agent could be drafted by as many as 12 teams. Bidding began. Grich was there with a bucket.

"The timing was perfect," he says. "It couldn't have been better. I'd played five years [at second base and shortstop with the Baltimore Orioles], so I was just hitting my prime. I was coming off my best season. I hadn't signed. I couldn't have planned it better."

He eventually agreed to a five-year contract with the California Angels for a total of $1.5 million. In the previous season with the Orioles, he had earned $68,000. Signing with the Angels allowed him to return home to Long Beach and become a commuter from the neighborhood where he was raised. The new contract gave him more money for playing baseball than he had ever dreamed existed. It was almost a joke. When the Angels played at Baltimore, he was booed, and he understood why people were mad. Injured while lifting an air conditioner before the 1977 season even began, he started slowly and ultimately missed the final two thirds of the schedule after undergoing back surgery. He was booed at Anaheim Stadium. Again, he understood why people were mad. All that money.

Weren't the people right? There were nights in the following years when he would pound his glove and look at the field and the stands and the sky and think his secret thought: Didn't anyone know? He would pay the owners to play this game, to be where he was. Maybe he wouldn't pay to play every day, seven days a week, but he would pay for, say, four out of seven. Yes, he would.

Grich became a free agent again after the 1981 season. Again, he was coming off a good year. Again, he was there with the bucket. It was raining even harder. Again, the Angels paid—this time $4 million over four years.

"I manage my finances by myself now," he says. "That's the one thing I do. I've been stung a couple of times, but I've made some good deals too. Especially real estate. Here in Long Beach."

Grich has been retired for three years. On this day, he thinks he will play golf. Maybe nine holes. Maybe 18. Maybe just hit some balls. On the weekend he will go skiing at Mammoth Mountain. Which car should he drive? He has three Porsches and two Mercedes parked in his garage. He has one friend who says that Grich should at least get a paper route to give himself a little discipline. He has another friend who owns a food-brokerage business and wants to make him a marshmallow salesman. Nothing heavier. Only marshmallows. In August 1987, Grich went with a friend on a trip to London to see the Rams play the Broncos in an NFL exhibition game. From there, they were off to play golf in Scotland at Troon, Turnberry and Prestwick. Then they went to Nice to parasail and on to Lake Geneva to water-ski. Then they went to Monte Carlo. Grich won $2,000 at the blackjack tables to help pay for the trip.

Divorced since the early days of his baseball career, he sometimes thinks he would like to marry again and start a family. Then again, he does have other things to do.

"I have a goal," Grich says.

Yes?

"I want to play *Golf Digest*'s 100 Best Courses in America."

Yes?

"I'm at 27."

Isn't this the way we expected it to be, once the floodgates of free agency had opened? Take off that baseball suit. Put on that bathing suit. So much money. The average salary in baseball in 1976 was $52,300; that first class of 24 free agents averaged $200,696, and that included a few guys like Royle Stillman, who signed with the White Sox for $25,000. For those at the head of the class, the money seemed so great that the operative term was Set For Life. "Look at these guys: They're Set For Life." The game, we suspected, would begin to spin out an unending line of still-young retirees with no particular-place to go. Free men. Free time.

Fourteen years have passed since then. Most of the players involved in the '76 draft are now out of the game and out in the world. Set For Life? The first returns have begun to arrive at the Set For Life anchor desk.

On Nov. 24, 1976, the night of the first free-agent draft at the Plaza Hotel in New York City, Minnesota Twins relief pitcher Bill Campbell went into the hotel bar with his agent. They were beckoned by Oakland A's owner Charlie Finley to a corner table. Come on over. Have a drink.

"I'd never met the man," says Campbell as he sits in a restaurant near his home in Barrington, Ill. "But he'd been one of the guys to draft me. We went over. He immediately started trying to make a deal. Right there. He offered a $100,000 signing bonus, plus $100,000 for three years. Said I had to sign before I left the table. I looked at my agent."

The agent was LaRue Harcourt; Campbell had found him simply by asking another Twins pitcher for a name. Harcourt and Campbell had decided to ask for a million dollars for four years. They weren't exactly sure what the market would be, but they knew that a year earlier Finley had nearly sold reliever Rollie Fingers to the Boston Red Sox for a million, until commissioner Bowie Kuhn quashed the deal. If an owner would pay another owner a million for a relief pitcher, then why wouldn't he cut out the middle man? Give the million to the pitcher. Harcourt told Finley they wanted a million.

"Finley started laughing," Campbell says. "He said, 'A million dollars! You know what? These dumb s.o.b.'s will give it to you.' He was swearing and laughing so much that the guy at the next table got all upset. Told Finley to cut it out. I thought there was going to be a fight. We finished our drinks and went to see some people at another table. A little while later, the waitress comes over with the check. I think Finley tried to stick us with his bar bill."

Forty-eight hours later Campbell was at a press conference in Boston. He was the first of the 1976 free agents to sign: a million dollars for four years.

It was a pinch-yourself moment. One year earlier he was handed a contract from the Twins for $22,000, the same salary he earned in 1975. He had asked for a raise to $30,000, but he would have signed for less. The final bluff from owner Calvin Griffith was, "Sign this contract or forfeit your chance to go to spring training." Campbell held strong, played out his old contract at $22,000 per and finished with a 17–5 record with 20 saves—and free agency. And then he was a millionaire. Or so it seemed.

"That's what people would call you—'a millionaire,'" he says. "You really weren't, not when you broke the contract down, but that was what people said. I could hear them. 'Hey, there goes the millionaire.'"

By the time the season started, the money was a spotlight over his head. How can any man make a million to play baseball? Campbell admitted in the newspapers that the money he was getting was "ridiculous." He was told to keep quiet. No. He said he could not help saying what he felt. The money was ridiculous. His first check in the minors had been for $189 for two weeks—and he thought he was stealing even then.

The Red Sox had raised ticket prices during that winter, and in a game early in the '77 season, a large sign was hung from the centerfield wall that read SELL CAMPBELL, BRING BACK $1.50 BLEACHERS. Campbell was shelled in that game. He was shelled often that spring. The money was on his mind.

"I had the feeling I had to strike everyone out," he says. "If I was going to be making so much more money, I felt I had to be so much better. It took me a while just to forget the money. To just go out there and pitch."

Campbell would start to warm up in the bullpen and people would throw things at him. His early performances with Boston were so bad that the fan who had painted the sign called him to apologize and invited him to lunch. Campbell said he would go if the fan would give him the sign. "I still have it in the basement somewhere," Campbell says.

That season and the seasons to follow became easier when he simply focused on pitching. He went from the Red Sox to the Chicago Cubs after the contract was finished, then he stopped in St. Louis and Detroit before a sore shoulder finished him in Montreal in 1986. The money? He mostly left that to Harcourt.

The tax laws were different at the time; income was being taxed at more than 50% in Campbell's new bracket. Harcourt talked about various shelters to save as much money as possible from the government. Campbell found he was involved with airplane leasing and software companies. He paid attention, but not enough attention. Wasn't his job to strike out hitters in the late innings? He had left college after one year, then was drafted into the Army and sent to Vietnam. He had signed his first baseball contract with a smile and a handshake in a booth at a Denny's restaurant in Pomona, Calif. Not exactly a background for high finance.

So he left things to Harcourt. Deficiency notices from the Internal Revenue Service began to arrive, and Campbell would hand them to his agent. What about this? He says Harcourt would tell him that there was no problem. Two years later, the IRS would call again. Now there were penalty charges added. No problem.

"My wife was the one who said she had a gut feeling that something was wrong here," Campbell says. "Unfortunately, her gut feeling was right."

He estimates he lost as much as $800,000 with Harcourt, who acknowledges that the tax shelters had gone bad. The problems have not ended. An ongoing case with the IRS probably will be settled in the coming year. Campbell might lose as much or more to the government in back taxes as he has lost already. He calls the case a dark cloud that will not go away.

"You can't say, 'I didn't do it,' because your name is on the papers," he says. "As innocent as I am, I'm still responsible for my affairs. And, yet jeez. Those guys from the IRS can be pretty tough. Did you read what they did with Redd Foxx? Took his house, all his property. His memorabilia. They even came in and took his jewelry off of him."

For the past two years, Campbell has been employed at a marketing firm in Chicago, on commission. His wife, Linda, has worked toward gaining her master's degree. For fun, he started pitching in an amateur baseball league, seven innings, drinking beer in the parking lot after the games. He says his arm felt surprisingly strong. During the winter, he pitched for Winter Haven in the new Senior Professional Baseball League in Florida. The arm still felt strong. He led the league in ERA.

"I made some calls afterward, to see if I could get a contract for a major league training camp," he says, 41 years old and planning to spend the afternoon baby-sitting his three kids and painting a bedroom in his house. "Nobody was interested. I understand. I'm getting old. They're going with the kids. I'm thinking now about Japan. I'm expecting a call today from a guy, as a matter of fact. I think it'd be a good thing, Japan. Get it out of my system. For once and for all."

He nods his head at the idea. Japan would be nice.

Some of the tales from the class of '76 resemble scripts from the old television series "The Millionaire." What did the players do with the money? Fourteen years. Which guys got richer? Which guys went bust? Those early contracts now seem like a bunch of winning lottery tickets. Here's the money, kid. Let's see what you can do with it. Aren't these stories a lot like the ones you read about the local janitor who picked a succession of birth dates and then, in a dizzy moment, saw them flashed across the television screen? What happened to baseball's first lottery winners? A lot has happened.

The retired couple hovers near the table where Steve Stone sits in the sports bar he owns in Scottsdale, Ariz. Stone is engaged in a conversation, but for this couple, age has overcome any lifelong battles with shyness. They stare at Stone from a distance of two feet. His other conversation does not matter to them.

"Steve," the man interrupts, "we're all the way from Kankakee."

"Glad to have you here," Stone says.

"Came all the way down here to see some baseball."

"I'll be over in a minute. We'll talk."

"No baseball. What are these guys doing, Steve? This is terrible."

"In a minute."

"Terrible, Steve."

This is the public life of the modern television face. Hey, don't I know you? Aren't we friends? Stone is used to such public intrusions by now. He worked with the ABC network for two years and has worked seven more years with Harry Caray at WGN in Chicago. The face sells. He owns parts of two restaurants in Chicago and parts of two sports bars here in Arizona. He will talk about the lockout and baseball with the people from Kankakee. Business.

"My father always used to tell me, 'Baseball will open the door for you,'" Stone says. "Well, it's true...but what I've found is that the opening is about two inches wide. To do anything, you'd better push yourself the rest of the way. That door can close awfully fast."

When the money came, he was ready to work with it. He was preparing for a life after baseball long before he was through with baseball. His mother had been a waitress at a succession of shot-and-a-beer taverns in Cleveland. His father had serviced jukeboxes. The appeal of owning a bar or a restaurant had been as strong as the appeal of pitching in Municipal Stadium against the Yankees. A bar was familiar territory.

"In 1973, I went to the White Sox," Stone says. "My first three seasons [with the Giants and the White Sox] had been 5–9, 6–8 and 6–11. I had the feeling that I wasn't going right to the Hall of Fame, if you know what I mean. I was looking for something."

In Chicago, he would study the operation of the various bars he visited. How would I run this place? What changes would I make if it were mine? One of the hottest spots at the time was R.J. Grunt's, a place that catered to athletes by giving them free beer. This was a convenient operation to study.

The owner was a young guy, Rich Melman. Stone decided Melman was going to be a business winner and offered to become his partner. Melman declined. What did Stone have to offer? He was a ballplayer. Stone went down the street to Melman's main competitor and took a job in the off-season. He came back to Melman a year later.

"Rich asked me why I'd gone down the street," Stone says. "I told him that first, I wanted to learn more about the business. Second, I wanted to prove to him that I was serious about this. He already had opened another restaurant. He let me become involved."

The corporation that was eventually formed was called Lettuce Entertain You. Restaurants were opened with names like Jonathan Livingston Seafood and Lawrence of Oregano. The famous Pump Room was added to the string.

Melman was the winner Stone had predicted. Stone had a piece of the success.

On the mound, he had moved to the Cubs for 1974 and '75 and found moderate success, but in 1976 he was bothered by arm problems. The Cubs never got around to signing him that year. This made him a somewhat reluctant—and not very attractive—free agent. His '76 record was 3–6 with a 4.08 ERA. Five teams drafted him, but only two showed any interest. The low-budget White Sox and owner Bill Veeck wanted him back because he was a bargain. The Texas Rangers had a more curious situation.

"Their general manager, Danny O'Brien, called and asked what I wanted," Stone says. "I breathed deep and told him I was looking for $75,000 for one season. O'Brien said he couldn't do that. I said, right away, 'All right, I'll settle for $60,000.' He said I didn't understand. I wasn't asking for *enough* money. He said Brad Corbett, the owner, wanted to pay a million dollars for a pitcher. Corbett thought this would be good public relations. I said that was fine with me. I would take a million. He said no. I said I would take $60,000 and they could tell everyone I was getting a million. O'Brien said he thought they could give Doyle Alexander a million dollars and Doyle would take it. And that's what happened. Doyle got the million."

Stone went to the White Sox for $60,000, the fourth-puniest free-agent contract of the 24 signings. He pitched for two seasons, then signed a four-year contract with the Orioles in 1978. His career took a wondrous jump in 1980 when he finished 25–7 and won the American League Cy Young Award, but the arm troubles grew worse and he retired a year later. He became better known after baseball than he had been while playing. Even when he won the Cy Young he somehow remained anonymous. He remembers opening the box that contained the award. "The drums were rolling. My heart was beating, and then I take the plaque out and I read, Steve... Carlton?" The inscription read, STEVE CARLTON, MOST VALUABLE PITCHER, NATIONAL LEAGUE. They'd mailed him the wrong Cy Young.

"The day after I retired, my agent got a call from ABC," Stone says. "They were wondering if I wanted to try some broadcasting. I jumped. I recognized that this was the brass ring, and that it could keep me around baseball."

His two sports bars in Arizona are called Harry and Steve's Chicago Grill. Broadcast partner Caray is also business partner Harry. The bars are shrines to Chicago sports. Ivy hangs from the wall in a re-creation of Wrigley Field. More visitors from the North, looking for a spring training that has stalled, wander in from the sun. Stone is waiting.

"I make more money now than I ever did from baseball," he says. "Sure." Set For Life?

"Yeah, if I never want to eat again—if I want to weigh about 106 pounds."

The old-time ballplayer would retire and open a tavern in the center of town, become a barkeep. The new ballplayer can be a restaurateur. One restaurant can become a string of restaurants. A chain. The amounts that can be gained are larger. The amounts that can be lost are also larger. Nothing, alas, is guaranteed.

His right arm sometimes locks on him. If he drives for a while, right hand at the top of the wheel, the arm will become frozen at a 90-degree angle. If he watches television, hands behind his head, the arm will become frozen again. If he tries to pass the peas or open the door or do any of the dozens of daily movements that ordinary people do, he will find that the arm is out of control. He will have to move his right arm with his left hand. Jump-start it. Adapt.

Wayne Garland needs surgery on his rotator cuff again.

"I'm just waiting for an appointment in Birmingham," he says. "The specialist. Dr. Andrews. I'm waiting for an opening. He's a busy man."

In a few weeks Dr. Andrews will have an opening and the surgery will be performed. The same surgery that marked the beginning of the end of Garland's days as a major league pitcher. It is a last cruel twist in his baseball career. Who needs a second rotator-cuff operation at the age of 39?

"I think sometimes it's not worth it, having the operation, going through the rehabilitation and everything again," Garland says. "But I want to be active. I want to be able to play tennis, to bowl. Or if I got a coaching job somewhere, I'd like to be able to pitch batting practice."

He could use the job. The money is gone. He is living in Lakeland, Fla., and wondering where he will land next. Maybe he will get a job working for a beer distributor. Maybe something in baseball. He worked in a Walmart last year. Then he worked in a freight room, lifting boxes. The best job was playing in the Senior League, pitching in Fort Myers, but that was where the arm blew out again. There will be no more pitching.

The day in '76 when he signed that stop-the-presses contract with the Cleveland Indians seems long, long ago. Two million dollars over 10 years. Who ever heard of such a thing? Ten years? Where is the security that was supposed to last forever? Where is the golden parachute? The damn thing never opened.

"It was unbelievable the way people reacted to the money," he says. "Every time my name was mentioned, it was Wayne Garland, Two Million Dollar Man. I think for the first years of their lives, my kids thought that was my last name. Two Million Dollar Man."

His timing was the best of anyone's in that first explosion of money. A hard thrower from Nashville, Garland finished 20–7 with a 2.68 ERA in '76 for the Orioles. He had played out his option. Twenty-six years old. He was a pitcher for the present and a pitcher for the long-distance future. Ten years, said the Indians. At the time, no one in any sport had ever been given such a long-term contract.

The money seemed so grand that real estate agents were calling as soon as he got home from the signing ceremony. Home-improvement contractors arrived with large, inflated estimates. Strangers on the street asked for loans. The president of a bank opened the doors on a Sunday just to complete a deal with him.

"All I would hear about was the money," he says. "My wife heard it even more. People would yell at her in the stands. One guy was yelling so much, yelling things like 'Hey, Wayne, how about a loan. Hey, how about some money,' that my wife turned around and handed him a hundred bucks. Told him to shut up."

It seems that no one ever considered that maybe a right arm wouldn't last for 10 years, maybe wouldn't even last for two. The first year was all right, a 13–19 finish for a Cleveland team that bore little resemblance to the talented Orioles. But in the second season he tore the rotator cuff. He underwent surgery, then rehabilitation. He never won more than six games in any of the three seasons that followed, and he was released in 1981. His arm has never been the same.

During those last seasons, the talk about money became ugly. Garland was reminded again and again by Cleveland general manager Phil Seghi that he wasn't worth the money he was being paid. While he was on the disabled list, Garland was required to travel with the team and sit in the stands with a walkie-talkie, detailing outfield shifts. Make-work. When he pitched again, his car was vandalized in the parking lot after bad outings. His case became the classic illustration of how mistakes can be made in signing a free agent. His nickname on the team was Fool. Fool for going to the Indians. Fool for signing a contract for all that money and all that pressure.

"The strange part," Garland says, "is it seemed to me I'd had more money in my pocket when I was making $23,000 than I did after I signed the contract. I never seemed to have any money."

His big investment was a 26-acre estate in Hunting Valley, an affluent suburb of Cleveland. The estate had a giant slate-roofed house, a swimming pool, a tennis court and a 12-stall barn. The plan was to rent out the stalls and care for horses, to make money from the estate. No one had bothered to mention that a zoning ordinance prohibited that sort of use. Attorneys got involved. Suits were filed. The case dragged on and was eventually settled out of court. The estate was sold at a loss.

He invested in the oil business. The oil business sagged. He invested in an indoor batting cage. The indoor batting cage became a casualty of his divorce, which was costly and public. His ex-wife, Mary, is a radio personality in Nashville. She talked about him on the air. The money simply disappeared. Garland declared personal bankruptcy two years ago.

"I remember getting the final payment on the contract in '86," he says. "It was almost a relief. Like, 'Well, that's over.'"

He says his experiences have helped him to mature, grow up. Given the chance, he says, he would do the same things again. He would sign the same contract. No regrets. The crazy money, it turned out, was not as crazy as it seemed. He really was making $200,000 per year. This season, 1990, the youngest rookies were making half that amount before they threw their first pitch or got their first hit.

"Nowadays, $200,000, you'd be a nothing," Garland says, recovering from the surgery and looking for a job. "God forbid somebody today wins 30 games and becomes a free agent. What would he get? Good luck to him."

Fourteen years. The money being heaped on the newest free agents has doubled, tripled, doubled again. Will Clark's $15 million contract for four years is not much less than all of the free-agent contracts in 1976 added together. Will it be enough money to make him bulletproof to make him—yes!—Set For Life? There are more advisers now to help a ballplayer, better-defined courses to follow. There is so much more money. Is it enough? Is it ever enough? Fourteen years. The early returns have arrived. More will follow. The stories are going to get better and better. Are they not?

The left hand holds the steering wheel. The right hand punches out Jose Canseco's number on the cellular telephone. The 300 ZX sports car with the dealer plates from Reggie Jackson Nissan, in Palo Alto, Calif., is zipping along the passing lane of Route 80 between Berkeley and Palo Alto. Jose is not at home. A taped message plays. Reggie Jackson is disappointed.

"The guy doesn't call me back," he says. "I have a deal going to make him a half-million dollars. You'd think the guy would call me back. I was at his house last week for three days, and still he doesn't call me back. I've called him four times."

Maybe Jose is busy? Maybe he has a lot of people calling to help him make a half million? Maybe Jose is the same way Reggie was in those baseball days—hotter than hot, swimming in deals? Maybe Reggie wouldn't have had time to call during his baseball days?

"Nah," Reggie says. "If Willie Mays had called, I would have called him back."

Business is business. Reggie never has been slow to do business, even when he was wearing a shirt with number 44 on the back. He always has been a business machine. He is a business machine now. What is it that he calls himself? A cash cow. He is a cash cow, and now there are no fences. He can roam wherever he wants and travel at the speed he wants. The speed is predictably fast.

He has been to Atlanta and Rochester and Miami and Charlotte and Philadelphia and Newport Beach in the past two weeks. He is going to Daytona for the weekend. He will be in Palm Springs to start the new week. What does he say? He is in the rat race. A cash cow in the rat race. He talks about accruing assets and accruing debts and needing a cash flow. Make that money move. He is moving it. There are houses in Berkeley and Newport Beach and Carmel and Aspen. There is the car agency. There are 12 warehouses. There are...cars.

He estimates there are more than 100 of them in one of his warehouses, classic cars, rare cars. They are kept, most of them, in plastic bags, looking as if they just came back from the cleaners. See this one? The red Ferrari? This is worth $600,000. See that white '69 Chevelle? $200,000. The cars in this one warehouse are worth more than $7 million. That is his estimate. The cars are like baseball cards, tradable and easy to convert into cash. Accrued assets.

"We're coming out with this," he says. He holds a bottle in front of him. The label says the product is called Reggie Wax.

Reggie Wax?

"Two years being developed," he says. "We're trying to raise five or six million right now to fund it."

Of all the '76 free agents, he was the most celebrated. He received the most money: $3 million for five years from the Yankees. He was the most successful after signing, finishing the 1977 season with his three-homer night against the Dodgers in the World Series. He made as much money off the field as he made on the field. He was personality as much as player. He was an endorsement package. More than anyone else, he was a look into the financial future.

"I could be set for life, sure," he says. "If I sold off the cars, sold a couple of houses, got rid of everything, I'd never have to work another day. But do you know how that would be? Borrrrring."

Business is as much a game as baseball ever was. He was stung when his Chevy dealership went bust in Berkeley. He was distressed when a warehouse fire wiped out 34 of his investment cars and six motorcycles a year ago. These were some bad times in the business game. That doesn't mean that he doesn't want to play anymore. He wants to play harder.

On this day, he visits his Nissan and Volkswagen agency. He has called a general meeting of the mechanics and secretaries from the service department. They gather around him, 22 men and three women. He talks about the goal of being the No. 1 service department in northern California, if not all of California. He talks about teamwork and neatness and brake jobs. The mechanics fidget. He is the boss. He says he doesn't want anyone smoking in any of the cars. Smoke in one of the cars and you're fired.

"I'm becoming more involved," he says afterward. "I want this to work. Part of me would like to be involved here every day. The other part says there are other things to do. I don't want to confine myself to one thing. Maybe that's the attention span of the athlete. I want diversity."

He complains to the manager of the agency that the sign in front is not large enough. The Reggie Jackson sign. He congratulates the manager on the fact that the plate-glass windows are much cleaner than they were on his last visit. He rubs a finger across some dust on a used car's hood. The cars should be cleaner. In the showroom, he congratulates a customer on the purchase of a new Cabriolet. In the parking lot, he makes another call from the cellular phone. The cellular phone is with him wherever he goes.

"In 1976, I wasn't thinking about any of this," he says. "Realistically, at the age I was, 28, you're living for the day, living for the right now. You're too involved in what you're doing. No one foresaw what was coming in salaries. Not the players. Not the management. I always had thought I'd be an Oakland A for my whole career, that I'd end like Al Kaline or Brooks Robinson. That just isn't going to happen anymore. It's sad, bad for baseball, but it's the truth.

"I do know that going to New York was what made me. That's where it took off. I say now that, as much as I wanted to stay an A, I should have died a Yankee. Just played a final game and died right there. I guess I'm just being romantic. I always thought I was the perfect Yankee. Too big for his britches. Someone people really could hate. I'm probably still too big for my britches."

He laughs at the image. Dead in the on-deck circle at Yankee Stadium after one final wave as the fans cheer him and boo him at the same time. He says he'll probably work at his present pace until his 50s, then relax. Who knows?

"I'm just going to keep going, keeping my face out there," he says. "Reggie Jackson, famous guy. Just talking to this magazine is helping me. Do you know how much it costs for a full-page ad in sports illustrated? This is business. Talking to you."

In walking through the auto showroom, he has picked up a pink balloon that is filled with helium. He stands in the parking lot and releases the balloon. Up and up it goes, into the blue afternoon sky. He stares. The balloon has become a little spot. Up and up. Smaller and smaller.

"Look at it go," Reggie Jackson says. "That thing is really moving."

The balloon disappears. He goes back to work.

JUNE 25, 2001

Waiting Game

Coming to bat cold and chafing at their second-string status,
pinch hitters often must make the most of one big swing

BY JACK McCALLUM

It's 3 p.m. on a May afternoon at Veterans Stadium in Philadelphia, an hour
before batting practice, four hours before the Phillies will take the field
to play the Milwaukee Brewers. "Where are Jordan and Ducey?" somebody
asks in a nearly empty Philadelphia clubhouse.

"Where do you think?" answers an attendant. "Down in the cage."

To be a pinch hitter, the job being performed by Kevin Jordan, Rob Ducey
and a host of other anonymous practitioners of this sweaty-palmed, knock-
kneed art, is to be a member of baseball's Breakfast Club. Talk to a major
league pinch hitter, and he'll offer a version of this sentiment: "As a pinch
hitter you have to work twice as hard as a regular player."

Pinch hitters sneak in extra licks whenever they can because they get
only one at bat per game. They take extra fielding practice because, on
occasions when they remain in the game after pinch-hitting, they could
be asked to fill in at one of several positions. (During his seven-year career
Jordan has played every infield spot except shortstop, and 13-year veteran
Ducey has manned each outfield position.) They track every pitch because
an opportunity to bat, if it comes at all, may present itself unexpectedly. All
the while they hope against hope that no matter how well they perform in
this role, one fine day they will be released from it.

Or they might be just plain released. When second-division teams start
to trim their rosters, pinch hitters are usually the first to go, and even

contenders treat them like pawns in a chess game. Witness the National League East-leading Phillies, who on June 6 gave Ducey his walking papers to make room for a power hitter from the minors; six days later Ducey hooked on with the division's last-place club, the Montreal Expos. Philadelphia's move surprised Ducey only slightly. Even when he contributed four pinch hits as the Phillies amassed a .297 pinch-hitting average (way above the league's average of .218 and second to the Atlanta Braves' .315), Ducey admitted he pored over box scores, paying particular attention to what other lefthanded-hitting reserves were doing. "When you're a 36-year-old bench guy like I am," he says, "you have to know what's out there."

What's out there is a cocktail of sweat and adrenaline, mixed in a tall shaker of obscurity. "When you're playing Wiffle ball in the park," says outfielder David Dellucci, one of a fearsome foursome of Arizona Diamondbacks pinch hitters, "do you ever hear anyone say, 'Hey, I want to be the pinch hitter'? It's a role that no one wants."

Then, too, the pay isn't spectacular, at least by the standards of pro sports. On an inflated New York Mets 2001 payroll, utilityman Lenny Harris, a 14-year veteran whose 142 career pinch hits through Sunday placed him eight from tying Manny Mota as baseball's alltime leader in the category, is earning $1.1 million. The highest-paid pinch hitter, at $1.5 million, is Arizona's Greg Colbrunn. He's been in the majors for 10 years and was a regular first baseman for the Florida Marlins in 1995 and '96.

A pinch hitter is like a field goal kicker: He's often asked to help his team in a make-or-break situation. Pinch hitters, though, also have to be capable in the field. "That's why pinch hitters fade in and out pretty quick," says Phillies bench coach Greg Gross, a superb pinch hitter in his playing days (143 pinch hits, third on the alltime list, during a career that lasted from 1973 through '89). With most teams carrying 11 or 12 pitchers now, Gross adds, "they don't have the luxury of keeping someone around who can't take the field."

The first pinch hitter is believed to have been Cleveland Spiders catcher Jack Doyle, who was sent up to hit for pitcher George Davies in a game against the Brooklyn Bridegrooms in 1892. He singled, and thus was born an art. The names of the great pinch hitters, cold-blooded creatures who thrived under the pressure of the late-inning at bat, hold a mystical place in baseball history. There was Moose McCormick of John McGraw's New York Giants, who used to hold up the game for three minutes while a trainer massaged his legs, and Frenchy Bordagaray, a grandly mustachioed Brooklyn Dodger. They were followed by, among others, Dusty Rhodes, who made his name with the New York Giants; Jerry Lynch of the Cincinnati Reds and the St. Louis Cardinals; Smoky Burgess of the Pittsburgh Pirates and the Chicago White Sox; Gates Brown of the Detroit Tigers; George Crowe of the Cardinals; Dave Philley of–who else?–the Phillies (and the Baltimore Orioles); and Rusty Staub of the Mets.

The patriarch of pinch hitting is Mota, now a Los Angeles Dodgers coach and mentor to the Dodgers' crack pinch hitter, Dave Hansen. "When I stood up there as a pinch hitter, I honestly believed I was the best hitter in the game," says Mota, who claims never to have taken a called third strike as a pinch hitter in his 20 big league seasons. "That's the only attitude to have."

The art of pinch hitting isn't as celebrated–or as necessary–as it used to be, especially in the American League, where the DH is a kind of full-time pinch hitter. (National League teams used an average of 261 pinch hitters last season, compared with only 114 for American League clubs.) Nonetheless, a number of players still excel at this perilous pursuit.

What little limelight is being directed at pinch hitters this year is falling mostly on Harris (12 for 37 as a pinch hitter through Sunday) as he pursues Mota's mark. Last year Hansen (103 career pinch hits) got the attention when he established a single-season record with seven pinch-hit home runs. "I promise you they were seven singles that happened to go out," says Hansen. "No pinch hitter can deliver home runs on demand." This year Hansen has been hampered by a broken left middle finger suffered in spring training, and through Sunday he was only 2 for 10. Two other good men in the pinch have been the Phillies' Jordan, who was hitting .400 (6 for 15, with a homer and five RBIs), and Chicago Cubs first baseman Julio Zuleta, who was batting .350 (7 for 20), with three homers and 13 RBIs.

The Diamondbacks have the major leagues' highest PH level. Indeed, they present what amounts to a 13-man lineup these days. First baseman Erubiel Durazo ("the shiniest tool in the box," as manager Bob Brenly puts it) blasted four pinch-hit home runs in April; through Sunday he had run that total to five and was batting .435 in the pinch. Dellucci was at .300 with two homers, and Danny Bautista, a part-time outfielder, was at .364 with one homer. The only Arizona pinch hitter who isn't tearing it up is Colbrunn, the one who was considered the most reliable at the start of the season. Before going on the disabled list on June 6 with a bruised right knee, Colbrunn was 1 for 18 as a pinch hitter; the one hit, however, was a home run. The four pinchmen, who last season wore T-shirts proclaiming themselves THE STUNTMEN, are seeking a new moniker this year–the Four Amigos? Four Diamond(backs) in the Rough? Four Guys Who Would Rather Be Playing Regularly?

Arizona's pinch-hitting scheme is fairly set. "If we need a pinch hitter leading off an inning, it's going to be either, depending on who's pitching, Dellucci [a lefthanded hitter] or Bautista [righthanded]," says Brenly. "If we have runners in scoring position, and a home run or an extra-base hit won't tie it or win it, it's probably going to be Dellucci. If I need a home run or an extra-base hit, it's going to be Durazo [a lefty] or Colbrunn [a righty]." Brenly admits that when Durazo kept going yard in April he factored that into his strategy. "It got to where I was going to save him until a home run would tie it or give us the lead," says Brenly. "That's how specialized it became."

Not that Brenly is complaining, but late in a tight game he does have to consider more options than most managers. During the pregame he scrutinizes the makeup of the opposition's bullpen. "If the other team's got two or three lefty relievers available, it's going to be hard for me to get Durazo in the game against a righthanded pitcher," says Brenly. So against the Braves early in the season, Brenly used Durazo as a pinch hitter in the fourth inning against righthanded reliever Jason Marquis, and Durazo responded with a sacrifice fly.

Pinch hitters would prefer that their managers spend time figuring out how to get them into the regular lineup. Those who become regular players are rather like community-theater thespians who get plucked for Broadway. They are the envy of their erstwhile fraternity brothers, a status currently being enjoyed by Pirates rightfielder John Vander Wal, who over the years has fretted about being used mainly as a pinch hitter, and San Diego Padres rightfielder Bubba Trammell, who recently proclaimed pinch hitting to be "the hardest thing I ever did." A number of great hitters might concur. Ty Cobb batted .367 for his career, .217 in the pinch; George Brett, with a .305 career average, was at .219 as a pinch hitter; and five-time batting champion Wade Boggs's numbers were .328 and .207, respectively.

Pinch hitters say that the most difficult aspect of the job is overcoming an inferiority complex: If you're by definition a pinch hitter, you're by definition not good enough to be a regular, and that gnaws at you. "Many players who are given a pinch-hitting role won't accept it," says Gross. "They end up sabotaging themselves."

Hansen agrees. "About three years ago [when he was with the Cubs], it came to me that pinch hitting was why I was up here," says Hansen, who has played all the infield positions and in the outfield during his 11-season career. "I decided to release all that hardheadedness. I was mad about not being an every-day player instead of accepting the fact that I could be a major league player as a pinch hitter. That's when I started to get good at it."

Pinch hitters estimate that they face a closer 90% of the time. Moreover, they're coming in cold against that 95-mph fastball or wicked splitter. They'll take a walk, but in the typical pinch-hit situation it's not as if the hitter has the luxury to work the count. "Athletes live for the excitement and the adrenaline," says Hansen, "but, man, when you consider the typical pinch-hitting situation—ninth inning, men on base, closer on the mound, game on the line—sometimes you get a little bit more than you need."

Further, VanderWal (116 pinch hits and 16 pinch homers, the most among active players) has a theory that a pinch hitter gets only one good pitch to hit per at bat, which means one good pitch per game. Colbrunn agrees. "You take or foul off that one pitch," he says, "and you've got an uphill battle."

Dellucci believes the most difficult facet of pinch hitting is that your chances are few and far between. (The season record for pinch-hit plate appearances is 94, set by Staub in 1983.) "If you don't drive in a runner or move a guy along," says Dellucci, "maybe you don't get another chance to redeem yourself for three or four games. So it sits with you."

Gross used to play a mental game with himself. "I got about 50 pinch-hit at bats per season, so I'd chop them into five 'seasons,'" says Gross. "If I was, say, 0 for 9, I'd want to get the 10th real quick. It was like, O.K., thank God that's over with. Now I can start a new season."

Here's another fear, one that may be unique to pinch hitters: They worry about becoming too good at what they do. "If you do it successfully, then you're thought of as *just* a pinch hitter," says Dellucci. "That's the worst thing that can happen."

Pinch hitters fill their days and nights with routine. "Surprise is the enemy of the pinch hitter," says Hansen. "[You're always asking] Who's in the pen that day? How's he been throwing? What's my likelihood of seeing him? I learned more about the intricacies of baseball when I became a pinch hitter than I did as a regular."

In the third inning Durazo will go either to the batting cage to hit off a tee or to the locker room to swing in front of a mirror. Colbrunn and Bautista usually join him, and Durazo picks their brains for pointers about opposing pitchers. Dellucci likes to jump on the stationary bike in the fourth inning, pedaling away while he watches the game on the clubhouse TV. "One thing you worry about is getting up there, getting a hit and then pulling a muscle because you've been sitting around," says Harris, who also rides the bike during games. As with the Diamondbacks' pinch hitters, Jordan often finds himself in the locker room, stretching and swinging. He takes a lot of what he calls "dry swings" or "shadow swings," getting the timing down on his compact stroke.

With all that peripateticism during the game—Gross had a rule that he never sat still for longer than a half inning—one might think pinch-hitting lore is rich with stories of pinch hitters sneaking in a quick hand of clubhouse rummy or being in the middle of relieving themselves when the call comes. Forget it. Unlike closers, their late-game counterparts, pinch hitters tend not to be flakes. Most of them got the job precisely because they are, first, disciplined, studious hitters and, second, desperate to stay in the bigs and know they can't afford to blow a single opportunity. "I didn't want to become a pinch hitter," says the 27-year-old Durazo, who was a regular as a rookie in 1999 but now sits behind Mark Grace, "but they know I'll do anything to stay here."

There have been pinch-hit surprises over the years. In the 1960 World Series, New York Yankees manager Casey Stengel sent Dale Long up to bat for third baseman Clete Boyer in the *second inning* of Game 1. Long flied out, and the Yanks were without Boyer, a sterling gloveman, for the rest of the game, which they lost 6–4.

The lefthanded-hitting Gross recalls the night in '79 when Phillies skipper Danny Ozark had him hit for righthanded-batting cleanup man Greg (the Bull) Luzinski with the bases loaded. "Other than my first at bat in the majors, it was the most nervous I had ever been," says Gross, who delivered a sacrifice fly. What was the Bull's reaction? "I can't say because I stayed away from him," says Gross. "Pinch hitters, you see, can't get too cocky."

SEPTEMBER 6, 2021

Keep Your Eye on the Balls

Is this "game-used" baseball/bat/glove/urinal/
cornstalk legit? Consult the little silver sticker. And
then thank the legion of authenticators behind it

BY EMMA BACCELLIERI

The major league ballpark has really only one job that demands keeping an eye on the ball.

The hitter *should*, of course. And the catcher, too. But for them, watching the baseball is a means to an end rather than an actual requirement. *The umpire?* Close, but he has limited jurisdiction; he isn't asked to track the ball all over the diamond. If he's working home plate his eyes are peeled to call pitches, but he doesn't have to stay fixated on the ball for, say, a tag at second base. And while managers, fielders and fans are all looking on with varying degrees of attentiveness, they're generally watching *the game*, which is very often different from watching *the baseball*. That leaves one very small group of observers who will never relax their gaze.

Tasked with certifying the authenticity of items from every game—including, naturally, lots and lots of baseballs—there are at least two authenticators at every major league contest from spring training through October. Their work receives added attention when it comes to a milestone home run or a big moment, such as the World Series. But they are in stadiums every single day, tracking notable objects, documenting them with an intricate note-taking system and tagging them in a way that escapes tampering. While their work is done largely behind the scenes, it has become a more visible, ingrained part of the sport in recent years, and as

279

MLB's authentication program marks its 20th anniversary this season, the job is bigger than ever. What was once a laser-focused attempt to curb fake memorabilia is now a sprawling daily enterprise that tracks the journey of (*almost*) every single baseball.

And more. The program's legion of baseball detectives authenticate upwards of half a million objects each year, including jerseys, caps, belts, cleats, bases, lineup cards, stadium dirt—you name it. They have verified the legitimacy of at least one set of urinals (following the demolition of the Cardinals' old Busch Memorial Stadium in 2005) and a few stalks of corn (from the *Field of Dreams* game last month in Dyersville, Iowa). Some of these keepsakes end up in the Baseball Hall of Fame, others go to individual club archives or players' rec rooms, and many more are made available to fans. (The urinals, though perhaps historic in their own way, went to a private collector, not to Cooperstown.) Altogether, the program is part security initiative, part historical documentation, part revenue engine. And it starts with the authenticators, embedded in every park, who try never to take their eyes off the ball.

"It's in the way you take notes, the way you watch," says MLB's director of authentication, Michael Posner, trying to encapsulate his field. "You watch a game very differently than you've ever watched a game before."

It started with the FBI. In April 2000 the bureau announced that it had completed the first phase of what it called Operation Bullpen, a national probe into forged autographs and other fake sports memorabilia.

Investigators estimated that at least half of the items for sale across the industry were in some way counterfeit—possibly much more than that, even up to 90%. If you had what you believed to be a signed, game-used Mickey Mantle bat...well, *no*, the odds were that you actually didn't. And while the FBI was in charge of taking down sham dealers, leading to 63 separate charges and convictions, MLB, really, was at the center of everything. The national pastime, after all, had inspired the operation's name. Padres star Tony Gwynn and Cardinals slugger Mark McGwire even assisted in the investigation by verifying their signatures for the FBI and pointing out fakes. (Gwynn was spurred to action after he walked into an official Padres gift shop in Encinitas, Calif., and found that *even in a team store* there were alleged Tony Gwynn–autographed items that he knew he'd never signed.) The league, though, had no system for verifying memorabilia at scale, and after such a public embarrassment, a means of weeding out obvious fakes was needed. So MLB's leaders decided to take action.

Behold, the authentication program.

When it all began, in 2001, there was no blueprint for how, exactly, one would crack down. No other league had a program of the size that MLB was eyeing. (And baseball's version today is far more robust than those of other top leagues.) "The first years we were just trying to clean up something that had become a really big problem," says Posner, who has been with the program almost since the beginning. By '06, after a few seasons of working out the kinks, MLB had landed on the basic outline of the operation that's still in use today. Which looks like this:

Baseball's authenticators are required to have experience in law enforcement. Their work is like evidence collection in that it relies on a chain of custody. They must trace where and how an object changed hands throughout a contest in order to verify it as game-used. (The best authenticators, Posner says, tend to have worked as forensic accountants, where record-keeping and attention to detail are crucial.) The jobs are never openly listed; candidates are recruited by word of mouth and hired through a third-party company, and they undergo extensive training, with a goal of limiting turnover. Many of the 220 authenticators who work with MLB today have been around since almost the beginning.

Each club has its own director of authentication, and some team programs are more robust than others, so that the exact shape of the work can vary from stadium to stadium. But the basics are similar. Every day begins with a meeting to go over the game plan: Is there a player or some other personnel who's close to a statistical milestone of any sort? Could anyone be making their major league debut? Is there something else special about the game—a themed jersey, an addition to the coaching staff— or anything otherwise memorable about the environment?

Those items join a list of everyday fare: lineup cards, broken bats, perhaps some bases or jerseys.... And dozens and dozens of baseballs. Those balls make up the majority of the items handled by the program each year. They also show the profound, exacting rigor of its system.

The chain of custody can be easy enough to follow for a hat or for a set of bases—items that largely remain attached to a specific person or, better, stay stationary on the field. There isn't usually much to track. But for a baseball? A ball is involved in every single play, changing hands as a matter of course, ever a risk to leave the field and slip into the crowd. To authenticate a game-used ball is to bear witness to each and every moment of its major league life—an act of constant vigilance.

"You're so focused on the baseball as an authenticator that you really don't pick up some of the other things going on," Posner says. "You have to be very involved for every pitch."

Perched beside the dugouts, authenticators take notes as they track each ball, waiting for the moment when it is discarded or swapped out or otherwise removed from the field. If this part of the job seems redundant in the age of Statcast, note: Those cameras and radars can determine launch angle and exit velocity down to the decimal point, but they can't distinguish between one cowhide orb and the next. That's still the domain of the authenticator alone. And it's an area where human institutional knowledge helps. Skilled authenticators will remember that Pitcher A likes to ask for a new ball every time he gives up a hit, or that Pitcher B has a groundball-heavy style that will keep them busy with infield action.

Once a ball leaves a game, the physical stage of authentication begins. If an authenticator is satisfied that they have chronicled a ball's every move, they'll retrieve it, either themself or through a ball boy or ball girl. They'll affix a tiny silver sticker—a hologram bearing a unique string of letters and numbers—to its surface. And they'll log their record of the ball's life in a unique MLB system, akin to an app.

As recently as five years ago, the process would have stopped at that point, but now there's a new wrinkle: The relevant pitches and plays are matched with the corresponding data from Statcast. Today, if you were to type the code on that little sticker into MLB's authentication database it would unlock a record, not just of the ball's final play, but of all its plays—"actually going into the detail of *This is the pitcher that threw it, this was the batter, this was the speed it was thrown at, this was the exit velocity*," says Gavin Werner, director of retail and authentication for the Giants. "It creates this deeper, richer picture of how that baseball was being used. I think you can really remember it in a more significant way."

And that's just for one ball. Repeat 50 times per game, or more, and add in at least one set of bases and lineup cards. That's on an average night. But a perfect game? A milestone hit? A special jersey collection? You're easily looking at more than 100 items authenticated on a given game day.

The program ensures that someone documents the artifacts attached to every surprise bit of baseball history—each no-hitter and multi-home-run game and unassisted triple play—and from every day of baseball, period. And this authentication has become the standard for any sale or display of memorabilia. Even if a player has something of his own that he just wants to keep for posterity, the importance of getting that little sticker is now widely understood. (Technically, team-issued objects like jerseys and hats belong to each club, whereas personal gear like batting gloves or cleats belong to players—but teams generally try to build a two-way street so there's no dispute over who gets to keep a given item. "Players know we're going to put them first; if there's anything significant, we will always try to honor their requests," says Werner, whose Giants share a cut of any authenticated item that is sold with the player whose name is on it, even if the item was originally provided by the team, like a jersey.)

In the end, this all adds up to one dramatic blow to the fake-game-used-merchandise market. (Posner estimates that just one phony has come across his desk in the last five years.) In addition to chasing out the counterfeiters, however, the sheer volume of items catalogued has created a notable retail force for teams and for the league, which Posner sums up as "a very nice offshoot of cleaning up the fraud." If an object is authenticated but isn't requested by a player, the club archive or the Hall of Fame—most objects are not—it will often be made available for purchase at auction or by direct sale. And in its tiny silver sticker it will carry the story of its major league life.

There is one common situation in which it's all but impossible to maintain a chain-of-custody record for a piece of baseball history: when it flies into the crowd. The balls with the most exciting fates, in other words, are often the ones least likely to get authenticated.

"We have more than a few videos of people switching out baseballs," Posner says, explaining how stadium scrums can stymie the authentication process on home runs. "People have [balls] from batting practice, or they bring in a ball and they want to keep the real one and throw back the fake one."

As a result, authenticated home run balls are especially hard to come by. Dingers are generally stickered only when the ball ricochets out of the stands, back onto the field, in view the whole time. One recent exception: During the 2020 pandemic season, with its empty stadiums, the majority of home runs were authenticated for the first time.

Even then, though, the chain-of-custody standards ensured that authentication could be tricky. Jordan Field, the Tigers' director of player relations and authentication, recalls being told before a home game against the Brewers last September that Milwaukee slugger Ryan Braun was trying to collect as many of his own authenticated home run balls as possible, for his personal collection, as his career winded down. In the seventh inning Braun launched one toward the Comerica Park stands, which were swept clean after batting practice, leaving Field with what should have been an easy pickup. Instead, Field watched as the ball soared toward the home bullpen...and directly into a trash can.

Which is how Field ended up leaning over the left-field railing with an odd request for Detroit's pitchers below: *Could one of you please reach into that trash can? And if you find one baseball in there*—only one, of course, because Braun's ball couldn't be authenticated if there were two—*could you please pass it up?*

The trash can held just the one baseball. Field had it authenticated. And Braun got his memento.

Those specific circumstances seem unlikely to recur. And with fans in the stands again, the authentication of home run balls is once more a rarity. Still, Posner and his crew wondered last month whether there might be an opportunity for one more unobstructed home run haul, at the *Field of Dreams* game in Iowa, where long balls would disappear into the corn rather than into a crowd of potential collectors. Alas, "the way the corn was planted, the immensity of it and the height of it, the ball would literally just disappear," he laments. In the end, the authenticators did find baseballs among the stalks, but—such are their standards—they couldn't be *completely* sure that any given ball was a specific home run, not one from batting practice. And so Posner & Co. settled instead on authenticating some of the corn itself.

Another exception in the aversion to authenticating home run balls: the occasion of a major milestone, like when a player reaches No. 500. For the Tigers' Miguel Cabrera, the process worked like this: After he hit No. 499, on Aug. 11, baseballs stenciled with an M and a serial number were cycled in for each plate appearance so they could be easily recognized but also to establish an order in which they would be used. Each ball also bore a unique marking that could be seen only under something akin to a blacklight. (The specific fluid and light used for this process remains an MLB secret. "The covert marking you cannot find—I guarantee you—with a blacklight. It won't work," says Posner.) The ball boy or ball girl would visit the umpire before and after each of Cabrera's plate appearances, dropping off and picking up the special balls. The pitcher could not throw them to any other batter.

All of which ensured that authenticators would be able to verify the ball. But first they would have to retrieve it from whoever caught it, which has occasionally proved tricky in the past.

Cabrera hit No. 500 on Aug. 22, against the Blue Jays in Toronto. For every game of their road trip the Tigers had reserved an empty suite, where they could host a potential home-run-catching fan, both for security purposes (no one wanted to see the fan get swarmed), and for a chance at an intimate—and, ideally, persuasive—meet-and-greet with the slugger.

"We were not prepared to purchase the baseball," says Field. "The plan was to create an experience for the fan, with Miguel, that would have been so memorable that presenting the baseball to him in person after the game would have been an easy decision."

And it worked. The ball went back to Cabrera and the Tigers—*after* authenticators had verified it and applied a hologram sticker, of course. That afternoon, though, the ball itself was just one of 183 items authenticated, including a bucket of dirt from the right-handed batter's box, all of the unused marked balls, every champagne bottle from the postgame clubhouse celebration and everything worn by Cabrera. (Detroit's equipment manager had packed an extra No. 24 uniform—all the way down to the belt—for the road trip, knowing that Cabrera would have to give his up as soon as he hit No. 500.)

The same process is followed in the event of a 600th or a 700th home run. After that "you start getting into Babe Ruth, Hank Aaron territory—we start to do a bit more marking," says Posner. It's also used when someone approaches 3,000 hits, which means that Field and Cabrera, who's sitting on 2,964, will likely be doing this all over again next year.

These are the kinds of massive moments the program was made for. But asked for his favorite authentication of the summer, Posner throws a curveball. When White Sox reliever Liam Hendriks was miked up at this summer's All-Star Game in Denver, fans on television got to hear him pitch through a creative string of profanities. They also got to hear how he reacted to his first strikeout.

"I wanna get that ball authenticated!" he yelled as the baseball returned to him after going around the horn. Hendriks motioned for a new one, tapped the surface of the old one, tossed it in the direction of the authenticator by the dugout and hollered: "Hey! Little sticker!"

MARCH 31, 2021

Remembering the Best (and Worst) of Pitchers at the Plate

On the eve of what is likely to be the final season without
a universal DH, let's remember the glorious spectacle—
heroic and/or ridiculous—of pitchers hitting.

BY STEVE RUSHIN

In the grillroom of McArthur Golf Club in Hobe Sound, Fla., this winter, two retired pitchers were talking baseball. Jim Kaat pitched 25 seasons in the big leagues, in four decades, for six teams, while one-time Phillies prospect Bill Parcells topped out as a teenager in New Jersey, only to become a football coach of some renown. Still, both men fondly recalled the oversize sweats—some were feed bags fashioned into baseball pants—they wore to practice sliding in the 1950s should they ever have to leg out a double. "We wanted to be baseball players, not pitchers," says Kaat, 82. "We wanted to learn to bunt, slide, run the bases and help ourselves out with the bat."

Major league pitchers have been batting for 150 years now. Their walk-up music, in the mind's ear, is "Entry of the Gladiators," the theme of the Ringling Bros. and Barnum & Bailey Circus, for pitchers have often looked silly at the plate. Last season they laid down their weapons entirely when the National League used designated hitters, as the American League has done since 1973. Pitchers are unlikely to bat at all in 2022, when the universal DH is expected to be enshrined permanently in a new collective bargaining agreement. That leaves 2021 as their final trip around the bases, a valedictory lap for men who tend to run awkwardly, wearing warmup jackets, after reaching on an error, or a dropped third strike, or some form of suspected chicanery. In 1964 the severely nearsighted Reds pitcher Ryne Duren was accused by the Cardinals of thrusting his knee into a pitch to reach first base. It was more useful than his bat. As one writer put it, "[Duren] couldn't hit the ground with a safe."

If this is the obituary for pitchers as batters, there are multiple causes of death, including asphyxiation. With every inelegant swing, Brooklyn pitcher Preacher Roe choked up a little higher on the bat, his hands slowly climbing the barrel like a koala ascending a eucalyptus trunk. Deep into a count, Roe risked having more lumber below his fists than above them. He was so lost at the plate that the left-handed pitcher tried switch-whiffing. "Roe often would take two strikes hitting right-handed, then finish the strikeout left-handed," his Dodgers teammate Pete Reiser told a reporter after Roe retired in 1954 with 215 strikeouts in 620 at bats. "Anything to try to change his luck."

Roe wasn't unlucky as a hitter. He was un-good. Most pitchers are. A difficult enough task for everyday players, hitting is infinitely more challenging for anyone attempting to do it every fourth or fifth day. "When the other players on the club are taking their licks in batting practice, the pitchers are sprinkled around in the outfield and delegated to chase fly balls," noted *Los Angeles Times* baseball writer and foreign correspondent Harry A. Williams. "Chasing balls for other people is not calculated to benefit a man's batting eye."

That was in 1913, after which a few pitchers *did* do significant damage with a bat. Babe Ruth used to make an annual bet with Yankees pitcher Lefty Gomez that Gomez wouldn't get five hits on the season, a wager Gomez usually ended up winning, by a narrow margin, in late September. One afternoon Ruth handed Gomez his own bat and told him to a hit a home run with it. While attempting to knock the dirt from his spikes in the on-deck circle, Gomez smashed himself in the ankle instead and had to be hospitalized. But at least he hit something. At least he *held* something—that Ruthian Louisville Slugger, full of latent energy. Some pitchers couldn't be bothered schlepping 42 ounces to the plate.

On April 2, 1982, A's righthander Steve McCatty approached the batter's box in Yuma, Ariz., in the final week of spring training. Oakland manager Billy Martin didn't want his ace to risk injury by swinging—or God forbid, to get a hit and have to run the bases—so McCatty strode to the plate with a 15-inch bat, purchased that night at the souvenir stand, an effort umpire Jim Quick found humorous but beneath the dignity of even a Cactus League game. A batboy brought McCatty some real lumber, which Cat left on his shoulder as he watched three pitches sail by. Quick, quickly, punched him out.

"In my opinion, there is nothing as dull in baseball as watching pitchers try to hit," said Hall of Fame first baseman George Sisler, who played during the Warren G. Harding Administration, by which time it was already long-established that pitchers—like the anti–Venus de Milo—were valued for only their arms. "A pitcher isn't expected to hit, and he knows it," Tigers pitcher Bill Donovan said in 1908. "Therefore, he doesn't pay attention to that end of the game."

As a rookie with the Phillies in 1980, Bob Walk wasn't paying attention to that end of the game when he absentmindedly strolled to the plate with no bat at all, packing light for what he must have known would be a brief round trip from the dugout. Most pitchers bring a bat to the plate for the same reason kids bring a glove to the bleachers: on the slim hope they'll get to use it to some positive effect.

"Pitchers can't hit," Casey Stengel once said. "You can't even teach 'em to bunt." So perhaps it is time—long past time—to confine them to the mound, to take away their bats, to turn the whole pitching profession into Lumber Liquidators.

But what of the guys who *could* hit? Hall of Fame Braves lefty Warren Spahn clobbered 35 long balls in his career, the third most all-time among pitchers. He hit at least one home run in every NL ballpark. "We've made nonathletes out of pitchers," he complained to *The New York Times* in 1999, the same year his successors in the Braves rotation were featured in a famous Nike commercial. Greg Maddux and Tom Glavine, envious of Cardinals slugger Mark McGwire, pumped iron and took batting practice before declaring, in front of *Melrose Place* heartthrob Heather Locklear: "Chicks dig the long ball."

The Angels' Shohei Ohtani pitches and plays DH with equal proficiency. "Adding to my HOF credentials," tweeted pitcher Dan Haren, who had a perfect day at the plate for the Diamondbacks in 2010, "I'm the last pitcher in history to have a 4 hit game." Pitcher Madison Bumgarner, who has 19 career home runs, was so at ease as a Giants slugger that he blew a celebratory snot rocket after crossing the plate with his first grand slam in 2014.

Still, most pitchers who hit safely get seeing-eye singles, which may be why Cardinals flamethrower Bob Gibson drew a pair of peepers on his bat. Gibson hit a home run into the upper deck in San Diego in 1971, though he chalked up that blast to a juiced ball. "Under normal circumstances," he said, "I'd have to hit a ball, then chase it and hit it again to get it that far."

Still, Gibson batted six points above the Mendoza Line over 17 seasons and hit 24 home runs, one of them in the 1967 World Series. He continued hitting prodigious dingers in Old-Timers' Games, rocketing one into the upper tank at Busch Stadium in 1991 while batting left-handed as a goof. Gibson, a right-handed hitter, was 56 at the time.

More often, though, the pitcher's slot in the batting order is like the ballad at a heavy-metal concert: a cue to use the restroom. "The time to get a hot dog and a beer is when the pitcher comes to bat," Joe Altobelli said when he was managing the Orioles, but the fan who acted on that impulse risked missing a spectacle—heroic or ridiculous, possibly both at the same time. When Roe, a year before retirement, hit one over the fence in Pittsburgh, his Dodgers teammates Jackie Robinson, Ralph Branca and Roy Campanella lay down a carpet of towels to guide him into the dugout as if he were a movie star strolling into a premiere, which he was, in a manner of speaking: It was Roe's first—and last—dinger.

In 1963, baseball writer Neal Russo of the *St. Louis Post-Dispatch* compiled a partial list of pitchers—including the Cardinals' Clint Rehm as well as the Dodgers' Sandy Koufax and Hank Behrman—who had singled cleanly to the outfield but were thrown out at first base after standing too long in the batter's box gazing in wonder and disbelief at the ball they had just put into play.

There is a cognitive dissonance when pitchers connect with the ball, a disbelief in some cases. "The impossible has happened!" Mets announcer Gary Cohen shouted when Bartolo Colon, who more often swung out from under his helmet, went yard at Petco Park in 2016. Over a thunderous ovation from the crowd in San Diego, Cohen said, "This is one of the great moments in the history of baseball!" It was a wry bit of hyperbole; Cohen had ages of time to fill as Colon circled the bases. "I wanna say it was one of the longest home run trots I've ever seen," said analyst Ron Darling. "But I think that's how fast he runs."

Colon's dinger was also a victory lap for hurlers, perhaps the last great triumph of a pitcher at the plate, one final blow to disprove—however briefly—Addie Joss's ancient theory of why pitchers can't hit. Joss, who pitched for Cleveland in the first decade of the last century, said that a man accustomed to watching a ball go away from himself cannot comprehend a ball coming toward him.

Tony Cloninger could. On July 3, 1966, at Candlestick Park in San Francisco, the hard-throwing Braves righthander hit two grand slams against the Giants, then added a gratuitous single. Cloninger had nine RBIs, one for every inning he pitched in a complete-game, 17–3 win. He became the first player in NL history to hit two grand slams in a game and remains one of only 13 players in either league to do so.

And even that was not the finest two-way performance ever wrought by a pitcher. Rick Wise no-hit the Reds in Cincinnati on June 23, 1971, while belting two home runs in the Phillies' 4–0 win. His bat was dispatched to Cooperstown, where it was displayed under glass like King Tut's death mask, a relic of mythical fascination.

For many pitchers, the home run was the greater achievement than the no-hitter. At 40, Nolan Ryan hit the second home run of his 27-year career on May 1, 1987, the same night he took a no-hitter into the sixth inning against the Braves. "Realistically, the odds are not very good," he said of throwing another no-no. "I would think better than hitting another home run, though." He was right. Four years later to the day, Ryan threw his seventh no-hitter. He never went yard again.

Jack Kofoed, a sportswriter from 1912 until his death in 1979, saw nearly everyone play during the decades that baseball was America's pastime. "I used to think the worst hitter I ever saw was Eppa Rixey," wrote Kofoed, of the Phillies pitcher who went 1-for-26 (with a double) in 1914. But then he saw Ryne Duren: "Rixey was a regular Joe DiMaggio compared with [Duren]."

Duren made a spectacle of himself, in spectacles, for 10 seasons, three of them with the Yankees. He might throw his first warmup pitch 100 mph to the backstop, then use a handkerchief to theatrically clean his glasses. (He owned seven pairs.) Catcher Elston Howard painted his own nails with Mercurochrome just so Duren could read the signs. When Duren was on his knees, repairing the mound with his hands, Gus Triandos of the Orioles asked Yogi Berra what Duren was doing. "Trying to find the rubber," Berra replied.

For a man who could hardly see, Duren managed seven career hits. Three of them came in one season, in 1963. But he wasn't the worst-hitting pitcher of the 1950s and '60s, when Tigers lefthander Hank Aguirre boasted of winning an anti–Silver Slugger—what he called a Lead Bat. His swing was, in the words of the writer Milton Richman, that of a man "flailing away futilely at the plate like someone trying to swat houseflies off his nose." Aguirre once received a five-minute standing ovation at Tiger Stadium for getting a base knock.

Like Duren, Giants righthander Ron Herbel wore glasses at the plate, but they didn't help. There was no Herbel remedy. He got six hits in nine years, half of them in a torrid 1967 season, when Herbel went 3-for-28. Bob Buhl went oh-for-1962, when—as a member of the Braves and Cubs—he was hitless in 70 at bats. In a 15-year career, Buhl batted .089 and slugged, if that is the right word, .091. The fans weren't *Buhl*ing; they were booing.

Many pitchers, however, were proud of their prowess at the plate, even if those skills were a fading memory of their high school days. With two outs and two on in the bottom of the eighth inning of Game 2 of the 1965 World Series, Dodgers pitcher Ron Perranoski pitched around Twins second baseman Frank Quilici to get to Kaat, who felt mildly insulted. He singled up the middle to extend Minnesota's lead to 5–1 and seal the win.

On his 1973 Topps card Kaat is racing out of the box, bat still in hand, a baseball player, not a pitcher. That was the year the DH came to the AL, robbing fans of more glorious moments like this one: White Sox pitcher Billy Pierce, on his '56 Topps card, is two steps out of the box, looking back with pride at the ball he has just put into play. It is five feet in front of home plate.

It was another White Sox pitcher, reliever Terry Forster, who was, by one measure, the best hitting pitcher of all time. David Letterman infamously called him a "fat tub of goo," but Forster's lifetime average of .397 over 16 seasons is the highest among pitchers with at least 50 at bats and 15 years' experience.

"It's embarrassing to see pitchers who can't bunt, who can't slide, who can't run the bases without spraining an ankle," says Kaat, Forster's former teammate. Kaat was hitting .289 with the Twins in July 1972 when he broke his left wrist while—despite all that practice—sliding into second to break up a double play. That's how it is with pitchers. Getting on base was often more harmful than striking out. In 1973 a 37-year-old Gibson tore cartilage in his right knee while scrambling back to first base on a line drive to third. Twelve years later, reigning NL Cy Young winner Rick Sutcliffe went on the DL after injuring his left hamstring while trying to beat the throw to first and avoid a double play. Until that moment, Sutcliffe said, "I didn't know a hamstring existed."

There was often a perverse pleasure watching pitchers hit, or try to. As with so many other of the game's traditions—twi-night doubleheaders, no pepper signs, fans tearing up sod in postseason celebrations—we don't miss them until they're gone. "The way they're...bastardizing may not be the right word, but the way they're *tinkering* with the game, with analytics and shifts and some other proposals?" says Kaat, who won 283 games and got 232 hits. "...I'm kinda sad to see it."

That goes for pitchers' being stripped of their bats, too. Koufax, Kaat's counterpart in Games 2, 5 and 7 of the 1965 Series, was a career .097 hitter. In '55, his rookie season with Brooklyn, Koufax made 12 plate appearances and struck out all 12 times. There was a sad poignancy whenever he slipped out of his warmup jacket before entering the box, like a palooka prizefighter publicly disrobing before taking a certain beatdown. Batting humanized the finest pitcher of his generation. His rotation mate Don Drysdale was a beast: His .300 average in 138 at bats led all Dodgers regulars in 1965. But Koufax was so poor at the plate that he gave up golf. "When you're a bad hitter like me, you want to swing hard at something," he said, "so when I play golf, I try to tear the cover off the ball." He feared his violent drives were hurting his shoulder and stayed off the links during the baseball season.

Kaat, meanwhile, plays golf almost every day. He plays the way Roe struck out: left-handed and right-handed, often both in the same round. Working on Kaat's golf swing not long ago, the club pro at McArthur told him: "Make believe there's a guy playing third base and you're hitting a line drive down the left-field line."

That's a sight we haven't seen often enough—a pitcher roping one down the line—but soon we'll be robbed of even subtler pleasures, like a pitcher's taking three strikes and then his seat. There was something noble, pure, even purposeful about a pitcher's striking out. In a game that's already too long, pitchers' fanning expeditiously served a vital purpose. When Braves pitcher Larry McWilliams struck out twice in the same inning of a 1979 game, he performed a public service. Jose Canseco wasn't a pitcher, but he also struck out twice in one inning, and what he said after should be chiseled on the headstone of every pitcher who swung in vain: "Somebody's got to make the outs."

DECEMBER 22, 2008

Take Me Out to...the Winter Meetings in Vegas, Baby, Vegas

Baseball's annual swap meet was a mere sideshow to the circus of showgirls, rodeo, slots and neon kitsch, but it ultimately delivered a $161 million jackpot, a 4 a.m. free-agent signing and a 12-player—12!—trade. (Plus the usual frenzy of rumors, half-truths, outright lies and the stem-winding stories from the old baseball men)

BY JOE POSNANSKI

Midnight at the Bellagio, and the slot machines are ringing, the Big Six wheel clicks, blackjack dealers are dispensing 13s, and Lou Piniella poses for a photograph with a Chicago family in town to catch the Vegas Christmas spirit. A cocktail waitress looks for the man who ordered the 7 & 7, and she can't find him, so several baseball men nobly raise their hands and chips to save the fair maiden and her orphaned drink. Dice tumble, ice clinks, cards pop, scouts argue about a player who has been out of the game for 20 years, baseball writers stalk the scene like Depression Era hoboes pressing their noses against a restaurant window. Smoke chokes the air, and three women who look to be just off the set of *The Real Housewives of Orange County* wander through the scene wearing "dresses" (quotation marks necessary), stopping traffic, but only for a moment, because then talk of a three-team trade heats up. The voice of Sinatra croons *Let's Face the Music and Dance* over the casino sound system, and Tommy Lasorda asks if anyone's heard any more about the Jake Peavy deal. More than anything, however, my feet are killing me, absolutely killing me, because I didn't take to heart the advice of the king.

The king of this year's baseball winter meetings in Las Vegas is an 81-year-old scout for the Kansas City Royals named Art Stewart. He is barely 5'7", and he never played at a level higher than semipro in Chicago, but he's the Sinatra of the baseball bat pack, the chairman of the hoard, the guy behind the guy behind the guy. He has been coming to the winter meetings for 45 years, going back to his scouting days with the New York Yankees, back when he signed the outfielder Norm Siebern by throwing in a working stove for Norm's mother. Art knows everybody, and everybody knows Art, and he will admit that the game has changed, the money has changed, even the baseball people have changed. But there's one thing that hasn't changed, one rule that never changes, and it is this: The secret to the winter meetings is to stand on your own piece of carpet.

"Don't stand on the bare floor," he says. "You have to protect your feet."

You laugh? Don't laugh. See, it's midnight at the Bellagio, and what's happening? All those people who did not find their place on the carpet, all of those eager baseball men who have spent the last five or six hours downing drinks and recalling ballplayers who haven't played in 20 years and proposing deals and standing on the marble floors, well, now their feet hurt. Look at them shifting back and forth. "They're dropping like flies," is how Art puts it, and he adds that over his many years, he's seen countless good guys make bad baseball trades simply because their feet hurt.

"There are tricks to the trade," Art says. "You bet. Tricks to the trade."

Las Vegas is not a baseball town, of course. Vegas is a boxing town. Vegas is an event town. Vegas is a tuxedo town, a chandelier town, a Cher town, a magician's town, a dirty-joke town. Vegas is an on-the-rocks, Siegfried-and-Roy, white-tiger, *Danke-Schoen*, cigar-smoking, *Ocean's-Eleven*, roller-coaster-through-the-lobby, Eiffel-Tower-replica town. Vegas is the kind of place, as Boston Red Sox senior adviser and baseball oracle Bill James says, where it costs more to get an Internet connection in your room than to have an escort sent up. When you say World Series here, people think poker.

Maybe that's why there isn't a single sign in the lobby of the Bellagio hotel and casino indicating that the winter meetings are happening here. Baseball people have gathered almost every winter since 1904—it may even go back a few years before that—and the meetings have been a point of major interest in New York City* and Chicago and New Orleans and everywhere else.

The origin of the winter meetings, like the origin of baseball (and the origin of Las Vegas, for that matter), is hazy. But you can probably say the official winter meetings began on Dec. 15, 1911. That was the day that cranky Chicago Cubs owner Charles Murphy became convinced that St. Louis Cardinals manager Roger Bresnahan was trying to steal his first baseman Victor Saier. And so, in the lobby of the Waldorf Hotel in New York City, in full public view, Murphy spent a very long time screaming at Bresnahan, calling him a liar and a thief and promising to run him out of the game. It was quite a scandal. And everyone looked forward to the winter meetings in 1912.

Point is, you get all these baseball executives together, and the drinks start flowing, the talk gets animated, money starts changing hands, human beings get traded, and it is quite a show—the winter meetings have always been the biggest rodeo in town.

Only in Vegas this week, there is a bigger rodeo, the Wrangler National Finals Rodeo, and everywhere you turn, leathery men in cowboy hats and Volkswagen-sized belt buckles argue on cellphones about whether to go see Donny and Marie at the Flamingo or the showgirls at the Luxor's *Fantasy* revue. It is the cowboys' town this week. Baseball is an afterthought.

"We get a lot of top professional baseball players in to see the show," says Lance Burton, Master Magician and a staple at the Monte Carlo. "Pete Rose has been in several times."

Ah, yes, Pete Rose. He is the one enduring connection between the game and the Strip—he is baseball's Mr. Vegas, its Elvis. Several days a week, every week, year round, he appears at the Field of Dreams store in the Caesar's Palace next door to the Bellagio. He signs autographs, poses for pictures, tells stories and occasionally sells an apology ball for a few hundred bucks—that's a baseball on which he inscribes, I'M SORRY I BET ON BASEBALL.

"I'm the best deal in Vegas," Rose says. "Think about this: When you go see Bette Midler, will she take a picture with you? Will she put her arm around you? Will she sign an autograph for you? No. I give you all that."

When it is pointed out that, technically speaking, he doesn't sing or dance, he shrugs. "Maybe I can," he says. Alas, at the last minute, even Pete Rose cancels his scheduled appearances while the winter meetings are going on. No reason is given. He might just want the whole town to himself.

Inside the Bellagio it looks like the opening bar scene from *Casablanca*, when everyone is trying to cut a deal. ("And bring fifteen thousand francs in cash. Remember: in cash.") Baseball people huddle by the elevators, outside the Café Gelato, near the Bellagio Gallery of Fine Art, between the slot machines, around the piano bar, speaking quietly so as not to be overheard, though nobody would really understand them anyway. There's a beautiful economy to the conversations of baseball men—team executives with titles like "special assistant" and "special projects coordinator," the scouts, the writers. The rhythms of the dialogue are familiar to anyone who has ever watched a Mafia movie.

Baseball writer: So when did you get in?

Special assistant: Little while ago. You?

BW: Same.

SA: It's a zoo, huh?

BW: Yeah. Zoo.

SA: Zoo.

BW: You hearing anything?

SA: Naw. All quiet.

BW: What about that thing?

SA: Dead.

BW: I heard there's movement.

SA: Wait. Which thing?

BW: Baltimore.

SA: Yeah. It's dead.

BW: Too bad.

SA: Yeah. What you hearing?

BW: Maybe Arizona.

SA: Yeah, I heard something.

BW: You think?

SA: I don't know.

BW: Depends on the third guy.

SA: I didn't know there was a third guy.

BW: Yeah.

SA: Well, a third guy—that could be interesting.

BW: Oakland could get in too.

SA: Wait. Which thing are we talking about?

And so on.

Day 1: Nothing happens

There are two progressive jackpots at these winter meetings. Well, there are more than two, but nobody expects such big-ticket sluggers as Mark Teixeira or Manny Ramirez or Adam Dunn to sign with teams anytime soon, not with everybody but the Yankees moaning about the baseball economy. The biggest jackpot is the big free-agent lefthander Carsten Charles

Sabathia, CC for short. He could be the heaviest pitcher in baseball history,* not that his weight has anything to do with it; Sabathia won the Cy Young Award in 2007. He was even better in '08, especially after he was traded in July from the Cleveland Indians to the Milwaukee Brewers (11–2, 1.65 ERA after the deal, delivering the Brewers their first playoff appearance in 26 years).

That title of heaviest pitcher usually goes to Jumbo Brown, a reliever for five teams from 1925 through '41. Jumbo was listed at 295 pounds. Sabathia is officially listed at 290—but there are reasons to believe that his official weight would be overturned upon further review.

Sabathia was so good in Milwaukee that the Brewers are cashing in all of their savings bonds, pulling out the money they stuffed into mattresses and borrowing from various grandparents in an effort to keep him. The down-market team has reportedly offered him $100 million for five years, a staggering sum, almost double the salary they have ever offered a player. But because the Yankees are said to be interested, nobody believes the Milwaukee money will be nearly enough.

The second jackpot is 27-year-old righthander Jake Peavy, who has the second-best ERA in baseball over the last five years, behind that of Johan Santana, who at the moment is the highest-paid pitcher in baseball. Peavy is the property of the San Diego Padres, but that's what baseball people call a "fluid situation." The Padres are owned by John Moores, and he is in the midst of a nasty divorce from Becky, his wife for 45 years.

Divorce details are not public, of course, but rumors fly. Most assume that Moores will have to sell the team and split the money. Therefore, most assume that the Padres will have no choice but to deal Peavy and his $70 million contract. Therefore, most assume that the Chicago Cubs will get Peavy. There are a lot of assumptions at the winter meetings.

Then, as one baseball executive says, "The good thing about these meetings is that I don't know s---, but I look around and I realize everyone around here knows even less."

Here's how dead it is on Day 1: The big story seems to be the Detroit Tigers' trade of two minor league pitchers to the Texas Rangers for part-time catcher Gerald Laird. "I think he's the type of guy that may not only hit doubles, but he'll hit triples," Detroit manager Jim Leyland says. And to show you how slow things are, I write this down.

The pulse of the winter meetings has slowed over the years. General managers used to meet in hotel lobbies, have drinks and make trades they would regret in the morning. In 1974, late at night, Philadelphia Phillies G.M. Paul Owens traded catcher Bob Boone to Detroit for three players. In the morning, though, he pulled out of the deal on the concrete legal claim that he had probably had a few too many when he agreed to the deal. "How do you unshake a handshake?" Detroit general manager Jim Campbell asked angrily. But that's how it was—everybody sort of made the rules as they went along.

Now, it's different. General managers mostly stay in their swanky Bellagio suites alongside trusted scouts, sundry statisticians, a fridge filled with bottles of water, and a bank of computers. They look out over the Vegas skyline; they communicate by texting; and they run every trade and free-agent possibility through simulators and accountants. They talk around deals, refuse to be pinned down and exchange lists of players to choose from. Stinking lists.*

*The late Syd Thrift, a longtime scout and G.M. for the Pirates, Orioles and five other teams, used to hate when other general managers gave him lists—"Lists are for grocery stores," he'd say. "Make me an offer."

And it has all grown so complicated, so distant, so jittery. Most executives seem afraid to make a bad trade, afraid to face the instant wrath of the newspapers and talk-radio hosts and bloggers. There are no pigeons left in baseball. It's safer to stay indoors.

"You know what Pat Gillick told me?" said Allard Baird, the onetime Royals G.M. and now an assistant to Theo Epstein in Boston. "I asked him why he got out [in November], after he won the championship in Philadelphia. He said, 'Allard, nobody trades anymore. And that was the whole fun of it.'"

There's another rule that Art Stewart picked up in his half century plus in this crazy game: Never leave before the last pitch is thrown. He learned that 50 years ago in Chicago Heights, Ill., on a day when scouts went to check out a young pitcher named Jerry Colangelo—the same Jerry Colangelo who would one day own the Arizona Diamondbacks and the Phoenix Suns. Colangelo got knocked out in the second inning, and all the other scouts headed for another school to look at another prospect.

A new kid came in, one whom everybody called Warm Up because he never got to pitch. Well, Art thought the kid threw pretty well. He stayed—and later signed him. The kid was Jim Bouton, who won 21 games for the Yankees in 1963.

It's 1 a.m. Vegas time, and Art's standing on the carpet, and he's welcoming people like he's in a wedding receiving line.

"We've got to get this deal done," Cubs manager Lou Piniella shouts as he wraps his arms around Stewart's neck.

"Well, if you change a couple of names on your end, we can get it done," Art says.

"Arthur, are we still talking?" Los Angeles Dodgers ambassador Tommy Lasorda asks.

"You bet, Tommy," Art says back. "We're open for business."*

**"We're open for business"* is a reference to one of the great stories in the history of the winter meetings. It was 1975, the meetings were at the Diplomat Hotel in Hollywood, Fla., and the owners had (against their better judgment—and on the second vote) allowed showman Bill Veeck to repurchase the Chicago White Sox. They were worried that Veeck, who in his previous life as an owner had sent a midget to the plate, would make a mockery of the game.*

The next day Veeck and his general manager, Roland Hemond, set up a table and phones in the lobby of the Diplomat. And they posted a homemade sign that read: OPEN FOR BUSINESS. BY APPOINTMENT ONLY. Then Veeck and Hemond sat there for 14 straight hours and made four trades, the last one—Bee Richard to St. Louis for Buddy Bradford and Greg Terlicky—just seconds before the midnight deadline. And the crowd cheered.

What's amazing about Art is how excited he is, even late at night, even after all these years. He pulls out his legal pad and scribbles names and numbers and gossip and lies. He talks the way baseball people talked in the old days; there's urgency in his voice. For everyone else, every sentence is conditional, every offer a trial balloon, every overture merely a conversation starter. Just as Veeck and Thrift were, Art Stewart is a man of action.

"Hello, Dayton," Indians G.M. Mark Shapiro says the next morning when he phones his Royals counterpart, Dayton Moore. "I hear you need to talk to me."

"Well, I'm always happy to talk to you, Mark," says Moore, who wasn't expecting the call.

"No, I thought it was urgent," Shapiro says. "I was told you needed to talk with me immediately."

Moore smiles and shakes his head. "Let me guess," he says. "You were talking to Art."

Day 2: Peavy talk heats up; Brian Cashman leaves town

No, general managers can't set up in the lobby anymore. The place is crawling with agents trying to get a little face time for their players, kids just out of college who desperately want to work in a major league front office, former players who are trying to get back into the game, fans looking for a recognizable face and sportswriters who are desperate to find something, anything, that resembles news. If G.M.s showed up, it would be like the Beatles getting mobbed in *A Hard Day's Night*.

So with the men who make news locked in their suites, the Bellagio lobby turns into a rumor echo chamber. The first big rumor to make the rounds on Day 2 is that Yankees general manager Brian Cashman slipped out of Vegas and headed for San Francisco to meet with Sabathia. Nobody seems quite sure how Cashman made it out of the hotel without being noticed. "He must be like James Bond," says one baseball scout, though nobody is quite sure what he means.

The other persistent echo is that Peavy is going to the Cubs. According to the grapevine, the deal is all but done. The trouble is that some say it's a two-team trade, others say it is a three-team trade, and for a while it is even rumored to be a four-team trade.

After so many hours the talk begins to overwhelm you, and the only way to escape the madness is to pull a Cashman, get out of the hotel, go down to Fremont Street—a $25 cab ride from the Bellagio—and catch a little bit of what Vegas used to be. You can see Binion's and the Golden Nugget and the neon cowboy smoking a cigarette on top of the Frontier. Here it's a bit rundown and seedy: exotic dancers, sad-looking men slumping at craps tables, wrinkled women who pull the lever on the side of the slot machine rather than pushing the more convenient MAX BET button in front.

There is no sign of baseball anywhere—nobody wearing a baseball cap, nothing baseball-related for sale, no one talking about the Gerald Laird trade. Two women dressed like mermaids stand outside a casino named Mermaids, and I ask if they have ever heard of Brian Cashman. They have heard of Cashman, but they seem to be confusing him with Big Jim Cashman, a classic character who helped build Las Vegas. They do not care about baseball. They do offer me beads to wear.

Day 3: CC signs; Peavy deal blows up; an old-fashioned baseball trade saves us

Everyone knows that the Red Sox and the Yankees do not like each other, but seeing the "You sunk my battleship" looks on the faces of Boston officials in the moments after New York signs CC Sabathia (seven years, $161 million) tells a more complete story. "You have to understand," one Red Sox official says, "they won last night. Sure, we knew there was a good chance they would sign CC. We planned for it. But now that it has happened, I can tell you, it's like a punch to the gut. We never stop competing with the Yankees."

Within minutes his Blackberry buzzes, and he is summoned to the Red Sox suite. And just minutes after that, the rumor hits the Bellagio floor that Boston is serious, very serious, about trying to sign super slugger Mark Teixeira.

The general sense throughout Day 3 is that these meetings are a dud. Yes, in the wee hours of Day 2 the New York Mets signed closer Francisco Rodriguez, who saved 62 games for the Angels last season, and baseball men are talking about the Metropolitans' finally being collapse-proof in the last weeks of September. We'll see about that. Yes, the Sabathia signing livens things up for a moment. But the Peavy trade crashes and burns and leaves Cubs G.M. Jim Hendry walking through the casino muttering, "I'm not trading seven players for one."*

This leads more than one wise guy to suggest that the Cubs could not have traded seven players to the Padres anyway. It would need to be an even number so that the players could be split evenly in the divorce.

Alas, third-day Vegas numbness has set in. The first time I came to Vegas, maybe 10 years ago, the cab driver pointed out at the MGM Grand and New York, New York and the Mirage and all the rest, and he said, "You see all these big and shiny buildings. I want you to remember something when you're here, and never forget it: Losers built this town."

That realization tends to hit home on the third day in town, that day when the slot-machine bells start to pound against ear drums, and everything smells like cigarettes, and you forget what the sky looks like, and the Caligula-inspired buffets no longer seem especially charming, and you wonder why anyone would pay 50 bucks a ticket at the Imperial Palace to see impersonators of Donna Summer and Justin Timberlake. Most people probably would not pay that money to see the originals.

Minnesota Twins manager Ron Gardenhire walks around in a beige sports coat that he apparently picked up in one of the Bellagio stores. "You know what I paid for this?" he asks as he reaches out to let you feel the material. "I paid $580. I could have bought three jackets at Target for that."

Just when it seems as if the baseball–Las Vegas connection never quite clicked, something happens. A rumor. A three-way deal. Lots of players. And there's a little bit of a baseball buzz in the bar by the craps tables. Then a lot of buzz. The scouts talk louder. The writers work the room. Managers play slots.

The word finally comes down. It's a 12-player deal. Twelve players! The Mets are getting a reliever with the most interesting name in baseball, J.J. Putz. The Indians are getting a reliever with the least interesting name in baseball, Joe Smith. The Mariners are getting six players, four of them with last names that begin with C.*

Carp, Carrera, Chavez, Cleto—it looks as if Seattle didn't want to plunge too deeply into the Baseball Register.

"Best thing I can say about this trade, guys, is it's an old-fashioned baseball trade," Mets G.M. Omar Minaya tells reporters. "Here we are in the year 2008 and talking about millions of dollars, and this is how trades were done. Just a pure baseball trade."

So true. A pure baseball trade. And it brings a little celebration to the final night of the winter meetings.

Art Stewart hears all the names that announce just how long he's been at this crazy game—Art, Artie, Arthur, Stew, Stewie and, of course, Mr. Stewart. Baseball men congratulate him because he just won another award: Midwest Scout of the Year. Art has reached that point in his life when people want to keep giving him awards.

Art is recalling the first time he saw Bo Jackson hit after he had drafted the Auburn star for the Royals in 1986. Bo had not swung a bat in months, but the first pitch he saw he slammed over the centerfield fence. The ball whacked off the scoreboard, some 450 feet away—it was one of the longest home runs any of the onlookers had ever seen. Bo hit the next pitch even farther. The great major league scout Buck O'Neil was among the observers that day, and he famously said he'd only heard that sound, that unmistakable crack of the bat, twice before. "The first time was Babe Ruth. And the second time was Josh Gibson."

Art's eyes are a little bit watery now, and you might think it's from the lateness of the night or the emotion of the story or the cigarette haze, but no. He's thinking about Donna. They met at a ball game, of course. Another scout had tried to make a move on her, but he worked for the wrong club. "There's only one team," Donna said. "And that's the New York Yankees." Art worked for the Yankees. He and Donna were married for 47 years.

They were made for each other. He scouted; she traveled with him. He worked the lobbies; she listened for rumors. Sometime in 2007 they were at a game when she said her back throbbed. The doctors said she had breast cancer. She died last February.

Everyone felt sure that Art would not make it back to the game after that. "She was my life," he said, and for the first time baseball seemed empty to him. He did not want to go to spring training. He felt that way for a long time. But then he came back to the game—because he realized that baseball makes him feel closer to her.

"Donna would love this here," he says, and all around him are baseball men drinking and lying and proposing deals that'll never happen. Over the speakers Sinatra sings again; this time it is *I Could Have Danced All Night*. Art closes his eyes and remembers that he and Donna had seen Sinatra at the Golden Nugget not so many years ago. They had front-row seats. Someone in baseball had gotten those seats for them.

"This is a great town," he says. "And this is a great game." With that, some baseball people wander over to talk deals, and Art Stewart comes to life again.

"Hey," he calls out to me after a while, "how are your feet?" As he mentions it, I realize that my feet are throbbing. I look down and see that Art Stewart is standing on the carpet.

THE MODERN AGE

AUGUST 22, 2016

The Metrics System

New technology has produced massive piles of data about everything that happens on a baseball diamond. For both players and MLB front offices, all kinds of answers are in there—finding an edge is all about asking the right questions

BY ALBERT CHEN

One afternoon in May, Diamondbacks third baseman Jake Lamb was engrossed in his daily pregame routine inside the clubhouse when he stopped, suddenly, in front of a TV screen. He had overheard an unlikely topic of conversation on the afternoon MLB Network show: a somewhat obscure second-year player on a middling team who was a having an unremarkable season. The talking heads were diving into a list of players whose average exit velocity—the speed at which a ball comes off a bat—had improved the most from the 2015 season, and they were discussing the hitter who'd seen the greatest jump. The player atop the list, to the surprise of the analysts and to Lamb himself, was Jake Lamb.

Lamb does not like to clutter his head with information; the daily team stat sheets have no use to him. His philosophy is that the categorizing of a hitter's batted balls into "outs" or "hits" on a given night is more or less a dice game—a fielder makes a remarkable play, or happens to be standing in the right spot, and what should be a hit becomes an out. "If I hit the ball hard, I count it as a hit," Lamb says. "If I hit two balls hard, at the end of the night I was 2 for 4, even though on the scorecard I was 0-fer. If you look at the result, you're going to drive yourself crazy."

Over the winter, after a somewhat disappointing 2015 rookie season in which he hit .263 with six home runs in 107 games, Lamb overhauled his approach at the plate; he added a leg kick and lowered his hands so that when he started his swing, they were moving in a straighter plane through the strike zone. Though he felt he was squaring up the ball better early in the '16 season, the results didn't reflect that—that day in May his slugging percentage was .500, and even Lamb was beginning to question the effectiveness of his new style.

But now, standing in front of the TV, he was looking at a number—his 93.7-mph average exit velocity, which ranked higher than that of Bryce Harper, Miguel Cabrera and Lamb's star teammate, Paul Goldschmidt—that told a different story. Lamb was doing precisely what he'd set out to do with his new swing: He was absolutely murdering the baseball. "Here was something telling me, don't change a thing," he says. "I'm doing everything right."

Exit velocity is a measurement that comes from MLB's Statcast system, which deploys radar equipment and high-resolution cameras to track every movement on a baseball field. Statcast information from every ballpark became available in 2015, though teams had been quietly using some of the data it produces in their player evaluations even before that. In the Rays' organization, players sitting in an auditorium on the first day of spring training are told that hitters in that franchise are not measured by batting average but by batted-ball exit velocity. ("It's a term they use exclusively, like nothing else matters," says one former Rays player.) In 2014 the Mets' front office, after agonizing over the choice between Lucas Duda and Ike Davis as the team's first baseman of the future, settled on Duda in large part because of his superior exit velocity. (Duda hit 57 homers over the next two seasons in New York, before going on the DL with a stress fracture in his back this May; Davis has struggled to stick in a major league job.) Scan a ranking of the leaders in exit velocity at any point in a season, and you will find the game's most famous mashers—Giancarlo Stanton, David Ortiz, Miguel Cabrera—but also a smattering of underappreciated players who possess hidden skills.

Players such as, for instance, Lamb. Arizona's third baseman stuck to his new approach, and not only did the hits begin to fall in, but during one stretch in May and June he mashed 16 home runs over a 45-game period. At the All-Star break he was leading the National League in slugging percentage. "I'm trying to barrel up the ball and hit it as hard as I physically can," says the 25-year-old, who was slugging .561 with 24 home runs at week's end with an average exit velocity that ranked high on the Statcast leader board among NL regulars. "Exit velocity tells you what you need to know. I think it's a cool stat, and you're talking to someone who doesn't exactly care for stats."

"Exit velocity is one new metric out of potentially hundreds—it's just scratching the surface of what we expect to do," says Cory Schwartz, MLB. com's vice president of statistics. Schwartz is one of the original employees of Major League Baseball Advanced Media (BAM), which was created under then commissioner Bud Selig in 2000 as the league's tech start-up. BAM now does everything from maintaining team websites to powering instant replay to producing the streaming live video service, MLB TV, which turned BAM into a tech powerhouse. Today it owns the NHL's digital rights; is the streaming service provider for ESPN, HBO and the WWE; and has spun off its tech operation in a deal that would give the new stand-alone company an estimated value of over $3 billion. In many ways Statcast represents BAM's boldest undertaking to date: a big-data initiative that's limited only by the imagination of those turning to it with questions. Every baseball play is tracked to the microsecond and produces an almost infinite stream of data, from the spin of the ball as a pitch hurtles toward home plate (spin rate) to the velocity and angle of the batted ball to the movements of every defender on the field.

On an August afternoon in the BAM offices, in a former cookie factory in lower Manhattan, Schwartz and a group of analysts were in a meeting room deconstructing a single play from the previous night's Yankees-Mets game. On a screen at the front of the room was BAM's internal diagnostic tool, a data-packed user interface which offered a visual representation of outfielder Brett Gardner's failed attempt at an inside-the-park home run to start the game. With everyone gazing up at a large chart with lines tracking the movement of every individual on the field, the room felt like a NASA control center. The data ran across the screen, including the trajectory of the ball (30.3-degree launch angle, 401.4 feet); the time of the exchange and distance on the throw by rightfielder Curtis Granderson (0.87 seconds, 180 feet); cutoff man Neil Walker's exchange time and throw distance (0.63 seconds, 160 feet); and Gardner's home-to-home time (max speed of 20.1 mph, 14.9 seconds around the bases, the fastest home-to-home time of the season, though he was still thrown out). "The fact that Gardner got thrown out, was that a smart decision [by the runner] and just a good play by someone in the field?" asks Schwartz. "That's the part we want to deconstruct."

Two systems merge to create Statcast's complete picture: the Danish company Trackman, which has a system based on missile defense technology, uses radar to measure the ball's movement by tracking the speed of the seams at 40,000 frames per second. A system operated by ChyronHego, a German company, measures the movements of the individuals on the field.

"We want to incorporate all the elements into what we do," says Tom Tango, BAM's senior database architect, looking up at the screen. "The third base coach, when he has to make the decision, he has to figure out what the odds are of [his runner] being thrown out. Now when this outfielder is 180 feet away from the runner and the runner has to decide [whether] to go, we'll be able to construct a chart and say: At that point he's got a certain percentage chance of being safe."

Last season was the first in which this technology was active in all 30 major league stadiums, officially launching what those at BAM loftily refer to as "the Statcast era," an age in which exit velocity will become as ubiquitously cited as pitch velocity (those readings already flash at some ballparks, including Dodger Stadium and Progressive Field) and measurements take out the subjectivity in player evaluations with what statheads call "outcome independent" metrics. It is an era that has been largely mischaracterized by the media. Statcast is *not* the next Moneyball—in fact it goes in the other direction. The earlier movement was about identifying trends from piles of data in order to exploit market inefficiencies. Statcast, instead, measures individual players down to the fraction of a second, to tell us precisely what we are seeing.

Statcast data is being applied in two main ways: in game broadcasts, targeted at fans and media, and in player evaluation within teams. It has the potential to offer a better picture of what happened on the field, why it happened, and even what *will* happen—uncovering players who are due for a breakout or bounce-back season, like Lamb or Miami's Marcell Ozuna, who struggled last year but was a top 20 player in exit velocity, and this season was a first-time All-Star. The job of the team of analysts BAM has assembled over the last year, a who's who of all-stars from the world of sabermetric analysis, is to decide what questions to ask of the massive data set. Tango, who previously consulted for teams (most recently the Cubs), has invented a number of metrics, including fielding independent pitching (FIP), and is focusing on what's long been the holy grail of baseball statistics: fielding metrics. He's identified Statcast data that could make popular defensive statistics like Ultimate Zone Rating obsolete. ("We're close," says Tango, who, with info on players' starting position in the field, now has the final piece of the puzzle.) Writer and analyst Mike Petriello was a popular columnist at the analytics site Fangraphs and now writes articles for MLB.com that are driven by Statcast data. He gets queries from front office executives and even players: When veteran outfielder Chris Coghlan was dangling as a free agent, he wanted to know what he could do to improve his defensive

Statcast numbers. A third analyst, Daren Willman, a former college player based in Houston, was running the site Baseballsavant.com, which scraped Statcast data from the MLB sites and offered it up, with analysis, to fans. Willman received a cease and desist letter from MLB; instead of shutting him down, however, the league decided to hire him. Willman now spends his time creating visualizations with Statcast data, the kind of visualizations that some organizations are beginning to use behind closed doors to show players what adjustments they need to make.

Willman's work gets to that other way the data is being applied: by teams, internally, in player evaluations. One less obvious area is injury prevention. General managers, for instance, can see how a pitcher's stuff has changed over time; in the weeks leading up to the trade deadline, at least one front office balked at trading for Royals closer Wade Davis at the last minute because of his fading spin rate, even though his velocity remained steady. Just days before the deadline Davis ended up on the DL with a flexor strain.

Every MLB organization now has an analytics team in place to try to figure out what to do with all the data that comes from 2,430 games—roughly 750,000 pitches—a season. The 30 teams are using the data in 30 different ways, but they do all share this: an unwillingness to talk about what it is they are doing with it.

"It's an arms race, with all the different areas to explore. As teams find benefits they're gaining a competitive advantage that they want to hold very close," says Greg Cain, BAM's senior director of sports data. "It even colors how we receive requests for information from clubs. A lot of times we'll get a long list to kind of hide what they're looking for."

The challenge is to know what to look for. "It's so massive, it's just about asking the right questions," says Willman. "As far as the answers: The answers are all there."

Cole Figueroa was a perfect fit for the job, and not just because he was the 25th guy on the Pirates' 25-man roster. Figueroa, a Pittsburgh utility infielder through the season's first half, is deeply interested in analytics— he can code and has even run his own studies on how players with his skill set tend to age. And so, at the start of this season, when MLB allowed teams to use iPads in dugouts for the first time, Figueroa was the obvious guy to man those tablets during games. "There is so much information," he says. "Besides your coaches and manager, it's become the best resource."

For the Pirates, one of the most aggressive teams with defensive shifts, it was no longer necessary for players to memorize fielding positions before a game as if they're cramming for a test. Pitchers now watch video of opposing hitters in between innings, and vice versa. "The way a hitter can look at spin rate, for instance," says Figueroa. He would show a teammate, just before his at bat, video of the opposing pitcher. "If a guy has a high spin rate, you're going to know you've got to be thinking something down in the zone. You know that the ball is going to jump on you a little bit more—that's the perceived velocity. You're going to have to be ready a little bit sooner."

Like spin rate, exit velocity and launch angle have become a part of the everyday vernacular in front offices and even in clubhouses. This off-season Cubs third baseman Kris Bryant made changes at the plate with the goal of adjusting his launch angle; he wanted to get his swing flatter, so that he could turn more foul balls into hits. "You get into all these numbers, and I think my launch angle this year has definitely gone down from last year," Bryant, who's emerged as an MVP candidate, told reporters. For players at the other end of the spectrum, the new data could have even more of an impact. "I'm not 6'3", I don't run like a deer; my advantage is trying to find little openings in data, little edges that can help me prolong my career," says Figueroa.

Whether Statcast would become a true game changer—more than a cool toy for baseball nerds, more than glittery window dressing for broadcasts—was always going to depend on how it would be applied behind closed doors and on practice fields. Lamb, for one, couldn't tell you the first thing about launch angles or optimal swing planes, or, until recently, exit velocity. "If I were struggling, yeah, exit velocity is something I'd look to now," Lamb says.

It was late July, and after his midseason explosion, a slump was coming. Lamb went 0 for 24 over one stretch. But ignoring those ugly results, he changed nothing, and the hits began to fall again. A new hot streak—back-to-back home run nights in early August, a 9-for-28 run to start the month—soon began. Lamb, and anyone who'd taken the time to take a closer look at the new data, could have told you. It was only a matter of time.

JUNE 4, 2021

'This Should Be the Biggest Scandal in Sports'

The inside story of how rampant pitch-doctoring in
MLB is pumping pitchers up and deflating offenses

BY STEPHANIE APSTEIN AND ALEX PREWITT

To understand the fiasco of baseball's 2021 season, which people around the game describe as sullied by rampant cheating to a degree not seen since the steroid era, all you have to do is pick up a ball.

Then try to put it back down.

One ball made its way into an NL dugout last week, where players took turns touching a palm to the sticky material coating it and lifting the baseball, adhered to their hand, into the air. Another one, corralled in a different NL dugout, had clear-enough fingerprints indented in the goo that opponents could mimic the pitcher's grip. A third one, also in the NL, was so sticky that when an opponent tried to pull the glue off, three inches of seams came off with it.

Over the past two or three years, pitchers' illegal application to the ball of what they call "sticky stuff"—at first a mixture of sunscreen and rosin, now various forms of glue—has become so pervasive that one recently retired hurler estimates "80 to 90%" of pitchers are using it in some capacity. The sticky stuff helps increase spin on pitches, which in turn increases their movement, making them more difficult to hit. That's contributed to an offensive crisis that has seen the league-wide batting average plummet to a historically inept .236. (SPORTS ILLUSTRATED spoke with more than two dozen people; most of them requested anonymity to discuss cheating within their own organizations.)

From the dugout, players and coaches shake their heads as they listen to pitchers' deliveries. "You can hear the friction," says an American League manager. The recently retired pitcher likens it to the sound of ripping off a Band-Aid. A major league team executive says his players have examined foul balls and found the MLB logo torn straight off the leather.

In many clubhouses across the sport, the training room has become the scene of the crime: Pitchers head in there before games to swipe tongue depressors, which they use to apply their sticky stuff to wherever they choose to hide it, then return afterward to grab rubbing alcohol to dissolve the residue. Even that is not always sufficient. One National League journeyman reliever, who says he uses Pelican Grip Dip, a pine tar/rosin blend typically used by hitters to help grip their bats, has been flagged at airport security.

"They swab my fingers—and this is after showering and everything—and they're like, 'Hey, you have explosives on your fingers,'" he says. "I'm like, 'Well, I don't, but I'm sure that I have something that's not organic on there.'"

The MLB rule book bars pitchers from applying foreign substances to baseballs, but officials have so far done little to curb the practice. (MLB declined to comment but says it is focused on the issue.) Meanwhile, as high-speed cameras and granular data have made it clear that doctoring the ball makes it almost impossible to hit, baseball has found itself dripping with sticky stuff.

"This should be the biggest scandal in sports," says another major league team executive.

As MLB dawdles, and batting averages dwindle, the use of substances has become all but institutionalized. One NL reliever, who says he does not apply anything to the baseball because sticky stuff disrupts the feel of his sinker, says his pitching coach suggested this year that he try it. An AL reliever, who says he uses a mixture of sunscreen and rosin, recalls a spring-training meeting in 2019 in which the team's pitching coach told the group, "A lot of people around the league are using sticky stuff to make their fastballs have more lift. And if you're not using it, you should consider it, because you're kind of behind." The clubhouse attendants of at least one minor league team, according to a player, stock cans of Tyrus Sticky Grip, another product intended to keep hitters from accidentally flinging their bats, and distribute them to pitchers who ask. The NL reliever who uses Pelican says he played for a team that hired a chemist—away from another club—whose duties include developing sticky stuff.

An SI analysis of Statcast data suggests that one team in particular leads the industry in spin: the defending world champion Los Angeles Dodgers.

According to the data, L.A. has by a large margin the highest year-to-year increase of any club in spin rate on four-seam fastballs, which are considered a bellwether pitch. In fact, the Dodgers' four-seam spin rate is higher than that of any other team in the Statcast era. There is no proof the Dodgers are doctoring baseballs, but nearly across the board, their hurlers' spin rates on that pitch have increased this season from last.

The Dodgers declined to comment.

Souped-up spin exists far beyond L.A., though. Across the league, some pitchers hide gunk on the brim of their cap, in their jockstrap, on their shoelaces. But most no longer bother to be so crafty. Turn on almost any baseball game these days and you can see a pitcher digging into his glove between pitches, coating the ball with his preferred concoction.

"It's so blatant," says the AL manager. "It's a big f--- you. Like, what are you gonna do about it?"

Never in the history of Major League Baseball has it been so hard to hit the ball. The league batting average would be the worst full-season number of all time. Nearly a quarter of batters have struck out, which would also be the feeblest performance ever. The AL manager recently admitted to himself before a game that he expected his team to whiff a dozen times. One of the team executives says that against some pitchers, he is proud of his hitters for just making contact.

MLB introduced a new baseball this year, one that was designed to increase offense but seems instead to be suppressing it. (*Baseball Prospectus* found that the new ball, which is about 1% lighter than the old one, is spinning faster, making it harder to hit, and flying less far once struck.) Many hitters are still ramping up from a truncated 2020 season. After a year with the universal designated hitter, pitchers are back at the plate, dragging down numbers. All these factors contribute to the drought. But mostly, people around the game blame sticky stuff.

"If you want to talk about getting balls in play and kind of readjusting the balance of pitching and offense, I think it's a huge place to start," says an NL reliever who says he does not apply anything to the baseball because he believes that is cheating. "Because it seems to have created these basically impossible-to-hit pitches."

Initially, pitchers mostly sought grip enhancements. Brand-new major league baseballs are so slick that umpire attendants are tasked with rubbing them before games with special mud from a secret spot along a tributary of the Delaware River. Pitchers also have access to a bag of rosin, made from fir-tree sap, that lies behind the mound. Hitters generally approve of this level of substance use; a pitcher who cannot grip the baseball is more likely to fire it accidentally at a batter's skull.

But it has slowly, and then quickly, become clear that especially sticky baseballs are also especially hard to hit. For more than a decade, pitchers have coated their arms in Bull Frog spray-on sunscreen, then mixed that with rosin to produce adhesive. They have applied hair gel, then run their fingers through their manes. They have brewed concoctions of pine tar and Manny Mota grip stick (essentially, pine tar in solid form), which are legal for hitters trying to grasp the bat. A lawsuit brought late last year by a fired Angels clubhouse employee alleged that the Yankees' Gerrit Cole, the Nationals' Max Scherzer and the Astros' Justin Verlander were among the users of one such substance. (The suit has been dismissed and is being appealed; SI reached out to each player through his agency but did not receive replies.)

More recently, pitchers have begun experimenting with drumstick resin and surfboard wax. They use Tyrus Sticky Grip, Firm Grip spray, Pelican Grip Dip stick and Spider Tack, a glue intended for use in World's Strongest Man competitions and whose advertisements show someone using it to lift a cinder block with his palm. Some combine several of those to create their own, more sophisticated substances. They use Edgertronic high-speed cameras and TrackMan and Rapsodo pitch-tracking devices to see which one works best. Many of them spent their pandemic lockdown time perfecting their gunk.

"Guys have been using stuff for years," says Marlins rightfielder Adam Duvall, "But I think recently it's almost become an art. Guys are getting really good at it."

Experts do not entirely understand why sticky stuff works so well, but they agree that it does. The addition of any substance to the surface of an otherwise mostly smooth projectile will make it behave unpredictably—Gaylord Perry's spitball helped get him to the Hall of Fame—but tackier products have even more promise. For one, says one of the NL relievers, gluing the ball to your hand gives you more control over when and how you release it.

"I think that a good portion of the increased velocity is because guys can throw pitches at 100% all the time," he says. "They can rear back and literally throw with everything they've got and still have a reasonable amount of control because of the sticky stuff. I think if the ball feels a little slick, your mechanics have got to be a little better; you've got to stay within your means a little bit more."

But the biggest benefit of using sticky stuff is the way it contributes to spin. The faster a baseball spins, the more potential for movement it has. And movement is what makes a baseball so hard to hit. If a pitcher can harness that added spin, he can make his fastball appear to rise as it reaches home plate, so the hitter swings under it.

One way to increase spin rate is to increase velocity. Another is to apply shear force to the ball, probably by adjusting finger strength. It is possible to make modest gains, especially on breaking pitches, through improving the efficiency of a pitcher's grip and delivery. But the most effective means is to produce friction, and the best way to do that is to smear gunk on the ball.

"You can just create and leverage [friction] better if you have some sort of a substance, whether that's legal or illegal," says a pitching expert who works for an independent facility and also consults for an MLB team. "So guys are chasing, yes, more spin, but it's not the raw spin itself that's making the pitch better. It's what that raw spin affords, which is more total movement, potentially."

For hitters, all this suddenly acquired extra movement is catastrophic. What was an elite spin rate in 2018 is now average. The added spin means that the average four-seam fastball drops nearly two inches fewer this year than it did in '18, according to Statcast, making it appear to hitters as if it's rising. So far in '21, facing fastballs down the middle thrown at 2,499 revolutions per minute or fewer, hitters have batted .330. Facing fastballs down the middle thrown at 2,500 rpms or more, they have batted .285. And the percentage of high-spin fastballs has increased threefold since '15.

"I'm tired of hearing people say that players only want to hit home runs," says Rockies rightfielder Charlie Blackmon. "That's not why people are striking out. They're striking out because guys are throwing 97 mile-an-hour super sinkers, or balls that just go straight up with all this sticky stuff and the new-baseball spin rate. That's why guys are striking out, because it's really hard not to strike out."

Hitters spend their entire careers building a library of pitches, explains Garrett Beatty, who teaches physiology and applied kinesiology with a focus on sports at the University of Florida. Because they have only 200 to 400 milliseconds—about the blink of an eye—to decide whether and where to swing, they have to extrapolate where the pitch will end up, based on all the pitches they have seen in their lifetimes.

"There's some [pitchers] where, if you swing where your eyes tell you, you won't hit the ball, even if you're on time," Blackmon says. "I have to go out there and if my eyes tell me it's in one place, I have to swing to a different place. Which is hard to do. It's hard to swing and try and *miss* the ball. But there's some guys where you have to do it, because their ball and the spin rate or whatever is defying every pitch that you've seen come in over the course of your career.... I basically have to not trust my eyes that the pitch is going to finish where I think it's going to finish and swing in a different place, because the ball is doing something it has no business doing."

Hitters are bothered on a mechanical level. They are bothered on a moral one, too.

"It is frustrating because there's rules in this game," says Duvall. "I feel like I've always been a guy that's played by them, and I expect that of others, too."

Before his career ended in infamy amid the Black Sox scandal, Eddie Cicotte baffled opponents throughout the early 20th century with his signature "shine ball," coating it with talcum powder that he'd poured in his pants pocket; decades later, in addition to saliva, Perry lubed up with Vaseline and K-Y Jelly. But only a handful of hurlers have ever been caught in the act and punished, most recently when relievers Will Smith (of the Brewers) and Brian Matsuz (Orioles) were ejected and handed eight-game suspensions, less than one week apart, in May 2015. Last week, when umpire Joe West noticed a mark on the brim of Cardinals reliever Giovanny Gallegos's cap, he confiscated the hat but left the pitcher in the game.

If players have been doctoring the ball for a century, why is this all coming to a head now? Nearly everyone interviewed for this story mentioned one person in particular: Dodgers righthander Trevor Bauer.

In 2018, Bauer seemed to accuse the Astros of applying foreign substances to baseballs in a cryptic tweet replying to a comment about Houston's rotation. "If only there was just a really quick way to increase spin rate," he wrote. "Like what if you could trade for a player knowing that you could bump his spin rate a couple hundred rpm overnight...imagine the steals you could get on the trade market! If only that existed..." (Houston denied the allegation.) He complained to reporters that by ignoring the problem, the league was sanctioning illegal behavior.

Bauer said he had done tests in a pitching lab and found that sticky stuff added about 300 rpm to his four-seam fastball. He wrote in a *Players' Tribune* essay that after eight years of trying, "I haven't found any other way [to increase spin rate] except using foreign substances."

He also tried to make his point on the field: He used Pelican in the first inning of a 2018 start and watched his four-seamer, which usually averaged about 2,300 rpm, tick up to 2,600 rpm. After the first inning, that number dropped back to normal.

"If I used that s---, I'd be the best pitcher in the big leagues," he told SI in 2019. "I'd be unhittable. But I have morals."

From March through August of that year, his four-seamer averaged 2,358 rpm, according to Statcast. In September, it jumped to 2,750. In 2020, when he won the Cy Young Award for the Reds, it was 2,779. This season, the first of a three-year, $102 million deal that makes him the highest-paid pitcher in history, it's 2,835.

Before Bauer's spin rate jumped, he had an ERA of 4.04 and the 228th-best opponent batting average, at .241. Since the increase, those figures are 2.31 and an MLB-best .161. *The Athletic* reported in April that the league had collected several balls from Bauer's first start that "had visible markings and were sticky." Asked about the report at the time, Bauer said, "MLB is just collecting baseballs to do a study. Like, they're not doing anything with them. No one's under investigation, or no one's—like, just these gossip bloggers out here, writing stuff to try to throw water on my name or whatever." (The league is indeed collecting balls from every pitcher for analysis, and there has been no finding that Bauer did anything wrong.)

Through both his agent and the team, Bauer declined to make himself available for an interview. Manager Dave Roberts says he does not know if his players use sticky stuff.

Los Angeles this year is Spin City, according to the SI analysis. In March, the league sent a memo to teams to warn them that it would begin studying the problem, collecting those baseballs for analysis and using spin rate data to identify potential users of foreign substances. Officials have focused on four-seam spin rate, because breaking pitches can sometimes be enhanced naturally. But four-seamers are thrown with the hand and wrist behind the ball and with true north-south backspin, so there are fewer variables.

SI found that through June 2, the Dodgers had the highest increase in year-to-year four-seam spin rate, at 7.01%. The next highest was 4.21%, by the White Sox. That increase and that gap are enormous. The Red Sox came in third, at 4.01%; the Nationals fourth, at 3.07%; and the Yankees fifth, at 2.94%. The league-average increase has been 0.52% this year. (All clubs declined or did not respond to requests for comment.)

Some of this surely relates to personnel. L.A., for instance, traded away Dylan Floro and Adam Kolarek and did not re-sign Pedro Baéz, all low-spin pitchers. They signed Bauer and Jimmy Nelson and traded for Garrett Cleavinger and Alex Vesia, who all spin the ball. Still, every active Dodger pitcher except one has a higher spin rate than he did last year.

L.A.'s four-seam spin rate is 97 rpm higher than that of any other team in the Statcast era. The 2020 Reds, Bauer's former team, and a group that calls itself Spincinnati—because of their development of pitchers with high spin rates—rank second. (When SI asked for an interview with a Cincinnati pitcher about sticky stuff, longtime Reds PR chief Rob Butcher refused to make the request to the player. "I am not asking him to participate in your project," Butcher wrote in an email.)

Whether or not Bauer is using sticky stuff, other players around the league have taken note of his success and have begun experimenting. In 2018, Bauer compared the use of foreign substances to that of steroids: MLB looks the other way while those unwilling to cheat put themselves at a disadvantage. Other people in the sport echo him.

"People need to understand the significance of spin," says one of the team executives. "It is every bit as advantageous as a [performance-enhancing drug]—except it has been sanctioned by the league and there are no [harmful] consequences for your body."

"We're just doing the same thing we did during the steroid era," says the other team executive. "We were oohing and ahhing at 500-plus-foot home runs.... A 101-mile-an-hour, 3,000-rpm cutter, isn't that the same thing as a 500-foot home run? It's unnatural."

"It's like steroids," says one of the NL relievers. "For us that refuse to use sticky [stuff], we get pushed out, because 'you don't have great spin rate.' Well, no s---, because I don't cheat."

The tacit approval leaves everyone doing difficult moral math. At the moment, umpires generally rely on managers to request that they check a pitcher. Managers largely refuse to do so, in part because they know their own pitchers are just as guilty, and in part because they worry their team may someday acquire the pitcher in question. Executives and coaches who personally abhor the practice do not see much benefit in telling their own pitchers to knock it off, knowing that will accomplish little more than losing games and angering their employees. Fringe pitchers tell themselves that everyone is doing it—indeed, that the league's clumsy management of the game all but requires it.

"MLB has been changing the balls for so many years now and it's so inconsistent with how they're rubbed up and what the seams feel like and how stretched the leather is and everything," says an NL reliever who says he uses a mix of pine tar, Mota stick and rosin. "The only thing that's consistent is what we put on our fingers."

And they understand that they are being evaluated in an environment in which everyone else is using it. Four minor leaguers have so far this season been caught with substances, ejected and suspended for 10 games. (After one of those incidents, says a player who was there, relievers on both teams headed to the clubhouse to switch out their gloves.) Those punishments are supposed to send a message, but players hear a louder one.

"The calculus is whoever gets outs better gets to play major league baseball," says the NL reliever who says he uses Pelican. "There's some guys that might have a moral dilemma about it, but I'm not one of those guys. It's not bad for your health. Steroids...could kill you. That's different than washing your hands of stick at the end of the game."

Meanwhile, the league is weighing rule changes designed to increase offense. The minor leagues have begun experimenting with larger bases, a ban on infield shifts and a limit on pickoffs. If any of these show promise, the majors could adopt them.

"They talk about rule changes," says one of the team executives. "I think people would be absolutely shocked if they actually enforced this, how much you'll start to normalize things without rule changes."

Bauer has in the past suggested that the league legalize everything, and there is merit to that approach: Many of these substances are hard to police. But legalizing everything would only make pitchers even more dominant and the game even less watchable.

Most other people around the sport want the Spider Tack gone. Rawlings, which produces MLB baseballs, has experimented for years with a precoated ball such as the ones used in Japan and South Korea. MLB has sent prototypes to a handful of teams in spring training over the years; they reported that the tack wore away too quickly. That process is ongoing. Some pitchers propose a universal substance, developed and distributed by MLB, much the way rosin is.

The AL manager suggests a TSA-style screening in the bullpen, then a 10-game suspension for anyone caught with anything afterward. One of the team executives supports suspending skippers for their players' infractions. Managers generally did not make enough money as players to retire comfortably; pulling their game checks, he says, would turn them into hall monitors. Several players bring up the idea of escalating suspensions for pitchers. "At some point," says the first NL reliever, "you should just get kicked out of the [league]."

People familiar with the league's plans say that stepped-up enforcement is forthcoming—despite some teams' attempts at subterfuge. Once baseballs are out of play, they are supposed to be thrown into the home dugout, where they can be collected by MLB for analysis. Some teams, observers note, have tried tossing especially sticky balls into the visitors' dugout. Meanwhile, league officials plan to begin punishing offenders. Days or weeks from now, they will encourage teams to police their clubhouses, then instruct umpires to start checking pitchers more frequently. Offenders are to be ejected and suspended 10 games.

"Pitchers are shortsighted if they're not mad [about sticky stuff]," says Marlins reliever Richard Bleier, who says he has never used anything more than sunscreen and rosin because he wants to feel proud of his career. "Like, 'Oh, we don't want hitters to hit'—well, look what's happening now. Hitters aren't hitting, and now everybody's going to be penalized."

Not everyone agrees. Three minor league pitchers tell SI they use sticky stuff and they don't feel guilty about it. "We're all trying to make the big leagues, and if that's what it takes to get there, that's what it takes," says one. "They want the guys with the best stuff, and the guys with the best stuff are using something." So he digs his fingers into his team-issued can of Tyrus, and he heads to the mound.

MARCH 23, 2021

Kim Ng Made History. Now Comes the Hard Part

After years of being passed over, in November Ng became the first woman to be named GM of a North American professional men's team. Landing the Marlins job was a breakthrough, but Ng knows that to keep it—and help others like her follow—she'll have to win

BY STEPHANIE APSTEIN

Kim Ng knew people would care. When she became the Marlins' general manager in November, she expected a few hundred messages, some calls, an exhausting number of interview requests. Instead the response nearly incinerated her phone battery: She got thousands of messages. Michelle Obama tweeted about her. President Joe Biden asked her to speak at an event following his inauguration. (She accepted.)

All these people told her what her career move meant to them, and to their daughters. But most of them could not begin to understand what it meant to Ng. She had wanted this title for decades, but the minute she accepted it, it ceased to be about her. As she likes to say, a weight had been removed from one shoulder—and placed on the other. Now the pressure is on Ng to win, not just for herself but for those whose future opportunities may hinge on her performance.

And almost none of her well-wishers knew this: When Miami CEO Derek Jeter first phoned to talk about her dream job, Ng wondered how to say no.

She had gotten this call many times—she ballparks double digits. A team was looking for a GM, and would she like to interview? Some owners

323

just wanted to check a box: We talked to a woman, and a Chinese American woman at that! No major North American men's sports franchise had ever hired a woman as GM, and no one of East Asian descent had ever run a baseball team; just interviewing her made a team look progressive. Ng knew what they were doing, but she still prepared for the meetings—15 hours a day for weeks—as if they were all giving her an honest shot.

Now Jeter was on the phone, asking to talk. He had just ousted Michael Hill, whom Ng, now 52, had known for years. She had been working for Major League Baseball's central office for close to a decade, and she had made peace with the idea that she would never sit in one of the 30 big chairs. "Always going to be the bridesmaid," Ng says. Some of that was self-protection, she acknowledges now. But she really believed that her career would be complete without the title, that she did not need the validation of MLB's fraternity of owners.

"I think that takes a certain self-confidence, right?" she asks. "To say, 'It is what it is. And I'm not going to let myself necessarily be defined by that.'"

She told Jeter she would think about it. She spoke to Joe Torre, special assistant to commissioner Rob Manfred and her boss at MLB. Torre had been their mutual coworker two decades ago, when they won three straight World Series with the Yankees—Jeter as shortstop, Torre as manager, Ng as assistant GM. *You know Derek*, Torre told her. *This isn't a token call. If he's asking, you know it's serious.*

She appreciated Torre's support. But this time, she wasn't worried that the interview was fake. She was worried it was real.

Jeter had known Ng for 22 years, but he could not truly understand what it was like to be her. The lines on her résumé—seven years starting out with the White Sox, one as the director of player records and waivers for the American League, 13 as assistant general manager for the Yankees and Dodgers, and 10 as MLB's senior vice president of baseball operations—do not tell her whole story. Everywhere she went, nobody looked like her.

"Every day, for 31 years in her job," says her husband, Tony Markward, "she has to go in and, to any new person she meets, she has to make the case for why she belongs there."

Ng had a typical childhood for a baseball fan: She slept under a poster of the 1978 Yankees and played stickball in Queens, then was the MVP of her softball team at the University of Chicago. But when she started an internship with the White Sox after the '90 season, she was still the woman in a man's game. Coworkers called her Honey and asked her to get them coffee. She shrugged them off. She took a white legal pad with her everywhere; assistant GM Dan Evans, who hired her, knew that if he saw her scribbling notes in the morning, she would stop by his office in the afternoon with a question: *Why did you do that?* Evans was 30. He wasn't always sure why he had done that. "She really was helpful to me," he says. "She forced me to inquire to myself as to why I had the opinions [I had]."

The focus of her internship was computer administration and salary arbitration. Evans told her she could make herself indispensable by learning the arcana of the collective-bargaining agreement. "She separated herself immediately," he says. By the time she was 25, he would tell people, once Ng was out of earshot, that she would be baseball's first female GM.

In 1997 she left the White Sox for the AL office, where she spent hours on the phone explaining the minutiae of the major league rule book to team executives. A young Yankees assistant general manager named Brian Cashman was impressed enough that when he was elevated to GM in '98, he hired Ng as his assistant. "Right away, [I thought], *Well, I'm used to calling Kim all the time*," Cashman says now. "*It would just be so easy if I could just have her in the office next to me.*"

On the conference call announcing her hiring, someone asked, "Kim, are you after Brian Cashman's job?"

"No," she said. "Brian and I are good friends, and I am really looking forward to working with him. He is a good man."

Cashman, cackling, revealed himself as the questioner. Later on the call, Ng acknowledged that she hoped to lead a team one day. "I didn't realize it was quite possible until recently, but I think it's out there," she said.

Over the next three years, the idea tugged at her. Ng wasn't after Cashman's job, but she wanted to be a general manager somewhere, so she decided to let her contract expire at the end of the 2001 season. After Game 5 of the World Series, with the finale at Yankee Stadium that year, she and Markward sat for hours behind home plate as the cleaning crew turned off the lights. She loved it there. But she knew she had to leave.

She took the same position with the Dodgers, by this time run by Evans, who offered her expanded responsibilities. Torre, who managed the team from 2008 to '10, laughs now, thinking of how heavily they leaned on her knowledge of rules and regulations. Bill Bavasi, Los Angeles's player development chief when Ng arrived and the former Angels GM, says, "I wouldn't cross the street without talking to her."

When the club asked her to set up a video system for major leaguers to review at bats, she set one up for the minor leaguers, too. No franchise had ever done that. Nearly everyone who talks about her offers a version of this thought: She is generally the smartest person in the room, but she rarely acts like it.

"I mean this with the utmost respect," says Logan White, the scouting director when she worked in L.A. "She is a great plagiarizer. She doesn't have to be the inventor of it. She's going to go, *Oh wow, that works. Let's use that.*"

Ng was savvy enough not to complain about the challenges of being a woman in baseball and smart enough to know she had to meet them. When Evans put her in charge of negotiations with Japanese lefthander Kazuhisa Ishii in 2002, she met extensively with Acey Kohrogi, L.A.'s director of Asian operations. She practiced every detail of how to comport herself in Japan, down to how to hand his representatives her business card: holding it in two hands, with the writing facing them. In Tokyo, Kohrogi says, "She was right on the money." Ishii signed with the Dodgers.

Most of all, Ng observed. "She kind of reminds me of a really, really good scout," says Vance Lovelace, who scouted for the Dodgers. "You can't listen if you're always talking."

Ng trained herself to be a general manager, even as she wondered whether she would ever get the chance. She would notice which low-level employees seemed intimidated and give them small assignments as a way to build their confidence and identify their strengths. When Evans was fired before the 2004 season, Ng, then 35, stayed on to work for 31-year-old Paul DePodesta. That fall, some 10 minutes after the team Evans built won the NL West for the first time in nine years, his phone rang. It was Ng, standing in a champagne-soaked clubhouse. She passed the phone around, and player after player thanked Evans. A year later, L.A. fired DePodesta and interviewed Ng for the job. The team chose industry veteran Ned Colletti instead. She stayed on as assistant GM—and briefed Colletti on employees she thought he should persuade to remain.

She showed that she could outwork the boys, and she showed that she could out-boy them. At company golf tournaments, Ng refused to play from the ladies' tees, then smoked her drives down the middle of the fairway. She hosted cookouts after Sunday afternoon games. She somehow knew the grimiest dive bar in every road city.

"I'm sure you've grown up hearing that you don't have to like a person to work for them; you just have to respect them," Bavasi says. "I never have bought that. I think you have to like them. She got a long way with guys like me and Logan [because] listen, man, we're not the most enlightened people in the world. So I think it mattered that she was likable."

In spring training 2002, at Dodgertown in Vero Beach, Fla., Bavasi filled a wardrobe-size box with fireworks and headed to an abandoned golf course behind the dormitories. He jammed PVC pipe into sand traps and set off the explosives. White, the scouting director, recalls Bavasi using bottle rockets;

Bavasi insists they were mortar fireworks. Whatever they were, they shot some 75 feet into the air.

Once he had the system down, he invited Ng and White along.

"You like to blow s--- up?" she asked.

"Well, no, I don't blow things up,'" Bavasi said. "I light fireworks off."

"When I was a kid," she said, "I lit a dumpster on fire." (She was eight; it was an accident.)

Most nights they made their mess and then went home, but one night they heard sirens. Evans, reading on his patio, guffawed as he took in the scene: His 33-year-old assistant general manager, his 44-year-old player development chief and his 39-year-old scouting director fleeing in golf carts, pursued by the Vero Beach Police Department.

No matter how well Ng fit in, people in baseball seemed to see her more as a passenger than a driver. She would attend meetings alongside a Dodgers subordinate, Chris Haydock, and the people on the other side of the table would ignore her and address him. "She brought me to take notes!" Haydock says. "It was crazy."

She was not just a woman in a man's sport. She was also an Asian American executive in a game with hardly any. At the 2003 general managers' meetings in Arizona, Mets executive Bill Singer approached Ng and asked where she was from. "I was born in Indiana and I grew up in New York," she told him. "Where are you *from*?" he repeated. When she said her family was Chinese, he began babbling in a caricature of an accent. (News of their encounter got out, and Singer publicly apologized a few days later, claiming he had been on a low-carb diet. The Mets fired him.)

In 2011, Torre left L.A. to head baseball operations for MLB and immediately set about persuading Ng to come with him. "I really wasn't concerned with what she was going to do for us," he says. "I just wanted her over there."

It was an unconventional move for an aspiring GM, but Ng was an unconventional candidate. She saw working for MLB as a chance to network. She ran the international operations, putting her in contact with decision-makers for every team and expanding her knowledge of scouting and player development. Still, overhauling the signing process in the Dominican Republic has little in common with building a modern roster.

Ng kept her skills sharp by creating her own challenges. Tasked with renewing contracts with the Caribbean winter leagues, she instead reached out to all 30 major league teams, solicited ideas and revamped the program.

She has held various titles in her career but has always been subtly reminded of this one: Asian American woman. Every compliment seemed to begin with, "I had my doubts, but..." She tried to focus on the *but*. Over the years, she would come home and mention some indignity: She had overheard a stray comment, someone had spoken over her, someone had tried to take credit for her work. Markward would encourage her to make a fuss. "That's not how I do things," she would say.

Ng tried not to dwell on questions of fairness. "People are going to see what they see, and you just have to deal with it," she says. "I have been able to navigate that path. It's not easy. Particularly being a woman, first and foremost. There's this whole idea of inclusion, or 'Is she allowed here? Is she allowed there?' And I think those have been obvious obstacles that I've had to overcome or endure on a fairly regular, consistent basis.... I have to deal with it, and I do."

She felt her gender affected her treatment in baseball more than her ethnicity did. But Ng understood she owed it to fellow Asian Americans to represent them, too. Last summer, on an MLB call discussing racism and social justice, she described the glares she received in public from people who believed Asian people were to blame for the coronavirus. Chief baseball development officer Tony Reagins, who is Black, was struck by the parallels between her experiences and his. "I didn't look at it that way until she vocalized it," he says. "That's real."

Through it all, Ng clung to the belief that her work was all that mattered. And she was right, mostly. She had risen up the ranks—just not as high as she dreamed. She worked so hard to be the perfect No. 2 that people in the industry began to see her as just a No. 2.

She interviewed for so many GM jobs that she lost count. She also lost faith. Before every interview, she locked herself in her office to prepare, committing to memory the swings of the club's teenage prospects and the reputations of its strength coaches. She surveyed friends in the game. She brainstormed the front-office team she would bring with her if hired. Meanwhile, Markward, who co-owns a winery in Oregon, was always convinced she would get the job; while she studied a team's farm system, he would study neighborhoods in their new city: Where would they live? Where would they eat? Then they would both watch the team hire a man.

"One of the toughest things is you're not sure if the interview is real, but I still felt the responsibility to go through most of them," Ng says. "I didn't interview for every single request, but I did feel a responsibility to keep doing it, to keep the idea of a woman taking over that position as a possibility."

With every rejection, her friends ran out of words. In 2014, when Ng was at MLB, the Padres chose A.J. Preller over her. A few days later, when she took 10 or so subordinates to dinner, everyone seemed to stare at the table.

Finally she ordered a round of drinks. "Enough!" Ng said. "It stinks that I didn't get the job, but let's do this. Ask whatever questions you want."

Her work was all that mattered, she kept telling herself. She just needed to interview with somebody who knew her work. And that was what scared her when Jeter called.

"You think, *What if?*" Ng says. "*What if I don't get it and it's Derek?* Derek knows me.... That's fear of failure to the nth degree."

If he didn't want her, maybe it was because she wasn't good enough.

Still, Ng accepted his offer, as usual, and she spent hours studying, as always. It went well. Her colleagues at MLB noticed a barely disguised smile. Still, a few days later, when Jeter called back, that fear of failure clutched her. Ng decided to give him what she calls her "last-ditch effort," a half-hour monologue about her experience and her character and her promise that she would always try to do the right thing. She was talking to the most respected player of his generation, but she was also talking to all the men who had overlooked her, who had doubted her, who had taken credit for her work. And she was talking to herself. After 10 minutes, Ng took a breath. In that pause hung the weight of 30 years of trying to prove she belonged.

"Kim!" Jeter cut in. She had it wrong, he explained. He wasn't calling to go over her résumé. He was calling to add to it. Kim Ng was the new general manager of the Miami Marlins.

Ng has already made history. But she did not set out to make history. She set out to be a general manager. This might be her only chance.

All GM jobs offer obstacles—the position is generally open because the last person who held it has been fired—but Miami's is especially challenging. The NL East is the only division in which every team can credibly claim it is trying to win this season. The Marlins unexpectedly finished 31–29 last year, good enough for a spot in the expanded playoffs, and advanced to the Division Series. A losing season this year would surely be viewed as a failure, but principal owner Bruce Sherman has shown no willingness to spend. Cot's Contracts estimates the Marlins' 2021 payroll at $57 million, No. 28 in MLB. (The Mets rank third at $193 million, the Phillies fourth at $187 million, the Nationals fifth at $182 million and the Braves 14th at $130 million.)

The team can also be secretive: Jeter declined, through a spokesperson, to be interviewed for this story, and the same spokesperson listened in on Ng's interview.

Most of Ng's franchise-executive experience is with powerhouses in New York and Los Angeles. She will have to be creative and disciplined with the low-budget Marlins. But she sees a team with a talented young core, one of the game's strongest farm systems and only $6.5 million committed in 2022.

Along with the obvious obstacles, she offers another: The decade she was at MLB, she points out, is the one when the game changed more than in any other in history. Technological and strategic updates have made it almost unrecognizable to old-timers. Still, Ng believes her diverse experience in so many facets of baseball could give her an edge over, for example, a scouting director or quant who ascended straight to the top job.

"I think as a general manager, probably the most important thing is that you have a little understanding of a lot of different areas," she says. "You're like the conductor of an orchestra."

If the orchestra falters, the conductor will be fired—and it will be harder for the next woman to land a GM job. She feels that pressure. And even if the orchestra triumphs, she will probably watch men reap the praise. Within the industry, there were already whispers that any Marlins GM would actually be *third* in the hierarchy, behind both Jeter and vice president of player development and scouting Gary Denbo. (Jeter and Denbo have been close since 1992, when Denbo managed him in rookie ball.)

Ng is also uniquely ready for the inevitable criticism that every general manager receives. People have questioned her ability her whole career; they didn't even think she was qualified to be an *intern*. She recounts dealing with sexist slights as a "regular occurrence."

She adds, "You have to have patience. You have to educate, you have to redirect. And when all of those fail, look out."

After Ng got to Florida in January, people kept asking how the job felt. It feels...*comfortable*, she decided. Transactions, scouting reports, personality management—none of it is new. All those years, she wondered if she would become a GM. Once she did, she realized she had been doing the job all along.

The Ohtani Rules

The most amazing thing about the greatest season baseball
has ever seen? The Angels' two-way sensation doesn't act
like being a pitcher and a hitter is anything special

BY TOM VERDUCCI

The frog in the well knows nothing of the sea.
　　　　　　　　　　　　　　　—Japanese proverb
GREATEST SHOHEI ON EARTH
　　　　　　　　　　　　　　　—American T-shirt

The phone of Ippei Mizuhara, friend and translator to Shohei Ohtani,
buzzed with a text from Angels manager Joe Maddon late on the night
of Aug. 18. This is what passes for the determinative daily diagnostics of
whether Ohtani can physically withstand the rigors of pitching and hitting
in the same season unlike anyone before him.

"How does he feel?" Maddon texted.

This diagnostic check carried more than the usual curiosity about
whether Ohtani could DH the next day or required a day off. Ohtani had just
played the most Ohtani game of all Ohtani games: eight innings of pitching
with eight strikeouts while hitting his 40th home run in a 3–1 road win over
the Tigers.

Ohtani hit his home run 110 mph and 430 feet off a breaking ball in
the top of the eighth, making him only the second hitter this year to hit a
breaking ball that hard and that far in the eighth inning.

In the bottom of the inning, Ohtani threw a fastball 98.1 mph to strike out Victor Reyes. Only two other starting pitchers this year had registered a strikeout with a pitch that hard that late in a game: Gerrit Cole and Jacob deGrom.

If you had only nine minutes, five seconds to understand why Ohtani, 27, has pulled off the most amazing season in baseball history, this was your window. Eight innings deep into a mid-August night, Ohtani hit one pitch 430 feet with his last swing and threw another 98.1 mph with his last fastball. *Cliffs Notes* to an epic.

"I'm old school, or whatever you'd like to call it," says Angels bench coach Mike Gallego. "I don't talk this way about anybody. But what he's doing this year you will never see again.

"Unless it's by Ohtani."

Upon receiving the text, Mizuhara checked with Ohtani. He had thrown 90 pitches when Maddon replaced him with closer Raisel Iglesias to start the ninth. After the game Ohtani iced his elbow and shoulder while he met with 27 reporters over Zoom before returning to the team hotel. The next game would be here in about 13 hours. Maddon waited on a reply text.

"It's a very easy method," Maddon says. "I told him he is in charge of this. I asked him for absolute honesty, and he has gotten mine in return. Me, [GM] Perry [Minasian], Shohei and Ippei, we all sat down in spring training and decided there would be no specific limitations to pitching and hitting. Shohei explained to me that he would let me know. When his legs felt tired, that's when he may need a day. That hasn't happened."

This would be the biggest test yet: Could Ohtani play the day game after a night game after the longest outing of his major league pitching career? Maddon's phone buzzed. It was Mizuhara with a reply.

"He is all good for tomorrow! Thank you for taking him out there Joe!! Great win."

Mizuhara closed with a trophy emoji.

Done. Ohtani decided he was playing, just like that.

"There are no controls," Maddon says. "He owns the joystick."

It is a far cry from how the Angels handled Ohtani in past years, when they used complex data to monitor his energy level, sleep, soreness and nutrition—right down to how many times he dove back to first base on a pickoff attempt—to decide when he should play. Any deviation as little as 5% in his energy level would cause the Angels to issue a "yellow light" of caution on his use.

"They broke the glass house," Gallego says. "They let him go play baseball and don't hold him back in any manner. Because of that, he feels the game."

Ohtani threw 77% strikes against Detroit. He threw only 21 balls to 28 batters. It was only the second time this season a pitcher navigated eight innings with eight strikeouts on 90 pitches or fewer. After the other occasion, the pitcher, Zack Greinke of Houston, took five days of rest. "It takes two or three days for a normal pitcher to recover from the stress," Gallego says.

Ohtani batted leadoff the next afternoon. He had two hits, two walks, two runs and a sacrifice fly. At 6'4" and 210 pounds, he beat out his 14th infield hit. In just one of the many amazing-but-true Sho-stopper stats, by the end of August, Ohtani had hit the most homers 430 feet or more (15) and had the second-fastest home-to-first time (4.10 seconds), behind Atlanta second baseman Ozzie Albies, who is eight inches shorter and 45 pounds lighter.

Babe Ruth was the benchmark for two-way players, rare as they have been. But Ruth never was a full-time two-way player for more than three consecutive months; he did it for a stretch in the 1918 season and again in '19. Ohtani is six months into his double duty. And yet, the wonder of Ohtani isn't merely that he is doing the two disciplines. Instead, it's that he is adding elite performance and beautiful aesthetics to this skill show. He is playing at such a high level that he is a virtual lock to be named American League Most Valuable Player, and he deserves consideration for the Cy Young Award as the league's best pitcher.

Entering play Tuesday, Ohtani has 44 home runs, one behind Vladimir Guerrero Jr. for the most in the majors. If Ohtani wins the home-run race with Guerrero, he would become only the fifth player to lead MLB outright in homers and steal 20 bases, which would put him in the company of only Willie Mays, Mike Schmidt, Jose Canseco and Alex Rodriguez. Ohtani also is on pace to become only the ninth pitcher to strike out at least 10 batters per nine innings with a winning percentage of at least .810 over 20 starts or more.

Combine the two disciplines, and Ohtani occupies a solitary place in the Venn diagram of baseball history. He is the only player to strike out 100 batters and hit more than nine home runs, the only All-Star named to the game as a pitcher and a hitter, the only All-Star pitcher (he started and won the game) to bat leadoff, and the only player since Statcast tracking began in 2015 to hit six 500-foot home runs in the All-Star Home Run Derby—the day before he threw a fastball clocked at 100.1 mph in the game.

"I was pretty amazed by him last night," Tigers manager A.J. Hinch said the morning after the Aug. 18 extravaganza. "To see it in person is something I'll always remember. He was pretty artful in his pitching approach, mixing his pitches early—incredible strike throwing—and then leaned on velo late in the game. His stuff got better as the outing went on.

"His power is enormous. He hit the most majestic homer I've seen in a while. I'm mostly amazed at the ease he plays with. He doesn't try too hard or give the impression that he is stressed physically or mentally. Completely under control. His conditioning has to be elite."

Ohtani endured injuries and surgeries to his elbow and knees in his first three seasons. After last season, with rehab work finally behind him, he strengthened his body, especially his lower half, while changing his diet based on blood work to determine what foods best fueled him. He felt so good that he led the charge at that spring training meeting to finally discard the governors on his workload.

Freed, the caged bird soared. His two-way duty is a labor of love. He had decided when he was 18 years old to be a two-way player. He told MLB teams when he was a free agent that a condition of his signing was to be a two-way player. The narrow American mind that equates specialization with advancement completely misses the essence of Ohtani when it suggests he should pick one discipline and max it out. Ohtani is successful precisely because he is not specializing. You should no more encourage Ohtani to forsake one discipline than you would ask Springsteen to knock off either the singing or the songwriting. His heart fills with joy from doing both, and it is in that Zen-like place when all of us are at our best.

"He's got a great sense of humor and is always laughing and joking easily," Maddon says. "Compared to last year, it's night and day. Last year he was not enjoying himself. He always appeared to be somewhat stressed. This year is exactly the opposite. There is a joy about his game."

People crowded around the Comerica Park visitors' bullpen to watch Ohtani warm up for the Aug. 18 start.

"When he warms up people always get close and want to watch his routine," Angels pitching coach Matt Wise says. "It's an event. I definitely have taken some moments where I step back and just go, 'Wow.'"

The spectators had better not dally. Ohtani first takes batting practice in an indoor cage, staying off the field to conserve energy and avoid the regimented schedule of on-field batting practice. Then, on nights he is pitching, he heads to the bullpen. He warms up by throwing balls of various weights against a wall as Mizuhara measures their speed to make sure he is reaching the proper exertion level. When he climbs the mound, Ohtani throws only about 20 pitches, about half what most pitchers throw.

"He really sets the tone for himself," Wise says. "He definitely gets down to the bullpen a little earlier than most pitchers because he is also hitting first or second. He's pretty used to it. He throws around 20 pitches, takes a nice stroll to the dugout, puts his helmet on and gets to work.

"The way he is saving energy and effort, it's incredible. Even his bullpens [between starts] are very, very light. [They] are just to feel the slope of the mound with the ball coming out of his hand."

The genius of Ohtani as a pitcher is in his artistry, a compliment rarely afforded someone who can throw 100 mph. Wise and catchers Max Stassi and Kurt Suzuki will review opposing hitters with Ohtani and Mizuhara before a game. "He's extremely intelligent, open to information, and his memory is very strong," Wise says. But when the game starts, Ohtani goes more by feel than by script.

Against the Tigers, for instance, he averaged 93.5 mph with his fastball in the first two innings and 97.8 mph in his last three. He complements it with four secondary pitches: curveball, slider, cutter and a split-finger fastball that acts as his changeup. It is thrown about 10 mph slower than his fastball with 34 inches of vertical drop.

Of all the pitches thrown at least 400 times by all the pitchers since Ohtani joined the majors, his splitter is the most difficult pitch to hit. Batters have hit just .069 against Ohtani's split, with only 11 hits over four years—none of them home runs.

The sharpness and touch Ohtani exhibits on five pitches are astounding given that he can devote much less maintenance to his mound work than pitcher-onlys. Ohtani throws a baseball the way da Vinci wielded a paintbrush. There is a serene beauty, an ease of movement and effort, in the brushstrokes of his craft. And there is a brilliant deception in the technique.

Ohtani is borrowing from da Vinci's technique of *sfumato*, the exquisite blending of shades and colors that are almost imperceptible to the human eye. Translated literally from Italian, it means "vanished" or "evaporated." *Sfumato* is what puts the mystery in Mona Lisa's smile—and the deception in Ohtani's pitches.

Asked what impresses him most about Ohtani's pitching, Wise says, "His ability to throw such a wide range of fastballs. He's effective through the range of about 90 to 100, and he throws them effectively in the zone. That to me is incredible. Most guys can't do that. He can dial it up whenever he wants.

"I have a 13-year-old son. And I tell him, 'If there is a delivery to emulate, it would be his.' He throws pretty. He's a large person that moves like an elite athlete. He is an elite athlete. His delivery is very fluid. To me it's about as perfect as it gets."

Ohtani was a competitive swimmer growing up. He has the broad shoulders, narrow waist, long levers, lean strength and freakish flexibility of Michael Phelps. After Ohtani throws a pitch, his right hand slaps against the back of his left oblique, an ideal, maximum range of deceleration that saves wear and tear on his arm and shoulder—like easing a plane to a stop after landing on a long runway rather than slamming the brakes on a short one.

As a hitter, Ohtani starts and finishes with two hands high, with the barrel of the bat tapping the back of his right shoulder on his majestic finish. In one midsummer stretch, Ohtani became the first hitter in American League history to hit 16 home runs in 21 games. More than one out of every three fly balls he has hit this year has been a home run (34.4%, the highest rate in the AL).

"What we're looking at is something special for the world to see," Gallego says. "At the plate he's Barry Bonds. When Barry was hitting his 73 home runs, every swing he took, everybody would take a deep breath. Either he just missed it, or it was a home run. That's how this guy is. I never had that feeling with another hitter, other than Bonds.

"And yet this guy is also a Cy Young candidate. There's nobody close to him. We're comparing him to Babe Ruth, but I don't think even that does him justice. He's the best player I've ever seen on a day-to-day basis, and I've seen some Hall of Famers, like Rickey Henderson. To be able to do what he's doing right now, and to do it every day, it blows me away."

Ohtani is good for business, and not just the T-shirt business. A 2021 Ohtani All-Star jersey autographed by Ohtani (but not worn by him) sold by MLB Auctions for $130,210, setting a record for the highest-priced item sold in the two decades of the service. The previous record was set just three days earlier—for an Ohtani game-worn Angels jersey that went for $121,800.

In a 60-day midseason window, MLB generated $450,000 in new sponsor deals directly related to Ohtani, most of which were tied to the All-Star Game broadcast in Japan.

In Japan, MLB games with Ohtani rate 256% higher than non-Ohtani games. Social media posts featuring him have a 267% greater reach.

In Taiwan, Facebook posts featuring Ohtani generate 921% more engagement than non-Ohtani MLB posts. Angels games account for 30% of the games shown there and perform 80% better than games without him.

In Korea, his posts get 188% more likes.

In addition to the plethora of T-shirts, you can buy Ohtani birthday cards (IT'S SHO BIRTHDAY), coffee mugs, pillows, hats, hoodies, beach towels, ornaments, laptop sleeves, phone cases, water bottles, earrings, throw blankets, tote bags and, in keeping with the times, face masks. One hundred and two years after the Babe quit the two-way gig because he found it too tiring, Ohtani is a true international brand and—if only the Angels could build a playoff team—the face of baseball.

"He comes across as very authentic," Hinch says. "I loved his act watching the All-Star Game from afar. He's such a good player to celebrate."

Ohtani smiled through what had to be an exhausting two days in Denver for the All-Star festivities—the Derby, the game, one interview after another. At one point while snaking through a pre-Derby crowd ringing the field, Ohtani was bumped inadvertently on the shoulder by a heavy, shoulder-mounted television camera. Ohtani quickly turned and asked the camera operator whether he was all right. He earned $150,000 from the Derby, all of which he gave to 30 Angels training and front office staff members.

He is fastidious about keeping his surroundings neat; he picks up bits of loose trash in the dugout and on the field. He casually flips the ball to himself on the pitcher's mound, just as you might see a Little Leaguer do. He makes sure to politely greet the opposing catcher and home plate umpire when he takes his first at bat of a game.

"He goes out there with these huge expectations on him, and he's just playing a game for the Angels," Maddon says. "Tokyo is New York. He plays in a large market on the West Coast. Every kid wants to watch him and do what he does. And yet he handles it all so well.

"The guys on the team really love him. They appreciate his abilities. But they love him because he is so respectful and humble. When you hear his high-pitched giggle in the dugout, everything is right in the world."

Japanese proverbs are works of art when painted with Zen calligraphy on mulberry paper. The artist becomes one with the meaning the characters create.

Americans guffaw over punny T-shirts.

The proverb about the frog in the well is about how the limits of experience limit us. The frog in the well has no idea about the vastness of the ocean. The message is to get out into the world.

In baseball, to get outside the well is to break from the American way of specialization, a confinement in which kids as young as 12 years old become pitcher-onlys, in which the average relief pitcher throws just 19 pitches per appearance, in which teams use 35 pitchers per team per year, and in which Ohtani, when he reached 100 innings in mid-August, had thrown more innings than 89% of all pitchers.

It is tempting to think Ohtani is changing that world. But to believe that this is the start of something—that kids wearing SHOHEI OHTINY onesies will grow up in a world with more two-way players—is to believe that there are others who are this talented, this hypermobile, this driven, this humble, this joyous.

"Not that I've seen. It's hard to imagine," Maddon says. "Not with that combination of skill on the mound and at the plate. And don't forget the speed.

"What he has done is he has started a trend of more people believing they can do it. He's knocked down that barrier. In professional baseball there might be some more openness to try it with different people. But you're not going to see it. Not like this. This is more than a once-in-a-lifetime player. This is a once-in-a-century player—or more."

What Ohtani is doing is so rare that there is an underlying fragility to it. What happens when The Most Amazing Season There Ever Was turns plural? The answer is informed by Ohtani's physique and fitness and by his joy to both pitch and hit. "You see it in how he runs, how his body moves," Maddon says. "This is a big man, but he runs at a really high level, like an NFL wide receiver. There is fluidity in his body. There's no tension. He competes freely.

"I believe by doing both he's not going to get overloaded or overwhelmed or grind too hard on one thing. Once a mind expands it does not revert to its original shape. Doing more things, by not bogging down the mind with one thing, lends itself to discipline."

Says Gallego, when asked whether the Year of Ohtani is sustainable: "Why wouldn't it be? The guy's in great shape. He's as strong as an ox and runs like a gazelle. He's a superhero."

Then again, why even ask the question? We are watching Ohtani, but are we paying attention to him? Because if we are, we know that he is not only gifting us with the most amazing season ever, but he is also reminding us of the wisdom and beauty of staying in the present tense. Only when we get outside the well do we experience the true vastness of the world. Limits fall away.

JUNE 30, 2014

Houston's Grand Experiment

There are rebuilding projects...and there's what the Astros are trying: an unprecedented burn-the-house-down overhaul. Can it work? By October 2017, it might seem silly to ask

BY BEN REITER

In the late 1980s, when people got too drunk and were kicked out of the other casinos in Lake Tahoe, they ended up at High Sierra, a place where there was no such thing as being too drunk. Sometimes they staggered over to a blackjack table manned by a young dealer named Sig Mejdal.

Mejdal was an undergraduate at UC Davis, studying mechanical engineering and aeronautical engineering. During the summers he'd head 120 miles west, clip an oversized bow tie to his collar—"Looked like a dead cat around your neck," he says—and sling cards at Tahoe's seediest betting house. He loved the job. It was fun, it was social, and he learned things that he could not back in the lab at Davis. He learned that human beings do not always make decisions that serve their own long-term self-interest, even when they are equipped with a wealth of experience and knowledge of the mathematical probabilities that ought to guide their choices.

Blackjack is a probabilistic game. For any combination of cards, the player's and the dealer's, there is an optimal action for the player to take to increase his chances of winning—or, as is generally the case, of losing less. Sometimes the course of action is obvious: You hit a 10 no matter what the dealer is holding. Often, though, players know what they *ought* to do—but they do something else because their intuition has told them to. "Hitting a 16 against a dealer's seven, it doesn't feel right," Mejdal says. "With a hundred-dollar bet, it feels even less right. But that doesn't mean it isn't right."

Sometimes players would ask other dealers what they ought to do with a difficult hand. The dealer would, without meaning to, offer the wrong advice. "This person sees a million hands a year, with immediate feedback," Mejdal says. "I thought that illustrated well the limitations of human capabilities."

Mejdal, who is now 48 and married with a stepson, would go on to earn two master's degrees from San Jose State, in operations research and cognitive psychology. He would perform research for NASA in which, essentially, he disproved the perceived utility of napping. All along, though, Mejdal's mathematically driven career had stemmed from his passion for the most mathematically driven of sports: baseball. In 2003, when he was 37, he read Michael Lewis's Moneyball, and he realized that there might be a place in the game for someone like him.

Soon Mejdal was sending out résumés and proposals in an attempt to land his dream job. He traveled to the 2003 winter meetings, in New Orleans, hoping to get a general manager's attention. Finally, in '04, one of his pitches caught the eye of a baseball executive whose CV was almost as unusual as his: Jeff Luhnow, who had joined the front office of the Cardinals the year before.

Like Mejdal, Luhnow had two undergraduate degrees (in chemical engineering and economics, from Penn), as well as a master's (an M.B.A. from Northwestern) and a varied professional career. He had designed suits intended to protect troops from nuclear, biological and chemical warfare. He had helped start an Internet business, PetStore.com, and another that produced customized apparel on a large scale. He had also spent five years as a management consultant at McKinsey & Company, and he believed that one engagement (in the company's parlance) he'd worked on there had prepared him for his job in baseball more than any other. The project involved advising one of the world's largest casino operators.

"I learned a lot about how the gaming industry works, and about probabilities," says Luhnow, a trim 48-year-old with neat gray hair. "How if you have a large number of occurrences, even though luck is involved, you can still make things pretty predictable. For the player, when you do start to follow your gut, or you've had a couple drinks and think you've seen a lot of 10s, you're just basically giving the house back some money. The odds are the odds."

Luhnow hired Mejdal to run the franchise's new analytics department in 2005, around the same time that Luhnow was elevated to director of amateur scouting. Over the next seven seasons the Cardinals would draft more players who became big leaguers than any other organization. Of the 25 players on the team's World Series roster last October, 16 were drafted under Luhnow's watch. But he was not in St. Louis to see the Series, because in December '11 the new owner of the Astros, Jim Crane, hired him to be Houston's general manager.

Luhnow brought Mejdal aboard to be his director of decision sciences. The new director of amateur scouting was Mike Elias, a 31-year-old Yale graduate who had worked in the Cardinals' scouting department. The new assistant GM would be David Stearns, a 29-year-old Harvard graduate who had most recently worked for the Indians. The new director of pro scouting would be Kevin Goldstein, who had been a respected writer for *Baseball Prospectus* but had never worked in pro baseball.

The job facing Luhnow was different from the one he'd faced in St. Louis. There he had to keep a healthy organization healthy. In Houston he was asked to figure out how to defibrillate a club that was dying.

The Astros reached the World Series in 2005, but in '10 they finished at least 10 games below .500 for the third time in four years. In '11 they went 56–106, their worst record to that point. Their club's longtime core was gone—Lance Berkman and Roy Oswalt had been traded; Jeff Bagwell and Craig Biggio had retired. Worse, the farm promised no quick replenishments. Before the 2010 season, *Baseball America* ranked Houston's minor league system as the game's worst.

Luhnow and his men envisioned a decision tree, with that 56-win team at its roots and a sustainable championship club at its tip. Their only goal, with Crane's blessing, was to reach the top as quickly as they could. That meant every decision they made, no matter how painful, would be based upon the probability that it would be helpful in the long term. They would, in other words, hit on 16 against a seven every time. "We didn't want to be mediocre for a decade," says Elias. "We wanted to be really good as soon as possible."

They would not make cosmetic decisions, such as wasting money on a free agent or hanging on to a veteran who might instead be converted into future assets, in an effort to keep up appearances. This was partly a financial decision: When Crane bought the team from Drayton McLane, it was running, sources say, an annual deficit in the tens of millions. Crane was not driven to spend more than necessary while the team was losing—a period he planned would last no longer than a few years.

"You look at how other organizations have done it, they've tried to maintain a .500 level as they prepare to be good in the future," says Luhnow. "That path is probably necessary in some markets. But it takes 10 years. Our fans have already been on this decline, from 2006 to 2011. It's not like we're starting fresh.

"Would it be the right strategy for somebody else who had a great farm system and up-and-coming players already at the big league level? No. But for us, it was. When you're in 2017, you don't really care that much about whether you lost 98 or 107 in 2012. You care about how close we are to winning a championship in 2017."

It is one thing to commit to only making decisions that will lead to a long-term goal, and another to figure out *how* to make those decisions. Blackjack is an exercise in hard probabilities. Evaluating baseball players is something else. Some information you can gather about a baseball player is hard: how fast he can throw a fastball, how quickly he can reach first base. But much of it is soft: how diligently he will work, how his power stroke might develop, how likely he is to become injured. "How do you combine the soft information with the hard information in a way that allows you to make the best decisions?" asks Luhnow. "That is the crux of what we're trying to do here."

They are trying to do it in a way that synthesizes quantitative and qualitative information about players. This represents an evolution from the processes that Billy Beane's A's used a decade ago—at least as they were described in *Moneyball*. "For all the wonders that the book did, the portrayal was a dichotomous one," says Mejdal. "It's either the scouts or the nerd in the corner of the room. But from the very beginning in St. Louis, Jeff framed it as an *and* question. The question was not which one to use, but how to combine them." The goal is to use all that information to produce a metric that will render a decision on a player as simple as the one in blackjack: hit or stay.

To that end Mejdal and his analytics team—which has grown to four and occupies a room in the Astros' offices that they have named the Nerd Cave and decorated with a Photoshopped image of scientists examining Vladimir Guerrero in mid-swing—created an evaluation system that boils down every piece of information the Astros have about prospects, and about every player for that matter, into a single language. The inputs include not only statistics but also information—much of it collected and evaluated by scouts—about a player's health and family history, his pitching mechanics or the shape of his swing, his personality. The system then runs regressions against a database that stretches back to at least 1997, when statistics for college players had just begun to be digitized. If scouts perceived past players to possess attributes similar to a current prospect, how did that prospect turn out? If a young pitcher's trunk rotates a bit earlier than is ideal, how likely were past pitchers with similar motions to get hurt?

The end result is expressed as a numerical projection which roughly translates into how many runs a player can be expected to produce compared with what the team is likely to have to pay him—a single value partly derived from a player's stats but mostly from scouting reports. "They're not asking us to be sabermetricians," says Ralph Bratton, a Texan with a thick white mustache who has spent a quarter century as an Astros scout. "They're asking us to do what we've always done." The twist is that Luhnow's front office processes that information differently and makes decisions largely based on the result—even when that result, like a directive to hit a 16, feels wrong.

The Astros' decisions since the end of 2011 seem to have genuine promise. The farm system is now ranked among the game's best. The major league team, buoyed by recent promotions of top prospects like outfielder George Springer (who energized the club with both his constant dance moves and his 13 home runs in his first 58 games) and first baseman Jon Singleton, went 15–14 in May, its first winning month since September 2010. Springer and Singleton have complemented holdovers like diminutive second baseman Jose Altuve (who is batting .336 with an AL-leading 26 steals), but more impressive has been the improvement of the young staff. Since May 1 the Astros have an ERA of 3.75, the league's sixth lowest, behind suddenly maturing starters like 26-year-old Dallas Keuchel (2.45), 24-year-old Jarred Cosart (2.84) and 24-year-old Brett Oberholtzer (3.32).

The progress made in the last few years, however, has come at a cost. The Astros are not a restaurant that, when faced with dwindling returns, can shut down, renovate, hire a new chef, reimagine the menu and relaunch. They had to stay open for business. Business has been bad.

In Luhnow's first two seasons in charge, the Astros were 106–218. They drew a combined 3.3 million fans to Minute Maid Park—an attendance figure they had nearly reached in 2007 alone, when they topped three million. Several games have gotten local TV ratings of 0.0. The franchise has been accused of violating the most basic element of a baseball team's social compact—that it tries its best to win every game—and has angered the players' union with its low payrolls ($22 million as of Opening Day 2013, the lowest in the majors; $44 million this season, the second lowest). The team has even been made fun of by Alex Trebek, on *Jeopardy!* The answer, last November: "The large valve used to control wellbore fluids on oil rigs is this 'preventer'; the Astros could have used one." The question: "What is a blowout preventer?"

One result of their poor performance was that the Astros this year became the first team to have the first pick in three consecutive amateur drafts. This was never a goal, they insist, but a by-product of their long-term plan. Even so, it represented an opportunity. The right player might be the finishing piece on the championship teams they envision. They dreaded making the wrong decision.

To clubs picking first overall—one-one, in baseball shorthand—high school pitchers are terrifying. They have displayed a greater chance of flaming out, due to injury or a failure to develop, than any other category of player. "There have been some wild successes," says Elias, "but the list of those picked high is littered with injuries and disappointments."

Between 1965, the first year of the draft, and 2013, clubs picked a high school hurler one-one just twice. In 1973 the Rangers chose a lefthander from Houston named David Clyde. Arm injuries ended Clyde's career when he was 26; he had a record of 18–33 and an ERA of 4.63. The Yankees tried again in 1991, when they selected a southpaw from North Carolina named Brien Taylor. Taylor tore up his shoulder in a fight in 1993. He would become one of three one-ones to never play in the majors at all.

The Astros had decided on less volatile categories of players with their two previous one-one picks. In 2012 they selected a 6'4" high school shortstop from Puerto Rico named Carlos Correa. The pick surprised the industry, but Elias had deep convictions about Correa from scouting him extensively when he was with the Cardinals, Mejdal's system liked him, and Correa had indicated that he would sign a contract that would be relatively cheap for a one-one. This year Correa was rated by *Baseball America* as the sport's seventh-best prospect, although he is now on the DL with a leg injury. Last year the Astros went with Stanford righthander Mark Appel, considered as risk-free a pitcher pick as has ever been made. This spring Appel was *BA*'s 39th-rated prospect, though he has a 10.48 ERA through 22⅓ innings in Class A this year. He has had tendinitis in his right thumb and an appendectomy, underscoring that the ride isn't always smooth even for the safest of prospects.

As 40 members of the Astros' front office staff—including Luhnow, Elias, Stearns, Goldstein, Mejdal and the other inhabitants of the Nerd Cave, all of their scouts and certain special assistants like Biggio—assembled in a conference room on the second floor of Houston's old Union Station, which abuts Minute Maid Park and contains the club's offices, they knew this year could be different. It was 10 a.m. on June 4, the day before the draft, and the men were there to provide their expert opinions on the six players who were still in the running for one-one. Two of the prospects were high school pitchers. "All right," said Elias, who was running the meeting, "this is your opportunity to air it out."

For the next 100 minutes the room discussed the prospects one by one. As each player's name was announced, his video clips were projected on a screen. First, the area scout who was responsible for the player would introduce him. Then anyone else who had seen him—Elias, national cross-checker David Post, special assistants—would chime in. Luhnow, who had also seen each of the six in person, would ask questions. Analyses of the player's swing or pitching mechanics, to which coaches within the organization contributed, would be read aloud. Finally, Mejdal's team would weigh in with its statistical projections.

It became clear that while the room liked each of the players very much, they were narrowing their focus to four: Carlos Rodon, a lefthander from N.C. State; Alex Jackson, a slugger from Rancho Bernardo High in Southern California; and Brady Aiken and Tyler Kolek, the high school pitchers.

A year ago Rodon had been considered almost a sure thing to go one-one, but a slightly down junior season had engendered some doubts in the industry about his command and efficiency. You wouldn't have known it based on the report that Tim Bittner, the area scout who had covered him, delivered. "The big thing for this guy is he has a pitch you don't see normally: it's a 70-grade slider"—out of 80—"at 88 to 91 miles an hour," Bittner said. "It's a weapon. It's a weapon now, it's a weapon on all levels." Mejdal's team revealed that one of the players to whom their metrics suggested Rodon was comparable was Chris Sale, the White Sox' ace and an annual Cy Young candidate.

You could sense the scouts' views of Jackson before the discussion of him had even begun. He had hit 47 home runs in high school. "Mmmm," they grunted, each time he unleashed his violently powerful swing on the video screen. "Mmmm." "Physically, he looks like Magglio Ordoñez," the area scout said. "A three or four hitter. Potentially hits 30 homers, with a .300 average."

"What about his swing?" Luhnow asked.

"Graded 80 out of 80," came the reply.

Area scout Brad Budzinski was similarly unequivocal about Aiken, a 6'4" lefty from San Diego's Cathedral Catholic High who had committed to play at UCLA and who threw a mid-90s fastball to go with a plus curveball and changeup. "I love everything about this kid," Budzinski said. "To me, we're getting possibly the next Andy Pettitte. Makeup-wise, I feel like it's Peyton Manning on a surfboard. A lot of people say they want to be a Hall of Famer, but I believe for this kid it's a realistic goal."

"If the stuff stayed the same as it is right now," said Post, "it's more than enough to pitch and have success in the big leagues."

Though Mejdal's department does not incorporate high school statistics into its formula—they are too misleading—it recited Aiken's stats anyway: "K's per nine of almost 17."

"Did he say 17?" one of the scouts in the back of the room whispered.

Kolek was also an attractive option. He stands 6'5" and weighs 260 pounds, and his fastball touches 102 miles an hour. "The stuff is as good as we've ever seen from a high school kid," Elias said. "I think we can all agree this is as seriously as we've considered taking a high school righty, and with good reason."

Kolek had attended Shepherd High, less than an hour northeast of Minute Maid Park, and the allure of drafting a local boy was considerable. "They've got a cool setup out there on their ranch," Elias told the room. "They've got a pond to fish in. They've got tractors that they drive around, chasing animals."

Elias grew up in the Washington, D.C., suburbs, the son of a Secret Service agent, and his novice description of hunting drew laughs from the outdoorsmen in the room. "Now, where are you from, Mike?" boomed a deep Texan voice. It belonged to Nolan Ryan, who is the father of Astros president Reid Ryan and serves as an executive adviser to the club.

"Nolan, how hard did you throw at his age?" a scout asked the alltime strikeout king, who had watched Kolek pitch in person.

"There weren't radar guns in those days," Ryan said. "But I can tell you, Nolan Ryan wasn't even close to what this kid is as a senior in high school."

The meeting drew to a close at 11:40 a.m. "All right, it's a good group," Luhnow said to his 39-man brain trust. "Flip a coin now, or later?"

"If we take one of the high school pitchers, we have to be really [convinced] that this guy is the guy, and that's not real easy to settle on," Elias said later. "Especially when you've got other good options." The Astros' decision engine had one more day to make its choice.

The Astros anticipated backlash against the rebuilding effort they planned to conduct with a purity that to their knowledge had never before been attempted. They have received it. It came most fiercely at the end of last season, after they had traded away the last of their mature assets in closer Jose Veras, outfielder Justin Maxwell and starter Bud Norris. They finished out the season with a 15-game losing streak. Their record, 51–111, tied for the majors' worst in a decade.

Before the season they'd hired a manager they felt was the right man to guide their players through such a stretch. Bo Porter understands the necessity of losing, or at least he professes to. "We had to go through that," says Porter, who is 41. "The biggest mistake organizations can make is the misevaluation of their own players. Had we not gone through what we went through last year, we wouldn't be where we're at today, because we'd still be trying to figure out who can we move forward with, who do we need to cut ties with."

Even though Luhnow intellectually understands why his Astros must lose, he maintains that doesn't make it any easier. "The hardest part for me is when people think we don't care," he says. "We desperately care. Would I prefer to be able to do this with losing 70 games a year instead of 100? No question about it. Do I think it's possible? I really don't."

As for concerns about the payroll, "we feel we're going to have the resources we need to add the appropriate players to complement what we have to win when we need to win," Luhnow says.

Other criticisms have surfaced more recently. In an article published in the *Houston Chronicle* on May 25—the day, as it turned out, the Astros began a seven-game winning streak—beat writer Evan Drellich detailed the ways in which, as the headline read, RADICAL WAYS PAINT ASTROS AS 'OUTCAST.' "They are definitely the outcast of major league baseball right now, and it's kind of frustrating for everyone else to have to watch it," Norris, who was traded to the Orioles last July 31, told Drellich. "When you talk to agents, when you talk to other players and you talk amongst the league, yeah, there's going to be some opinions about it, and they're not always pretty."

The criticisms fell into two categories. The first was that the Astros' analytics-based approach dehumanizes players. "It was a difficult thing for me to read, because I spend so much time personally getting to know our players, and so does our staff," says Luhnow. "There is a perception that anybody who is doing analytics in a serious way is doing that at the expense of the human element. It's just not true, in our case."

Adds Mejdal, "We realize these are human beings, not widgets. As far as assigning a number to a person—well, I assume you get a salary? Do you feel dehumanized because your boss has put a number on you?"

The other criticism stemmed from the Astros' use of new competitive tactics, such as a heavy reliance on extreme defensive shifts. The club's proprietary database—christened Ground Control by Elias's wife, Alexandra—contains not just projections of the future value of every player but also spray charts for every hitter on every count against every type of pitch thrown by every type of pitcher, as well as the probabilistically optimal way to position defenders in each scenario. This sometimes leads to shifts in which, say, the Astros' second baseman plays well to the left of second base against a pull-happy righthanded hitter—a violation of traditional baseball norms, though one that's becoming more common across the game.

Mejdal puts the Astros' tactics into perspective. "A year ago, with the defensive positioning that was going on, we were in the top half dozen, and there was tremendous pushback," he says. "Well, the rate at which we shifted last year, that would be below average in the major leagues now. Innovation, by definition, suggests change will be taking place. If there's change taking place, it's not likely going to feel right at first. If it felt right, it would have been done a long time ago."

The Astros' leadership bristles at the notion that it thinks it knows how to operate better than anyone else. All it knows is what it believes to represent best long-term practices, based on the information it has acquired and processed. "We're far from perfect," Mejdal says. Even what they believe to be optimal decisions often don't work out. Sometimes a righthanded pull hitter goes the other way. Sometimes players they discard, or decline to draft, turn into stars. "Sometimes you hit on a 16," Mejdal says, "and if you stayed, you would have won."

As 6 p.m. Central approached on the evening of Thursday, June 5, the majority of the Astros' scouting and analytics staff milled around the club's draft room. The metal walls were covered with magnets, each bearing the name of an amateur player. The staffers were waiting, like the rest of the baseball world, to see who the team's leadership would pick one-one. The day before they had dressed in khakis and oxford shirts, but now they wore suits and ties. If there was any need to remind them of the caliber of player they hoped to draft, there was the dinner they had just been served: Nolan Ryan Beef Brisket and Nolan Ryan Jalapeño Sausages.

Finally, at 6:05, Elias emerged from Luhnow's office, where he had been huddling with the GM, Stearns and Mejdal. He nonchalantly slapped the magnet bearing their pick's name at the top of the draft board. Minutes later commissioner Bud Selig announced the pick from the MLB Network studios in Secaucus, N.J. On the fuzzy big-screen TV mounted at the front of the room the Astros' scouts watched as the player, whose reaction the network's cameras were covering live from his home, buried his face in his hands.

"Oh, no!" a scout called out. "I don't want him to cry!"

There would be no tears from Brady Aiken, whose name was printed on Elias's magnet. Soon, Brad Budzinski, the young scout who had followed Aiken since he was 15, was accepting congratulations—"That's your guy, Budz!"—and handshakes. "A lot of seasoned scouts have never even had a first-rounder, let alone a one-one," Budzinski would say.

Luhnow tried to call Aiken on his cellphone, but Budzinski had given him the wrong number. "How well do you really know this guy?" a smiling Elias teased the scout. Then Luhnow appeared to connect. "Hey, Brady, it's Jeff Luhnow with the Astros," he said, as everyone listened in expectantly. Luhnow paused for dramatic effect. "Give me a call back when you get this." Laughter reverberated off the room's metal walls.

The decision to select Aiken over Kolek, Rodon and Jackson—who would be picked second, third and sixth, respectively—had not been a last-minute one. "We decided the morning of the draft," Elias says. "The mere fact that we were willing to take a high school pitcher one-one for the third time in history, even though the first two didn't pan out, showed us how strongly we agreed. We feel good enough about our farm system, that there's enough coming, that we don't want to look back in 10 years and say, 'We passed on the best high school lefty ever just to get something a little quicker.'"

Years of scouting reports, regressed in Mejdal's system, all suggested that Aiken was the draft's best player. Picking someone else simply because he was not a high school pitcher would have been the equivalent of staying on 16 against a dealer's seven. That is not something Luhnow's Astros do.

Luhnow knows there is a chance that Aiken—and, indeed, his own venture in Houston—might not work out. "There are injuries and declines in performance," says Luhnow. "Then there's the luck of playing games. Still, with all those unpredictable variables, I feel pretty good that we're putting ourselves in a situation where if we were to do this a million times, the odds would be in our favor to succeed."

Luhnow, however, does not discount the value of simple fate. "A memorabilia collector gave me the SPORTS ILLUSTRATED from my birth week in 1966," he says. "The issue came out on June 6. My birthdate is June 8. You know who's on the cover? The Houston Astros. ASTROS IN ORBIT, it says. Unbelievable."

In the draft room there were more immediate matters at hand. Not only did the Astros have 40 more picks to make, but they also were at the moment playing against Albert Pujols and the Angels. "We're losing 1–0," Craig Biggio announced, holding his smartphone aloft.

"Already?" said Luhnow. "How'd that happen?"

"Albert hit a sac fly."

It wasn't long before the Astros started scoring themselves—three RBIs came off the bat of Springer—and were on their way to their ninth win in their last 12 games.

"Oh, good, more points!" Mejdal deadpanned, glancing up at a TV.

"They're not points, Sig," said Kevin Goldstein.

Mejdal, like Luhnow, knows that even a long string of correct, intricately considered decisions might not turn out favorably. "What if we don't have good results?" he says. "I love my job in baseball. It would be terribly disappointing. But all we can control is the process, and I'm confident we're creating good processes and making good decisions.

"The rest," Mejdal says, "is hope."

MARCH 15, 2023

Playing for the Yankees Has Its Perks. In-Flight Internet Is Not One of Them

Tragically, one of the world's most valuable sports franchises doesn't provide complimentary Wi-Fi to its millionaire employees

BY STEPHANIE APSTEIN

TAMPA—Gerrit Cole had dreamed of playing for the Yankees since he was a kid, and in so many ways the experience has been exactly what children envision: the crisp pinstripes, the retired numbers, the Bleacher Creatures.

But one thing surprised him when he got to New York after signing a nine-year, $324 million deal before the 2020 season: The fourth-most valuable franchise in sports charges players for internet access on the team plane.

"It's your fault," longtime center fielder Brett Gardner told him. "Your contract is too big, so they can't pay for the Wi-Fi."

Technically, it's Delta that does the charging, approximately $9 per flight. (Delta also offers free iMessage and WhatsApp.) But the Yankees, whom Forbes estimates are worth $6 billion, do not cover the cost. A person familiar with the prices of such things said an in-flight Wi-Fi plan for one team for one year costs approximately $40,000—or about the price of four Cole pitches.

A very serious and embarrassingly exhaustive survey of the 30 MLB teams could identify only one other team that regularly makes its players pay: the Reds. (Some teams provide free Wi-Fi on their usual jet but do not cover the cost when they fly a different plane.)

Of the world's problems, this ranks, obviously, near the top. A couple dozen millionaires have to scrape together some $350 annually if they want full connectivity in the air. So you can understand why many of them have tried to work around the issue.

"I've got T-Mobile," said right fielder Aaron Judge, who is coincidentally a spokesman for that company. T-Mobile offers customers free Wi-Fi on Delta flights. Judge added that the Wi-Fi question did not factor into his decision to consider switching teams in free agency, because "I've got T-Mobile, so I don't have to worry about it."

So does reliever Michael King—and crucially, so do his parents, whose family plan he still uses. Last season, reliever Lucas Luetge, now with Atlanta, sat next to him on the plane and realized King was blessed with the luxury of Googling anything he wanted for nothing.

"So I gave him my sister's phone number," said King. "My sister got a text saying, 'Are you authorizing this?' 'Yep!' I got the code for my sister's number to give to Lucas."

The New York Yankees, brought to you by Michele and Jim King.

Unfortunately, the Kings have only the two children, so the other players have to make their own decisions. (The team does allow coaches and other staffers to expense the cost.)

"I didn't pay for it, on principle," said righty Jameson Taillon, who spent two years with the Yankees before signing with the Cubs this winter—not, he said, because of the Wi-Fi issue. He added, "I will say, also, the Yankees fly on a pretty cool custom plane with poker tables and stuff. So I would take that over free Wi-Fi, if I'm being honest."

Still, their peers across the league cannot believe the Yankees suffer such indignity. "Who told you that?" asked Phillies catcher Garrett Stubbs, who said he had never heard of such a thing. "I think they're messing with you."

Fellow Phillie Brandon Marsh, the team's hirsute center fielder, just shook his head sadly. "That sucks," he said. "And they have to shave their face."

Marlins center fielder Jazz Chisholm burst out laughing when he heard what the Yankees endure; when he boarded his first team flight, in 2020, he dutifully entered his credit card information in the Wi-Fi portal, then lamented aloud, "Bro, the Wi-Fi didn't even fricking work and I paid 10 bucks!" His teammates laughed and explained that the Marlins provide players a code; in his next paycheck, he found that $10 reimbursed.

Players from one other team, though, can relate to the Yankees' plight. In 2019, shortstop Kyle Farmer, who had just been traded from the Dodgers, had a drink or two at a club party and asked Dick Williams, then the Reds' president of baseball operations, why the team would not spring for the Wi-Fi. "He said, 'Too short of flights,'" Farmer, now a Twin, remembered. Farmer did not follow the logic; he responded by declining to pay for Wi-Fi until he hit arbitration and had a little more money.

Reliever Lou Trivino, who was traded at last year's deadline from the famously frugal A's, was surprised to learn that his old team had one up on his new one. (He added, though, that although the Wi-Fi was free in Oakland, it often didn't work.)

"You know Zack Greinke, when he talks about guacamole?" Trivino said, referring to Greinke's outrage that his favorite burrito place had increased its prices. "It went up 25 cents, and he won't pay for it. [I'm the same.] On principle, I'm not paying the 25 cents for guacamole." (Greinke would surely point out here that the guacamole price actually increased 30 cents.)

So Trivino instead uses the flights to engage in an almost anachronistic pursuit: He reads. Last year he tore through Thomas Sowell's 704-page tome, *Basic Economics*. He recently turned his attention to a book about Christianity. He appreciates the break from his phone. "Sometimes I sit there and I just scroll," he said. "I delete my Instagram every week and I get it back in a week and my screen time shoots up two hours and I'm like, *This is ridiculous!*"

Reliever Clay Holmes said he too enjoys the opportunity to spend an hour or two unplugged. He does sign up for the free iMessage, though, because, he said, "My wife sees other wives getting texts and she's like, 'You must have Wi-Fi!'"

But some players need the Wi-Fi for more than poisoning their minds with social media. Catcher Kyle Higashioka buys the Wi-Fi on most flights so he can study for the next opponent. He considered purchasing a monthly pass but calculated that because he tends not to bother on short trips, it was cheaper for him to pay each time. He has never investigated the possibility of expensing the cost.

"To be honest, I've never had a real job, so I don't even know how that works," he said. He added that he was not offended that the team made him pay. "I mean, who says that's required as a job perk, you know?" he said.

General manager Brian Cashman agreed.

"I think most of our players can afford it," he said.

This is a fair point. But the job of the press is to comfort the afflicted and afflict the comfortable, so sports illustrated continued to pursue this important story. (In this case, the comfortable are afflicted.)

And there is good news coming to the Bronx: Delta recently introduced free Wi-Fi on some flights for fliers who subscribe to its rewards program.

("I'm a SkyMiles member!" Higashioka said brightly when informed of this development.) As for the other flights: Manager Aaron Boone, who pays for and does not expense a monthly Gogo account, said he was unaware many other teams cover the Wi-Fi. He wondered gravely whether the Yankees' policy might cost them free agents. "We're gonna have to get on that," he said. Journalism changes lives.

MARCH 11, 2021

The Last Ordinary Inning

A Rays-Phillies spring training game, which was in
progress as MLB decided to postpone its season last
March, became the last major event to wrap up before
American sports paused due to the pandemic

BY EMMA BACCELLIERI

MLB's last at bat before the coronavirus was Ruben Cardenas's first.

The outfielder—22 years old and in the low minors with the Rays—stepped into the box for his first career plate appearance in a major league spring game. With two outs in the bottom of the ninth, he'd been brought in as a pinch-hitter; many players get their first spring at bats this way, in the late innings of a game after the starters have been removed. But this was an ordinary setup under extraordinary circumstances. The game was the last ongoing event in major U.S. professional team sports, and if Cardenas got on base, he would keep sports alive for just a little bit longer.

It was almost 4 p.m. on March 12. The NBA had suspended its season the night before due to COVID-19. In the morning, statements came from almost every other major sport: MLS, the NHL, the ATP and WTA, various conference basketball tournaments across the NCAA, U.S. Soccer. Even out-of-season leagues made announcements. The NFL said it would cancel its annual league meeting, and the WNBA said it was considering alternate scenarios for its draft next month. But spring training games started on time. As the hours ticked by, news about the virus became bleaker, with growing reports of positive tests and community closures, and these games felt increasingly anachronistic—a relic of a world that seemed to be slipping away by the minute.

MLB finally made an announcement a little after 3 p.m. The league would postpone the regular season and suspend spring training indefinitely–after the six games that were already underway had finished. It was an odd situation even by what was then a quickly shifting definition of "odd": NBA games had been called off the previous night just before tip-off, and a handful of NCAA games had been shut down that afternoon at halftime, but no other athletes had been allowed to keep playing after learning that it would be their last time doing so for the foreseeable future. This was a weird liminal space that belonged only to baseball.

These last six games finished one by one, until professional baseball consisted of only a slow-moving contest between the Phillies and the Rays, winding down to its last batter.

This was Cardenas–who'd tried to tune out dugout chatter about the league announcement as he concentrated on the chances for his first spring at bat. (He'd appeared in one game the previous spring as a defensive substitute but had not had an opportunity to hit.) He came to the plate with the immediate status of the sport resting on his shoulders. And he struck out looking.

"I was so frustrated that I struck out because that was my first real at bat," he says. "I was so frustrated that honestly I wasn't even thinking about anything else. And then once I got in the locker room and got on my phone–I was like, *Oh, wow, I just struck out to end major league spring training.*"

The final innings of spring games are clunky affairs by design. The score doesn't matter; the box score, loaded with substitutions, is full of players that even the most dedicated fans might not recognize. It can feel like the very definition of meaningless baseball. (This year, under MLB's protocol for COVID-19, these innings might not even exist: Managers can agree to shorten a spring game to five or seven innings in an acknowledgement that, really, those last few frames don't do much for anyone.) To watch the end of those games on March 12, against a backdrop of increasingly grim news, was to wonder the same question with each passing minute: Why hasn't this whole thing been shut down yet?

But for the players–minor leaguers, by and large, unsure of what would come next–these innings were their last chances to do their jobs.

There was no formal announcement in the stadium that spring training had been suspended. Phillies first baseman Rhys Hoskins said after the game that he had heard from a fan in the stadium; Rays manager Kevin Cash said that he found out from a staffer who happened to have his phone on him in the dugout. In the bullpen, Phillies reliever Jonathan Hennigan–who would come in for the ninth and throw the final pitch of spring training—learned the news around the sixth inning from a fan walking past the 'pen.

"Some guy was arguing back and forth with us about it," Hennigan says. The relievers knew what had happened the night before in the NBA; they understood that it was likely only a matter of time before baseball would get the same message. But that the sport would be suspended then, in the middle of a game, and they'd hear it first from a fan? "We're like, Man, there's no way, they're not just going to shut down baseball like that—impossible, you know?"

With no physical signifiers that anything had changed, the game looked identical to the one they'd played yesterday and the day before that. But it was hard to shake the weirdness that came with the knowledge they wouldn't be playing again tomorrow. There was nothing to do but keep going, until, eventually, they were the only ones left playing.

"We all started at one o'clock," Rays radio broadcaster Neil Solondz says of the last six spring games. "But our game lasted so long that you're realizing, Wow, we're the last one, and we don't know when we're playing again.... By the end of the game, you didn't even know what the next day was going to be like."

Hennigan says that he barely remembers warming up for the ninth. (For him, like Cardenas, the day felt like a milestone: It was just his second career appearance in a spring game and his first time starting a fresh inning.) He walked to the mound thinking about a line that he'd been told since he was a kid—pitch each game as if it's your last—and wondering whether it might apply in a different sense here.

His leadoff hitter was infield prospect Xavier Edwards. The 20-year-old had entered the game in the sixth inning—shortly after rumors about the suspension started flying around the dugout, meaning that he had a sense of the moment when he stepped on the field, wondering when he'd get to do it again. "It was kind of like the end of a season, you know, last game, this is it, we're going to go home for a while," he says. "It was like that, but not knowing how long we'd be gone for."

Edwards swung at the first pitch he saw and made contact for an infield single—a move that made it briefly seem as if, maybe, this game would keep on going, and baseball would last a bit longer. But it wrapped up quickly from there. Outfielder Randy Arozarena grounded into a fielder's choice. Catcher Michael Pérez flew out to right. And then it was down to Cardenas.

"That's your ballgame," Solondz declared on the broadcast as the outfielder struck out on a pitch on the outside corner. "And we don't know how long it'll be our final ballgame."

The players shook hands for the last time. And Solondz signed off: "We went from telling a story," he says now, a year later, "to just following along like everybody else."

Afterward, in the locker room, players learned officially what they had been hearing around the field for the last hour. But there was no sense yet of what it actually meant. They didn't know whether they'd be able to stay in town to work out, or whether they'd have to go home immediately, or whether they'd be called back at their spring complexes in weeks or months or not at all. Edwards remembers teammates leaving gear in their lockers with the belief that they'd return in two weeks. He suspected otherwise—"I was like, I'm just going to be on the safe side, and I'm going to bring everything with me."

Hennigan held on to the baseball that he'd used to strike out Cardenas. He didn't know what he'd do with it—if it had been worth grabbing at all, if this would be a brief hiatus or a historic break, if his last pitch of spring training would eventually mean something to anyone other than him.

Soon, the team closed its complex in Florida, and he was sent home to Texas, where he set the ball on his mantel. It's still there—a reminder of baseball's last ordinary inning.

UNFORGETTABLE MOMENTS

End of the Glorious Ordeal

Henry Aaron gracefully endured the pressure of the
chase, and then stopped it with one lash of his bat

BY RON FIMRITE

Henry Aaron's ordeal ended at 9:07 p.m. Monday.

It ended in a carnival atmosphere that would have been more congenial
to the man he surpassed as baseball's alltime home-run champion. But it
ended. And for that, as Aaron advised the 53,775 Atlanta fans who came to
enshrine him in the game's pantheon, "Thank God."

Aaron's 715th home run came in the fourth inning of the Braves' home
opener with Los Angeles, off the Dodgers' Al Downing, a lefthander who
had insisted doggedly before the game that for him this night would be
"no different from any other." He was wrong, for now he joins a company
of victims that includes Tom Zachary (Babe Ruth's 60th home run in 1927),
Tracy Stallard (Roger Maris's 61st in 1961), and Guy Bush (Ruth's 714th
in 1935). They are destined to ride in tandem through history with their
assailants.

Downing's momentous mistake was a high fastball into Aaron's
considerable strike zone. Aaron's whip of a bat lashed out at it and
snapped it in a high arc toward the 385-foot sign in left-centerfield.
Dodgers centerfielder Jimmy Wynn and leftfielder Bill Buckner gave futile
chase, Buckner going all the way to the six-foot fence for it. But the ball
dropped over the fence in the midst of a clutch of Braves' relief pitchers
who scrambled out of the bullpen in pursuit. Buckner started to go over
the fence after the ball himself, but gave up after he realized he was

outnumbered. It was finally retrieved by reliever Tom House, who even as Aaron triumphantly rounded the bases ran hysterically toward home plate holding the ball aloft. It was, after all, one more ball than Babe Ruth ever hit over a fence, and House is a man with a sense of history.

House arrived in time to join a riotous spectacle at the plate. Aaron, his normally placid features exploding in a smile, was hoisted by his teammates as Downing and the Dodger infielders moved politely to one side. Aaron shook hands with his father Herbert, and embraced his mother Estella. He graciously accepted encomiums from his boss, Braves Board Chairman Bill Bartholomay, and Monte Irvin, representing Commissioner Bowie Kuhn, who was unaccountably in Cleveland this eventful night. Kuhn is no favorite of Atlanta fans and when his name was mentioned by Irvin, the largest crowd ever to see a baseball game in Atlanta booed lustily.

"I just thank God it's all over," said Aaron, giving credit where it is not entirely due.

No, this was Henry Aaron's evening, and if the Braves' management overdid it a bit with the balloons, the fireworks, the speeches and all-round hoopla, who is to quibble? There have not been many big baseball nights in this football-oriented community and those few have been supplied by Aaron.

Before the game the great man did look a trifle uncomfortable while being escorted through lines of majorettes as balloons rose in the air above him. There were signs everywhere—MOVE OVER BABE—and the electronic scoreboard blinked HANK. Much of centerfield was occupied by a massive map of the United States painted on the grass as an American flag. This map-flag was the site of a pregame "This Is Your Life" show, featuring Aaron's relatives, friends and employers. Sammy Davis Jr. was there, and Pearl Bailey, singing the national anthem in Broadway soul, and Atlanta's black mayor, Maynard Jackson, and Governor Jimmy Carter, and the Jonesboro High School band, and the Morris Brown College choir, and Chief Noc-A-Homa, the Braves' mascot, who danced with a fiery hoop.

This is not the sort of party one gives for Henry Aaron, who through the long weeks of on-field pressure and mass media harassment had expressed no more agitation than a man brushing aside a housefly. Aaron had labored for most of his 21-year career in shadows cast by more flamboyant superstars, and if he was enjoying his newfound celebrity, he gave no hint of it. He seemed to be nothing more than a man trying to do his job and live a normal life in the presence of incessant chaos.

Before this most important game of his career he joked at the batting cage with teammate Dusty Baker, a frequent foil, while hordes of newsmen scrambled around him, hanging on every banality. When a young red-haired boy impudently shouted, "Hey, Hank Aaron, come here, I want you to sign this," Aaron looked incredulous, then laughed easily. The poor youngster was very nearly mobbed by sycophants for approaching the dignitary so cavalierly.

Downing, too, seemed unaware that he was soon to be a party to history. "I will pitch to Aaron no differently tonight," said he, as the band massed in rightfield. "I'll mix my pitches up, move the locations. If I make a mistake, it's no disgrace. I don't think the pitcher should take the glory for No. 715. He won't deserve any accolades. I think people will remember the pitcher who throws the last one he ever hits, not the 715th."

Downing's "mistake" was made with nobody out in the fourth inning and with Darrell Evans, the man preceding Aaron in the Braves' batting order, on first base following an error by Dodger shortstop Bill Russell. Downing had walked Aaron leading off the second inning to the accompaniment of continuous booing by the multitudes. Aaron then scored on a Dodger error, the run breaking Willie Mays' all-time National League record for runs scored (after the home run, Aaron had 2,064).

This time, with a man on base, Downing elected to confront him *mano-a-mano*. His first pitch, however, hit the dirt in front of the plate. The next hit the turf beyond the fence in leftfield.

"It was a fastball down the middle of the upper part of the plate," Downing lamented afterward. "I was trying to get it down to him, but I didn't. He's a great hitter. When he picks his pitch, he's pretty certain that's the pitch he's looking for. Chances are he's gonna hit it pretty good. When he did hit it, I didn't think it was going out because I was watching Wynn and Buckner. But the ball just kept carrying and carrying."

It was Aaron's first swing of the game—and perhaps the most significant in the history of baseball. It was also typical of Aaron's sense of economy. On Opening Day in Cincinnati, against the Reds' Jack Billingham, he tied Ruth with his first swing of the new season. But this event, noteworthy though it may have been, was merely a prelude, and Aaron recognized it as such.

"Seven-fourteen only ties the record," he advised well-wishers at the time. And in yet another ceremony at home plate, he reminded everyone, "It's almost over."

Aaron's innate dignity had been jarred in that opening three-game series by the seemingly irresolvable haggling between his employers Bartholomay and manager Eddie Mathews, and Commissioner Kuhn. Bartholomay and Mathews had hoped to keep Aaron out of the lineup for the entire series so that he might entertain the home fans with his immortal swats. When Kuhn suggested forcefully that it was the obligation of every team to put its best lineup on the field at all times and that any violation of this obligation

would be regarded by him as sinful, Mathews and Bartholomay relented—
but only partially. After Aaron tied the Babe, Mathews announced that he
would bench him for the remaining games of the Reds' series, saving him
for the adoring home folks.

This brought an iron rebuke from the commissioner: Aaron would play
or Mathews and the Braves must face "serious consequences." This message
was delivered after the Saturday game, in which Aaron did not play. Aaron
was in the lineup for 6½ innings on Sunday, striking out twice and grounding
weakly to third in three at bats. The stage—and a stage it seemed—was set
for Monday night.

It rained in Atlanta during the day, violently on occasion, but it was warm
and cloudy by game time. It began raining again just before Aaron's first
inconsequential time at bat, as if Ruth's phantom were up there puncturing
the drifting clouds. Brightly colored umbrellas sprouted throughout the ball
park, a brilliant display that seemed to be merely part of the show. The rain
had subsided by Aaron's next time up, the air filled now only with tension.
Henry wasted little time relieving that tension. It is his way. Throughout his
long career Aaron had been faulted for lacking a sense of drama, for failing
to rise to critical occasions, as Mays, say, or Ted Williams had. He quietly
endured such spurious criticism, then in two memorable games dispelled it
for all time. And yet, after it was over, he was Henry Aaron again.

"Right now," he said without a trace of irony, "it feels like just another
home run. I felt all along if I got a strike I could hit it out. I just wanted to
touch all the bases on this one."

He smiled slightly, conscious perhaps that his words were not sufficient
to the occasion. Then he said what he had been wanting to say since it became
apparent that he would eventually pass Ruth and achieve immortality.

"I feel I can relax now. I feel my teammates can relax. I feel I can have a
great season."

It is not that he had ever behaved like anyone but Henry Aaron. For this
generation of baseball fans and now for generations to come, that will be
quite enough.

JANUARY 2, 1956

The Year, the Moment and Johnny Podres

There was no Roger Bannister in 1955, towering above the crowded field of sport like an Everest, but there was a yellow-haired youngster from the Adirondacks who provided sport's most rousing moment of the year—and its most significant

BY ROBERT CREAMER

The ninth was Johnny Podres' inning. The anticipation of victory rode on every pitch. The first batter tapped the ball back to the pitcher's mound and Johnny, plucking the ball from the netting of his glove, threw him out. In Yankee Stadium 62,000 people leaned forward to watch Johnny Podres face the next man. He raised an easy fly to left field and was out. (Fifty million or so TV watchers were holding their breath now too.) The third man took a called strike (the stadium crowd exploded with noise), took a ball, swung and missed (an explosion from coast to coast), took a second ball high, fouled one, fouled another. The Brooklyn Dodger infield moved restlessly, fidgeting. Podres threw again, a big, fat, arrogant change-up that the batter topped on the ground. After a half century of waiting the Brooklyn Dodgers were champions of the world.

The grandfather of Johnny Podres climbed out of the mines of czarist Russia and came to America in 1904, the year after Cy Young and the Boston Red Sox beat Hans Wagner and the Pittsburgh Pirates in the first World Series. The chances are excellent that Barney Podres had never heard of Cy

365

Young or Hans Wagner, or of the Boston Red Sox or the Pittsburgh Pirates, or of the World Series, or even, for that matter, of baseball. He was 24, and he had been working in the mines for 10 years.

In America he found his way to an iron-mining community in upstate New York in the rough foothills of the Adirondacks near Lake Champlain, married a Lithuanian girl and took his broad back and big hands down into the mines again. Forty-six years, two wives and eight children later he came out of the mines for the last time.

Now he sits in his weather-beaten house in the company village of Witherbee, N.Y., ailing from "the silica," the miner's disease, his great hands folded. His story is neither rare nor extraordinary; it has been repeated in one form or another in millions of American families. But it has a close relationship to the reasons why SPORTS ILLUSTRATED this week salutes the old man's grandson as its second Sportsman of the Year, to succeed Roger Bannister as the one person—of the millions active in sports all over the world in 1955—who was most significant of the year past.

For in the old man's lifetime sports has grown from a minor diversion for a leisurely handful of people to a preoccupying influence in almost every country on earth.

Consider Joe Podres, son of old Barney and father of Johnny, the Sportsman of the Year. Like his father, he went down into the mines in his youth. But working conditions in the mines have improved, like working conditions almost everywhere, and a man has more time that is his own. Joe Podres spent a good deal of his free time playing baseball. He worked all week and played ball on Sundays, or whenever the local team could schedule a game. He was a topflight semiprofessional pitcher for 25 years, until he reluctantly retired three years ago at the age of 43. Sports earned him no money to speak of ("Eight dollars in eight years," is one family joke about it), but the competition and the pride of victory over a quarter century did a great deal to offset the exacting drudgery that goes with simply digging iron ore. And it provided the key that opened the way for his son to make come true a modern version of one of those old legends of beggars and kings and gold pots in the cabbage patch that were told for centuries by miners, farmers, peasants and other wishful Old World dreamers.

Today, even the dream is different. It does not deal with beggar boys becoming kings, or knights on white chargers. The boy kicks a football along Gorky Street and imagines himself booting the winning goal for Spartak in Dynamo Stadium in Moscow. He belts a hurley ball along the rich turf with a slick of Irish ash and thinks how grand it would be in Croke Park in Dublin saving the All-Ireland title for Cork. He stands on the edge of a street in a village in Provence as the Tour de France wheels by and sees himself pedaling into Parc des Princes Stadium in Paris, miles ahead of Louison Bobet. He throws a ball against the battered side of a house and dreams of pitching Brooklyn to victory in the World Series.

Johnny Podres, with three other high school boys, drove out of Witherbee in August 1949, and 265 miles south to New York City to see the Brooklyn Dodgers play a baseball game with the Boston Braves. It was the first major league game Johnny Podres had ever seen.

"We sat way up in the upper-left-field stands," Podres recalls. "Newcombe was pitching. The Dodgers had the same guys they have now: Robinson, Reese, Campy, Hodges, Furillo, Snider. I've always been a Brooklyn fan, and that day I made up my mind, I'm going to pitch for Brooklyn."

Johnny planned to see the Dodgers play again the next day but it rained, and the day after that when the Dodgers were playing again, some other youngster was sitting in the upper-left-field stands daydreaming of playing in the majors. John Podres was back in Witherbee, still a high school kid rooting for Brooklyn. While the Dodgers went on playing, winning and losing pennants, John Podres went on to become captain of his high school basketball team, to pitch his high school team to its league championship, to date, to dance, to hunt deer in the hills outside of town, to fish through the ice of Lake Champlain in the winter.

Then the major league scouts came around and the dream began to come true for John Joseph Podres. Two or three clubs were interested in him for their minor league farm clubs, but for one reason or another John did not sign. His father says, "I think he was just waiting for Brooklyn to come along." Come along they did, and Johnny signed a contract and, in 1951, went off to the Dodgers' farm system. He won 21 and lost five in his first year, later caught the eye of Dodger Manager Charley Dressen and in 1953 was indeed pitching for Brooklyn in a World Series. That, however, was far from being the magic moment, because young Podres was driven from the mound by the New York Yankees, who were beating Brooklyn again, for the fifth time in five World Series meetings.

John Podres is on good terms with luck, however, despite a chronic bad back and a midseason appendectomy. Last fall, as most of the world knows, he got a second try at immortality. Fittingly enough, it was on his 23rd birthday. Brooklyn had lost the first two games of the World Series— and Johnny himself had not finished a game since early summer—but he was the right man in the right place that day. The Yankees could not rattle him, nor could they connect solidly against his arrogant blend of fast balls and lazy-looking slow ones. The Dodgers not only won that game but the next two to take the lead in the Series and approach the brink of incredible victory.

Then they lost the sixth game, woefully. People in Brooklyn were saying, "those bums," and not in tones of rough affection. Rather it was an expression of heartbroken anger and frustration, that they should have come so close only to lose again. They had always lost to the Yankees in the World Series. They had always lost to everybody in the World Series. They were losing now. They would always lose.

At this propitious moment the grandson of old Barney Podres stepped forward, bowed to the audience and promptly became the hero of the year. It was the setting of the dream of glory, and Johnny Podres knew exactly what to do. He beat the Yankees for a second time, shut them out without a run in that old graveyard of Brooklyn hopes, Yankee Stadium itself. Johnny Podres pitched with his ears shut. The explosive noise of the crowd, the taunts of the Yankee bench never got through to him. "I guess I didn't really hear the noise," says Johnny, "until I came up to bat in the ninth." By that time the noise was for Johnny Podres, pitcher, and it was time for him to hear it.

In winning—and this was, in retrospect, the most exciting and fascinating thing about the Series—Johnny became the personification, the living realization of the forgotten ambitions of thousands and even millions of onlookers who had pitched curves against the sides of their own houses and evoked similar visions of glory, only to end up at the wheel of a truck or behind a desk in an office. What was happening transcended any game, or any sport...

...The Russian more often than not ends up in a factory turning out heavy machinery for the state; he keeps his emotions under control until he can get to his seat high up on the side of Dynamo Stadium where he can yell his heart out for Spartak. The Irishman puts his hurley stick away and tends dutifully to the farm, except when he can get down to Cork City to shout for Cork against Tip or Limerick. The Frenchman uses his cycle only to ride back and forth from home to shop to café; but the day the Tour goes through his village he's back on the curb again, watching, watching, as the wheels fly by. Dreams die hard.

And so, when the country boy from the small mining village stands alone on the mound in Yankee Stadium in the most demanding moment of one of the world's few truly epic sports events, and courageously, skillfully pitches his way to a success as complete, melodramatic and extravagant as that ever dreamed by any boy, the American chapter of the International Order of Frustrated Dreamers rises as one man and roars its recognition.

There were others in the world of sport eminently fitted for the robes of Sportsman of the Year. But nowhere else in that vast, heterogeneous and wonderful world did such a moment exist in 1955 as that of the seventh game of the World Series. Nowhere else did a man do what he had to do so well as Johnny Podres did that day. Nowhere else in all the world did sports mean as much to so many people as it did the day John Podres beat the Yankees.

NOVEMBER 4, 1991

A Series to Savor

In a World Series of delicious drama, the Minnesota
Twins barely bested the Atlanta Braves

BY STEVE RUSHIN

The truth is inelastic when it comes to the 88th World Series. It is impossible
to stretch. It isn't necessary to appraise the nine days just past from some
distant horizon of historical perspective. Let us call this Series what it is,
now, while its seven games still ring in our ears: the greatest that was ever
played.

Both the Minnesota Twins and the Atlanta Braves enlarged the game
of baseball, while reducing individual members of both teams to humble
participants in a Series with drama too huge to be hyperbolized. There were
five one-run duels, four of them won on the game's final play, three extended
to extra innings—all categories that apply to the ultimate, unfathomable
game played on Sunday night in Minneapolis, in which a 36-year-old man
threw 10 innings of shutout baseball in the seventh game of the World Series.
Grown men were reduced to tears and professional athletes to ill health in
the aftermath of the Twins' winning their second world championship in
five seasons.

This was the winners' clubhouse: An hour after Jack Morris beat the
Braves 1–0 for the title, Twins pitcher Kevin Tapani broke out in a red rash.
"I'm surprised if I don't have ulcers," said infielder Al Newman, slouched
lifelessly on a stool. "I think I'll get checked out."

Across the room, Morris lay propped against a television platform,
pondering the events of the previous days. "I don't know if it will happen

tomorrow or the next day," he said, "but somewhere down the road, they're going to look back on this Series and say...."

Say what, exactly? Morris, like the scribes spread out before him, was overwhelmed by the thought of describing all that had transpired, and he allowed his words to trail off into a champagne bottle. The bubbly had been broken out by clubhouse attendants shortly after 11:00 p.m., when pinch hitter Gene Larkin slapped the first pitch he got from Alejandro Pena to left center, over the head of Brian Hunter, who, like the rest of the Atlanta outfield, was playing only 30 yards in back of the infield in an effort to prevent Minnesota's Dan Gladden from doing precisely what he did: bound home from third base in the bottom of the 10th, through a cross-current of crazed, dazed teammates, who were leaping from the third base dugout and onto the field.

Even Atlanta second baseman Mark Lemke, whose name had become familiar to the nation earlier in the week, was moved, in defeat, by the momentous nature of the game. "The only thing better," he said, "would have been if we stopped after nine innings and cut the trophy in half."

Impossibly, both the Braves and the Twins had loaded the bases with less than two outs in the eighth inning and failed to score. Improbably, both threats had been snuffed with mind-boggling suddenness by double plays. Atlanta was done in by a slick 3-2-3 job courtesy of Minnesota first baseman Kent Hrbek and catcher Brian Harper. The Twins were stymied by a crowd-jolting unassisted DP by Lemke, who grabbed a soft liner off the bat of Hrbek and stepped on second. So by the bottom of the 10th, when Harper, seeing Larkin make contact, threw his batting helmet high into the air in the on-deck circle and Gladden jumped onto home plate with both feet, the switch was thrown on a 30-minute burst of emotion in the Metrodome stands, an energy that, if somehow harnessed, would have lit the Twin Cities through a second consecutive sleepless night.

For it was only 24 hours earlier that Minnesota centerfielder Kirby Puckett had virtually single-handedly forced a seventh game by assembling what has to rank among the most outrageous all-around performances the World Series has ever seen. Puckett punctuated his night by hitting a home run in the bottom of the 11th inning off Atlanta's Charlie Leibrandt. The solo shot gave the Twins a 4–3 win and gave Puckett's teammates the same "chill-bump feeling" Braves manager Bobby Cox confessed to having had in Atlanta, where the Braves had swept Games 3, 4 and 5 earlier in the week to take a three games to two lead into Minneapolis.

Hrbek was reduced to a 10-year-old when the Series was tied last Saturday night; Sunday morning would be Christmas Day. "Guys will be staring at the ceiling tonight," he said following Game 6. "They won't even know if their wives are next to 'em. I know I won't. She won't want to hear that, but...."

Minnesota hitting coach Terry Crowley was reduced to a doddering man in long underwear that same evening, pacing a small circle in the clubhouse, head down and muttering to no one, "It's unbelievable. Unbelievable."

And Twins manager Tom Kelly fairly shed his skin in the aftermath of that game, wriggling from the hard exterior he has worn throughout his career and revealing himself to be, like the rest of us, both awed and addled by all he had witnessed. "This is storybook," Kelly said. "Who's got the script? Who is writing this? Can you imagine this?"

Understand what Kelly and 55,155 paying customers had just seen Puckett do beneath the dome. In addition to his game-winning home run, he had singled, tripled, driven in a run on a sacrifice fly, stolen a base and scored a run of his own. In the third inning he had leapt high against a Plexiglas panel in centerfield, hanging there momentarily like one of those suction-cup Garfield dolls in a car window, to rob Ron Gant of extra bases and Atlanta of an almost certain run.

After the game had remained tied at three through the eighth, ninth and 10th innings, Cox brought in lefthander Leibrandt to face the righthanded-hitting Puckett, who was leading off in the bottom of the 11th. Why Leibrandt? He had won 15 games in the regular season, Cox pointed out later. But Cox may as well have said what was on everybody's mind—that it didn't matter whom he put on the mound to face Puckett. The man was going to hit a home run no matter what. That was the only logical conclusion to his Saturday in the park. Puckett did just that, and the tortured Leibrandt walked off the field, his face buried in the crook of his right arm.

Afterward, teammates filed almost sheepishly past Puckett's locker, some shaking his hand, others embracing him, most of them without any words to say. This 5'8" escapee of one of North America's worst slums—Who is writing this, anyway? Who did imagine this?—acknowledged he was having difficulty grasping the enormity of the evening. "Ten, 30, 50 years from now, when I look at it, it might be different," he said. "Right now? Unbelievable, man. Unbelievable."

Yes, this Series was baseball's most epic tale. It included twin props—the Minnesota fans' fluttering hankie and the Atlanta fans' chopping tomahawk—that grew equally tiresome as the Series grew increasingly enervating. And it was a tale that engaged two teams that, preposterously, had finished last in their divisions a year ago. Yet, similar as they were, the teams had two distinct followings for the Series: The nationally cabled Braves were America's Team, while the Twins became Native America's Team.

After the Twins put a stranglehold on the first two games of the Series, which had opened on Oct. 19 in Minneapolis, by producing game-winning dingers from two bottom-feeders in their batting order—Greg Gagne and Scott Leius? Who is writing this?—the Series went south in geography only. Before Game 3, Native Americans picketed Atlanta-Fulton County Stadium, protesting from behind police lines that the Braves' nickname and the team's tomahawk-chopping fans were disrespectful to their people. Ticket holders approaching turnstiles were implored by placard-bearers to, among other things, "Repatriate remains to ancestral burial grounds!"—which is a difficult thing to do between pitches. "No one," said Atlanta pitcher John Smoltz, "is going to stop this city from having fun right now."

Likewise, no gun-toting yahoo was going to stop Hrbek from having his usual hellacious good time in the ballyard. His mother, Tina, was telephoned at 3:30 a.m. on the eve of Game 3 by an anonymous moron, who told her that her son would "get one between the eyes" in Atlanta. Yet Hrbek, who in Game 2 had leg-wrestled Gant from first base to tag him out and kill a rally, came to Georgia wary of nothing more than...gingivitis. He tipped his cap to the bloodlusting crowd that booed him during introductions, tomahawk-chopped the fans from the top step of the Minnesota dugout and blithely flossed his teeth during live TV interviews. All the while he went one-for-Dixie and found the time to reconcile the joy of playing in the Series with the anguish of a death threat. "This game sucks," he said, "but it's a lot of fun."

Their villain already cast, 50,878 Braves fans showed up for Game 3, the first World Series game ever played within 500 miles of Atlanta. When it finally came time to play ball, y'all, and the first pitch was thrown by 21-year-old Braves starter Steve Avery at 8:38 p.m., flashbulbs popped throughout the park like bursts of white lightning. "I feel sorry for Dan Gladden," said Braves first baseman Sid Bream later of the Twins' leadoff hitter. "He was probably seeing 5,000 baseballs thrown at him."

For each flashbulb, there was photographic evidence for a fan that he or she was present the night the largest cast ever to appear in a World Series game put on the longest-running night show in Series history. When the curtain dropped four hours and four minutes later at 12:42 a.m. after a record 42 players had traversed the stage, Atlanta reserve catcher Jerry Willard would pronounce himself "exhausted." And he was one of two position players on either roster who didn't play.

When Chili Davis, pinch-hitting against Pena, squeezed off a two-run tracer bullet to leftfield in the eighth inning, the game was tied at four. It would go to extra frames and send scorekeepers into a hopelessly dizzying spiral of pinch hitters, double switches and defensive replacements, thus birthing the biggest box score the World Series has ever known.

Before the bottom of the 12th, Braves catcher Greg Olson told Lemke, a career .225 hitter with a dwarflike presence at the plate, that Lemke—a.k.a. Lumpy, a.k.a. the Lemmer—would get the game-winning hit that inning. Olson is a Minnesota native who spent 13 days with the Twins in 1989, during which time he was given the T-shirt, emblazoned with a caricature of Puckett, that Olson wears beneath his uniform to this day. Lemke, having no such talisman to draw upon for strength, pretended not to hear his teammate's prediction. "But I said to myself, 'Ehhhh, I don't think so,'" said the Lemmer later. This recollection came, of course, shortly after Lemke had singled to drive in rightfielder David Justice, who scored inches ahead of Gladden's throw and Harper's tag.

With Lemke's late game-winner, bedlam and then bedtime ensued in Atlanta. The Braves were 5–4 victors, and Lemke, at his locker, looked longingly at a bottle of Rolaids the size of a sweepstakes drum. "I get big-time heartburn," he said as just one of several cardiologically concerned members of the Braves. As Justice put it: "If we win the World Series now, I think you're going to see some guys have heart attacks in here. I really do."

Eighteen hours later, as baseball commissioner Fay Vincent settled into his special overstuffed, faux-leather easy chair along the first base line and prepared to take in Game 4, he needed only a reading lamp and a stand-up globe to look completely at home. And that was all an observer needed to do on this night: Look at home, to the thick and transfixing traffic at the plate. It was there, in the fifth inning, that Harper tagged out Lonnie Smith in a bone-rattling collision and, moments later, put the touch on Terry Pendleton as Pendleton tried to score on a not-wild-enough pitch that bounded in front of home plate.

In the top of the seventh, Minnesota's Mike Pagliarulo hit a solo homer to break a 1–1 tie. In the bottom of the seventh, Smith did the same to retie things. Stomach linings could be heard eroding throughout the stadium before Lemke, who wears a PROPERTY OF UTICA COLLEGE INTRAMURALS T-shirt under his uniform, slugged a one-out triple in the bottom of the ninth. One batter later, Willard emerged from the dugout to pinch-hit.

Willard's parents, Faye and Jerry Sr., had arrived two days earlier from Port Hueneme, Calif. They had driven three straight days to Atlanta, only to see their son sit on the bench during the most populous World Series game ever played. Coach Cox, why don't you play my son? You play all the other kids. On this night, however, Willard would heroically fly out to shallow rightfield, just deep enough to allow Lemke to tag up from third and slide past Harper, who appeared to tag him out as the two made contact. In fact,

Harper never laid the leather on the Lemmer, and another page in the epic was turned. "Same two teams here tomorrow," Skip Caray dryly told his radio audience as he signed off following Atlanta's 3–2 win.

Game 5 was a godsend for both teams, though Minnesota wouldn't acknowledge that at the time. The Braves' 14–5 tomtom drumming of the Twins at last broke the skein of hypertense games that had endangered the central nervous systems of all those who had been watching them. On the Atlanta side, Smith tied a Series record by homering for the third consecutive game. On the Minnesota side, Kelly removed oh-fer rightfielder Shane Mack from his lineup and rendered him Mack the Knifeless as well. "We hid the razor blades," said Kelly of Mack, who was so disconsolate after the benching that "he was ready to cut his throat."

After the Twins had taken their Game 5 punishment, Atlanta fans stayed at the stadium to send off their team, and the players enthusiastically embraced the crowd in this love-in. The Braves were fully expected to return from Minneapolis with a world championship, what with Avery pitching on Saturday against Minnesota starter Scott Erickson. The former was so cool that when former President Jimmy Carter introduced himself in the Atlanta clubhouse following Game 5, Avery responded, "Howyadoin'." The latter, meanwhile, had posted a lukewarm 5.19 ERA in the postseason. And yet....

Erickson allowed only five hits in six innings in Game 6, though various Braves scorched balls right at Twins infielders or launched missiles that landed millimeters foul. But give the Twins credit. "If you got any pride at all, and your back's against the wall, you're going to fight your way out," said Puckett, who was raised in the crime-infected Robert Taylor Homes on Chicago's South Side and who fought his way out of Game 6 with two fists. Said the man afterward, "I'll get my rest when I'm dead."

Twins reliever Rick Aguilera picked up the win, just as he had in the dramatic sixth game of the 1986 Series as a member of the New York Mets, cannibalizing the Red Sox and Bill Buckner. What is it about Game 6? Boston's Carlton Fisk hit his unforgettable body-English home run off Cincinnati's Pat Darcy in the 12th inning of Game 6 in '75. And while the Red Sox went on to lose Game 7, they are as inextricably linked to that Series as are the Reds. The same unforgotten status would be bestowed upon Sunday's loser, no doubt. "Whatever happens tomorrow," Puckett said haltingly on Saturday, "it's been a great Series. I mean, I want to win. But if we don't, I'm just honored to be a part of this."

Morris would concede no such thing. "In the immortal words of the late, great Marvin Gaye," he said on the eve of Game 7," 'Let's get it on.'" And that they did, the Braves and the Twins. Morris outlasted the 24-year-old Smoltz. On this night it appeared he would have outlasted Methuselah.

When the seventh game and the Series had finally been bled from the bodies on both sides, when the two teams had stopped their cartoon brawl, raising ridiculous lumps by alternately slugging each other over the head with a sledgehammer, when all of 60 minutes had passed after the last game, Pagliarulo stood wearily at his locker. "This was the greatest game," he said. "How could the TV guys describe it? They had a chance to win—but they didn't. We had a chance to win—but we didn't. Then we did. I kept thinking of the '75 Series tonight. This is why baseball is the greatest game there is."

The greatest game there is. The greatest games that ever were.

It Happened

RIP, Curse of the Billy Goat. In a Game 7 for the ages, the Cubs overcame the resilient Indians to win their first title since 1908 and wash away the last vestiges of the longest title drought in American sports

BY TOM VERDUCCI

The drought, as all eventually do, ended with help from above. Rain, glorious cool rain on a strangely warm November evening, fell on Progressive Field in Cleveland just as the Cubs were about to flush away their 108th consecutive season without a World Series title, in their most harrowing manner yet.

The rain fell not in a deluge or in buckets, but in a gentle spray, as if the timer on heaven's sprinklers had kicked in. It fell with the minimal amount of force necessary to coax umpires into stopping the seventh game of the 112th World Series just after nine innings had been completed in a 6–6 tie. Grounds crew personnel began the choreography of pulling the tarpaulin over the infield. Both teams repaired to their clubhouses to wait out the delay.

The last players to leave the Cubs' dugout were reliever Aroldis Chapman and catcher Willson Contreras. The 28-year-old Chapman throws a baseball harder than any man alive. At 6'4" and 215 pounds he is, in the words of his manager, Joe Maddon, a mass of "wrapped steel," and he was weeping. Contreras walked by his side with an arm around Chapman's broad shoulders. The woeful picture did well to capture the sentiment of Cubs Nation at the moment, a brotherhood of tears and misery.

It was Chapman who in the previous inning, with Chicago four outs away from the title and ahead 6–3, had allowed a run-scoring double and a two-run homer to the first two batters he faced, Brandon Guyer and Rajai Davis. The lead and any semblance of optimism Cubs fans can allow themselves dissipated that quickly.

"Guys, weight room! Won't take long!"

The deep, purposeful voice rang out loudly.

What happened next is a story that will be told a hundred years from now, just as the oral history of the last century overflowed with tales of Babe Ruth's called shot, flubbed grounders, pet goats, black cats, deflected foul balls and assorted other misdeeds and pratfalls that defined Cubs baseball. How this story differs from all the others over the previous 107 years is that it ends with Chicago winning the World Series.

That's right: The Chicago Cubs are World Series champions. Shout it from the rooftops of Waveland and Sheffield. The last time anybody spoke such words, Joshua Chamberlain, a hero at the Battle of Gettysburg, was alive. That such a development could be real is amazing enough. But how it happened was nothing short of astonishing.

"I said before the Series that a sweep wouldn't do it," said Cubs principal owner Tom Ricketts. "It would have to be something epic. And that was epic, wasn't it?"

Said first baseman Anthony Rizzo, "That rain delay was the most important thing to happen to the Chicago Cubs in the past 100 years. I don't think there's any way we win the game without it."

The man with the deep, purposeful voice was Jason Heyward, the $184 million rightfielder who was batting .106 for the postseason after a disappointing year in which he hit .230 with seven home runs. As the players left the first base dugout and went down a corridor that leads to stairs up to the clubhouse, Heyward called them into a long, rectangular weight room off the hallway.

Maddon saw them and kept walking back to his office. He rarely has meetings with his players—only about three of them in the past 10 years, he estimates. So the manager didn't bother to inquire about what was going on in the weight room.

"It's crazy how things happen for a reason," he says. "I love when players have meetings; I hate when I do. So they had their meeting, and the big part of it was, We don't quit. We don't quit."

Cubs president Theo Epstein met with the manager in his office to confer about their pitching. Maddon had already improvised by inserting Jon Lester into the fifth inning in relief of Kyle Hendricks with Cleveland's

Carlos Santana at first base and two outs. In a pregame strategy session the last thing Epstein and Maddon agreed upon was that Lester, because of his mental block throwing to bases and his limited history of relief work, would enter a game only at the start of an inning.

But Maddon abandoned the agreement because he wanted the lefty to face lefthanded-hitting Jason Kipnis. However, Kipnis reached on an infield single that was compounded by a throwing error from catcher David Ross that left Kipnis at second and Santana at third. Lester then bounced a wild pitch that allowed both runners to score—the first such play in a World Series since 1911—to cut the lead to 5–3. Lester, however, recovered to pick up nine outs without further damage.

While Epstein met again with Maddon during the rain delay, his phone buzzed with a text. The message instructed him to meet in a suite behind home plate with Peter Woodfork, MLB senior vice president of baseball operations, about the anticipated length of the delay. Epstein walked out of Maddon's office and down the stairs. As he passed the weight room on his left, however, Epstein suddenly stopped. He saw his entire team—no coaches—so he remained outside and listened. Heyward was leading the meeting.

"We're the best team in baseball, and we're the best team in baseball for a reason," Heyward said. "Now we're going to show it. We play like the score is nothing-nothing. We've got to stay positive and fight for your brothers. Stick together and we're going to win this game."

Other players began to speak up.

"Keep grinding!"

"Chappy, we've got you. We're going to pick you up."

"This is only going to make it better when we win."

Epstein smiled. Only moments earlier, when Davis had hit his dagger of a home run off Chapman to tie the game with two outs in the eighth, Epstein's heart sank.

"You blow a three-run lead with four outs to go..." Epstein says. "I'm thinking five years of sacrifice and hard work by so many people is about to go by the wayside."

Epstein took over the Cubs after a contentious divorce from the Red Sox following the 2011 season. Starting with Chicago's Instructional League teams that winter, he set about changing the Cubs' culture so that rather than expecting to lose, members of the organization expected to thrive and win through camaraderie and attention to detail. "That's so Cub" became shorthand for playing baseball the right way. Overhearing the players-only meeting, Epstein suddenly lost that doomsday feeling Davis's home run had triggered.

"It snapped me back," he says. "It reminded me of how much I admired them and how tough they are, how connected they've stayed with each other, and the great things human beings can accomplish when they set out to achieve for other people, not for themselves.

"That's something that made this organization what it is now. From my position I can see it: the sacrifice the scouts make when they drive the extra miles to get that last look at a player, the minor league coaches putting in extra hours, the big league coaches crushing video, the players working on their weaknesses, picking their teammates up. That's what makes a great organization. That's Cub.

"Right then I thought, We're winning this f------ game."

Says Rizzo, "All game long I was burning nervous energy. I was a wreck. I thought about all the people in Chicago and how much this meant to them. But after we had that meeting, I knew we were going to win. It was only a matter of how and when."

The clock approached midnight when the rain began. The delay lasted only 17 minutes, not much longer than the time it took to unroll the tarp and then roll it back up. The timing was crazy. The Cubs and the Indians had combined this year to play more than 400 games, including spring training, and with the score tied after nine innings in the final game of the World Series, they were forced to take a break. It was the ultimate dramatic pause in the telling of a story, perhaps a final wink and nod from the baseball gods before fortune really turned for the Cubs.

"A little divine intervention never hurt," Epstein says.

Before heading back to the field, Maddon sat behind his desk in the visiting manager's office, the one with two open packages of dark-chocolate bars and an 8×10 picture of Hall of Fame Orioles manager Earl Weaver, which served as both inspiration and totem for Maddon throughout the World Series. Then he grabbed a faded periwinkle-blue Angels cap—the outdated one with a wings logo—and stuffed it into the back of his waistband and underneath his hoodie.

The hat belonged to his father, Joe, or as they knew him around Hazelton, Pa., Joe the Plumber. Joseph Anthony Maddon worked 60 years at C. Maddon & Sons Plumbing and Heating, a family business begun in the 1930s by Carmen Maddon, an immigrant from Italy. Five sons followed. Many of the pipes in Hazelton were serviced by the Maddon boys. Three of them, including Joe, who often would be found with a Phillies Cheroot cigar between his teeth, raised families in the apartments above the shop on 11th Street.

Joe the Plumber died in April 2002, when the oldest of his three children was bench coach for the Angels. Six months later Anaheim won the World Series. During the clinching Game 7, Joe would sneak back to the clubhouse and rub his dad's hat for luck. In the ninth inning he brought the hat to the dugout, facing the field, Joe says, "so he could see the last out of winning the World Series."

Fourteen years later, Maddon and the hat were in the dugout for the finale of another Game 7. "It's incredible how this all plays out sometimes," he says. "You have to believe in order to see things, and I do believe. But it was great to have my dad there for two World Series victories."

Maddon and Epstein had already decided that righty Jake Arrieta, who had started and won Game 6 the previous day while throwing 102 pitches, would relieve the weary Chapman in the bottom of the 10th inning.

The first batter to come to the plate after the rain delay was Kyle Schwarber, the 23-year-old designated hitter who is the swaggering definition of "That's so Cub." Epstein and general manager Jed Hoyer took Schwarber with the fourth pick of the 2014 draft, a choice some experts derided as a reach because Schwarber, a catcher-outfielder, seemed best suited to DH.

In the third game this year Schwarber wrecked two ligaments in his left knee when he collided in the outfield with centerfielder Dexter Fowler. Doctors told the Cubs he would be lucky if he could play by the second half of the winter league season. But Schwarber attacked his rehabilitation with gusto and even attended routine scouting report meetings for catchers about how to attack opposing hitters, a practice he continued in the postseason.

"I just love baseball," Schwarber says, when asked why an inactive player would take such an active role in game-planning. "I'm always looking for ways to get better, so that can only help."

On Oct. 17, Schwarber flew to Texas for his six-month checkup. He received medical clearance to begin hitting. Eight days later he started Game 1 of the World Series.

Schwarber came off six months of inactivity to hit .412 against the Indians. In serving as the DH he learned a routine to get himself sharp between at bats. He would hit off a tee in an indoor cage, then hit off a pitching machine cranked to more than 100 mph.

"I want to get myself ready to hit velocity," he says.

Because of the meeting, Schwarber did not hit in the cage before his leadoff at bat in the 10th against righthander Bryan Shaw.

"I had already faced him [four] times," Schwarber says. "I knew what was coming."

On a 93-mph cutter on the second pitch of the at bat, Schwarber rifled a single through the shift against him on the right side. Maddon sent Albert Almora Jr. in to run for Schwarber.

The next batter, third baseman Kris Bryant, had been fighting cramps all night. He received treatment on his right arm between innings. His legs throbbed.

"Never had cramps on any level playing baseball," Bryant says. "Just a lot of nervous energy in Game 7, I guess."

Bryant blasted a long fly ball that chased Davis to the wall in centerfield where he made the catch so deep that Almora tagged up and advanced to second base.

"Just instinct," Almora says. "As a centerfielder myself, once I read that he's coasting and camping underneath the ball, I know he's going to catch it and I have time."

Cleveland manager Terry Francona opted to intentionally walk Rizzo, who was 2 for 2 against Shaw, to pitch to leftfielder Ben Zobrist. When the Series began Maddon called Zobrist "the perfect protector" for Rizzo, preferring his switch-hitting bat behind Rizzo's lefthanded stick.

Shaw jumped ahead of Zobrist 1 and 2, then threw a nasty inside cutter that Zobrist fouled off in the manner of someone shooing bees. Shaw came back with another cutter, this one away, and Zobrist sliced it down the leftfield line for a double, chasing Almora home. After an intentional walk to shortstop Addison Russell, catcher Miguel Montero knocked in another run with a single, putting the Cubs ahead 8–6.

Arrieta no longer was needed for emergency duty. With a lead Maddon gave the ball to Carl Edwards Jr., a 25-year-old 48th-round pick who was, in Epstein's words, "the third player in a trade" with the Rangers in 2013.

Edwards retired the first two batters but couldn't get the last out. He walked Guyer and gave up a run-scoring single to Davis. Maddon removed Edwards and brought in Mike Montgomery, his fifth pitcher of the night. "He loves throwing here [at Progressive Field]," Chicago pitching coach Chris Bosio said of Montgomery. "He just loves the dirt and the slope of the mound—it's a little flatter—so we liked him there."

Montgomery, 27, had never saved a major league game among his 75 career appearances, postseason included, and here he was being asked to save the title of the century. A July trade acquisition from the Mariners, Montgomery embodies what Epstein and Hoyer seek.

"We try to find players just before they are about to pop," Epstein says.

They had been fishing for bigger names on the trade market, but pro scouting director Jared Porter and director of major league scouting Kyle

Evans kept pushing for Montgomery. In a year, they told Epstein, he would be a solid four-pitch starter.

The Cubs' World Series roster was chock-full of those about-to-pop acquisitions, including Game 7 starter Hendricks and Rizzo (2012 trades), setup man Hector Rondon (2012 Rule 5 pick), pitchers Arrieta, Edwards, Pedro Strop and Justin Grimm (2013 trades), Russell (2014 trade) and Montgomery (2016 trade).

The World Series came down to Montgomery against little-used Michael Martinez, a utility player hitless in three postseason at bats. Martinez tapped a slow roller toward Bryant, whose left foot skidded on the wet grass as he set himself to throw. In any of the previous 107 years, the slip might have caused an errant delivery, extending the inning toward greater infamy and deeper heartbreak.

But for the Cubs there are two epochs now: What came before the rain and what came after. Bryant whipped the ball accurately to Rizzo, who squeezed it for the final out.

It was a cleansing rain.

Maybe the night had to be this dramatic—a midnight passing shower, a seventh game requiring more than nine innings—to end the biggest burden in sports.

"Right now," bench coach Dave Martinez, a former player for the Cubs, said after Game 7, "I think about the parents and the grandparents—all the people who waited for this day and the many of them who never lived to see it. I hear it all the time from fans: 'My dad is spinning in his grave.' They tell stories about loved ones who rooted for the Cubs and never saw them win. Those are the people I think about—and all the players who came before us, guys like Ernie [Banks] and [Ron] Santo."

Maybe the whole Series had to be this dramatic. Chicago fell behind three games to one. Only three teams, and none since the 1979 Pirates, had overcome such a deficit to win the championship on the road. The Cubs trailed 1–0 in Game 5, six innings from elimination. But that's when Bryant homered and Rizzo doubled on back-to-back pitches, the building blocks to a three-run fourth inning that was just enough to win 3–2, the jump start to the comeback.

Before that game, facing elimination, Rizzo stripped down to nothing and shadowboxed around the clubhouse as *Rocky* played on the TV monitors. "Got to go the distance!" he shouted. He stepped to the plate in the first inning that night to the movie's theme song.

By the time Chicago reached Game 7, Rizzo had an entire pregame lounge act working in the clubhouse. Besides the *Rocky* pantomime, he

sang or quoted inspirational words from movies such as *Any Given Sunday,
Little Giants, Miracle* and *Remember the Titans*, among others, while the
clubhouse stereo blasted AC/DC.

That's the way the Cubs prepared for and played baseball—with an
insouciance that couldn't be bothered with nonsense about goats and
curses.

"I think that's why they did it," says David Ross, the 39-year-old backup
catcher who hit a home run in Game 7, his last game before retirement.
"They're young players who have been successful their whole careers, so
they expect to succeed."

Maybe to be a Cub meant something entirely new this year. How fitting
that it was Heyward, a bust as far as the production he returned on the
franchise's investment in him, who pulled the team together in its moment
of crisis.

"Jason doesn't say much," Bryant says, "so when he does, it gets
everybody's attention."

When informed it was Heyward who called the meeting, Epstein said,
"That's amazing—that he stayed not only connected to this team, but in the
middle of everything and despite his offensive struggles, he stepped up. It
speaks to his character and professionalism."

Says Heyward, "I'm fortunate to come from great parents and a great
family. No matter how tough it was for me at times this year, I think I gave
something to this team with my character, and I think this team gave
something to me."

Game 7, before the first pitch was thrown, carried the heaviest weight of
any World Series game ever played, if only because the two franchises had
gone a combined 176 years without winning the title. The next-closest World
Series Game 7 with so much unrequited history behind it came in 1975, when
the Reds and the Red Sox brought 92 years of waiting into their finale, won
by Cincinnati.

Once played, this game became even bigger. It will go down as one of the
most epic games in baseball history: four hours, 28 minutes of stomach-
turning drama—and a 17-minute interlude that changed history.

To be a Cub today means something very different than what was
commonly known. It was the motivation Maddon brought to the club last
year, and reinforced this spring when he adopted Embrace the Target as
the team's motto.

"I love tradition," he said. "I think tradition is worth time mentally, and
tradition is worth being upheld, but curses and superstitions are not.

"So it's really great for our entire Cubdom to get beyond that moment
and continue to move forward, because now based on the young players

we have in this organization, we have an opportunity to be good for a long time, and without any constraints, without any of the negative dialogue.

"The burden has been lifted. It should have never been there in the first place, I don't think, but now we can move forward."

Cubdom, as Maddon would call this nation of the yearning, is transformed. All it took was 108 years, and one of the greatest baseball games ever played.

SEPTEMBER 24, 2007

A Death in the Baseball Family

Mike Coolbaugh, the first base coach of Double A Tulsa, was a baseball lifer with an abiding love of the game—until a foul ball struck him. Since then, people at all levels of the sport have struggled to grasp how and why he died

BY S.L. PRICE

At first Tino Sanchez figured he had no choice but to quit baseball cold. Would anyone have blamed him if he'd stayed holed up in his hometown of Yauco, Puerto Rico, for the rest of the season? Forever? He'd gone there to be with his wife, Maria, for the birth of their first child, and as they waited he tried to take in the soothing words of friends and family. *Come on, Tino, it wasn't your fault.* The Colorado Rockies' front office told him not to hurry back, but the game that had been his life kept exerting its pull. So even though the baby—due to arrive on the same July day they rolled Mike Coolbaugh away in a hearse—stayed in Maria's belly, and even though his nerves still jangled, Sanchez returned. To the blast-furnace heat of a Texas League afternoon. To the visitors' clubhouse in the Dallas suburb of Frisco. To another dusty dugout, 17 days after he hit the foul ball that killed his coach.

A breeze wafts through the quaint confines of Dr Pepper Ballpark, promising a cool that never comes. Sanchez sits on the far right side of the vinyl-covered bench, three of his Double A Tulsa Drillers teammates hovering. It's 4:42 p.m., more than two hours from the first pitch, but

386

already the same terrifying guilt that had left Sanchez buckled is at work again. In his first game since pulling the line drive that fatally struck the 35-year-old Coolbaugh in the first base coaching box, Sanchez is still getting accustomed to a macho subculture's clumsy stabs at sensitivity, to his bewildering new identity as both perp and victim. No one has yet informed Sanchez that Coolbaugh's older brother, Scott, is at the park today—and that he's the coach on the mound in a gray T-shirt throwing batting practice for the Frisco RoughRiders.

Scott grooves a pitch, a batter swings and the ball flies into shallow rightfield, toward a cluster of Drillers. "Heads up!" someone shouts, and then two more voices say it again. Sanchez flinches, his gut twisting until he sees the ball plop in the grass. His teammates notice his reaction. They act as if they don't.

"How are you, Tino?" asks one. "Daughter?"

"Not yet," Sanchez says. "And my wife, she's big. She's 40 weeks."

Someone somewhere flips the stadium's speakers on; cheery pop music muffles the grunts and cracks, and for 25 minutes the day seems almost routine. Sanchez is the second man up for Drillers batting practice. Hitting righthanded, he bunts twice, runs to first base. The music stops. Two teenage girls start singing into a microphone next to the stands, practicing *The Star-Spangled Banner*. Sanchez rounds third base as they harmonize about the flag forever waving, then hops back in the cage. Batting lefty, he pulls a ball foul along the first baseline. Everyone tries to ignore that, too.

Sanchez is a utilityman, at 28 the oldest player on the team, so it's no shock that he doesn't start. In the bottom of the first inning he sits in the dugout, gauging whether the coaches are taking their positions farther from home plate. When the RoughRiders' first base coach turns, Sanchez sees the name COOLBAUGH on his back.

"Is that Mike's brother?" he asks a teammate.

"Yeah, that's Scott."

Sanchez had written a letter to Mike's widow, Mandy, and asked a teammate to deliver it at the funeral, but heard nothing back. Now he feels a slight panic: What do I do? What should I say? How will Scott react? But in this dugout, this stadium—in this world, really—there's no one who has the answers. In the top of the eighth a Driller is ejected, and manager Stu Cole tells Sanchez to get ready. He has never reached the majors and probably never will. In 11 minor league seasons he has played in games that decided championships, games that seemed vital to his career, games during which he was distracted by family troubles. But nothing like this.

In the bottom of the eighth Sanchez trots out to first base and fields a few grounders. Then the moment he's been dreading comes; before he looks he can feel Scott Coolbaugh walking up the line to the coach's box. The Drillers lead 3–2, and the crowd of 6,853 has thinned. A man eats peanuts; a child sleeps on his mother's shoulder. On any field, anywhere, there could be no more emotionally charged moment than this one, but the fans don't seem to notice. While Coolbaugh takes his position in the box, Sanchez readies himself not 15 feet away. In the Tulsa dugout, two pitchers shake their heads at the eerie sight of two men yoked by tragedy and separated by one thin line of chalk. One of the pitchers thinks, *This whole thing is just unreal.*

For a moment or two, Sanchez and Coolbaugh are close enough to hear each other whisper. But Coolbaugh doesn't want to distract Sanchez during the game, and Sanchez, with no idea what Scott is thinking, can't stop his mind from racing. He wants to apologize, grieve, console, be consoled, say something, anything. He steals a glance at Mike Coolbaugh's brother. He fields the first out, a pop-up. The bases load, then Frisco ties the game, but Sanchez can't focus. Mostly he looks at the dirt by his feet. The inning ends. The two men run off in different directions without saying a word.

Coolbaugh doesn't go out to the field in the bottom of the ninth. At first that's a relief to Sanchez, but then he wonders if Scott can't bear to be near him, if the Coolbaugh family will ever forgive him, if his future seems doomed to unfold in the space between two unanswerable questions.

"Why me?" Tino Sanchez asks. "Why him?"

News of the accident at Dickey-Stephens Park in North Little Rock generated shock and horror across the nation. Mike Coolbaugh's death in the ninth inning of Tulsa's 7–3 loss to the Arkansas Travelers had every earmark of a freak event, a lightning strike: no way to stop it, no way to explain it. The last fatality caused by a baseball in a professional game—the pitch that killed Cleveland Indians shortstop Ray Chapman in 1920—still serves as a cautionary tale of how quickly a toy can turn into a deadly projectile. But in that case the ball had been doctored. Coolbaugh's death seemed more random, a feeling compounded by the presence of three people all too familiar with the impact a ball can have.

Up in the press box and doing color commentary for the Travelers was general manager Bill Valentine, a former major league umpire who, 40 summers before, had been behind the plate in Fenway Park when a fastball from California Angels pitcher Jack Hamilton pulped the face of Boston Red Sox outfielder Tony Conigliaro, damaging Tony C's eyesight forever. Drillers pitching coach Bo McLaughlin had his major league career effectively ended in 1981 when a Harold Baines line drive caved in his left cheek. And two months earlier Tulsa pitcher Jon Asahina suffered a fractured skull and a shattered eardrum when a batter at the same Little Rock park drove a ball into the left side of his head. If the impact had been an inch or two in another direction, Asahina was told by neurosurgeons who viewed his CAT scans, he might not be standing today.

Some observers suggest—and Asahina insists—that Coolbaugh, in just his 18th game as a first base coach, was focusing on the lead of Drillers base runner Matt Miller and not on the batter in the second before Sanchez made contact. Inexperience might have been a factor, but one seemingly offset by the fact that Coolbaugh constantly preached about the dangers posed by foul balls. "He was more worried about it than anybody I've ever met," says Mandy. In 2005, when Mike was playing with Triple A Round Rock, he was about to settle into his crouch at third when he noticed Mandy visiting a friend in the seats behind the base. Before the pitcher could wind up, Coolbaugh walked off the field and insisted that she move somewhere safer. "So when people say he was turned the wrong way, I just can't believe it," she says. "He was so aware of what a ball could do. God plucked him. There's no way he would've let a foul ball kill him."

For those closest to Coolbaugh, "God plucked him" is the most palatable explanation for what happened in Little Rock. Within the game itself that Sunday night, so many things had to line up: hits, runs, calls. Heading into the eighth inning the Travelers held a one-run lead, a choice situation for their sidearming closer, righthander Darren O'Day. But Arkansas scored three in the bottom of the inning to erase the save opportunity. Bill Edwards, a more conventional righty, took the mound. Would O'Day have thrown the same pitches as Edwards? No. Would it have mattered?

Miller led off the ninth for Tulsa with a single to right. Up to the plate came Sanchez. Edwards threw three consecutive balls; one more and everyone would be safe. "The 3-0 pitch," recalls Drillers play-by-play man Mark Neely, "was a very borderline strike on the outside corner. I'm not blaming this on the umpire. But with all the strange things that had occurred to get to that moment.... Many times—though umpires would never say this—on a 3-0 count the strike zone does expand. That was a perfect example: A borderline pitch on the outside corner that was called a strike and made it 3-1."

It was 8:53 p.m. Coolbaugh leaned over to Miller, standing on first. "We're down a couple runs, so don't get picked off," he said. "Freeze on a line drive." Then Mike Coolbaugh said his last words: "If you're going first to third, you've got to be sure."

Miller took a lead. Edwards brought back his arm. Miller took another step.

A fastball inside, the kind of pitch that always gave Coolbaugh trouble as a hitter. Sanchez, batting lefty, swung a fraction of a second too soon, and the ball blasted off his bat. "A rocket!" Neely shouted into his microphone.

"I don't remember a ball being hit that hard, that fast," says Valentine, who has been working in baseball for 56 years. "He really got every bit of it."

Even though he knew the ball was foul, Sanchez kept watching as it hooked behind first. Coolbaugh threw up his hands as if to defend himself, and tilted his body slightly back.

"It's so crazy," Sanchez says. "It seemed like the ball followed him."

Mike Coolbaugh's baseball career began with an accident. Football was his first love. As a highly touted senior quarterback for San Antonio's Roosevelt High, he was sitting in the locker room when his head coach, hurling a clipboard in what was meant to be a motivational rage, hit him square in the face. His nose deeply gashed, Coolbaugh couldn't wear a helmet and missed vital games; the coach was fired, Coolbaugh's family sued and settled out of court. Recruiters from Texas, LSU and Wisconsin stopped calling. Coolbaugh turned to baseball, became a power-hitting third baseman and was drafted 433rd by the Toronto Blue Jays in 1990.

He spent his first 10½ years bouncing among six organizations: four years in A ball, three in Double A, nearly four in Triple A. He made three All-Star teams, was voted a team MVP, broke the Southern League record for RBIs in a season. He sat and watched as callow talents, bad teammates and, yes, plenty of superior players elbowed past him. Soon Coolbaugh was 29 and thinking his chance at the majors would never come. "Just one day," he would tell Scott. "To get called up for just one day."

God knows, he had worked for it. When Mike was in high school and Scott in college at Texas, teammates had come to work out in the family backyard in San Antonio once or twice, never to return. "Camp Coolbaugh," they dubbed it, and they didn't mean days spent dangling a toe out of a canoe. The boys' dad, Bob, a precision tool-and-die man, was a onetime high school talent from Binghamton, N.Y., who'd turned down an invitation to a New York Yankees tryout because he knew he wasn't good enough. He would make sure his sons never felt that way. The boys loved sports, all sports, but Dad knew baseball, and his rule about playing it was simple: If you won't help yourself by practicing 100%, then you'll help me pull weeds or wash the car—100%.

Scott began running a three-mile course at age 12, and when the smaller, wiry six-year-old Mike would bolt ahead of him, Scott would gasp, "Don't you beat me or I'll kick your tail!" Bob set up a pitching machine in the backyard, tinkering with it until it could fire at 110 mph, and each boy would take 300, 400 cuts—to start the day. Their sisters, Lisa and Linda, were put to use fielding grounders, feeding balls. "Sprint work, running, swinging an ax into a tree stump," Scott says of the workouts. "He'd have us hit into a stump 200 times before we went to bed. We got through the stumps so quick, he dulled the blade. There were a lot of hard times, but it created a work ethic."

Bob couldn't help trying make his young tools ever more precise. If Mike or Scott went 3 for 4, Bob needed to know what went wrong that one at bat. Scott absorbed the constant analysis and prodding quietly, but Mike couldn't. He was hard enough on himself already. "That's what kept those two going," Scott says. "You'd put them in a room together, and they'd argue like they were about to fight, but that's what made their relationship, and they accepted it. They both said their piece and walked away."

Bob will forever be bitter about his boys' small-time careers—Scott, a corner infielder, played 167 big league games from 1989 through '94—certain they were jobbed by the powers that be. Baseball? "A curse on the Coolbaugh family, as far as I'm concerned," Bob says. Mike hit 256 home runs in the minors, and if he agonized over not getting his break, he never resented the good players who got a shot. He could be dour: "A lovable grouch," Astros second baseman Chris Burke, a former minor league teammate, called him. But Coolbaugh's dark moods would always pass. "Listen to me complain," he would say. "Like I've got it bad."

Finally, on the afternoon of July 15, 2001, he got his day. Coolbaugh was heading for the batting cage in Durham, N.C., when Indianapolis Indians manager Wendell Kim stopped him. "I don't think that's a good idea," Kim said. "It wouldn't be good for you to get hurt just before you go to Milwaukee."

Coolbaugh warned him not to joke. "Better get packed," Kim said. "You're going to be late for the plane."

Mandy and Mike had been a couple since 1996 and married since 2000. She knew him to have cried only four times: on their wedding day, on the days their two sons were born and on the day he got called up, after 1,165 games in places like St. Catharines, Ont.; Knoxville, Tenn.; and Huntsville, Ala. "We did it," Mike said in a voicemail, between sobs. "We finally did it. We're going to be up there."

The next day Coolbaugh had a cab drop him at Milwaukee County Stadium at 9 a.m. A security guard told him no one would arrive until 11. He had nowhere to go. So the guard gave him a tour: up and down the concourses in a golf cart, out to the perfect field, into the hushed clubhouse. Coolbaugh found his locker, with a Brewers jersey hanging in it: number 14, his name stitched with care across the back.

He played 39 games with the Brewers. None were as sweet as the first two. In his first at bat, with Mandy in the stands, he smacked a pinch-hit double. The next morning the couple woke to find that Mike's father; his mother, Mary Lu; and his sisters had arrived after an all-night drive from upstate New York. "My dad's here today," Mike told one sportswriter. "I'm going to have a good game." In his second major league at bat he drove a 3 and 1 pitch from the Chicago White Sox' Jon Garland into the leftfield stands and ran around the bases as if it were the most normal thing in the world. The whole Coolbaugh family was crying. "Just that one at bat," Mandy says, "he didn't need anything else."

No, Coolbaugh needed what all competitors need: more. Milwaukee gave him a taste of playing at the pinnacle, with its plush hotel rooms, a $320,000 salary and, most of all, respect. He finished the season with two home runs and a .200 average, and now, it seemed, all those years of work might pay off. Even after the Brewers released him that October, Coolbaugh felt he belonged in the majors. He hooked on with St. Louis the next spring, ravaged Grapefruit League pitching and seemed sure to head west with the Cardinals. Instead, the St. Louis brass opted for the multidimensional, if less productive, Eduardo Perez—a decision that shocks Perez to this day. When manager Tony La Russa called Coolbaugh over with the news that he was being sent down again, Coolbaugh began to jog away. "You're not going to catch me," he said, laughing outside and groaning within. "This is not going to happen."

But it did. Coolbaugh played five games for St. Louis as a September call-up, hit .083 and would never appear in a major league city again. "To me it's one word: opportunity," says former Houston Astros general manager Tim Purpura. "It just never came for him at the right time. He had the talent. There just wasn't the opening."

It's a truism of minor league ball that anyone who plays it for a long time must be a team guy, good for clubhouse chemistry. Coolbaugh played 17 seasons in the bushes for nine organizations, and no one ever said a harsh word about him. Clubs gave him chances well past his sell-by date. He played in Korea in 2003, got hurt, then surfaced in the Astros' farm system. In '04 he reached Triple A New Orleans, only to get off to a poor start. One night in Omaha he struck out three times, and the team bus passed him walking the 10 miles from ballpark to hotel. "He's got his head down and he's talking to himself," Burke recalls. "Here he is, with a thousand games in his career, but he couldn't handle the fact that he was in a bad rut."

Coolbaugh climbed out and hit 30 home runs that season. It wasn't nearly enough: Morgan Ensberg had a lock on third base in Houston. Coolbaugh was back in Triple A in 2005,hitting 27 homers and driving in 101 runs for Round Rock. "I'm not going to let them beat me," he told Scott.

The Astros had every intention of calling him up in September, but in late August, Coolbaugh took an inside pitch on his left hand, breaking a bone. In the spring of '06, on the first day of big league camp with the Kansas City Royals, a fastball shattered his left wrist. He toyed with playing in Mexico this spring but gave it up after a week. His playing career was done.

Still, Coolbaugh wanted to keep his battered hand in. He tried to land a rookie league coaching job with Houston, but execs there felt his demeanor, while fine for seasoned players, might not be right for fresh-faced youngsters. Coolbaugh didn't have, as Burke says, a "warm-and-fuzzy *Field of Dreams* love of baseball." There were times when Coolbaugh, like any self-respecting player, hated the game for its politics, all the gut-wrenching failure. He took business courses online, but baseball was what he knew; he had a family to feed and a baby on the way. His sons, five-year-old Joseph and four-year-old Jacob, wanted to see him in uniform again. When hitting coach Orlando Merced left Tulsa for personal reasons and the job opened up in May, Mike interviewed and waited—but didn't say a word about it to Mandy until he actually got hired.

"He didn't want to jinx things," she says. "It felt like we were always being jinxed in his career."

Coolbaugh joined the Drillers on July 4, introducing himself at the batting cage in San Antonio. "I always had trouble getting away from inside pitches," he told the players. The team's hitting improved almost instantly. With his quiet sincerity, Coolbaugh gained the players' trust. "You just felt him," says Asahina. "He had that warrior energy, very stoic. I was very careful: I would only ask him crisp questions. I wanted to let him know I'm not here talking about last night or women in the stands. No: It's baseball."

Here was a guy who wanted them to succeed, like "a family member," says Sanchez, who had worked as the de facto hitting and first base coach before Coolbaugh's arrival. "When somebody got a hit, it was like he got a hit. When somebody struggled, he said, 'Hey, let's do this or that.'" Like Coolbaugh, Sanchez had been victimized by injuries and the numbers game. Like Sanchez, whose daughter, Isabella Sophia, was born on Aug. 18, Coolbaugh was expecting a child—and was sure it would be a girl. On July 21, the day before he died, Coolbaugh took Sanchez out to lunch at a Mexican restaurant. "We couldn't stop talking about baseball," Sanchez says. "After I told him I was going to have a baby, his face changed. He told me that it's the most beautiful experience I would go through. That's when I knew how much he really loved his family."

The last time Scott Coolbaugh saw his brother, he stopped by Mike's house in San Antonio. Mike had been with the Drillers less than a week. It's really starting to click, he told Scott. They spoke of the Drillers' Aug. 8 game in Frisco, and how cool it would be to face each other on the field again. "I'm looking forward to seeing you," Mike said.

When a bat hits a pitch flush, the ball gains speed. Asahina's sinker ranges from 88 to 91 mph, but a field-level radar gun measured the speed of the ball at 101 mph just before it struck the side of his head. The ball that crushed Bo McLaughlin's cheekbone hit him at 104 mph. McLaughlin has a tape of that game and swears that the microphone hanging from the press box picked up the sound of bones breaking. He needed two operations to reconstruct his face. His left eye socket is wired in five places. McLaughlin lives in Phoenix, and whenever temperatures hit 113° or 114°, the metal gets so hot that the whites of his eyes turn red.

Did Mike Coolbaugh know what hit him? McLaughlin remembers every instant of his accident. Asahina, on the other hand, seems to have experienced a protective amnesia. "I don't recall seeing the ball off the bat or anything else," he says. "It's like something in your deep subconscious says, *No, you're not supposed to see this*. So I don't."

Eyewitnesses declared that they saw the ball strike Coolbaugh in the temple. But the sound of impact wasn't that of ball on bone; it was more muffled, and a preliminary autopsy released two days later found that the ball hit Coolbaugh about half an inch below and behind his left ear. The impact crushed his left vertebral artery—which carries blood from the spinal column to the brain—against the left first cervical vertebra, at the base of Coolbaugh's skull. Squeezed almost literally between a rock and a hard place, the artery burst. A severe brain hemorrhage ensued. Mark Malcolm, the Pulaski County coroner who performed the autopsy, says he's never seen a case like it in his 21 years of work. "Man, that's a one-in-bazillion chance," Malcolm says. "A half a hair in either direction and it wouldn't have killed him."

Coolbaugh fell to his back, his hands landing on either side of his head. Sanchez bolted out of the batter's box and up the first base line, reaching Coolbaugh first. Coolbaugh's eyes were rolling up into his head. His mouth spewed a whitish foam; his body convulsed. Sanchez backed up, sank to his knees and dropped his head into his hands.

The two team trainers and the three doctors who came out of the stands raced to the prone figure. Within seconds Coolbaugh had stopped breathing. He was given oxygen and hooked up to a defibrillator. An ambulance was called, and Cole had Asahina run into the clubhouse, retrieve a trainer's first-aid pack and carry it out to first base. It was the first time Asahina had stepped on a field during a game since his own accident 12 weeks before.

Sanchez was standing now, praying for Coolbaugh to be O.K. He also begged God, *Please don't do this to me.* Then he heard someone near Coolbaugh say, "Don't go, Mike! Come back!"

The ambulance took him. Though Coolbaugh still had a pulse when he arrived at Baptist Health Medical Center, doctors determined that his life ended at the moment of impact. "He may have heard the crack of the bat, but that's it," Malcolm says. "I think he had no knowledge."

Cole received the news soon after in his office but didn't inform the players until a good 90 minutes later, after he'd been to the hospital and back. In the meantime Sanchez buttonholed everyone he could, asking if they'd heard anything. When the manager finally announced that Coolbaugh was dead, Sanchez started flailing. "I think I fractured my hand here," he says, pointing to the bottom of his right hand, "because I couldn't control it; I started punching everything. I hit the floor. I walked away and I went down, because I couldn't stop myself. I went down."

The phone rang in the Coolbaugh house in San Antonio around 9:15 p.m. Mandy had friends over to watch a movie, and when she saw it was Mike's cellphone, she answered quite appropriately for a pregnant woman whose mile-a-minute boys were finally down for the night. "Mike, you know I have people over here," she said instead of hello. "What do you *want*?"

The instant she heard the voice of Drillers trainer Austin O'Shea, Mandy knew the news was bad. Mike called himself whenever he got hurt. O'Shea told her only that Mike was at the hospital. He didn't want some insensitive MD telling her out of the blue that her husband was already dead. "You need to come up here," O'Shea said.

But a doctor phoned before she left for Little Rock. For Mandy the rest of the night was a blur. She got up early and saw that reports of Mike's death were on TV; the first camera crew came to her door at 7 a.m. Mandy knew she had to tell the boys quickly. When they woke up, she and Mike's mother sat in their bedroom, with the baseballs listing their birth weight and height, and their dad's Milwaukee and St. Louis jerseys on the wall. Mandy told them Daddy was hit by a ball, and God took him to heaven. "Well, if Daddy's up in heaven now, can I play with his bats?" Joey asked.

Mandy Coolbaugh is still irked by the way she answered the phone that night. But it's just like baseball to leave her with regret on top of grief. "This game will step on your neck and keep stepping on it," Burke says. "But something like this is almost too much to take."

Tino Sanchez kept sinking. There was a five-hour bus ride back to Tulsa, a tearful team meeting the next day, a night of torment in his apartment. He didn't sleep. He turned off his cellphone. Everyone kept repeating that it wasn't his fault. "People don't understand," Sanchez says. "They're still telling me that it was an accident, and that's been very supportive. But whether it was my fault or not, literally I killed a human being."

He would stare off, having clear flashbacks of his lunch with Coolbaugh, of looking to the coach for reassurance during his next-to-last at bat—every image from the moment they met to when the ambulance rolled away. Too many thoughts: *Coolbaugh's family. His sons. His wife, his wife, his wife.* Guilt engulfed Sanchez those first 48 hours. He felt as if he were drowning. "Mike is dragging me," he told a friend. "He's taking me with him."

The Rockies sent him home to Yauco. Sanchez began to calm, to sleep. He decided to go back to the Drillers because he felt he owed the organization and his teammates for standing by him, because he wanted to honor baseball and Coolbaugh. When he rejoined the team in Frisco, he almost felt ready.

But then came that strange dance with Scott Coolbaugh at first base, the silence, the guilt flooding back into his gut. The game ended, and as Sanchez was gathering his glove, a teammate pointed to two women along the rail who wanted a word. The stands emptied as he walked to a spot just by the on-deck circle. Scott's wife, Susan, introduced herself and Mike's sister Lisa. Sanchez removed his hat and put out his hand, eyes stinging. Lisa's knees wobbled; she wasn't sure she could speak. Mike had spoken to the family, had said how proud he was of this one player on the team named Tino. She wanted him to know that. She reached out, crying too, and they grabbed each other tight.

It was about 10:30, two strangers touched by mercy. Lisa told Tino that the family was doing well. She said they didn't blame him. She cried again and said they would all get through this together. The stadium lights went dark. And for the first time since Coolbaugh died, Sanchez felt lighter.

He'll never be completely free. "I took his life away," Sanchez says, "and he took a part of my heart with him." But when Scott Coolbaugh stopped Sanchez during batting practice the next afternoon and repeated his sister's words and told him to call whenever he needed, it helped. When Mandy approached him outside the clubhouse in Tulsa in mid-August, it helped even more. That the Coolbaughs could push past their profound pain to comfort—no, absolve—him seems like a miracle, proof of grace. "Everything that's got to do with love is God," Sanchez says, "and that was pure love."

They saved him. Of that alone he's sure.

In the baseball world, the reaction to Coolbaugh's death went far beyond what would be expected for a player so obscure. It wasn't just because of the accident's freakish nature. Coolbaugh had played for so many organizations that, for many people, he'd become emblematic of how arbitrary the sport could be. More than $100,000 in donations have poured into the foundation formed to help his family. Not just from fans, but also from major leaguers who know that just one broken hand could have derailed their careers too—players who fear what Coolbaugh represented. He was the guy who always gets a flat tire on the way to the job interview, the one who never could get a break. He was minor league baseball, and who grew up wanting to be that?

Yet off the field Coolbaugh was an object of envy. He took his two boys with him everywhere, couldn't seem to breathe without holding them. And when O'Shea frantically scrolled through Coolbaugh's cellphone directory that Sunday, it wasn't hard for him to find Mandy's number. He came upon the nickname Gorgeous and knew to hit SEND.

"As a husband? He was perfect," Mandy says. "He just did everything right. He was the one who made sure we got to church every Sunday, who made sure the kids prayed before every meal, who tucked them in at night. He would leave me surprises everywhere. If he left before me for the season, he would leave handwritten notes, but he would hide them under pillows, in shorts, drawers, suitcases, a book I was reading. Saying things like, 'I'm going to miss you, but we'll be together soon. I love you.' He would call every night no matter how late it was just to tell me he loved me. When we had our kids, he wrote two songs describing our life. I was in labor, and he sat in the hospital and took out a notepad and wrote them down and would sing them to me. He sang all the time."

Mike built the crib and the changing table from scratch and installed the catcher's-mitt light in the boys' room. The only time in 10 years that Mandy and he disagreed, she says, was over the third child. Mandy wanted one, while Mike worried that they couldn't afford another. She figured that the battle was lost, but on the day she learned she was pregnant, he couldn't have been happier. Money would be tight; he didn't care. Tears roll down her face as she speaks of it: Mike always put her first. "But I know you want this," he said.

"So there are days I question it," she says of his death. "Why would God want this to happen to the kids? I have no doubt it would've been easier for everybody if it had been me instead of him, because Mike would know where to go from here. He would know what to do."

He always made the decisions, after all, which is why his behavior this past spring seemed so jarring. Mike turned 35 in June, and indulged in midlife-crisis standards like calling old friends he hadn't spoken to in years. But he also had become fixated on death. Cancer had killed Mandy's mother in 2003, but not until recently had Mike wanted to know details of the moment she passed, how much pain she endured. He talked about buying burial plots for himself and Mandy. He insisted that Mandy, who never even knew his salary, learn how to handle the household finances in case "something happens to me." Just weeks before Little Rock, he spoke about her having a baby after he died. For the first time, too, he wanted her to sit out in the front yard and watch while he showed Joey and Jake how to play baseball. "If something ever happens to me," he said, "I want you to remember how to teach them to hit."

"Mike, you're not playing anymore," Mandy told him. "We're home. Nothing's going to happen to us."

Mike never let the boys mess with his equipment. Now Joey puts on his father's spikes and refuses to take them off. Now he wears his dad's oversized T-shirts all day. One day recently when Joey was hitting the ball, he told Jake, "Get out of the way. I don't want you to get killed." That was about the time he started badgering Mandy about Mike's black bat, the one in the attic. She didn't know what Joey was talking about, but, finally worn down, she climbed up there the night of Aug. 10. Joey followed her and pointed to a black Louisville Slugger. "There it is!" he cried. A scrawl on a piece of masking tape wound around the handle identified it: the bat Mike used for his first major league hit, July 16, 2001.

The next morning Joey stands in the front yard swinging the black bat that's nearly as long as he is tall. His father taught him well. His swing is smooth. He lines the first three pitches 20 feet over the grass.

At times like these, Coolbaugh's death makes almost no sense. It's easy to see the accident as merely a random occurrence. For believers, though, the coincidences, premonitions and precursors are signs of a plan: causal lines and connections revealed only after the fact, like a spiderweb after rain.

Or maybe it's nothing so grandiose. Mandy mentions all the tributes from Mike's peers, the hundreds of e-mails from around the world, the fact that the Drillers have retired his jersey. "If he went out any other way, would he have gotten all the respect he has from this?" she asks. "If he was in a car crash? When he wasn't called back to play, he said, 'I put in so many good years. I wish I could at least have the respect that I was a good player.' And by dying on the field, he did."

Now a DVD tribute is playing on the TV, and she's identifying the images as they fade in and out: Mike with his grandfather, Mike and Mandy mugging in a photo booth, Mike and Mandy dancing at their wedding, the last family photo, Mike's first home run, Mike walking in the surf with his sons. "His last day with the kids," she says. "He took us to Corpus Christi beach. Then he took a long walk with me. He hated sand between his toes, but he wanted to take a long walk. We walked for about an hour, the kids running in front."

It seems a brutal trade: A husband and father dies prematurely in return for a little respect. Mike Coolbaugh's wife, expecting a third child in October, is alone. His sons cling to empty clothes and the fading echo of a summer sea. Who can say why? It will have to be enough to know that in the most obscure corners, compassion lives and success has nothing to do with fame or money or even greatness. It will have to be enough to understand that such a notion is easy to forget, until a good man's dying forces the world to pay attention at last.

JUNE 15, 2015

No-No Regrets

Three years after he gave fans one of the great nights in
Mets history, Johan Santana is still struggling to get back
on a major league mound. But he's not the one haunted
by the limits he pushed past for one moment of glory

BY PHIL TAYLOR

Suppose the devil offered you this bargain: You can have one unforgettable
night doing what you love to do, but in exchange, you will never again be
able to do it nearly as well. Would you take that deal? No? What if he added
this: You can bring joy to thousands of people who will be forever grateful
to you. But your future will be full of surgeon's scalpels and solitary
workouts in a futile pursuit of what you used to be. Would you sign on the
dotted line?

Here's another, even more difficult question: What if you had to make
that choice for someone else?

Rain was in the forecast on June 1, 2012, the radar showing that it could
pass over Citi Field sometime during the game, which did not bode well for
Johan Santana. It is difficult for any starting pitcher to get back on the
mound after sitting through a delay, and Santana knew he would not even
be allowed to attempt it. It was his 11th start after missing an entire season
due to major shoulder surgery, and his 33-year-old left arm was too valuable
for the Mets to take such a risk. If the weather caused a mid-game stoppage
of any length, he would be done for the evening. No one would want to take
the chance that he would come back and get injured.

But Santana didn't concern himself with that as he began to prepare in the Mets' bullpen. Pitching, he often said, was about being in the moment, about clearing your mind of everything except the next pitch. He concentrated instead on the way he felt as he started to throw, lightly from in front of the mound at first, then harder, from a full windup when he backed up onto the rubber. Normal. He felt normal. After the months of rehab, of strengthening his arm with elastic resistance bands, triceps extensions, dumbbell flys and dozens of other exercises, after working diligently to regain his velocity and command of his pitches, he didn't take that feeling for granted.

Before the 2010 surgery to repair a torn capsule in his shoulder, there had been pain when he threw, and after the procedure, even though the discomfort was gone, the anticipation of it was not. He began throwing again in early 2012, and it had taken him weeks to be able to release the ball freely, without worry. But now everything was the way it used to be when he was the best pitcher in baseball, when he won a pair of American League Cy Young Awards with the Twins before he was traded to the Mets in February 2008 and signed a six-year contract extension worth $137.5 million. He had thrown a shutout in his previous start, a four-hitter against the Padres in which he threw just 96 pitches, striking out seven and walking no one. It was a clean and efficient performance, his best game since he'd been back, and it dropped his ERA to 2.75. The biting of fingernails over Santana's health had given way to discussion about whether he might make the All-Star team. In a way, it was a good sign that the pregame crowd for this Friday evening game against the Cardinals was sleepy and relatively sparse. It meant that his starts had become routine again.

When Santana finished warming up, he jogged to the dugout, where he went through his series of elaborate handshakes featuring individualized choreography with each teammate. He was never one of those pitchers who went into an intense, unapproachable cocoon on the days he started; he was gregarious and relaxed until the moment he stepped on the mound, when he became all business.

In the first inning he induced fly balls from Rafael Furcal and Matt Holliday and struck out Carlos Beltran, the former Met whose return to Citi Field for the first time since he was traded away the previous summer was supposed to be the game's main story line. But Santana walked David Freese and Yadier Molina in the second, and his fastball seemed to have a mind of its own, refusing to hit his desired spots. In New York's bullpen, Santana's fellow pitchers were in agreement that he did not have his best stuff, that tonight would be a battle. He managed to escape without giving up a run, striking out Matt Adams and Tyler Greene to end the inning, and then he breezed through the third on nine pitches. Santana could tell the Cardinals' hitters were overeager because his fastball velocity, which at his peak had sat at 92–95 mph, was down to around 90. They were jumping out of their shoes to hit the pitch, so he used that to his advantage, getting them to lunge at his changeup, which had always been his signature pitch.

That third inning went so quickly that outfielder Andres Torres patted Santana on the knee when he came in and sat down in the dugout. "You're rolling now," Torres said. "We just need the rain to hold off."

Santana shrugged. "I'm just gonna pitch," he said. "Whatever happens, happens."

After managing the Astros and the Angels in the 1990s, Terry Collins had been mostly out of the majors until the Mets hired him in 2010 to be their minor league field coordinator, overseeing the skill development of the team's farmhands. That's what Collins was doing during spring training that year in Port St. Lucie, Fla., when he first met Santana. "One day the big club was on the road, and I was helping run some drills with the minor league kids and some of the big league guys who stayed back," Collins says. "Not everybody was going a full 100 percent, so Johan stopped the drill and said, 'Hey, if we're going to do it, let's do it right.' He didn't yell it or scream it, just firm, no nonsense. And I'm thinking to myself, Wow, even with the Cy Youngs, the playoff games and everything else this guy has accomplished in his career, every single individual drill is still important to him."

Ever since, Santana had been an object of Collins's admiration, and he used the pitcher as an example to the minor leaguers of the kind of work ethic and attention to detail it took to be great. When Collins took over as the Mets' manager in 2011, he saw the grueling work Santana was doing to make it back from the torn capsule. Every major league pitcher who had suffered that injury—including Dallas Braden, Rich Harden, Mark Prior, Bret Saberhagen and Chien-Ming Wang—came back significantly diminished, if he came back at all. But Santana was beating the long odds against him, and Collins felt he had been entrusted to be the caretaker of something precious. "He was special," Collins says. "It was my job to keep him that way."

Before the Cardinals game, in his daily session with the local media, someone asked Collins what the maximum number of pitches Santana, whose season-high was 108, would be allowed to throw. Somewhere around 110, the manager had said. Maybe 115. Some fans and media felt that Collins overworked pitchers, especially his relievers, but he was determined that would not be the case with Santana.

It's safe to say that no one in the Mets' organization rooted for Santana's success more than Collins, which is why it is ironic that what became the most triumphant night of Santana's career was the most excruciating of Collins's. "It was without a doubt," he says, "the worst night I've ever spent in baseball."

In the great rethinking of baseball sparked by the sabermetric revolution, any number of traditional statistics—batting average, ERA, pitcher wins—have been devalued, exposed as the incomplete, often misleading measurements that they are. In some ways, the no-hitter is in the same category. On closer examination, it's hard to see why it's considered such a grand achievement when, in most cases, it's nothing more than a well-pitched game sprinkled with a little extra good fortune: A line drive is smoked right at an outfielder; a diving stop by an infielder turns a sure hit into an out; an umpire mistakenly calls a smash down the third base line foul when it should have been ruled fair.

A no-hitter is more a roll of the dice than a measure of greatness. Chris Bosio threw one but Pedro Martinez did not. Eric Milton threw one but Steve Carlton did not. Bud Smith threw one but Roger Clemens did not. A journeyman pitcher named Joe Cowley tossed a no-no for the White Sox in which he walked seven and allowed a run on a sacrifice fly. The quality of a no-hitter can vary so widely as to make the term in and of itself almost meaningless. And yet....

"Every pitcher wants to do it at least one time," Santana says. "There's something about it, the way you never see it coming. Once you start to get close, can you make the pitches you need to finish it? But mostly it's the surprise. The surprise makes it special."

The randomness helps give the no-hitter its mystique. By the late innings, everyone in both dugouts and in the stands is fully invested. You will either get the perfect payoff to all that anticipation ... or it will all come crashing down at the finish.

For the Mets and their fans, that finish had always been the same. Since the franchise's birth in 1962, that extra dash of no-hitter luck had eluded them. When Santana took the mound against the Cardinals, the team had played 8,019 games without throwing a no-hitter. The Padres were the only other team without one, but their franchise was seven years younger. The inability of the Mets to get a no-hitter, especially in light of how many great pitchers they had employed—Tom Seaver, Dwight Gooden and David Cone among them—was proof that God was not a Mets fan.

Any fan worth his psychosis knew about the no-hitter drought. In 2008, Mets fan Dirk Lammers, an Associated Press reporter, started NoNohitters. com, a blog devoted to the team's pursuit of a no-no. One of Lammers's earliest baseball memories was Seaver's no-hitter for the Reds in 1978.

Seaver had pitched 10½ spectacular seasons for the Mets before his trade to Cincinnati in '77, and in that time he had pitched five one-hitters—including the most famous Mets near-miss of them all, the 8⅓ perfect innings Seaver pitched against the Cubs before a little-known outfielder named Jim Qualls broke it up with a single in the ninth. A year and one day after Seaver joined the Reds, he finally threw the no-no. Of course.

"I was nine, and I remember thinking, That should have been the Mets," Lammers says. "I remember Gooden coming close for the Mets and the David Cone one-hitters. Then Gooden threw one and Cone threw one, a perfect game, actually, both for the Yankees. The Yankees. It was like, O.K., this is officially a curse."

Lammers didn't realize how many Mets fans believed in the curse until he started the blog. "I thought it was only me and a few friends who were desperate for this thing to end," he says, "but it turned out it was pretty much everyone who ever rooted for the Mets."

In the fourth inning Santana allowed a walk to Holliday but nothing else, and the Cardinals continued to help him by swinging early in the count. After throwing a total of 41 pitches in the first two innings, his pitch count was a more manageable 62 after four.

That was about the time Kevin Burkhardt, then the Mets' roving reporter during their local telecasts on SNY, noticed the zero on the scoreboard under the Cardinals' hit column. "He didn't have good control," Burkhardt says. "He was just kind of getting through it. But after the fourth, I was like, 'Wait a minute.' He got more intense, laser sharp." Santana opened the fifth by issuing his fourth walk, to Adams, before striking out Greene and Adam Wainwright and retiring Furcal on a line drive to left.

When Santana took the mound for the sixth inning, the no-hitter buzz was beginning in earnest. This being the Mets, there was a subtext of pessimism. Who would break it up? The despised Molina, a longtime Mets tormentor whose ninth-inning homer in Game 7 had beaten them in the 2006 NL Championship Series? Beltran, who had spent six-plus mostly brilliant years in centerfield for the Mets, a run that somehow never seemed good enough for a portion of the fan base? Beltran was leading off the sixth. Yes, it would probably be Beltran.

Sure enough, Beltran pulled a scorching ground ball past third baseman David Wright, and for a moment, the magic went out of the night. It was all over. But third base umpire Adrian Johnson threw his hands in the air signaling foul ball. After the game he would see what the television audience saw on replay, that the ball had clearly nicked the foul line just after it went past the bag.

"Did it?" Santana says now, winking. "I'm still not sure." Given that reprieve, he retired Beltran on a groundout in a one-two-three inning.

"I started to believe after the Beltran grounder, after the...I never like to say it was a blown call," Lammers says. "I wasn't there. I can't say for sure. And then, after Mike Baxter went into the wall for that catch."

No Mets player understood more about what a no-hitter would mean to the fan base than Baxter, who grew up in Queens in the shadow of Shea Stadium. His father, Ray, made the six-minute drive to the ballpark to see every Mets home game, and he was in the stands to see his son preserve Santana's gem by crashing headlong into the leftfield wall to gather in Molina's fly in the seventh inning. It cost Baxter a displaced right collarbone, a fractured rib cartilage and two months on the disabled list.

Like Santana, Baxter, who at age 27 was hitting .323 in a potential breakout season when he got hurt, had a hard time getting back to normal after his injury. The Mets waived him in 2013 and he was picked up by the Dodgers, who let him leave after the '14 season. He then signed a minor league contract with the Cubs, who called him up to the majors in May. "I can't say that the injuries slowed my career down, but obviously they didn't help," he says. "But regardless, it was worth it to be able to not only be there for the no-hitter, but to be a part of making it happen."

Santana is now in Florida again, at the Blue Jays' facility in Dunedin, not unlike the one in Port St. Lucie where Collins first met him five years ago. Toronto signed him in February to a $100,000 contract and brought him to spring training with the understanding that it would take weeks before he was ready to pitch in even an exhibition game. Maybe Santana's arm will cooperate enough for him to get major league hitters out again, or maybe not. There are no expectations, no time line. Still, there is no denying the progress has been slow. While he has lately been throwing from 120 feet, he has yet to throw from the mound.

There is no way to say with any certainty that the 134 pitches Santana threw on that night in 2012 caused the three years of struggles that have followed it. Maybe his arm was destined to break down on him no matter what he did. For Santana, that uncertainty is comforting.

"You can't say it was the right decision or the wrong decision," he says. "Because you don't know. No doctor ever told me, 'Oh, if you didn't throw so many pitches in this game or that game, your shoulder would not have been hurt again.' Maybe if I would have gotten knocked out in the fourth inning, everything would have been different, or nothing would have been different."

But there is no denying that something changed after June 1, 2012. In his next start, Santana was shelled by the Yankees, giving up four home runs in five innings in a 9–1 loss. Next came another five-inning start in which he surrendered four runs and labored through 96 pitches. He then had a stretch of several decent outings, but only got past the sixth inning once the rest of the season, when he held the Dodgers scoreless for eight innings on June 30. That game would prove to be the most recent win of his career, and the aberration in a horrid second half in which Santana had an 8.27 ERA in his final 10 starts. After he gave up 15 hits and 14 runs in a total of 6⅓ innings against the Braves and the Nationals in August, the Mets decided to shut him down. "My arm felt more or less O.K., but then I got inflammation in my lower back," says Santana. "Then you start overcompensating and it goes to your shoulder and your knees, and they decided to shut me down for the year."

The following spring Santana still wasn't throwing smoothly. An MRI revealed that he had the same torn capsule injury as before, and he underwent a second shoulder surgery on April 2, 2013. He never threw another pitch for the Mets, who exercised the $5.5 million buyout clause in his contract after the '13 season.

Santana remained unsigned until the Orioles gave him a contract in March 2014. He pitched well in spring training—until he snapped his Achilles tendon. So he went home to Venezuela, and as is typical of his optimistic nature, he considers the injury a blessing in disguise because it gave him more time to spend with his family. In January he reported to the winter league to see if he still had the passion, the desire to try for another comeback, and he quickly discovered that the fire was still there, even as he also experienced more shoulder soreness requiring still more rehab. His agent, Chris Leible, put out the word that Santana still wanted to pitch, and after several teams looked at him, the Blue Jays finally made him an offer.

When Santana finished the seventh inning against the Cardinals, he had thrown 107 pitches. The fans in Citi Field were all in now. The weather had cooperated—a light rain had come and gone—and now there was just the exquisite agony of hoping for a no-hitter.

For Collins, there was only agony. He was torn, a part of him hoping that a Cardinal would bloop in a hit so he could pull Santana. "I don't know if I said it, but I thought it," Collins says.

He went to Santana after the seventh and got the expected response. "I can do this," Santana told him. "I'm fine." Collins looked at him and said, "You're my hero."

"Thanks," Santana said. "Now go over there, because I'm not done working."

Collins talked to pitching coach Dan Warthen at the end of the dugout, and they decided they would have to let Santana make the decision. Every foul ball made Collins wince. Another pitch, and another. Everywhere there were minidebates going on about whether Santana should be allowed to go so far past his 115-pitch limit. "We're all down in the bullpen asking each other, 'Is he going to take him out? Is he going to leave him in?'" pitcher R.A. Dickey says. "'Would you take him out, leave him in?' I don't remember a single guy saying pull him. It was one of those moments. You have to let him go for it."

Collins felt the same way, but that didn't make it any less torturous to watch. "I was just sitting there hoping he'll get a couple of one-pitch outs," he said. "I was very aware of what the wear and tear of that night could do to him, and basically, that worst-case scenario happened. To throw that amount of pitches with that much pressure and that much adrenaline going, it can beat you down. And it did."

In the ninth, Holliday lined to center and Allen Craig flied to left, leaving Freese as the only man between Santana and the no-hitter. The count went to 3-0, then a strike, then another. Santana went back to his money pitch, the changeup, pitch 134.

Freese swung and missed. It was done.

In the bedlam, after catcher Josh Thole had jumped into Santana's arms, after he had been mobbed by his teammates, while 27,609 disbelieving fans chanted his name, Santana went into the dugout, where Burkhardt was waiting to interview him. "He hugged me and he just started crying," Burkhardt said. "All that he'd overcome, it just hit him. He knew what it meant to the fans here."

But was it a good trade, the no-hitter for, possibly, more healthy seasons? "If you had to choose, maybe you'd take more years," says Burkhardt, "but it's close."

"I think about that a lot," says Lammers. "If someone had offered me the choice: You can either have a no-hitter or Santana can pitch this many more games for the Mets...well, I'm glad I'm a fan and not sitting in the dugout as a manager. The choice would be that close. I don't know which way I'd go."

Collins has his wife's ticket stub from the game, autographed by Santana, framed in his home. It may have been the worst night of Collins's career, but it's still one he never wants to forget. "People still come up to me at banquets, on the street, wherever, and tell me they're glad I let him finish it," Collins says. "I'm glad they're glad. For me, the one thing it did is that one of the great competitive players I've ever been around got to have a great moment, and I was very happy for him."

As Santana left the clubhouse after the no-hitter, a security guard approached him. "He just gave me a hug and said that was from his dad. He said his dad was a Mets fan from Day One, and he thought he'd never see a no-hitter, and he told him, 'Give Santana a hug.' I mean, that's pretty emotional, right? Pretty special." Santana wrapped his arms around the security guard, embracing the man and the moment, not the slightest bit worried about whatever would happen next.

It's unlikely that Santana will ever have another night on a major league mound that rivals the no-hitter, but that isn't even his goal. "Just to be on a mound again in the big leagues, that's all I want," he says. "Starting, relieving, just to pitch again. Coming back is a challenge, and I love challenges. Is it going to happen? I don't know. But I'm taking my chances, and I'm giving it everything I have."

He has no regrets about anything that took place on that June night three years ago. "It's easy to criticize things after they happened," he says. "You don't have a crystal ball to say what's going to happen. I told Terry I felt fine, and I did. Even if an army had come to get me, I wouldn't have come out of the game. I love this game too much."

Santana knows that Collins still struggles with the decision he made that night. "Tell Terry he's a great manager and everything is fine, I'm fine," he says. "There's nothing for anybody to be sorry about. What happened, happened."

When those words are relayed to Collins, he is asked whether they help him feel more at peace with his choice. He allows himself a small smile.

"Not really," he says.

DECEMBER 12, 2004

At the End of the Curse, a Blessing

The 2004 Boston Red Sox staged the most improbable comeback in baseball history and liberated their long-suffering nation of fans

BY TOM VERDUCCI

The cancer would have killed most men long ago, but not George Sumner. The Waltham, Mass., native had served three years aboard the USS *Arkansas* in World War II, raised six kids with a hell of a lot more love than the money that came from fixing oil burners, and watched from his favorite leather chair in front of the television—except for the handful of times he had the money to buy bleacher seats at Fenway—his Boston Red Sox, who had found a way not to win the World Series in every one of the 79 years of his life. George Sumner knew something about persistence.

The doctors and his family thought they had lost George last Christmas Day, more than two years after the diagnosis. Somehow George pulled through. And soon, though still sick and racked by the chemo, the radiation and the trips in and out of hospitals for weeks at a time, George was saying, "You know what? With Pedro and Schilling we've got a pretty good staff this year. Please let this be the year."

On the night of Oct. 13, 2004, George Sumner knew he was running out of persistence. The TV in his room at Newton-Wellesley Hospital was showing Pedro Martinez and the Red Sox losing to the New York Yankees in Game 2 of the American League Championship Series—this after Boston had lost Game 1 behind Curt Schilling. During commercial breaks Sumner talked with his daughter Leah about what to do with his personal possessions. Only a few days earlier his wife, Jeanne, had told him, "If the pain is too much, George, it's O.K. if you want to go."

But Leah knew how much George loved the Red Sox, saw how closely he still watched their games and understood that her father, ever quick with a smile or a joke, was up to something.

"Dad, you're waiting around to see if they go to the World Series, aren't you?" she said. "You really want to see them win it, right?"

A sparkle flickered in the sick man's eyes and a smile creased his lips.

"Don't tell your mother," he whispered.

At that moment, 30 miles away in Weymouth, Mass., Jaime Andrews stewed about the Red Sox' losing again but found some relief in knowing that he might be spared the conflict he had feared for almost nine months. His wife, Alice, was due to give birth on Oct. 27. Game 4 of the World Series was scheduled for that night. Jamie was the kind of tortured fan who could not watch when the Red Sox were protecting a lead late in the game, because of a chronic, aching certainty that his team would blow it again.

Alice was not happy that Jaime worried at all about the possible conflict between the birth and the Sox. She threatened to bar him from the delivery room if Boston was playing that night. "Pathetic," she called his obsession with his team.

"It's not my fault," Jaime would plead, and then fall on the DNA defense. "It was passed down through generations, from my grandfather to my mother to me."

Oh, well, James thought as he watched the Red Sox lose Game 2, at least now I won't have to worry about my team in the World Series when my baby is born.

Dear Red Sox:
My boyfriend is a lifelong Red Sox fan. He told me we'll get married when the Red Sox win the World Series.... I watched every pitch of the playoffs.
—SIGNED BY A BRIDE-TO-BE

The most emotionally powerful words in the English language are monosyllabic: love, hate, born, live, die, sex, kill, laugh, cry, want, need, give, take, Sawx.

The Boston Red Sox are, of course, a civic religion in New England. As grounds crew workers tended to the Fenway Park field last summer after a night game, one of them found a white plastic bottle of holy water in the outfield grass. There was a handwritten message on the side: GO SOX. The team's 2003 highlight film, punctuated by the crescendo of the walk-off home run by the Yankees' Aaron Boone in ALCS Game 7, was christened, *Still, We Believe.*

"We took the wording straight out of the Catholic canon," club president Larry Lucchino says. "It's not We Still Believe. Our working slogan for next year is It's More than Baseball. It's the Red Sox."

Rooting for the Red Sox is, as evident daily in the obituary pages, a life's definitive calling. Every day all over New England, and sometimes beyond, death notices include age, occupation, parish and allegiance to the Sox. Charles F. Brazeau, born in North Adams, Mass., and an Army vet who was awarded a Purple Heart in World War II, lived his entire 85 years without seeing the Red Sox win a world championship, though barely so. When he passed on in Amarillo, Texas, just two days before Boston won the 2004 World Series, the *Amarillo Globe News* eulogized him as a man who "loved the Red Sox and cheap beer."

Rest in peace.

What the Red Sox mean to their faithful—and larger still, what sport at its best means to American culture—never was more evident than at precisely 11:40 EDT on the night of Oct. 27. At that moment in St. Louis, Red Sox closer Keith Foulke, upon fielding a ground ball, threw to first baseman Doug Mientkiewicz for the final out of the World Series—and the first Red Sox world championship since 1918. And then all hell didn't just break loose. It pretty much froze over.

All over New England, church bells clanged. Grown men wept. Poets whooped. Convicts cheered. Children rushed into the streets. Horns honked. Champagne corks popped. Strangers hugged.

Virginia Muise, 111, and Fred Hale, 113, smiled. Both Virginia, who kept a Red Sox cap beside her nightstand in New Hampshire, and Fred, who lived in Maine until moving to Syracuse, N.Y., at 109, were Red Sox fans who, curse be damned, were born *before Babe Ruth himself.* Virginia was the oldest person in New England. Fred was the oldest man in the world. Within three weeks after they had watched the Sox win the Series, both of them passed away.

They died happy.

Dear Red Sox:
Can you get married on the mound in, say, November at Fenway?

On its most basic level, sport satisfies man's urge to challenge his physical being. And sometimes, if performed well enough, it inspires others in their own pursuits. And then, very rarely, it changes the social and cultural history of America; it changes *lives*. The 2004 Boston Red Sox are such a perfect storm.

The Red Sox are SI's Sportsmen of the Year, an honor they may have won even if the magnitude of their unprecedented athletic achievement was all that had been considered. Three outs from being swept in the ALCS, they won eight consecutive games, the last six without ever trailing. Their place in the sporting pantheon is fixed; the St. Jude of sports, patron saint of lost athletic causes, their spirit will be summoned at the bleakest of moments.

"It is the story of hope and faith rewarded," says Red Sox executive vice president Charles Steinberg. "You really believe that this is the story they're going to teach seven-year-olds 50 years from now. When they say, 'Naw, I can't do this,' you can say, 'Ah, yes you can. The obstacle was much greater for these 25 men, and they overcame. So can you.'"

What makes them undeniably, unforgettably Sportsmen, however, is that their achievement transcended the ballpark like that of no other professional sports team. The 1955 Brooklyn Dodgers were the coda to a sweet, special time and place in Americana. The 1968 Detroit Tigers gave needed joy to a city teeming with anger and strife. The 2001 Yankees provided a gathering place, even as a diversion, for a grieving, wounded city. The 2004 Red Sox made an even deeper impact because this championship was lifetimes in the making.

This Boston team connected generations, for the first time, with joy instead of disappointment as the emotional mortar. This team changed the way a people, raised to expect the worst, would think of themselves and the future. And the impact, like all things in that great, wide community called Red Sox Nation, resounded from cradle to grave.

On the morning after the Red Sox won the World Series, Sgt. Paul Barnicle, a detective with the Boston police and brother of *Boston Herald* columnist Mike Barnicle, left his shift at six, purchased a single red rose at the city's flower market, drove 42 miles to a cemetery in Fitchburg, Mass., and placed the rose on the headstone of his mother and father, among the many who had not lived long enough to see it.

Five days later, Roger Altman, former deputy treasury secretary in the Clinton Administration, who was born and raised in Brookline, Mass., flew from New York City to Boston carrying a laminated front page of the Oct. 28 *New York Times* (headline: RED SOX ERASE 86 YEARS OF FUTILITY IN FOUR GAMES). He drove to the gravesite of his mother, who had died in November 2003 at age 95, dug a shallow trench and buried the front page there.

Such pilgrimages to the deceased, common after the Red Sox conquered the Yankees in the ALCS, were repeated throughout the graveyards of New England. The totems changed, but the sentiments remained the same. At

Mount Auburn Cemetery in Cambridge, for instance, gravestones were decorated with Red Sox pennants, hats, jerseys, baseballs, license plates and a hand-painted pumpkin.

So widespread was the remembrance of the deceased that several people, including Neil Van Zile Jr. of Westmoreland, N.H., beseeched the ball club to issue a permanent, weatherproof official Red Sox grave marker for dearly departed fans, similar to the metal markers the federal government provides for veterans. (Team president Lucchino says he's going to look into it, though Major League Baseball Properties would have to license it.) Van Zile's mother, Helen, a Sox fan who kept score during games and took her son to Game 2 of the 1967 World Series, died in 1995 at 72.

"There are thousands of people who would want it," Van Zile says. "My mom didn't get to see it. There isn't anything else I can do for her."

One day last year Van Zile was walking through a cemetery in Chesterfield, N.H., when the inscription on a grave stopped him. Blouin was the family name chiseled into the marble. Beneath that it said NAPOLEON A. 1926–1986. At the bottom, nearest to the ground, was the kicker of a lifetime.

DARN THOSE RED SOX.

Dear Red Sox:
Thanks for the motivation.
—JOSUE RODAS, MARINE, 6TH MOTOR TRANSPORT COMPANY, IRAQ

Like snowflakes in a blizzard came the e-mails. More than 10,000 of them flew into the Red Sox' server in the first 10 days after Boston won the World Series. No two exactly alike. They came from New England, but they also came from Japan, Italy, Pakistan and at least 11 other countries. The New England town hall of the 21st century was electronic.

There were thank-you letters. There were love letters. The letters were worded as if they were written to family members, and indeed the Red Sox were, in their own unkempt, scruffy, irreverent way, a likable, familial bunch. How could the faithful not love a band of characters self-deprecatingly self-dubbed the "idiots"?

DH David Ortiz, who slammed three walk-off postseason hits, was the Big Papi of the lineup and the clubhouse, with his outsized grin as much a signature of this team as his bat. Leftfielder Manny Ramirez hit like a machine but played the game with a sandlot smile plastered on his mug, even when taking pratfalls in the outfield. Long-locked centerfielder Johnny Damon made women swoon and men cheer and, with his Nazarene look, prompted a T-shirt and bumper sticker bonanza (WWJDD: WHAT WOULD JOHNNY DAMON DO? and HONK IF YOU LOVE JOHNNY).

First baseman Kevin Millar, with his Honest Abe beard and goofball personality, had the discipline to draw the walk off Yankees closer Mariano Rivera that began Boston's comeback in the ninth inning of ALCS Game 4. Righthander Derek Lowe, another shaggy eccentric, became the first pitcher to win the clinching game of three postseason series in one October. Foulke, third baseman Bill Mueller, catcher Jason Varitek and rightfielder Trot Nixon—the club's longest-tenured player, known for his pine-tar-encrusted batting helmet—provided gritty ballast.

The love came in e-mails that brought word from soldiers in Iraq with Red Sox patches on their uniforms or Red Sox camouflage hats, the symbols of a nation within a nation. The cannon cockers of the 3rd Battalion 11th Marine Regiment built a mini Fenway Park at Camp Ramadi. Soldiers awoke at 3 a.m. to watch the Sox on a conference-room TV at Camp Liberty in Baghdad, the games ending just in time for the troops to fall in and receive their daily battle briefing.

A woman wrote of visiting an ancient temple in Tokyo and finding this message inscribed on a prayer block: MAY THE RED SOX PLAY ALWAYS AT FENWAY PARK, AND MAY THEY WIN THE WORLD SERIES IN MY LIFETIME.

Besides the e-mails there were boxes upon boxes of letters, photographs, postcards, school projects and drawings that continue to cover what little floor space is left in the Red Sox' offices. Mostly the missives convey profound gratitude.

"Thank you," wrote Maryam Farzeneh, a Boston University graduate student from Iran, "for being another reason for me and my boyfriend to connect and love each other. He is a Red Sox fan and moved to Ohio two years ago. There were countless nights that I kept the phone next to the radio so that we could listen to the game together."

Maryam had never seen a baseball game before 1998. She knew how obsessed people back home were about soccer teams. "Although I should admit," she wrote, "that is nothing like the relationship between the Red Sox and the fans in New England."

Dear Red Sox:
Your first round of drinks is free.
—THE LOOSE MOOSE SALOON, GRAY, MAINE

Nightfall, and the little girl lies on her back in the rear seat of a sedan as it chugs homeward to Hartford. She watches the stars twinkle in between the wooden telephone poles that rhythmically interrupt her view of the summer sky. And there is the familiar company of a gravelly voice on the car radio providing play-by-play of Red Sox baseball. The great Ted Williams, her mother's favorite, is batting.

Roberta Rogers closes her eyes, and she is that little girl again, and the world is just as perfect and as full of wonder and possibilities as it was on those warm summer nights growing up in postwar New England.

"I laugh when I think about it," she says. "There is nothing wrong with the memory. Nothing."

Once every summer her parents took her and her brother, Nathaniel, to Boston to stay at the Kenmore Hotel and watch the Red Sox at Fenway. Nathaniel liked to operate the safety gates of the hotel elevator, often letting on and off the visiting ballplayers who stayed at the Kenmore.

"Look," Kathryn Stoddard, their mother, said quietly one day as a well-dressed gentleman stepped off the lift. "That's Joe DiMaggio."

Kathryn, of course, so despised the Yankees that she never called them just the *Yankees*. They were always the *Damnyankees*, as if it were one word.

"We didn't have much money," Roberta says. "We didn't take vacations, didn't go to the beach. That was it. We went to the Kenmore, and we watched the Red Sox at Fenway. I still have the images...the crowds, the stadium, the sounds, the feel of the cement under my feet, passing hot dogs down the row, the big green wall, the Citgo sign—it was green back then—coming into view as we drove into Boston, telling us we were almost there...."

Roberta lives in New Market, Va., now, her mother nearby in a retirement facility. Kathryn is 95 years old and still takes the measure of people by their rooting interest in baseball.

"Acceptable if they root for the Sox, suspect if they don't, and if a Damnyankee fan, hardly worth mentioning," Roberta says.

On Oct. 27, two outs in the bottom of the ninth, Boston winning 3–0, Roberta paced in her living room, her eyes turned away from the TV.

"Oh, Bill," she said to her husband, "they can still be the Red Sox! They can still lose this game!"

It was not without good reason that her mother had called them the *Red Flops* all these years.

"And then I heard the roar," Roberta says.

This time they really did it. They really won. She called her children and called "everybody I could think of." It was too late to ring Kathryn, she figured. Kathryn's eyesight and hearing are failing, and she was surely sleeping at such a late hour.

So Roberta went to see Kathryn first thing the next morning.

"Mom, guess what? I've got the best news!" Roberta said. "They won! The Red Sox won!"

Kathryn's face lit up with a big smile, and she lifted both fists in triumph. And then the mother and daughter laughed and laughed. Just like little girls.

Dear Red Sox:
I really want to surprise my whole school and the principal.
—MAINE HIGH SCHOOL STUDENT, ASKING THAT THE ENTIRE TEAM VISIT HIS SCHOOL

"Is that what I think it is?"

The conductor on the 11:15 a.m. Acela out of Boston to New York, Larry Solomon, had recognized Charles Steinberg and noted the size of the case he was carrying.

"Yes," the Red Sox VP replied. "Would you like to see it?"

Steinberg opened the case and revealed the gleaming gold Commissioner's Trophy, the Red Sox' world championship trophy. Solomon, who had survived leukemia and rooting for the Sox, fought back tears.

The Red Sox are taking the trophy on tour to their fans. On this day it was off to New York City and a convocation of the Benevolent Loyal Order of the Honorable Ancient Redsox Diehard Sufferers, a.k.a. the BLOHARDS.

"I've only cried twice in my life," Richard Welch, 64 and a BLOHARD, said that night. "Once when the Vietnam War ended. And two weeks ago when the Red Sox won the World Series."

Everywhere the trophy goes someone weeps at the sight of it. Everyone wants to touch it, like Thomas probing the wounds of the risen Jesus. Touching is encouraged.

"Their emotional buckets have filled all these years," Steinberg says, "and the trophy overflows them. It's an intense, cathartic experience."

Why? Why should the bond between a people and their baseball team be so intense? Fenway Park is a part of it, offering a physical continuum to the bond, not only because Papi can stand in the same batter's box as Teddy Ballgame, but also because a son might sit in the same wooden-slat seat as his father.

"We do have our tragic history," says the poet Donald Hall, a Vermonter who lives in the house where his great-grandfather once lived.

The Sox specialized not, like the Chicago Cubs, in woebegone, hopeless baseball, but in an agonizing, painful kind. Indeed, hope was at the very breakable heart of their cruelty. From the 1967 Impossible Dream team until last season, the Red Sox had fielded 31 winning teams in 37 years, nine of which reached the postseason. They were good enough to make it hurt.

"It's probably the desperately cruel winters we endure in New England," Mike Barnicle offers as an explanation. "When the Red Sox reappear, that's the season when the sun is back and warmth returns and we associate them with that.

"Also, a lot has to do with how the area is more stable in terms of demographics than most places. People don't move from New England. They stay here. And others come to college here and get infected with Red Sox fever. They get it at the age of 18 and carry it with them when they go out into the world."

If you are born north of Hartford, there is no other big league baseball team for which to root, just as it has been since the Braves left Boston for Milwaukee in 1953. It is a birthright to which you quickly learn the oral history. The Babe, Denny Galehouse, Johnny Pesky, Bucky Dent, Bill Buckner and Aaron Boone are beads on a string, an antirosary committed to memory by every son and daughter of the Nation.

"I've known nothing different in my life," says David Nathan, 34, who, like his brother Marc, 37, learned at the hand of his father, Leslie, 68, who learned at the hand of his father, Morris, 96. "It's so hard to put into words. I was 16 in 1986 sitting in the living room when the ball went through Buckner's legs. We all had champagne ready, and you just sit back and watch it in disbelief.

"I was at Game 7 last year and brought my wife. I said, 'You need to experience it.' The Sox were up 5–2, and my wife said to me, 'They've got this in the bag.' I said, 'No, they don't. I'm telling you, they don't until the last out.'

"I used to look at my dad and not understand why he cried when they lost or cried when they won. Now I understand."

At 11:40 on the night of Oct. 27, David Nathan held a bottle of champagne in one hand and a telephone in the other, his father on the other end of the line. David screamed so loud that he woke up his four-year-old son, Jack, the fourth generation Nathan who, along with Marc's four-year-old daughter, Jessica, will know a whole new world of Sox fandom. The string of beads is broken.

David's wife recorded the moment with a video camera. Two weeks later David would sit and write it all down in a long email, expressing his thanks to Red Sox owner John Henry.

"As my father said to me the next day," David wrote, "he felt like a burden was finally lifted off of his shoulders after all these years."

He read the e-mail to his father over the telephone. It ended, "Thanks again and long live Red Sox Nation." David could hear his father sobbing on the other end.

"It's nice to know after all these years," Leslie said, "something of mine has rubbed off on you."

Dear Red Sox:
I obviously didn't know what I was talking about.
—FAN APOLOGIZING FOR HIS MANY PREVIOUS E-MAILS, ESPECIALLY THE ONE AFTER GAME 3 OF
THE ALCS, IN WHICH HE VERY COLORFULLY EXPRESSED HIS DISGUST FOR THE TEAM AND THE
PEOPLE RUNNING IT

It was one minute after midnight on Oct. 20, and Jared Dolphin, 30, had just assumed his guard post on the overnight shift at the Corrigan-Radgowski correctional facility in Montville, Conn., a Level IV security prison, one level below the maximum. The inmate in the cell nearest him was 10 years into a 180-year sentence for killing his girlfriend's entire family, including the dog.

Some of the inmates wore makeshift Red Sox "caps"—a commissary bandanna or handkerchief festooned with a hand-drawn iconic "B." Technically they were considered contraband, but the rules were bent when it came to rooting for the Red Sox in October. A few inmates watched ALCS Game 7 on 12-inch portable televisions they had purchased in the prison for $200. Most leaned their faces against the little window of their cell door to catch the game on the cell block television. Others saw only the reflection of the TV on the window of another cell door.

A Sox fan himself, Dolphin watched as Alan Embree retired the Yankees' Ruben Sierra on a ground ball to end the greatest comeback in sports history. Dolphin started to cry.

"Suddenly the block erupted," Dolphin wrote in an e-mail. "I bristled immediately and instinctively my hand reached for my flashlight. It was pandemonium—whistling, shouting, pounding on sinks, doors, bunks, anything cons could find. This was against every housing rule in the book, so I jumped up, ready to lay down the law.

"But as I stood there looking around the block I felt something else. I felt hope. Here I was, less than 10 feet away from guys that will never see the outside of prison ever again in their lives. The guy in the cell to my immediate left had 180 years. He wasn't going anywhere anytime soon. But as I watched him scream, holler and pound on the door I realized he and I had something in common. That night hope beamed into his life as well. As Red Sox fans we had watched the impossible happen, and if that dream could come true why couldn't others.

"Instead of marching around the block trying to restore order I put my flashlight down and clapped. My applause joined the ruckus they were making and for five minutes it didn't stop. I applauded until my hands hurt. I was applauding the possibilities for the future."

Dear Red Sox:
Any player who speaks Latin.
—REQUEST FOR A RED SOX PLAYER TO VISIT THE LATIN CLASS AT A MIDDLE SCHOOL IN NEWTON, MASS.

On the day after Christmas 2003, Gregory Miller, 38, of Foxboro, Mass., an enthusiastic sports fan, especially when it came to the Sox, dropped dead of an aneurysm. He left behind a wife, Sharon, six-year-old twin boys and an 18-month-old daughter. Sharon fell into unspeakable sadness and loneliness.

And then came October and the Red Sox.

Sharon, not much more than a casual fan before then, grew enthralled with the team's playoff run. She called her mother, Carolyn Bailey, in Walpole, as many as 15 times during the course of a game to complain, exult, worry, commiserate and celebrate. She even made jokes.

"My eyes need toothpicks to stay open," Sharon would say during the run of late games. "More Visine. I need more Visine."

Carolyn laughed, and her heart leaped to see her daughter joyful again. She had not seen or heard her like this since Gregory died.

"It was the first time she started to smile and laugh again," Carolyn says. "The Red Sox gave her something to look forward to every day. They became like part of the family."

The day after the Red Sox won the World Series, Carolyn wrote a letter to the team. In it she said of her daughter, "The Red Sox became her medicine on the road back from this tragedy. On behalf of my entire family—thank you from the bottom of our hearts."

Leah Storey of Tilton, N.H., composed her own letter of thanks to the Red Sox. Her father had died exactly one year before the Red Sox won the World Series. Then her 26-year-old brother, Ethan, died of an accidental drug overdose only hours after enthusiastically watching the Red Sox win ALCS Game 5. When the Red Sox won the World Series, Ethan's friends and family rushed outside the Storey house, yelled for joy, popped open a bottle of Dom Perignon and gazed up in wonder at a lunar eclipse, and beyond.

"To us, with the memory of Ethan's happy night fresh in our minds, those games took on new meaning," Leah wrote of Boston's run to the championship. "Almost as if they were being played in his honor. Thank you for not letting him down. I can't express enough the comfort we derived from watching you play night after night. It didn't erase the pain, but it helped."

Dear Red Sox:
I would even volunteer my time to clean up, do the dishes, whatever.
—FAN ASKING THAT THE SOX HOST AN EVENT WHERE PLAYERS GREET FANS 80 AND OLDER

On Oct. 25 the Sox were two victories away from winning the World Series when doctors sent George Sumner home to his Waltham house to die. There was nothing more they could do for him. At home, though, George's stomach began to fill with fluid, and he was rushed back to the hospital. The doctors did what they could. They said he was in such bad shape that they were uncertain if he could survive the ride back home.

Suddenly, his eyes still closed, George pointed to a corner of the room, as if someone was there, and said, "Nope, not yet."

And then George went back home to Waltham. Leah knew that every day and every game were precious. She prayed hard for a sweep.

On the morning of Game 4, which stood to be the highlight of Jaime Andrews's life as a "pathetic," obsessed Red Sox fan, his wife, Alice, went into labor. Here it was: the conflict Jaime had feared all summer. At 2:30 p.m. he took her into South Shore Hospital, where they were greeted by nurses wearing Red Sox jerseys over their scrubs.

At 8:25 p.m., Alice was in the delivery room. There was a TV in the room. The game in St. Louis was about to begin.

"Turn on the game."

It was Alice who wanted the TV on. Damon, the leadoff hitter, stepped into the batter's box.

"Johnny Damon!" Alice exclaimed. "He'll hit a home run."

And Damon, his long brown locks flowing out the back of his batting helmet, did just that.

The Red Sox led, 3–0, in the bottom of the fifth inning when the Cardinals put a runner on third base with one out. Jaime could not stand the anxiety. His head hurt. He was having difficulty breathing. He broke out in hives. It was too much to take. He asked Alice to turn off the television. Alice insisted they watch until the end of the inning. They saw Lowe pitch out of the jam. Jaime nervously clicked off the TV.

At home in Waltham, George Sumner slipped in and out of sleep. His eyes were alert when the game was on, but when an inning ended he would say in a whisper, which was all he could muster, "Wake me up when the game comes back on." Each time no one could be certain if he would open his eyes again.

The Red Sox held their 3–0 lead, and the TV remained off in the delivery room of South Shore Hospital. At 11:27 p.m. Alice gave birth to a beautiful boy. Jaime noticed that the baby had unusually long hair down the back of his neck. The nurses cleaned and measured the boy. Jaime was still nervous.

"Can I check the TV for the final score?" he asked Alice.

"Sure," she said.

It was 11:40 p.m. The Red Sox were jumping upon one another in the middle of the diamond. They were world champions.

George Sumner had waited a lifetime to see this—79 years, to be exact, the last three while fighting cancer. He drew upon whatever strength was left in his body and in the loudest whisper that was possible he said, "Yippee!"

And then he closed his eyes and went to sleep.

"It was probably the last real conscious moment he ever had," Leah says.

George opened his eyes one last time the next day. When he did he saw that he was surrounded by his extended family. He said, "Hi," and went back to sleep for the final time.

George Sumner, avid Red Sox fan, passed away at 2:30 a.m. on Oct. 29. He was laid to rest with full military honors on Nov. 2.

On the day that George Sumner died, Alice and Jaime Andrews took home a healthy baby boy. They named him Damon.

Dear Red Sox:
Thank you, 2004 World Series Champs, Boston Red Sox. It was worth the wait.
—CLOSING LINES OF THE OBITUARY FOR CYNTHIA MARIE RILEY-RUBINO IN A HAMDEN, CONN., NEWSPAPER, SENT TO THE TEAM BY ANOTHER FAN

Ballplayers are not social scientists or cultural historians. Quite to the contrary, they create an insular fortress in which all considerations beyond the game itself are feared to carry the poison of what are known generically as "distractions."

The Red Sox are not from Boston; they come from all corners of the U.S. and Latin America, and flew to their real homes immediately after a huge, cathartic parade on Oct. 30, during which normal life in New England was basically TiVoed for three hours. ("Three and a half million people there *and* a 33 rating on TV!" marveled Steinberg.)

There is an awful imbalance to our relationship with athletes, as if we are looking through a one-way mirror. We know them, love them, dress like them and somehow believe our actions, however trivial, alter the outcome of theirs, all while they know only that we are there but cannot really see us.

Howard Frank Mosher of Vermont was in northern Maine in the summer of '03 for a book-signing, during which he discussed his upcoming novel, *Waiting for Teddy Williams*, a fanciful tale in which the Red Sox (can you imagine?) win the Series; he heard a small group of people singing in the back of the bookstore. It sounded like, *Johnny Angel, how I love him*....

As Mosher drew closer he realized they were singing, *Johnny Damon, how I love him*.... What was going on? he wondered.

"We're performing an incantation," one of the men said. "Damon has been in a slump. We think it's working. He was 4 for 5 last night."

Crazy. How could Damon know this? How could any Boston player know that the Reverend William Bourke, an avid Sox fan who died in his native Rhode Island before Game 2 of the World Series, was buried the day after Boston won it all, with a commemorative Sox baseball and that morning's paper tucked into his casket?

How could Pedro Martinez know that on the morning of World Series Game 2, Dianne Connolly, her three-year-old son, Patrick, and the rest of the congregation of St. Francis of Assisi parish in Litchfield, N.H., heard the choir sing a prayer for the Red Sox after the recessional? "Our Father, who art in Fenway," the singers began. They continued, "Give us this day our perfect Pedro; and forgive those, like Bill Buckner; and lead us not into depression...."

How could Curt Schilling know that Laura Deforge, 84, of Winooski, Vt., who watched every Red Sox game on TV—many of them *twice*—turned the ALCS around when she found a lucky, 30-year-old Red Sox hat in her closet after Game 3? Laura wore it everywhere for the next 11 days, including to bingo. (And she's still wearing it.)

"I've only been here a year," Schilling says, "and it's humbling to be a part of the relationship between Red Sox Nation and this team. I can't understand it all. I can't. All I can do is thank God that He blessed me with the skills that can have an impact on people's lives in some positive way."

The lives of these players are forever changed as professionals. Backup catcher Doug Mirabelli, for instance, will be a celebrity 30 years from now if he shows up anywhere from Woonsocket to Winooski. The '04 Red Sox have a sheen that will never fade or be surpassed.

The real resonance to this championship, however, is that it changed so many of the people on the other side of the one-way glass, poets and convicts, fathers and sons, mothers and daughters, the dying and the newborn.

The dawn that broke over New England on Oct. 28, the first in the life of little Damon Andrews, was unlike any other seen in three generations. Here began the birth of a new Red Sox Nation, sons no longer bearing the scars and dread of their fathers and grandfathers. It felt as clean and fresh as New Year's Day.

Damon's first dawn also was the last in the fully lived life of George Sumner.

"I walked into work that day," Leah Sumner says, "and I had tears in my eyes. People were saying, 'Did he see it? Did he see it? Please tell me your dad saw it.' You don't understand how much comfort it gave my brothers and sisters. It would have been that much sadder if he didn't get to see it.

"It was like a blessing. One lady told me he lived and died by the hand of God. I'm not religious, but he was blessed. If he was sitting here, he would agree there was something stronger there.

"It was the best year, and it was the worst year. It was an unbelievable year. I will tell my children and make sure they tell their children."

The story they will tell is not just the story of George Sumner. It is not just the story of the 2004 Boston Red Sox. It is the story of the bond between a nation of fans and its beloved team.

"It's not even relief," Leah says. "No, it's like we were a part of it. It's not like they did it for themselves or for money or for fame, but like they did it for us.

"It's bigger than money. It's bigger than fame. It's who we are. It's like I tell people. There are three things you must know about me. I love my family. I love blues music. And I love baseball."

Sports Illustrated

THE VAULT SERIES

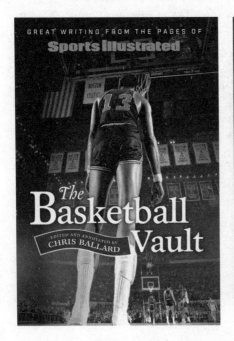

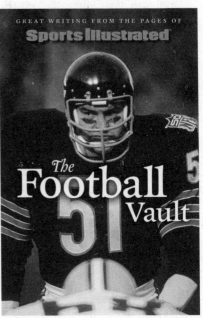

Available wherever books are sold